Lloyd George:
The People's Champion
1902–1911

Lloyd George in Chancellor of the Exchequer's robes, painted by Christopher Williams at Criccieth in the summer of 1911 (see pp. 338–40)

JOHN GRIGG

Lloyd George:
The People's Champion
1902-1911

Eyre Methuen
LONDON

First published 1978
by Eyre Methuen Ltd
11 New Fetter Lane, London EC4P 4EE
© 1978 John Grigg
Printed in Great Britain by
Butler & Tanner Ltd, Frome and London

ISBN 0 413 32620 9

Contents

Illustrations

ILLUSTRATIONS IN TEXT

Acknowledgments and thanks are due to Mr R. R. Carey Evans D.F.C. for the frontispiece; to the Radio Times Hulton Picture Library for plates 1a, 1b, 6c, 6d, 7b, and the illustrations on pp 199 and 319, to Mr Patrick Kearley for plates 2a, 2b and 2c; to the Mansell Collection for plates 3, 4a, 4c, 4d, and for the illustration on p 255; to the British Library for plate 5 and the illustration on p 36; to the Mary Evans Picture Library for plates 6a and 6e; to the Chamberlain Collection, University of Birmingham Library for plate 7a; to Bassano & Vandyk Studios for plate 8; to the Beaverbrook Foundation for the illustration on p 319 and to Robyn Wallis for her assistance in locating some of the pictures.

Abbreviations

D.L.G.	David Lloyd George
M.L.G.	Margaret Lloyd George
W.G.	William George
H.H.A.	Herbert Henry Asquith
W.S.C.	Winston Spencer Churchill
L.G.P.	Lloyd George Papers
N.L.W.	National Library of Wales
P.R.O.	Public Record Office
Letters	Lloyd George: Family Letters 1885–1936, edited by Kenneth O. Morgan

Acknowledgments

Ever since I first became interested in writing about Lloyd George I have had nothing but kindness from his daughter, Lady Olwen Carey Evans D.B.E., and his grandson, Owen, 3rd Earl Lloyd George of Dwyfor. Without their generous friendship and great practical help it would have been all but impossible to do the job at all.

Lady Olwen has helped me with documents and photographs, and above all has talked to me very frankly about the past. Lord Lloyd George has put his valuable collection of family papers at my disposal, and has given me constant encouragement. Both of them have left me entirely free to use what they have given me as I have thought fit.

I am more grateful to them than I can say, but in fairness to them – and to others who have helped me with personal recollections – it should be emphasized that I alone am responsible for judgments expressed in the book.

Mr D. L. Carey Evans allowed me to work on his great collection of letters before it was transferred to the National Library of Wales, by which it is now owned. I am very grateful to him for that kindness, as I am to his brother, Mr R. R. Carey Evans D.F.C., more especially for his permission to reproduce the portrait of his grandfather by Christopher Williams.

The Hon. William Lloyd-George gave me access to, and unfettered use of, his collection of family documents. To him, too, I am deeply grateful.

In 1974 I had the privilege of a Leverhulme Research Fellowship, which compensated me for the loss of freelance journalistic earnings while I applied myself to work on this book. To anyone without a regular academic or other salary such work presents serious difficulties, and I am conscious of my very great debt to the Leverhulme Trustees.

For copyright permissions, I have to thank above all the National Library of Wales and the Beaverbrook Foundation, with which I would couple the names of Mr David Jenkins C.B.E. and Professor A. J. P. Taylor F.B.A.

The letter from King Edward VII to Lloyd George given on pp. 210–11 is republished by gracious permission of Her Majesty the Queen.

For other copyright permissions I am indebted to the Hon. Mark Bonham Carter (Asquith), the British Library Board (Balfour), C. & T. Publications and William Heinemann Ltd (Churchill), the late Sir Ben Bowen Thomas (on behalf of the Executors of Ellis W. Davies), The Observer Ltd, by permission of the Oxford University Press, (J. L. Garvin), Miss Jennifer Gosse (Edmund Gosse), Viscount Harcourt K.C.M.G., O.B.E. (Lewis Harcourt, 1st Viscount Harcourt), the late Hon. Mark Kearley, his son Mr Patrick Kearley, and Viscount Devonport (Hudson Kearley, 1st Viscount Devonport), the Hon. Sir Steven Runciman F.B.A. and the University Library, Newcastle-upon-Tyne (Walter Runciman).

The Right Hon. Lord Boyle of Handsworth P.C., LL.D. read the typescript and made a number of very helpful suggestions, drawing on his exceptional store of knowledge and wisdom. He has my affectionate thanks.

Many other people and institutions have helped me – so many that any attempt to give a detailed list would be invidious. But I must record my gratitude to Jill Craigie (Mrs Michael Foot) for advice and documentation on the Women's Suffrage Movement; to Dr Prys Morgan for translating the D. R. Daniel memoir, and for his learned assistance on Welsh matters; and to the friendly, efficient staff of the London Library.

In addition, I can only say that no thanks are adequate for Miss Jean Walton who, apart from typing most of this book and much else relating to it, has been foremost among friends who have kept me up to the mark.

J.G.

Preface

My earlier book, *The Young Lloyd George*, ended at the zenith of Lloyd George's career as a back-bencher, when he courageously opposed the Boer War and survived it with his reputation greatly enhanced. This book carries the story on to the zenith of his whole pre-war career, 1911, when within the space of twelve months he achieved more, both in quantity and quality, than many leading politicians have achieved in a life-time.

Most of the book was written two years ago, but its completion was delayed partly because I went back, for a time, to regular weekly journalism, and partly because I was unhappy about the balance of the source material as between public and private. When writing about Lloyd George's early career I was denied access (as I am still) to the very important collection of family papers belonging to his nephew, Councillor W. R. P. George, and this was a painful deprivation. But to a considerable extent it was offset by the fact that I was allowed to make full use of the mass of letters (now in the National Library of Wales) inherited by Lloyd George's grandson, Mr D. L. Carey Evans. With so much evidence, largely in the form of letters from Lloyd George in London to his wife at Criccieth, I was able to check, amplify and illuminate the public record of his activities.

From the Boer War time onwards Margaret Lloyd George tended to be with her husband in London while Parliament was sitting, so he no longer had occasion to write her frequent letters charged with political gossip. Such letters would, of course, be of immense value for the time when he was President of the Board of Trade, and still more after he became Chancellor of the Exchequer and moved to the very centre of the political stage. Though he wrote extremely sparingly to colleagues, we know that he wrote often to his uncle and brother at Criccieth, but comparatively few of the letters have been published in the book by Councillor George's father, *My Brother and I*. Many problems might have been easier to solve if it had been possible even to read, without quoting, the letters which the Councillor holds; and, needless to say, permission to quote them as well would have enabled me to write a properly balanced book. But not even the lesser privilege was conceded.

Eventually, I believe, these crucial Lloyd George documents will be available to students, but not until Mr George has first made use of them himself in an unfolding work on his uncle. Two years ago he published an interesting first instalment, which reached the point of Lloyd George's entry into Parliament in 1890. Clearly it would be risky for some of us to hold up work in the hope of seeing the papers, because at the rate he is going the moment may not arrive until we are dead or in our dotage.

The book that I have now finished is, therefore, the best that I can do in the circumstances, and luckily – through the generosity of others – it contains quite a lot of new material. In addition, it may offer some novelty of interpretation or emphasis, and it certainly tries to present one of the most exciting and fruitful phases of Lloyd George's career on an appropriate scale, with plenty of his own words quoted. It seems to me that historical characters should, wherever possible, be allowed to speak for themselves, and all the more so when they speak as brilliantly as Lloyd George did. I have also tried to give fairly the views of other leading figures, so that readers can arrive at their own judgments which may differ from mine.

To turn to details, I should say that I am impenitent about putting references at the foot of the page, because few habits in serious modern publishing irritate me more than that of bunching references at the end of chapters or at the end of a book. If readers wish to know the source of a quotation or the authority for a statement in the text, they should be able to refer to it easily and without wasting their time. If they are not interested in such matters, there is, after all, nothing to stop them reading on. A footnote reference is no more offensive or distracting to the eye than the page number or running title at the top of a page.

A word about Lloyd George's name: his father's surname was simply George, and so, in law, was his. But he was given the names David Lloyd, and after losing his father in infancy was brought up by his mother's brother, Richard Lloyd. During his boyhood at Llanystumdwy he was known as David Lloyd to many of his neighbours, and as he grew up it was always his intention that he should be known to the world at large not as Mr George, but as Mr Lloyd George. One reason, no doubt, was a desire to please the uncle to whom he owed so much, and whose pride in him was unbounded. Just as he would describe himself, in later life, as having been educated at 'Llanystumdwy Church School and privately' – the last two words a tribute to Uncle Lloyd – so he would couple the name Lloyd with his patronymic.

He did not, however, hyphenate the names in his signature, though for quite a long time he allowed them to be hyphenated in works of reference. Presumably he did so in the hope that people would thus get into the way of using them together as his surname. He appears as 'Lloyd-George' in Hansard until April 1910, and in *Who's Who* until the edition of 1917. Thereafter his name was not officially printed with what, of another politician's name, he called the 'unearned increment' of a hyphen; and, whatever the College of Heralds may have wished, it is un-hyphenated in his title. (In his son Gwilym's family however – the cadet branch – the name *is* spelt with a hyphen.)

In due course I hope to complete my account of his life in two more volumes – the next ending at the Armistice or after the General Election in 1918, the last covering the rest of his life, including the four years of his peace-time Premiership. But I do not flatter myself that I am engaged in an attempt to write about him definitively. There is no such thing as definitive history, and even if there were I should not be capable of writing it.

J.G.

February 1978

ONE

An Unsettled Age

David Lloyd George was unmistakably an Edwardian, though he served his political apprenticeship under Queen Victoria and reached the zenith of his power under George V. History does not normally fall into clear-cut periods, and human beings do not readily fit into the neat patterns which historians and social scientists devise for them. But some periods are more identifiable than others, and in Britain the years from the turn of the century to the outbreak of war in 1914 form a very distinct epoch which, since it largely coincides with the reign of Edward VII, has been called the Edwardian age. It was then that Lloyd George came into his own as a politician, and more than any other politician of his time he seems to epitomise the character and outlook of Edwardian Britain.

The age was marked by feverish energy and a profusion of creative talent, by an acute sense of the impermanence of things, by the rejection of many traditional values, and by a curious blend of heroism and hedonism. Above all, it was marked by a growing sense of national insecurity. The Victorians may have had their doubts about Man's place in the Universe, but they had very few doubts about Britain's place in the world. With the Edwardians it tended to be the other way round. Having, in effect, substituted for Christianity some form or other of the religion of humanity, many of them combined an exaggerated self-confidence as individuals, and a rather naïve faith in the potential of the human race, with a realistic, even alarmist, view of the dangers by which Britain was beset.

The new century, closely followed by a new reign, brought into sharp focus what was already a vague, but disturbing, impression of change.

Forty years previously the oceans of the world were British lakes and the markets of the world British fiefs. The Royal Navy appeared to have made the world safe for the Free Trade system which, in turn, was thought to be a guarantee of ever-increasing prosperity. The German Empire did not yet exist, and the United States, still only partly developed, was on the brink of a near-suicidal civil war.

But within a generation the whole scene was transformed. Germany was united, economically a strong competitor, and, under a young Emperor of unstable character and restless ambition, a threat such as Britain had not known since the fall of Napoleon. The United States, its federal unity preserved and strengthened, its vast arable expanses producing an abundance of cheap grain, its young industries sustained by apparently unlimited mineral wealth, was becoming with every year a more formidable economic rival. The British people could see that their easy supremacy had gone for ever, and that unless they were careful they might lose their prosperity as well – even, conceivably, their independence.

In the short run the only major British industry to suffer calamitously from the new conditions was agriculture which, by the 'nineties, had settled into a deep decline. But some sectors of manufacturing industry were also feeling the pinch, and it was from these that Joseph Chamberlain was to receive his most enthusiastic support, when, in 1903, he launched his campaign for Tariff Reform. Yet the big staple industries continued to prosper in spite of foreign competition; to some extent, indeed, because of it, since the more enterprising firms were stimulated to diversify their products and improve their techniques. Inevitably Britain's rate of growth was slower than that of countries whose industrialisation was more recent, but the British economy was still very dynamic and the huge export of capital during the Edwardian period, though partly at the expense of industrial investment at home, helped to earn the country a consistent surplus on its balance of payments. Troubled though they were by the unfamiliar sensation of living in a competitive world, the Edwardians were not panicked by it into abandoning Free Trade; but they indulged in much heart-searching about the amateurishness and inefficiency of British life.

More serious – and rightly so – was their concern at the German challenge to British sea power, and the possibility that the country itself might be invaded. By its Navy Laws of 1898 and 1900 Germany revealed its determination to build a fleet which would not only menace Britain's trade routes but also, and more especially, threaten the security of the British Isles. The Edwardians reacted to this mortal threat with enormous programmes of naval construction and modernization, and during the period books were published, and widely read, in which a German invasion of Britain was projected. But the anxiety upon which such literature played did not drive British opinion into accepting the case for compulsory National Service, any more than anxiety about foreign trade competition induced acceptance of the case for Protection. The British continued to put their trust in a strong navy, and to show their rooted distrust of a large army, in spite of a terrific scolding from one of the great writers and prophets of the age, Rudyard Kipling:

> Given to strong delusion, wholly believing a lie,
> Ye saw that the land lay fenceless, and ye let the months go by
> Waiting some easy wonder, hoping some saving sign –
> Idle – openly idle – in the lee of the forespent Line.
> Idle – except for your boasting – and what is your boasting worth
> If ye grudge a year of service to the lordliest life on earth?[1]

Another comparable literary figure, whose genius was as distinctively Edwardian, shared Kipling's sense of impending doom, and his disgust at the blindness and small-mindedness of his contemporaries, but not his Imperialism. H. G. Wells was in theory a socialist and internationalist, in reality a Little Englander. Like Kipling, he believed that only a dedicated *élite* could bring salvation to the world, but he looked to an *élite* of pure scientists rather than to one of soldiers, engineers and proconsuls. To him the Empire seemed a discreditable encumbrance, and he had very little understanding of foreign countries or foreign people. His imagination ranged from Lewisham to Outer Space, but did not take in Lahore. It was, however, a very powerful imagination, and in his version of a prospective German attack upon Britain the attack is delivered from the air.[2] In another book he describes the countryside of his native Kent, evoking the precarious atmosphere of Edwardian England:

> It is like an early day in a fine October. The hand of change rests on it all, unfelt, unseen; resting for a while, as it were half reluctantly, before it grips and ends the thing for ever. One frost and the whole face of things will be bare, links snap, patience end, our fine foliage of pretences lie glowing in the mire.[3]

1. From *The Islanders* (1902).   2. H. G. Wells, *The War in the Air* (1908).
3. H. G. Wells, from *Tono-Bungay* (1909), ch. I, section 3. But not every Edwardian author was free from complacency. For instance: 'We live so safely now; we have nothing to be

As a master of science fiction Wells could grasp the new dimension of danger with which Britain was faced, while as a social novelist he gave expression to new forces stirring within a society to outward appearance still relatively static.

Allied to the fear of invasion was a sense of national degeneracy, a feeling that the country was rotten at the core; and this was a preoccupation which, from their different points of view, Imperialists and Little Englanders could share. The Boer War, which was going on when the Edwardian age opened, was traumatic in many ways and not least in its disclosure of the British people's physical unfitness. Of those who volunteered for the war at least one in three – some say a much larger proportion – had to be rejected on health grounds. The rate of infant mortality in London was 279 per thousand in 1899, or more than half the very worst figure recorded for a concentration camp during the Boer War, by which humanitarian consciences were outraged. As a result of the war an official committee was set up to report on Physical Deterioration, and although its conclusions (in 1904) were on the whole anodyne, public disquiet was not allayed. One of the principal aims of the Boy Scout movement – started, appropriately enough, by a Boer War hero – was to counteract national and Imperial decadence by improving the physique of British youth.

Advanced Liberal thinkers were equally exercised by the state of human decay which they observed at the heart of the Empire – the title, indeed, of a collection of essays by young Liberals, edited by Charles Masterman and published in 1901. Social reform was in the air, and the evidence brought to light by the Boer War gave added urgency to a movement already gathering momentum. The gross disparities of wealth in Britain were even more obvious in Edwardian times than they had been in the previous age, partly because the rich were tending to behave rather more ostentatiously, and partly because the condition of the mass of the people was being documented.[1] The value of unearned income increased by half during the period, while working-class earnings, which may have risen by

---

afraid of. When we have wars they are not in our own country. The police look after burglars, and even thunder is attended to by lightning rods. It is not easy for us to understand the frantic terror of those times, when, from day to day, every man, woman and child trembled in its shoes for fear lest "the French should come" . . .' (E. Nesbit, *The House of Arden*, ch. 4 – first published in 1908.)

1. As, for instance, in Charles Booth's *Life and Labour of the People of London* (1889–1903), and Seebohm Rowntree's *Poverty: a Study of Town Life* (1901).

as much as 40 per cent during the last quarter of the nineteenth century, came to a standstill because of higher import prices and lower productivity. A quarter or a third of the population was living in more or less abject conditions, while about a half of one per cent was enjoying a degree of affluence which now seems unimaginably high and paying taxes which now seem unimaginably low. The maldistribution of wealth was not only an offence against natural justice, but was probably also Britain's chief source of weakness in competition with the United States. The American home market would anyway have been larger than the British, because the United States had twice Britain's population; but American manufacturers had the additional benefit of a home market which was broader socially than Britain's and therefore more of a stimulus to mass production and standardization.

The Edwardians saw the physical fabric of their world changing very rapidly. By the end of the old century the telephone and typewriter were already established, if not yet in very extensive use. Electric light and electric trams had been introduced into some of the larger cities, and London had its first electric tube trains. But after 1900 more and more letters were typewritten, telephones multiplied, and the new invention of wireless telegraphy was developed. Electricity was used more widely for public lighting and transport, though its application to industry was still limited. The bicycle, its design constantly improving, achieved an immense popularity and enabled many town-dwellers to escape into the countryside. The motor vehicle, held at bay during the 'nineties by the operation of an archaic law, began at last to impose itself upon British streets and roads. In 1904 there were still 2,500 horse-buses in London alone, but the last London horse-bus was withdrawn from service on 4 August 1914. A year earlier there were 220,000 licensed motor vehicles in Britain, and between 1903 and 1909 the number of private motor cars increased from 23,000 to 100,000. Meanwhile an even more revolutionary change was occurring, as aeroplanes and dirigible airships appeared in the sky. On the ground, however, in the deep countryside, illusions of immutability could still be cherished. Beyond the railway station the horse still reigned:

> Only a man harrowing clods
>   In a slow silent walk
> With an old horse that stumbles and nods
>   Half asleep as they stalk.

> Only thin smoke without flame
> From the heaps of couch-grass;
> Yet this will go onward the same
> Though dynasties pass.[1]

Before long the tractor would destroy that idyllic picture.

Society was changing, but more slowly and less obviously than the environment. There were only about 170,000 civil servants in 1914 – most of them working in the very efficient postal service – but at the same time there were about a million domestic servants. Women were still under-privileged and exploited, but with more jobs available to them and, above all, with the spread of birth control their emancipation was at hand. Their demand for political rights was a notable feature of the Edwardian age. Labour was still very inadequately organized: at the beginning of the century only one-sixth of the total work force belonged to trade unions, and even in 1913 only a quarter. But towards the end of the period unions were legally better placed as well as numerically stronger than at the beginning, with the result that 1911–1913 was a time of unprecedented militancy. Moreover, Labour was emerging as an independent political force, with its own representatives in Parliament, though few anticipated the day – not far distant – when Labour would be able to form its own Government. Alcoholism, which for so long had enfeebled and degraded the working class, was markedly on the wane, while State or State-aided education was raising the level of popular culture, with important assistance from the public lending libraries.

Britain was still dominated by the landed gentry, the captains of industry and the professional middle class, but the masses were no longer content to be permanently submerged by the classes, and during the Edwardian period the ordinary people of Britain found in a member of the profes-sional middle class their most eloquent and effective champion.

1. Lines by Thomas Hardy, written as late as 1915.

TWO
Below the Snowline

When the Boer War ended Lloyd George had been in Parliament for twelve years. Almost as soon as he arrived at Westminster he made his name as an exceptionally lively and intelligent back-bencher, and also soon established a considerable reputation in the country as a platform speaker. Though at first it was tactically expedient for him to concentrate very largely upon Welsh issues, or upon general issues in which Wales was specially interested, his own view of politics was always far wider and his ambition unlimited. Never content to be a tribal leader like Parnell, he aimed at nothing less than the leadership of Great Britain.

In his opposition to the Boer War he had been acting beyond question as a national politician, taking his stand on an issue which, though bitterly controversial, was in no sense parochial. But before the war was over he became involved in a domestic controversy which made him once again appear to many as a narrow Welsh sectary, though at the same time it enabled him to return to the centre of Liberal Party politics and to resume close working relations with the Liberal Imperialists, from whom he had been separated by the war. This was the long struggle, in and out of Parliament, resulting from the Education Bill which Arthur Balfour presented to the House of Commons on 24 March 1902.

The background to the Bill was confused even by British standards. Until 1870 the initiative in school building was almost exclusively religious, but in that year the British State assumed responsibility, in the Forster Act, for providing elementary schools in areas where none were provided by the denominations. These schools were to be run by local boards elected for the purpose by the ratepayers; and religious instruction of a simple, undenominational kind was prescribed for them under the so-called Cowper–Temple clause. The board school system did not offend the Nonconformist conscience, and the 'British' schools founded as Non-conformist establishments were, on the whole, absorbed into it. But the Anglican and Roman Catholic schools remained outside, as 'voluntary' schools, and, in spite of vigorous building by the school boards, at the end of the century most of the children at the elementary stage were still being taught in voluntary – chiefly Anglican – schools.[1]

Meanwhile at the secondary stage most British children were not being taught at all. About 100,000 were being educated at 'public' or other endowed schools, and about 25,000 were receiving secondary education of a sort in 'higher-grade' schools provided by the school boards. In addition, during the last decade of the century a significant boost was given to technical education, the sphere in which Britain's competitive weakness, compared with other advanced nations, was most acutely felt. Responsi-bility for developing technical education was entrusted to the new county councils, and by 1902 nearly 450,000 students were attending technical schools or evening classes, representing a threefold increase within the past decade. All the same, the great majority of children were still receiving no post-elementary education of any kind.

Apart from the sheer inadequacy of the situation, thinking people were appalled by its incoherence. There were two separate categories of ele-mentary school, and at least three separate categories of secondary school, all dependent in some degree upon financial backing from the State. Yet the State occupied a nebulous position in the educational field. It gave direct aid to the voluntary schools without exacting in return any share in their management, while for the rest it operated through intermediate agencies, the school boards and the county councils. The elementary and higher-grade schools run by the school boards were basically rate-financed, with the State subsidizing the poor areas. Similarly, when the county and county borough councils were made responsible for technical education, the basic finance came from the rates but was supplemented by money from central funds – the so-called 'whisky money'[2] – which many councils

1. The figures in 1895 were: 2,446,000 children attending voluntary schools, 1,848,000 attending board schools. The upper age limit for compulsory attendance at elementary school was raised from 10 to 11 in 1893, and from 11 to 12 in 1899. In 1900 school boards were permitted, but not required, to raise the school-leaving age to 14. This did not become the compulsory leaving age until 1918.

2. So-called, because it derived from the additional duty on spirits introduced by Goschen in his 1890 Budget with the object of compensating licensees who were to be bought out.

also used for sending scholars to endowed, but often hard-up, secondary institutions. The universities, virtually independent of the State, were attended by about 20,000 students, but gave tuition to many more through their extension courses. Oxford, Cambridge and London, moreover, rendered a general service to the secondary schools, by acting as examining bodies and so determining the curriculum.

Many who fully recognized the value of academic freedom and diversity, and who did not at all hanker after a streamlined Napoleonic educational system, could nevertheless feel that a measure of rationalization was overdue. Lord Salisbury's last Government had been fumbling with the problem since it took office in 1895, but until 1902 lacked the will to tackle it comprehensively. Of the two Ministers responsible for education, the Vice-President of the Council, Sir John Gorst, was an ardent reformer, but also, unfortunately, a tactless and rather inept politician, while his superior, the Duke of Devonshire, was a dignified figurehead with no serious interest in the subject. In 1899 a Bill was passed establishing the Board of Education, and Devonshire was its first President; but although the Board had wider powers than had belonged to the Education Committee of the Privy Council, the system as a whole remained substantially unchanged. The Cabinet was inhibited by the fact that, of the two parties to the governing coalition, the Tories' chief concern was for the voluntary schools, whereas Joseph Chamberlain's allegiance was to the school boards. Such was the position when Balfour himself decided to give his mind to the problem.

His 1902 Education Act had the crucial effect of substituting for the old mishmash a unified system of control through local education authorities – committees representing county councils, county borough councils, councils of boroughs with a population in excess of 10,000, and councils of urban districts with a population in excess of 20,000.[1] The committees were to consist, as to a majority, of members elected by the councils, but were also to include a minority of lay members appointed by the councils on the nomination of various outside bodies.

In the Bill as originally drafted the committees were to be free to take

---

When that proposal came under heavy attack – not least from Lloyd George in his maiden speech – part of the money, together with part of the revenue from the beer duty, was earmarked instead mainly as a subsidy, through the county councils, to technical education. As such it was paid year after year, and in 1901–2 amounted to nearly £860,000.

1. London was omitted from the Bill, but was dealt with in separate legislation the following year.

over the functions of school boards, but before the measure was passed this provision was strengthened and taking over the boards' functions became obligatory rather than merely permissive. In other words, Chamberlain's pet authorities were abolished, and by a Government of which he was a leading member. The deed was done against his wishes, and he believed – not without reason, as events proved – that it would alienate many of his Liberal Unionist followers. But abolition of the school boards had been recommended only the year before in a Fabian tract, and Balfour must have hoped that his policy would divide the Left and so compensate him for the inevitable division on his own side. If so, he was disappointed, though the opposition was divided in another way, since the Irish naturally gave their support to a Bill which strengthened State aid for religious education.

To the voluntary schools the Balfour Act gave financial security in return for partial public control. Anglicans and Roman Catholics had the satisfaction of seeing their schools awarded a share of the rates, which the new education committees were to make available to them, on condition that they were up to standard. But this meant that they were brought within the unified system: like the former board schools and the technical schools, they were made subject to the education committees. Moreover, to qualify for a statutory grant from the State every voluntary school had to be controlled by a board of six managers, of whom two were to represent the local education authority. There was also to be public control, through the education committees, of secular instruction in the voluntary schools, and the committees' consent was required for the appointment or dismissal of teachers, though it was laid down that such consent should never be refused on religious grounds.[1]

All in all, the measure was a compromise between central and local, public and private, control. But it was a compromise which strongly favoured the expansion of public education, and Balfour deserves the highest credit for promoting it, more especially for remaining in charge of the Bill even after he had succeeded his uncle as Prime Minister in July 1902. It has been suggested that his interest in the Bill was purely partisan; that he sponsored it merely because it satisfied the Tories by meeting the financial needs of the Anglican schools and by abolishing the supposedly

1. The Kenyon-Slaney amendment, moved by a Conservative M.P. of that name, ensured that religious instruction in the schools should be strictly in accordance with the wishes of their founders – a safeguard against the ritualism which was thought to be infecting the Church of England.

extravagant school boards. But that interpretation does him a serious injustice. Certainly he calculated – and to a degree miscalculated – the benefits to his own party, but one cannot doubt that he was also influenced by loftier considerations. His personal commitment to the Bill owed much to the influence of Robert Morant, a civil servant of genius whose idealism was reinforced by the talent and ruthlessness necessary for worldly success. The child of a decorative artist and a headmaster's daughter, he was sent to Winchester, took a First in Theology at Oxford, and soon afterwards went to Siam, where he became tutor to the Crown Prince and was given the opportunity to try his hand at educational reforms for the whole country. His physical and moral stature earned him the nickname of Kroo Tai (Big Teacher), but fortunately for him – and for Britain – his career in Siam was cut short as a result of the international crisis of 1893, when Britain and France nearly went to war over Siam but eventually settled their differences at that country's expense. In 1895, after a spell at Toynbee Hall, Morant entered the British Education Department, but in 1902 was still no more, officially, than the Duke of Devonshire's assistant private secretary. In practice, however, he was the chief architect of Balfour's scheme, because Balfour, unlike Devonshire, was susceptible to his reforming zeal and found in Morant – as he later found in Chaim Weizmann – the sort of rationalizing mystic that he particularly admired.

Their combined efforts did the trick, but Balfour's was the more decisive contribution, because he had the political authority. He also cared as much as Morant did about education. Though in other respects his social conscience may not have been of the tenderest, as an intellectual he could not be indifferent to the wholesale waste of brain-power through sheer neglect. To the extent, moreover, that it was British brain-power that was being wasted, he could not be indifferent, as an Imperialist, to the effect of such waste upon the viability of the British Empire. At a time when Britain's alleged competitive weakness was a fashionable topic in board-rooms, common-rooms and drawing-rooms, Balfour's natural response was to give top priority, and his own dialectical resources, to the cause of educational reform.

As a schoolmaster's son Lloyd George had good reason to welcome a measure likely to increase the scope and efficiency of British education, and his first reaction to Balfour's proposals was, indeed, very different from the public attitude which he soon felt obliged to adopt. On 24 March, while the First Lord of the Treasury was still on his feet explaining the scheme and asking for leave to introduce the Bill, Lloyd George wrote to his wife:

> *5.30 p.m.* Balfour is developing a most revolutionary Education Bill. Sweeps away School Boards – creates the County Council the educational authority for the county & puts the School Boards & the Voluntary Schools under it . . . Up to the present I rather like the Bill. It is quite as much as one would expect from a Tory Government – in fact more than anyone could anticipate.

His one strong objection to the scheme as originally presented had very little to do with the religious issue, and would have seemed utterly perverse to a great many Liberals:

> Whole thing destroyed by making the whole Bill optional – it is left entirely to the discretion of each County Council![1]

Thus, instead of deploring the threat to the school boards, he only regretted its being, as yet, too feeble a threat.

The same evening he spoke in very mild terms to the correspondent of a Welsh newspaper:

> I am not unfavourably impressed with the Bill, judging it from a purely Welsh point of view. I am, however, assured by English Members that the Bill will be a bad thing for England, as the English county councils are not so interested in education as the Welsh county councils . . . There may be points in the Bill which I cannot agree with, and, until I have seen it in print, I must reserve further opinion.[2]

He did not take part in the brief discussion following Balfour's statement, nor was he one of the four Welsh M.P.s who opposed the Bill's First Reading.

Yet even before the full text was published the following night it must have been obvious to him that he would have to take a more militant line or forfeit all his accumulated credit as a spokesman for British Nonconformity. The *Daily News* leader on the 25th was a tirade against Balfour's

---

1. D.L.G. to M.L.G., 24 March 1902 (N.L.W., quoted in *Letters*, pp. 131–2).
2. *Western Mail*, 25 March 1902. In Frank Owen, *Tempestuous Journey* (p. 124), this interview is misquoted, the word 'unfavourably' appearing as 'favourably', so conveying the opposite of Lloyd George's true meaning.

scheme. Significantly entitled 'The Anti-School Board Bill', it was a resounding call to arms:

> The School Boards are to be destroyed because they stand for enlighten-
> ment and progress. Education is to be shovelled aside because it is the
> worst enemy of the present Government . . . It is to be the tool of the
> Church, the servant of the Treasury, and the slave of the capitalist . . .
> That is the vista opened out to us by schemes like this Bill. If it is not
> resisted with might and main by the Liberal party, then their work has
> indeed been in vain.

At the same time H. W. Massingham reported in his Parliamentary column that Dr John Clifford, who had listened to Balfour's statement from the Distinguished Strangers' Gallery, was already 'a strong opponent of the Bill'.[1]

Lloyd George could not afford to disregard these portents. The *Daily News* was the newspaper which he himself had secured for anti-Boer War Liberalism, when at the end of 1900 he had engineered its take-over by a syndicate including George Cadbury, the eminent Quaker and cocoa manufacturer. His success with Cadbury was symptomatic of his powerful appeal to English Nonconformists, whose support he was now in danger of losing if he did not join in the campaign against Balfour's Education Bill. Dr John Clifford was literally a John the Baptist among the Non-conformists of his day. He was a most eloquent Baptist minister, preacher and pamphleteer, whose chapel was in West London but whose influence was disseminated to every part of the country. His lively and largely self-taught mind was broader theologically than politically, and it may have been helpful to him to have a good political issue to reconcile him with fellow-Nonconformists whose fundamentalism he could not share, just as it became helpful to Lloyd George to be reconciled by a good sectarian issue with fellow-Liberals who supported the Boer War. In any case, however simple or complex Dr Clifford's motives, there could be no doubt that his declared opposition to Balfour's Bill was a factor of the first importance.

On 26 March the *Daily News* commented venomously upon the published text of what it called 'The Bishop's Bill', against which, accord-ing to Massingham, Liberal opinion was 'rapidly hardening and stiffening'; while the Revd Dr W. T. Townsend, President of the National Council of Free Churches, was quoted as saying that the Bill was 'most reactionary

1. *Daily News*, 25 March 1902: leading article, and 'Pictures in Parliament' by H.W.M.

in all its aspects', and as expressing 'the conviction that Free Churchmen throughout the country would offer their most determined opposition' to it. That afternoon there was a well-attended meeting of the Council's Education Committee, at which the Bill was roundly condemned. Afterwards the secretary, the Revd Thomas Law, was asked by a reporter if Wales was likely to suffer, and replied: 'It appears that the Bill has practically no relation to Wales, but it is expected that Welsh Nonconformists will stand side by side with English Nonconformists in opposing the measure.'[1] Another hint for Lloyd George.

Among practical politicians few have been less cowardly than he was, but even he had to recognize the difference between a tide which it was worth trying to resist, whatever the hazards, and a tide which it would simply be suicidal folly to resist. On the Boer War issue he had stood against a huge wave of public opinion, risking his reputation and, occasionally, his life. But he did not stand alone. Many shared his view of the war, and – more to the point – those who shared it were of the same political household as himself. His support came from Liberals and radicals who were his normal associates, while those who denounced him as a traitor were, in the main, his normal adversaries. If, however, he had persisted in his ambiguous attitude towards the new Education Bill he would not only have been struck by a wave of opinion and emotion comparable with the jingoistic wave with which he had to contend during the Boer War; he would also have known that the people who were being borne along by it were his own people, and that, by not joining them, he would soon be left stranded and probably perish in isolation. It would then be his friends, rather than his enemies, who would be cursing him as a traitor, and the Tories would have reason to rejoice at the gratuitous elimination of a formidable party opponent.

He therefore decided, not for the first or last time in his career, to make a virtue of necessity and to move in a direction which forces beyond his control dictated, while retaining as much initiative and freedom of manœuvre as circumstances might permit. So great was his success that he was soon regarded as the movement's Parliamentary leader. Far from appearing to be the slave of events, he appeared to be – and, in the tactical sense, undoubtedly was – their master.

Moreover, he accomplished the still more remarkable feat of persuading

1. *Daily News*, 26 and 27 March 1902. The latter issue also contained two letters from Dr Clifford, one written before, the other after, he had read the text of the Bill. The first was much shorter, but no less hostile to the Bill, than the second.

posterity, as well as his own contemporaries, that his fight against the Bill was utterly spontaneous – the gut reaction of a chapel-bred boy. In reality, his instincts were more secularist than Nonconformist. He rejected dogmatic Christianity of every kind, and had a special dislike for the Nonconformist kind, because he had a more direct experience of it than of any other and because its moral atmosphere was in many ways so alien to him. His statement to a Welsh friend – 'I hate a priest, Daniel, whenever I find him'[1] – should not be taken too seriously. He was never a good hater, and certainly did not always hate priests, whether Anglican or Roman Catholic. With Bishop Edwards of St Asaph, the most robust of the Welsh Church leaders, he was on terms of warm personal friendship; and in 1897, while on a visit to Rome, he had been much impressed by Pope Leo XIII. To be truthful, he would have had to admit that all ministers of religion were liable, as a class to irritate him, but that there were exceptions in every sect. His famous demonstration against saying the Creed at the Llanystumdwy church school which he attended as a boy – where, incidentally, he was very well taught and treated – would have been less warmly appreciated by orthodox Nonconformists had they realized that, even at the time, the Creed itself meant virtually nothing to him.

Tolerant by nature, he also had political grounds for tolerance on the Church schools issue. He had always wanted to get it out of the way so that Wales and the Liberal Party could concentrate upon urgent social reform. He could see that Balfour had gone as far as it was politically possible for a Tory leader to go towards establishing public control over the denominational schools. To a Welshman, the prospective fate of the school boards was not the tragic affair that it seemed to be to English Nonconformists, because in Wales the Bill confirmed and extended the functions of the local committees established by the Welsh Intermediate Education Act of 1889. (Hence Mr Law's statement that the Bill had 'practically no relation to Wales'.) Lloyd George was bored by sectarian squabbles and he knew that any campaign which gave an artificial stimulus to sectarian feeling in Wales would make life difficult for him in the event of a Liberal victory, since it would increase the Nonconformist clamour for Disestablishment while stiffening the resistance of Church people. Disestablishment was a cause to which he had to pay lip-service, but he had long been aware that it would never be passed by an unreformed

1. From D. R. Daniel's memoir of Lloyd George (N.L.W., quoted in *Letters*, Introduction p. 7).

House of Lords and that it did not matter enough to the British people as a whole to provide a suitable issue on which to force a show-down with the Second Chamber.

For these reasons, though as conscious as anyone of the scope afforded by the Bill for bashing the Tories and for re-creating Liberal unity, he would have preferred not to exploit it, other things being equal. But other things were not equal and he therefore set about exploiting it with his usual gusto.

At the end of the week which began with Balfour's statement to the House of Commons Lloyd George told his constituents at Pwllheli that the Bill 'tended to pander to priestcraft'.[1] This was his first reference to the religious issue and it marks the shift in his public line. But he was still in no hurry to become totally embattled. He needed time to prepare his arguments and his plan of campaign. An attack of laryngitis gave him an excuse for silence in the early part of April and, though present at the national conference of the Free Churches' Council on 15 April, he was not one of the speakers.[2]

But on the 24th he delivered, at Swansea, a full-scale onslaught on the Bill, claiming that in his whole experience of politics he could recollect no issue 'so thoroughly serious, so important, so far-reaching'. The questions involved 'went to the very root of free institutions'. Nonconformists were being 'forced to contribute towards propagating doctrines they did not believe in'. But he drew a politic distinction between Roman Catholic and Anglican schools: whereas the former were generally kept for Catholics only, Anglican schools were 'really State schools used for the purpose of proselytising Nonconformists'. If the Catechism were to be set above the Bible, it must be taught at the Anglicans' own expense. He asserted the supremacy, the all-sufficiency, of the Bible, with heavy emphasis on its social implications:

> There was once a time when the people of this country had mastered the Bible, and at the same time there arose in this country a monarch who taxed the people without their consent for purposes to which they objected. There also arose a State priesthood who wanted to exalt over all their extravagant pretensions. There was a famous Scripture reader with Welsh blood in his veins, of the name of Oliver Cromwell. He had

1. Quoted in *Daily News*, 29 March 1902.
2. The conference was held in St James's Hall, London, and was 'characterized by the greatest unanimity and enthusiasm' against the Bill (*The Times*, 16 April 1902).

mastered all the revolutionary and explosive texts in that Book, and the result was destructive to that State priesthood. The bench of bishops was blown up, the House of Lords disappeared, and the aristocracy of this land rocked as though an earthquake had shaken them.

Lloyd George told his wife that he would disappoint the audience at Swansea. 'They will expect brimstone. I will give them bread.'[1] In the event, he gave them plenty of both.

There was rather less brimstone, however, in his House of Commons speech on the Bill's Second Reading. The debate on this lasted for four days, from 5 to 8 May, and Lloyd George was the first speaker on the last day. His purpose, he said, was not to criticize the machinery of the Bill, but to present 'the Nonconformist case against the principle' of it. The Church of England had 'over 12,000 schools in the country', which were 'mission rooms' for proselytising 'the children of the poor'. In 8,000 parishes there were no alternative schools. Teachers in Church schools were, in effect, paid by the State, which meant that 'the patronage of 60,000 excellent appointments in the Civil Service' belonged to the Church. Yet out of two million children in Church schools, one million were Nonconformists; and in Wales, he did not neglect to add, Nonconformists constituted 'the vast majority'.

To the argument that the board schools were Nonconformist establishments, he replied that since they were controlled by the ratepayers, and most ratepayers were Anglican, it followed that most board members were 'denominationalists'. Whereas it was easy enough for a Churchman to be appointed teacher or even head teacher in a board school, staff appointments in Church schools were very largely dependent upon Church membership. But even in his new-found militancy Lloyd George was not prepared to make a fetish of the board schools. He would not, he said, object to their abolition if the authority which took their place were 'a representative authority', and if control of the schools were given to the people.

His peroration was an appeal to the Irish Members. He reminded them that the beneficiaries of the Bill were Ireland's enemies, its victims Ireland's friends. British Nonconformists had thrown over their 'most cherished leaders', such as Spurgeon, Bright and Chamberlain, for the sake of Ireland. They had been more true to the cause of Irish Home Rule than

1. D.L.G. to M.L.G., 21 April 1902 (N.L.W., quoted in *Letters*, p. 134). The statistics which he mugged up before the Swansea speech served as his working capital throughout the campaign.

Princes of the Roman Catholic Church had been. Would the Irish Members now help to pass an Act under which British Nonconformists would be 'sold up for rates . . . probably imprisoned'?

According to Massingham, Lloyd George's claim that the Irish owed more to British Nonconformists than to their own Church leaders was greeted with 'loud and assenting cheers from Mr Dillon and the whole Irish party'.[1] All the same, the Irish did not oppose the Bill's Second Reading, which was carried by 402 votes to 165, with many Irishmen, including Dillon and Redmond, voting in the majority.[2] Massingham also described the general effect of Lloyd George's speech in terms which proclaim the birth of a myth. The speech, he said, 'had the high interest of being a complete and sincere self-revelation'. Until Lloyd George spoke, Nonconformity had 'gone without a recorder and a champion', but he had taken 'the vacant place'. So he had, but with a strict economy of sincerity undetected at the time and, more surprisingly, overlooked by historians.

While Campbell-Bannerman, Asquith and other party leaders were united in denunciation of the Bill, one prominent Liberal back-bencher continued to give it qualified approval, though without actually voting for it. This was Richard Burdon Haldane, the future War Minister. Haldane was a passionate educationist, whose work as a promoter of British civic universities would alone entitle him to a place in the roll of fame. He was also personally attached to Balfour, as a fellow bachelor, Lowlander and amateur philosopher. Lloyd George, in his Second Reading speech, twitted Haldane on his contribution to the debate. The hon. Member for Haddington was 'politically speaking . . . above the snowline'. His counsel was 'very serene in its purity, but rather sterile'. Let him descend from the region of eternal snow and he would find it was not so easy as he thought to dispose of the religious problem. In fact, Haldane needed no instruction in the matter. To judge from their public utterances, he had been quicker than Lloyd George to see how vulnerable the Bill would be to sectarian attack. Unlike Lloyd George, he had intervened in the short discussion on First Reading when, after welcoming the proposed reform in principle, he had expressed the fear that religious controversy had not been laid to rest, because two-thirds of the voluntary school managers would not be appointed by the public authority. Lloyd George had failed to refer to this issue when he spoke to a journalist after the debate, but between First and

1. *Daily News*, 9 May 1902.
2. But in December the Irish abstained on Third Reading.

Second Reading his public attitude changed, as we have seen, rather abruptly. Haldane's remained constant. In his view, the Bill's merits outweighed its defects – a view which Lloyd George privately shared. Having reluctantly decided that he must, himself, take up a position below the snowline, he doubtless secretly respected Haldane for staying on the heights, just as Haldane probably understood why he was compelled to move to a lower altitude. In any case, their mutual goodwill was unimpaired.[1]

Between Second Reading and Committee stage the Boer War was brought to an end, and with it one of the most testing phases of Lloyd George's career. The new controversy was to serve him as well politically, but would cost him much less in emotional and nervous stress. He gave it his whole mind, but only half his heart. Yet he did not spare himself in the long Parliamentary struggle over the Bill, which was in Committee for a total of forty-nine days between early June and early December. During that time Lloyd George made about a hundred and sixty speeches in the House of Commons. They varied in length, but many were very substantial, and the figure does not include mere interruptions. His command of the subject and never-failing adroitness impressed his opponents as much as they delighted his own side, and Balfour was speaking for all, or nearly all, when he said that Lloyd George had played 'a most distinguished part', and had 'shown himself to be an eminent Parliamentarian', throughout the debates on the Bill.[2]

The Government's decision not to oppose an amendment making the assumption of power by L.E.A.s compulsory rather than optional might have embarrassed him a little – had he been the sort of person who was easily embarrassed – because the option clause had been the only thing he privately objected to in Balfour's scheme, when it was first expounded. But he now made a plausible case against the amendment, arguing that it would be 'a great mischief' unless preceded by a move to substitute democratic for denominational control of the voluntary schools. If the

1. About three weeks later Lloyd George wrote to his wife: 'Saw Haldane now for the first time since I chaffed him on the Education Bill. He sent me a copy of his Education Book just out & he told me that he meant to label it "Views from above the Snowline".' (D.L.G. to M.L.G., 28 May 1902, N.L.W., and *Letters*, p. 136.) The book referred to was Haldane's *Education and Empire* (1902).

2. Balfour's speech on Third Reading, 3 December 1902 (Hansard, Fourth Series, Vol. CXV, cols 1170–80). Lloyd George wrote next day to his wife: 'What a handsome compliment Balfour paid me . . . The general cheering in the House was very remarkable – the Tories being nearly as hearty as our own men'. (D.L.G. to M.L.G., 4 December 1902, N.L.W., and *Letters*, p. 138.)

Nonconformist grievance on that point were met, there would probably be no trouble about dropping the option clause. But the Government would not remove the grievance. He reminded the Tories of 'Ulster will fight and Ulster will be right', and asked how that doctrine differed from that of the Nonconformist who said he had a conscientious objection to paying rates for sectarian education.[1]

When the management of the voluntary schools was specifically discussed, on Clause 7, he was in excellent form. The party that professed to believe in the Empire was 'founding in England and Wales a system of education which would not be tolerated anywhere else in all our Imperial Dominions'. New Zealand and Canada, for instance, were 'reared on the secular system', whereas 'the great example of denominationalism' was Ireland. How could Britain hope to compete in the world with such a handicap?

> For the sake of teaching dogmas to children who cannot understand them, we, in the midst of our difficulties and the rocks that surround us, propose to put the chaplain on the bridge. It is a mad proposal.

Whether or not the proposal was mad, 'the chaplain on the bridge' was certainly a memorable phrase.[2]

After the recess Lloyd George achieved, by proxy, his most significant practical success during the passage of the Bill. On 12 November Sir Alfred Thomas proposed an amendment to Clause 12, to the effect that in Wales, as in England, the bodies responsible for education under the new law should be the county councils rather than the bodies set up under the Welsh Intermediate Education Act of 1889. Several members of the Welsh Parliamentary group were distressed at the idea of scrapping a system of which they were proud, and which was working well. But Lloyd George had his ulterior reasons, soon to be made manifest. By 'tremendous determination and driving force' he got his way at the private meeting,[3] and then shrewdly entrusted the amendment to the chairman, Alfred Thomas, who seemed relatively innocuous. Balfour was glad of the chance to be able to do something, as he thought, to appease the Welsh, and rather gratified by their apparent desire to assimilate the system of

1. Hansard, Fourth Series, Vol. CX, 9 July 1902: Lloyd George's speech, cols 1280-4. The amendment was carried 271-102 on a free vote. Joseph Chamberlain, for whose benefit the option clause had been included, was out of action at the time, having recently been injured in a cab accident. His son, Austen, voted against the amendment.
2. Hansard, Fourth Series, Vol. CXII, 7 August 1902: Lloyd George's speech, cols 1022-5.
3. Herbert Lewis's diary, 11 November 1902, quoted in K. O. Morgan, *Wales in British Politics, 1868-1922*, p. 187.

control in Wales to his English model. He therefore accepted the amendment, suspecting no booby-trap, and it went through after a brief discussion in which Lloyd George himself was careful to take no part.[1]

The Bill was sent to the House of Lords on 3 December and received the Royal Assent on 20 December. In the Third Reading debate Lloyd George adopted his own variant of the holier-than-thou ploy:

> I have only one word to add. There is a clear issue before the country. Public control – yes; and if you are going to teach religion in the schools, teach it from the Book which is acceptable to all Christians . . . Give the children the Bible if you want to teach them the Christian faith. Let it be expounded to them by its Founder. Stop this brawling of priests in and around the schools, so that the children may hear Him speak to them in His own words. I appeal to the House of Commons now, at the eleventh hour, to use its great influence and lift its commanding voice and say, 'Pray, silence for the Master'.[2]

As oratory this was doubtless effective, but as argument it was disingenuous. H. A. L. Fisher is surely right when he says that 'Religions are founded by laymen and organized by priests'.[3] There have to be people to organize and interpret, or there can be no living, lasting, coherent religious community. Without such people, Christendom would never have existed. There is little evidence that Jesus Christ himself realized he was founding an elaborate organization which would persist and proliferate through the ages. Indeed, there is some reason to think he was expecting the world to come to an end before everyone who heard him preach was dead. The divisions of Christianity reflect genuine differences of interpretation deriving from, and not capable of being spirited away by, assiduous study of the Bible. Lloyd George's appeal to the House of Commons was good politics, but too simple by half as a formula for religious education.

While the Education Bill was going through Parliament, the Nonconformist campaign against it in the country was growing in scale and

1. Hansard, Fourth Series, Vol. CXIV, 12 November 1902, cols 765–74. In 1898 Lloyd George had refused to stand against Alfred Thomas for the chairmanship of the Welsh group, partly because he was confident that Thomas would always be guided by him. Events proved him right.
2. Hansard, Fourth Series, Vol. CXV, 3 December 1902: Lloyd George's speech, cols 1112–23.   3. *A History of Europe*, ch. XIV.

QUEEN ARTHUR: *Won't someone take that man away? I do so dislike his style.* (Suggested by Wilkie's picture of John Knox preaching before Mary Queen of Scots.)

(*Mr. Balfour in a pamphlet published yesterday says that he doesn't like Dr. Clifford's style.*)

1. 'The Modern John Knox', *Westminster Gazette*, 5 December 1902 (Lloyd George shown sitting below Dr. Clifford)

intensity. On 12 June a star-studded deputation representing the Free Churches waited on Balfour, and an address was read to him by Principal Fairbairn, of Mansfield College, Oxford. In July, a by-election at Leeds demonstrated what the Education controversy was doing to party fortunes, when a Tory majority of over 2,500 was turned into a Liberal majority of over 750; the following month a Liberal candidate who was a Baptist came near to capturing Sevenoaks from the Tories: and in November Orkney and Shetland fell to the Liberals. Also in November a huge anti-Bill rally was held in London, at Alexandra Palace, with 15,000 people inside the building and 4,000 on the terrace.

At this rally Dr Clifford was given a tumultuous welcome. He was the chief Nonconformist hero of the hour, and his letters to the *Daily News,* published in pamphlet form, had a readership running into hundreds of thousands. In December Balfour himself replied to them in a short but exquisitely ironic open letter. Admitting the wide circulation of Clifford's pamphlet, he said that it could 'hardly be counted a waste of time to devote a few pages to the consideration of so important a masterpiece'. In his view, Clifford was the victim of his own rhetoric:

> Distortion and exaggeration are of its very essence. If he has to speak of our pending differences, acute no doubt, but not unprecedented, he must needs compare them to the great Civil War. If he has to describe a deputation of Nonconformist ministers presenting their case to the leader of the House of Commons, nothing less will serve him as a parallel than Luther's appearance before the Diet of Worms. If he has to indicate that, as sometimes happens in the case of a deputation, the gentlemen composing it firmly believed in the strength of their own case, this cannot be done at a smaller rhetorical cost than by describing them as 'earnest men speaking in the austere tones of invincible conviction'. The follies, or, if you please, the worse than follies, of a few parsons become 'typical of the whole situation' . . . In looking over the catalogue of epithets with which he has assailed this Education Bill and its authors, I find myself wondering on what linguistic resources he would draw had he to describe the Gunpowder Plot, or the Massacre of St Bartholomew.

Such elegant deflation must have given great pleasure to Balfour's more literate supporters, and may also have been quietly savoured by some of his political opponents, including – we may suspect – Lloyd George. All the same, it was probably unwise for a Prime Minister to argue thus with a critic who was not even a Member of Parliament. Whatever the merits of the case, in the short run Balfour's reply could hardly fail to add to Clifford's prestige.[1]

Yet all was not well in the Nonconformist ranks. United in fighting the Bill, they were by no means united when it came to fighting the Act. Clifford called for passive resistance, in the form of withholding payment of the Education rate for Church schools, and a large majority of the local Free Church councils at first supported his policy without giving much thought to the implications. In December, however, when the National Committee met in Birmingham to discuss the problem seriously, it appeared that a strong minority was opposed to any defiance of the law. Wesleyans, in particular, tended to recoil from the Clifford policy, and in other sects as well there were many who had qualms about it, with the result that it could not be made official Free Church policy. The Passive Resistance Committee which was set up to organize the 'No Say – No Pay' campaign was not a committee of the Free Church Council, though in the public mind the two were inevitably confused.

The Government could only benefit from the English Nonconformists' disarray, and the implementation of the Act was skilfully contrived to limit the scope for 'martyrdom'. For a start, the new law did not come into force until 1 April 1903, by which time the passive resistance movement had lost some of its initial ardour. Moreover, the movement itself was ill-considered and more or less doomed to end in anti-climax. The proportion of the rates applicable to the Church schools was so small that the withholding of it by a comparatively few people could not affect the financial viability of the scheme; nor, by the same token, could those who suffered distraint of goods to the value of the amount withheld appear to be making a very heroic sacrifice. Yet a total refusal to pay rates, which would have involved more substantial penalties, would also have involved the passive resisters in sabotaging public services of which they approved, and would have ensured their forfeiture of what little sympathy they may have commanded among the general public.

In the event, the Act worked smoothly in most English counties and municipalities. Passive resistance was confined to a few areas, and even in those areas did not reach unmanageable dimensions. By the beginning of 1904, 7,324 summonses had been issued against persons refusing to pay the

1. Dr Clifford's pamphlet – *The Fight Against the Education Bill: What is at Stake* – was published by the National Reform Union. A. J. Balfour's *Letter on the Criticisms of an Opponent* seems to have been published by himself: the printer was Eyre & Spottiswoode.

Education rate, or the proportion of it calculated to be for the benefit of the Church schools; and 329 distraint sales of goods had taken place.[1] At about this time a Passive Resisters' Anti-Martyrdom League was formed in Bradford, to pay the money which the resisters refused to pay and so to deprive their campaign of any effect. But such counter-measures were hardly necessary. For all practical purposes the campaign was a flop, and nobody who took part in it – least of all any leader of it – acquired the status of a martyr. There seem to have been only two cases of imprisonment, both trifling.[2] Dr Clifford and other instigators of the movement remained at large, attending mass meetings and ever more vehemently castigating the Act and its authors. But they were the sort of people, conspicuous then as now, who mistake political agitation for political action.

Lloyd George, however, was not that sort of person. Though he gave perfunctory moral support to the English Nonconformist militants – on the ground that they were taking the only course open to them, short of abject surrender – he could see that their campaign was futile, all the more so as Nonconformists were a minority in England. But in Wales, where they were a majority, he was determined that they should resist the Act more effectively. Faced with the spectacle of eleven Welsh county councils voting to follow the English example by simply denying rate aid to Church schools, he made it his business to change their minds and their mode of resistance. On 17 January 1903 he addressed a manifesto to the Welsh people, in which he offered his own alternative plan of campaign:

> . . . there is no greater tactical mistake possible than to prosecute an agitation against an injustice in such a way as to alienate a large number of men who, whilst they resent that injustice as keenly as anyone, either from tradition or timidity decline to be associated with anything savouring of revolutionary action. Such action should always be the last desperate resort of reformers . . . It behoves us also to think what the

1. *Annual Register, 1903*, ch. V, pp. 232–3. The number of distraint sales is not only small in itself, but also significantly small in relation to the number of summonses. Most of the passive resisters were obviously content to make their little gesture of defiance, and then pay up.

2. 'In March 1904 two ministers were committed to prison for non-payment of the Education rate. The Rev. Allon Poole of Southgate was sentenced to seven days' imprisonment, but escaped because someone paid the rate for him, while the Rev. W. H. Higgins of Coventry spent seven days in Warwick Gaol, for in order to avoid distraint upon his goods he had made them all over to his wife.' (E. K. H. Jordan, *Free Church Unity: History of the Free Church Council Movement*, 1896–1941, p. 94.) There appears to be no basis for the assertion in some other books that a considerable number of Nonconformists went to prison.

effect would be upon the education of the children . . . The interests of a whole generation of children will be sacrificed. It is not too big a price to pay for freedom, if this is the only resource available to us. But is it? I think not.

My advice is, let us capture the enemy's artillery and turn his guns against him.

He then explained in detail what he meant. Responsibility for administering the Act lay with the Welsh county councils, thanks to the Alfred Thomas amendment – which was as much as to say, though he did not say it, thanks to himself. It was essential for the councils to work together and to delegate some of their power to a Welsh central board. Outside nominees to local education committees must be from bodies which, like the councils themselves, were representative of the ratepayers. Voluntary schools should be inspected by competent architects or surveyors, who would report whether or not they were up to standard in the space provided for pupils, state of repair, ventilation, sanitation, lighting and facilities for play. If any were below standard – as Lloyd George knew many were – the local education authorities should refuse to become responsible for their maintenance until the defects were made good. 'The sectarian schools should be properly cleansed and clothed before they are allowed to associate on equal terms with more decently clad institutions.'

In addition, the Welsh L.E.A.s were to refuse rate aid unless the trustees of these schools would concede full public control and forgo all religious or political tests on the appointment of teachers. If any council were to grant rate aid without having first secured public control, Lloyd George had 'no hesitation' in advising Welsh Nonconformists to 'make the collection of those rates as difficult as possible'. And he concluded with a stirring appeal to Welsh national sentiment:

The Education Act of 1902 has presented Wales with its greatest political opportunity. It is exceptionally equipped . . . to take full advantage of this opportunity. Wales presents the spectacle of a well-ordered and highly disciplined community, where intense political and religious convictions produce no excesses which repel the most sensitive friend of good order . . . A patriotism which has not fallen into the fatal error of confounding depth of greed with breadth of outlook, or into the equally fatal error of imagining that war and politics are the only fields where a man can exhibit his love for his native land. A patriotism which for generations was almost purely literary before it became religious, which was religious fully a century and educational at least a generation before it annexed politics, and which, in adding new interests and activities to the national life, never forsook the old. If in this great struggle we are now entering upon Wales acts with a firm courage and a dignified restraint . . . it will emerge from the conflict with a national position surpassing the dreams of the line of prophets who foretold great things for 'Gwalia Wen' ere they passed to their rest under the shadow of its hills.[1]

Four days later, at Cardiff, he gave a further exposition of his policy. 'We must remember that, administratively, we are in power in Wales – and thank heaven for that.' They had to consider how far they could go, but in his view the Act was so badly drafted that they could go a long distance. 'I will not go a step beyond the strict limits of the law. I will give the pound of flesh – just one pound, and not a drop of blood. We should put a premium on popular control . . . For popular control – cash, and cash down. No popular control – no cash.'[2] His speech was loudly applauded, and most Welsh councils soon endorsed his plan of campaign.

Though he made out that he was taking his stand on the letter of the law, he was actually defying the law in letter as well as in spirit, on the reasonable assumption that it would not be enforced against a clear majority of the Welsh people. Having contrived, through the Alfred Thomas amendment, that the bodies most representative of Wales – the elected councils – should be responsible for administering the Act, he was able to play local democracy against legality, or one form of right against another. The Act afforded no legal justification for withholding rate aid indefinitely if church schools were judged, by the councils, to be below standard, or for withholding it at all if their trustees would not concede popular control. It was provided in the Act that L.E.A.s should have the power to inspect such schools, and that their managers were obliged to keep them in good repair and to carry out improvements as directed by the L.E.A.s – but subject to arbitration by the Board of Education in cases of dispute. Every attempt to amend the Bill so as to secure public management of the schools had been defeated, and the Act could not, therefore, be interpreted as giving L.E.A.s any legal right to demand control in return for cash. On the other hand, Lloyd George perceived that the

1. Address to the People of Wales, 17 January 1903. The full text is printed in Herbert du Parcq, *Life of David Lloyd George*, Vol. II, Appendix III, pp. 412–16.
2. Speech at Conference of the Welsh National Liberal Council, Cory Hall, Cardiff, 21 January 1903.

Welsh councils would have an important physical sanction, in that rate aid could only be disbursed by them, and a still more important moral sanction, in that they were democratically elected bodies against which the Government would hesitate to apply the rigours of the law. According to the Act, the Board of Education was entitled, after a public enquiry, to impose its will upon a defaulting L.E.A. by the procedure of mandamus, but in his Cardiff speech Lloyd George challenged the Government to use this procedure, if it dared: 'Will the Government mandamus the county councillors? I hope they will try it.'[1]

Having established a strong fighting position he thought next, as was his wont, of trying to end the conflict by negotiation. He would have been glad if this particular conflict had never arisen, and was certainly well satisfied with the kudos it had already brought him. To his mind, the best hope of a solution lay in the so-called 'Colonial compromise', whereby facilities might be provided outside school hours for the dogmatic religious instruction required by parents. Towards the end of March a conference was held in London between representatives, lay and ecclesiastical, of voluntary schools in the diocese of St Asaph, and representatives of the Welsh county councils. The points discussed were the form of dogmatic religious instruction to be permitted, the terms on which voluntary schools and county councils would agree to it, the appointment of teachers and the management of the schools. It is clear from the conference report that there was never any serious chance of all-round agreement, though Lloyd George and the Bishop of St Asaph bent over backwards to find a workable compromise. Unfortunately most of their colleagues and supporters, who responded readily enough to their public militancy, were less ready to follow them in their true character of moderates and realists. When an archdeacon taxed Lloyd George with some provocative remark he had made in a speech, he replied with disconcerting frankness: 'That was purely

1. On Lloyd George's copy of the Education Bill, preserved in the Lloyd George Papers, he has underlined the words in Clause 11 'and any such order may be enforced by mandamus', and has written in the margin the word 'Imprisonment'. He has also marked subsection 2 of Clause 13, which reads: 'All receipts in respect of any school maintained by a local education authority, including the annual Parliamentary grant, but excluding sums specially applicable for purposes for which provision is to be made by the managers, shall be paid to that authority'. (L.G.P., A/2/8/2.)

Du Parcq's statement (op. cit., Vol. II, p. 361) that Lloyd George 'had managed to get an amendment accepted which relieved a local authority from undertaking the upkeep of a school unless it was in proper repair' is totally untrue. By 1911, when du Parcq was writing under his subject's supervision, Lloyd George had no desire to appear to have preached sedition in 1903. But in fact he had.

a fighting speech. I had my war paint on then.' He also admitted that the Church would benefit, on school management committees, from the rivalry among Nonconformist sects. Members of smaller sects might often, he implied, support a Churchman rather than a Methodist. Such admissions failed to win the other side's confidence, though they may have jeopardised his own side's confidence in him.[1]

On some issues, however, there were signs of near-consensus at the London meeting, and if the Bishop of St Asaph had subsequently been able to carry Welsh Churchmen with him, Lloyd George would probably have been able to sell to Welsh Nonconformists a concordat on the maintained Anglican schools, of which the main features would have been an agreed syllabus for religious instruction in school hours, an arrangement for denominational teaching – about three-quarters of an hour a week – technically out of school hours, and an ingeniously fudged procedure for the choice of school managers.[2] But the Bishop did not succeed in winning general support for such a concordat even in his own diocese, let alone in the other Welsh dioceses which were more intransigent. So the attempt at peacemaking failed and Lloyd George had to reappear in his 'war paint'. In June he told an English audience that only the rich could afford to be ignorant. They had their cellars, but the only cellar accessible to the poor had but one key, an educated mind: 'I tell you that our business is to snatch the key from the girdle of the priest and hand it to the people.'[3]

Only two Welsh councils – Brecknockshire and Radnorshire, which had Tory majorities – refused outright to toe the Lloyd George line and voted rate aid, without conditions, to Church schools. He also had some initial difficulty with Carmarthenshire, but this was soon resolved. By and large Wales presented a formidably united front behind his leadership and for some months the Government stayed its hand, postponing enforcement of the Act in Wales until 1 February 1904.

Meanwhile party feeling was growing rapidly in the country, as Chamberlain's Tariff Reform campaign stirred traditional Liberalism to

1. Proceedings of Conference at Westminster Palace Hotel, 24 March 1903 (L.G.P., A/2/8/14). Among the St Asaph representatives were the Roman Catholic Bishop of Menevia, the Rev. Stephen Gladstone, a son of the G.O.M., and Stanley Weyman, the popular novelist. Herbert Lewis was among the Welsh county council representatives. Frank Edwards took the chair.
2. Lloyd George suggested, for instance, that for any vacancy the L.E.A. should submit three names to the managers, from which they would make their selection.
3. Speech at meeting of North Stafford Liberal Federation, Victoria Hall, Hanley, 18 June 1903, Lord Crewe presiding.

the depths and seemed to augur an early collapse of the Government.[1] English Nonconformists felt that their cause would soon triumph and were suspicious of any conciliatory moves, such as the St Asaph talks. In July 1903 they staged at the Albert Hall what was described as the largest indoor meeting ever held in London. Lloyd George was one of the speakers and said that the audience – over 17,000 people – was nearly three times as numerous as his electorate in the Caernarvon Boroughs.[2] The fighting spirit displayed on this and other similar occasions was aroused by the prospect – illusory, as it turned out – of an early general election, and was therefore matched by that of the Liberal leaders, who naturally wished to make the most of every available grievance while an election was impending. They already had plenty of evidence that the sectarian issue was worth many votes to them, and in what they assumed to be the fairly short time remaining before the nation went to the polls they intended to extract full value from the issue. In particular, they were determined to keep the Welsh revolt going, and to identify themselves with it unmistakably. At the end of November Campbell-Bannerman addressed a meeting in South Wales, at which he referred to Lloyd George as 'your foremost champion – yes, and the champion of us all against clerical pretensions and political injustice'.[3]

The crescendo of controversy distressed and alarmed Morant – now Permanent Secretary to the Board of Education[4] – who saw the great reform that he had done so much to promote imperilled. It was clear to him that the mandamus procedure could never be used against the Welsh councils, but it was also clear that, for the time being, the national leadership of the Liberal Party would discourage any attempt to make the Act acceptable to Wales. As he wrote to Herbert Lewis:

> One difficulty is that one hears the front Opposition bench do not want to see anything like a settlement arrived at, because the education cry is likely to be so useful at the General Election. If this be indeed the case

1. See Chapter Three.
2. Meeting of Free Churchmen held to protest, specifically, against the London Education Bill, 11 July 1903.
3. Speech at Newport, Mon., 30 November 1903.
4. He took up the appointment formally on 1 April 1903, having been Acting Secretary since 1 November 1902. There were also new Ministers at the Board since Balfour became Prime Minister in July 1902. Lord Londonderry was President in place of the Duke of Devonshire: he was another figurehead. The new Parliamentary Secretary in place of Sir John Gorst was Sir William Anson, who sat for Oxford University and was Warden of All Souls College there, but who carried no political weight.

the Unionists cd hardly *force* a bill thro', cd they, which was intended (as you suggest) to be a pacificatory settlement.[1]

This was written just after an event which made such a settlement less likely than ever – the local elections in Wales, which returned in overwhelming strength candidates pledged to demand the abolition of religious tests for teachers, and full public control of all maintained schools as the price of rate aid. Wales was now solid for the Lloyd George policy, and Lloyd George had reason to be proud of his achievement, which demonstrated finally and incontestably his pre-eminence among the Welsh Members. But he also had reason to hope that it would soon be possible to call the Welsh revolt off, on sufficiently favourable terms. Though it might suit other Liberal leaders that he should be confined, as it were, to the Principality – contributing to a Liberal victory by beating the tribal drum, while not unduly enhancing his reputation as a party spokesman on broader national issues – this did not at all suit Lloyd George. For some months past his speeches up and down the country had been devoted primarily to the case for Free Trade, and he wanted to be free to concentrate upon this and other themes of interest to the whole nation. Since it was beginning to appear that the Government might not, after all, be forced to resign in the near future, Lloyd George could only hope that it would make a big concession to Wales on the Education Act, and so both justify the Welsh revolt and justify his calling it off.

Thus when he raised the question in the House of Commons immediately after the Welsh elections his speech was unexpectedly restrained and emollient. He invited the Government to modify its position, but implied that it would be allowed to do so without too much loss of face.[2] At a meeting of Welsh county council representatives in early April he prepared them for battle, but was still more dove than hawk. 'If we are now compelled to face the disagreeable necessity of fighting this Act, it is not because we did not, in the first instance, seek the ways of peace . . .'[3]

1. Morant to Lewis, 13 March 1904 (Herbert Lewis Papers, N.L.W.). Lewis showed this letter to Lloyd George, who wrote three days later describing it as 'significant' and adding: 'He [Morant] came to me for a talk on Monday – Anson sought me yesterday. Both humble and conciliatory. Morant admits Mandamus is out of the question'. (D.L.G. to Lewis, 16 March 1904, same collection.)

2. Speech on motion to reduce vote on Estimates by £500, to draw attention to administration of Education Act, 14 March 1904 (Hansard, Fourth Series, Vol. CXXXI, cols 1004–15).

3. Conference at Llandrindod, 5 April 1904. In the same speech he referred to the Bishop of St Asaph's good work the year before: 'He met us and met us fairly – the best fighting man

But Balfour was in no mood to make life easier for himself – or for Lloyd George. At the end of April he brought in a Bill empowering the Board of Education, when any local authority was failing to discharge its statutory duties, to spend the necessary money over its head and then deduct the amount from its Parliamentary grant. What it might gain through denying rate aid to Church schools it would thus lose in the denial of grant aid for its own provided schools. This Education (Local Authority Default) Bill was soon nicknamed by its opponents the Coercion of Wales Bill.

As a result Lloyd George was inevitably pushed further out on a limb from which he had been hoping to dismount. His riposte to the Bill was to threaten that if the Government were to use the proposed new power against a Welsh local authority Nonconformist children would be withdrawn from Church schools and, 'if the need arose, from one-half to three-fourths of the existing Church Schools in rural Wales would be practically emptied in six or twelve months'.[1] Even Morant's resolution faltered under this threat, but Balfour's held firm.[2] He judged that moderate opinion would be outraged by the use of schoolchildren as cannon-fodder in a partisan, sectarian war, and no doubt he also regarded Wales as – from the Unionist point of view – electorally expendable. The Default Bill was carried by mid-August, with the Opposition creating a melodramatic scene in protest against the Government's closuring of discussion on the Committee stage. Lloyd George and a score of other M.P.s were 'named' by the Deputy Speaker.[3] Meanwhile a further peace initiative by the Bishop of St Asaph – this time in the form of a Bill introduced in the House of Lords – came to nothing because it failed to satisfy either side.[4]

Once again, Lloyd George gave the Welsh their marching orders at a great meeting in Cardiff, attended by a number of English Free Church leaders, including Dr Clifford. Resolutions were passed calling for a total boycott of Church elementary schools wherever the Default Act was applied, and for the education of Nonconformist children withdrawn from them in improvised school premises, out of funds to be raised voluntarily.

---

in the lot. The best fighters are not always the worst men at coming to terms'. He had himself, as well, in mind.

1. Interview, *North Wales Observer*, 6 May 1904.
2. Bernard M. Allen, *Sir Robert Morant: a Great Public Servant*, p. 223.
3. On 5 August 1904. The Bill became law on 15 August.
4. The Education (Transferred Schools) Bill, introduced in May and abandoned after its Second Reading in July. Lloyd George stayed with the Bishop at his Palace during the National Eisteddfod at Rhyl in September.

The day before he received, at Alfred Thomas's house, a deputation of Welsh teachers who were understandably anxious about their position, and assured them that the Emergency Committee which was being set up would have enough money 'to pay all the teachers in full, at any rate for some time to come'. The Government could not, he believed, declare the whole of Wales in default 'for at least six months' and could not itself survive for more than another 'eighteen months at the outside'. Welsh councils would, he was sure, re-engage every teacher who was given notice, but he could not guarantee compensation for any loss of earnings during the emergency: only that no teacher would starve. The deputation was so encouraged by his remarks that it passed a vote of thanks to him before leaving. Yet there was, surely, some contradiction between his assurance of full pay for an indefinite period and his refusal to guarantee more than bare subsistence. At the mass meeting next day he appealed unreservedly to the spirit of patriotic self-sacrifice – as he did on a more famous occasion ten years later, after the outbreak of war, when he appealed to a wider patriotism.[1]

Fortunately for him, the last stage of the Welsh revolt was limited both in time and in the sacrifices involved. If the Government had hung on for longer than he estimated, or if the Welsh people had been put to anything like the inconvenience that his oratory foreshadowed, he might well have emerged with ignominy from the whole affair. As it was, he managed to come out of it with credit, but only just. When the Government eventually resigned at the end of 1905 only three counties and two municipalities in Wales had suffered penalties under the Default Act, and only in Merionethshire had a substantial number of Nonconformist children been withdrawn from Church schools. The money raised to back the revolt was never fully spent and it is not at all clear what has happened to the balance.[2] But had the emergency lasted another year or more, with children all over Wales becoming dependent upon voluntary resources, it is unlikely that funds

1. Deputation of Welsh elementary-school teachers, received at Bronwydd, Cardiff, 5 October 1904. Convention of Welsh L.E.A. representatives, Park Hall, Cardiff, 6 October 1904.
2. William George, who took an active part in raising the fund, wrote much later that 'a few thousand pounds' were still lying dormant in a local bank, but that his nephew, Lord Tenby, and a retired county court judge, Ernest Evans Q.C. – the last of Lloyd George's nominees – were applying to the Crown for permission to use the money for Welsh educational and cultural purposes (*My Brother and I*, p. 193). There is no evidence, however, of any such permission having been obtained, or of the money having been disposed of in the manner favoured by Alderman George. It may still be lying on deposit in some Welsh bank.

would have been equal to the demands upon them and probable, therefore, that the revolt would have collapsed. Behind the façade of unity many doubted the wisdom of Lloyd George's policy, though only a few – among them D. A. Thomas and Bryn Roberts – were open critics of it. The Government's resignation occurred just in time to save the revolt from going bankrupt, literally and figuratively.

Even while it lasted, however, Welsh Nonconformists would have been less willing to follow Lloyd George but for a lucky, if from his point of view incongruous, development. This was a sudden religious revival inspired by a young miner, Evan Roberts, which swept the Principality from the autumn of 1904 until, roughly, the end of 1905. It then evaporated as swiftly and mysteriously as it had arisen, but meanwhile its timing could hardly have been more propitious for Lloyd George and he adjusted himself to it with a sanctimoniousness which must have imposed some strain upon his facial muscles, if not upon his conscience. At a meeting in his constituency, which was to have been political but under the influence of the revival assumed a religious character, he got up after prolonged hymn-singing and said that he could 'not intrude the inevitable strife of politics into such an atmosphere'. Yet he succeeded in mixing some politics with the unction:

I was travelling through France the other day and, picking up one of the most influential of the French papers, I saw a portrait of Evan Roberts and a sympathetic, appreciative article on the revival, displaying a remarkable insight into the real inwardness of the movement. In one of the French expresses a Frenchman in the same carriage as Mr Herbert Lewis, Mr Frank Edwards and myself discovered in the course of conversation that we came from Wales and the first question he then asked was: 'Will you tell me about the revival?' In Italy, we found the most important paper publishing a three-column article on the revival . . . The other day I was reading Dumont, a book on Mirabeau, and in the course of that great work the author, giving his reminiscences of the French Revolution, apologised for the inadequacy of the information, because he had not the knowledge that the events which he had witnessed with his own eyes were going to have such an effect upon the history, not merely of France, but of the whole of Europe. That is what one always feels about great popular upheavals which one witnesses . . . Even politically I rejoice in the revival. I am not referring to party politics as such, but I have observed that great reforms have followed great religious revivals, and it has been especially true of Wales . . . Every reformer must rejoice in a movement which strengthens the manlier qualities of the race.

Who but Lloyd George would have had the nerve to mention Mirabeau and the French Revolution in such a context? And who but Lloyd George could have got away with it? When he finished speaking the 'vast congregation' did not cheer, but sang 'Diolch, diolch Iddo'.[1]

The Education controversy of 1902–5 is an important rather than a glorious episode in Lloyd George's career. It was a pity that he had to take the line he did, because it was largely insincere. But he was acting under political necessity, of which he was adept at making a virtue. The Welsh revolt which he organized was not a clever evasion of the law, as has been generally believed, but a flat defiance of the law. What he persuaded the Welsh councils to do was more intelligent, but not more legal, than the English Nonconformists' type of passive resistance, which the Welsh were at first disposed to copy. Under his leadership they pretended to be obeying the letter of the law, instead of flaunting their disobedience, which made it easier for the Government to move against them slowly and with studied moderation. But it has to be understood that Ministerial reluctance to crush the revolt was due to weakness and canniness, rather than to any lack of legal excuse.

Throughout the controversy Lloyd George's ascendancy in Wales was plain for all to see, though he failed, as in the *Cymru Fydd* movement back in the 'nineties, to unite his compatriots politically to the extent that he would have wished. The proposal in his manifesto that the Welsh councils should transfer some of their power to a central board was taken up by the Board of Education in London, but disregarded in Wales. All the same, he was able to demonstrate his unrivalled political influence in the Principality, and this was useful to him in the larger arena of British politics.

Equally useful was his reconciliation with the 'Liberal Imperialists', which would have been brought about anyway by the Tariff Reform issue, but which was primarily due to the Education Act. Sir Edward Grey visited Caernarvon at the beginning of 1904 and spoke there of Lloyd

1. Meeting at Pwllheli, 17 January 1905, reported in *Caernarvon Herald*. 'Diolch, diolch Iddo' ('Thanks be to Him') was the refrain of a popular revivalist hymn. Ten days later Lloyd George was writing to Herbert Lewis: 'The Diwygiad [Revival] is immense. I am quite its slave. Its effect in Caernarvonshire is unparalleled sobriety.' (Herbert Lewis Papers, N.L.W.)

George's 'brilliant and effective part' in the fight against the Bill.[1] In March of the same year even Haldane supported Lloyd George in the debate following the Welsh local elections, and in August Asquith led the Liberal M.P.s from the Chamber in sympathy with Lloyd George's protest against the closure.

In playing the role of spokesman for outraged Nonconformity he was often led into statements which did not reflect his true opinion, and unfortunately one such statement has been quoted over and over again as a representative utterance of his. At a St David's Eve dinner in Liverpool, on 28 February 1903, the Mayor of Birkenhead proposed his health and referred to the excessive zeal of the Welsh for their 'little Bethels'. In the circumstances Lloyd George could hardly ignore the remark, and he dealt with it thus:

> Personally, I owe nothing to universities – I speak in all modesty and humility – nothing to universities, nothing to secondary schools. Whatever I owe is to the little Bethels. Let us utilize our educational machinery, but let us bring out the best that is in our little Bethels as well.

Quoted in context, the statement 'Whatever I owe is to the little Bethels' is not too misleading – because in the preceding sentence he implies regret at not having been to university or secondary school, and in the next sentence shows that he does not regard the 'little Bethels' as being either flawless in themselves or an adequate substitute for formal education. Yet it is that one statement which has echoed down the years, while the rest of the speech has been forgotten.[2]

Nobody, in fact, knew better than he did that his education, after he left the Llanystumdwy church school where he had been well grounded, owed nearly everything to his own efforts and the efforts of his uncle, and not very much to attendance at Nonconformist chapels. Admittedly his uncle was a Nonconformist minister, but what he did for Lloyd George was for the most part done at home, in the family cottage, or on their long walks together: his Sunday sermons counted for little by comparison. Lloyd

1. 5 January 1904.
2. Du Parcq (op. cit., Vol. II, p. 333) incorrectly gives the date of the speech as St David's Day, 1902 – i.e. before the Education controversy began. The mistake has compounded the false impression created by the 'little Bethels' passage, since it places the speech in a period before he had the special, compelling reason that he had in 1903 for exaggerating his commitment to Welsh Nonconformity.

The rest of the speech includes one passage which is, indeed, highly representative of his thinking: 'The Empire is simply a conglomeration of parishes; if every man serves his parish then he is serving the Empire.'

George enjoyed singing hymns, and could appreciate the style and delivery, if not very often the moral, of a sermon. But when as a boy he had to be a regular chapel-goer, he was undoubtedly more bored than edified by the experience.

His secularism, which was authentic, revealed itself in occasional complimentary references to what was happening in France, where the Combes government was carrying out a drastic separation of Church and State. But Britain was not France, nor was Lloyd George an anti-clerical fanatic like Combes. He wanted public control of Church schools, rather than their complete secularization. He was all in favour of basic religious instruction – by which he meant Bible teaching – in school hours, but would tolerate denominational or doctrinal instruction only as an extra-curricular activity. In other words, he was a genuine, but moderate and qualified, secularist.

The uniformity of the French educational system certainly did not attract him. Indeed, he criticized Balfour's Act for making the British system too similar to the French, in that respect:

> In France the Government is much more centralized than it is here. An Act of Parliament is passed, and the central authority says that, in every district, it is to be administered in the same way and in the same degree, without any regard at all to the difference in the temperament, the disposition, the prejudices or the opinions of the people themselves. In England, that is not the way; the administration of the law is much more decentralized . . . All I plead is that the grand old British Constitution should have its way with this Act.[1]

The argument was convenient politically, but cannot be dismissed as purely opportunistic, because it chimes with his dominant belief in unity through diversity.

Though he had to make much of the sectarian issue, there is abundant evidence of his real concern for education and of his pride in Wales's educational record, which he contrasted with England's record of trying to have education on the cheap:

> Denominational education means cheap education . . . the English zeal for education shrinks into an enthusiasm for religious dogma at the prospect of a sixpenny rate.

1. Speech at Victoria Hall, Halifax, 2 February 1903. Lloyd George began by saying that he had read in an old Welsh book that in the twelfth century Yorkshiremen and Welshmen were the only people in Britain who could sing in harmony.

Even Scotland, he said, had burdened itself less than Wales for the sake of education. In England, 7d. in the £ of rateable value was spent on education; in Scotland, 9s. 3d. in the £; in Wales, 11s. 7d. in the £.[1] Moreover, whatever he might say about the 'little Bethels', it shocked him that Britain should lag behind in university education. He pointed out that in Germany one in every 2,600 received some education of the sort, whereas in Britain the figure was only one in every 5,800.[2] It was clear that he did not regard the Nonconformist conscience as any substitute for a trained mind.

One significant by-product of the controversy was that Lloyd George was brought into contact with Robert Morant and made aware of his immense talent for creative organization. When the National Health Insurance Commission was being set up in 1911, Lloyd George thought he knew where to turn. Another by-product was that the bond of mutual respect which already existed between Balfour and Lloyd George was strengthened, and this, too, was to have great importance for the future. Balfour was a very tough politician and a Parliamentary virtuoso who could appreciate the quality of Lloyd George's opposition, while making due allowance for his mixed motives. Lloyd George recognized the historic value of Balfour's reform and the patience, determination and artistry with which he pushed it through. Fittingly, the next major legislative advance in British education was effected when Lloyd George was Prime Minister and Balfour a loyal member of his Cabinet.

1. Article in the *Independent Review*, September 1904.
2. Speech at Caernarvon, 16 December 1903.

THREE

Last Steps to Power

Throughout the Boer War, and for about two years afterwards, the Lloyd Georges' London home was 179 Trinity Road, near Wandsworth Common. They then moved to a house actually adjoining the Common, 3 Routh Road. Their windows were never broken during the war, in spite of jingo hostility to Lloyd George, probably because he was careful not to put his address in any work of reference – an early and justified case of 'ex-directory', which in recent times has become a tiresome affectation of many who wish to appear more important and sought-after than they actually are.

In other respects the family suffered considerably from the war. Lloyd George's eldest child, Richard, was given such a bad time by other Dulwich College boys, for being the son of a pro-Boer, that he had to be removed from the school and take sanctuary in North Wales, where he lived with his uncle William and attended the grammar school at Portmadoc. The daughters, Mair and Olwen, were not so victimized by their contemporaries and were able to stay in London, but they too had the feeling, never congenial to children, of being oddities, because they were not allowed to wear the patriotic favours which other children sported, and because they knew that their father was a bogeyman to many of their friends' parents.

For Margaret Lloyd George the war was a period of great anxiety. To her normal fear of London as a thoroughly unhealthy place was added the new fear that, by living there, her husband and children were exposed to the threat of physical violence. At the beginning of 1902, however, she was back in Wales awaiting the birth of her youngest child, since it was an inflexible rule with her that her children must all be born at Criccieth and delivered by her trusted doctor, Livingstone Davies. Lloyd George as usual lamented her absence, but it was convenient for him, in more ways than one, to be able to enlist the cooperation of Mrs Timothy Davies as an occasional mother-substitute for the children who remained under his care. This gave him an excuse for visiting 'Mrs Tim', and put him on the defensive in his letters to Margaret. 'I went to fetch Mair back home yesterday. *Don't tell me off, old Maggie.* I was a very good boy I can assure you. I have no fear of your cross-examination . . . & I know how with that sly eye of yours you watch every move & twitch of my telltale face.'[1]

The baby was born on 22 April 1902 and the next morning he wrote: 'I cannot put into words the thrill of joy & affection which passed through me on reading the telegram announcing that all had passed off well . . . How I would cover your sweet & pure & tender face with kisses.'[2] A month later he was discussing names for the child. 'Mrs Jones suggested "Ceinwen". A very pretty name. You please yourself about it. Either "Megan Arvon" or "Ceinwen Arvon". Both are very pretty names but I rather hesitate about having another "Beggan bach" – you would thus lose my pettest name.'[3] Margaret evidently did not regard this as a decisive objection and the child was called Megan Arvon.

Lloyd George's love of travel was undiminished. During the Boer War he spent two holidays on the Continent. The first, in September 1900, was at Fécamp in Normandy. Margaret did not go with him and was concerned to hear that the Timothy Davieses were staying nearby. But he did his best to reassure her. 'I've only seen them once. Tim was anxious I should stay there . . . But I preferred Harold Spender.'[4] On the Norman roads Spender tried to teach Lloyd George to ride a bicycle, but such was his clumsiness and awkwardness in such matters that he had several nasty falls and eventually broke the machine. In the summer of 1901 he was on the Continent again, visiting Salzburg, Vienna and Prague, but Margaret did not accompany him.

The following summer he went to Switzerland, again without Margaret.

1. D.L.G. to M.L.G., 24 March 1902 (N.L.W.). The words italicized are Welsh in the original. Later in the same letter, which was written from the House of Commons, he recorded his immediate reaction to Balfour's Education Bill (see p. 26 above).
2. D.L.G. to M.L.G., 23 April 1902 (N.L.W. and *Letters*, pp. 134–5).
3. D.L.G. to M.L.G., 24 May 1902 (N.L.W.).
4. D.L.G. to M.L.G., 7 September 1900 (N.L.W.). Spender was so slavishly devoted to Lloyd George that he cannot have been a very effective 'gooseberry'.

Spender was his companion, and Timothy Davies joined them at Zermatt –
but not 'Mrs Tim'. Lloyd George wrote to Margaret describing the Swiss
scenery and making a comparison which, however far-fetched, was the
most likely to arouse her interest. Lausanne, he said, was 'not unlike
Criccieth but steeper'; Lake Geneva was 'like Cardigan Bay'.[1] At Zermatt,
Spender was keen to climb the Matterhorn, but serious mountaineering
did not appeal to Lloyd George: he liked a good walk but not too stiff a
climb. All the same, he was able to report eating bread and cheese, and
drinking Apollinaris, with Spender on a 10,000-foot mountain top.[2] The
holiday in Switzerland was a refreshing interlude in his fight against the
Education Bill, and after the Bill had passed he went abroad again during
the Christmas recess – this time to Biarritz, and with Massingham.

It was not until September 1903 that he persuaded Margaret to accompany him on a foreign trip, when they went together to the Tyrol. But
her disinclination to leave England for foreign parts was about equal to
her reluctance to leave Wales for England. Her family used to remark that
when she was abroad she could hardly wait to be back in London, just as
when she was in London she was always pining to be at Criccieth. In
August 1904 Lloyd George returned to Switzerland, with his brother
William and D. R. Daniel. Unconvincingly he wrote to Margaret: 'A
holiday from home always bores me. The only exception was last year
& even then I was restless.'[3] At Basle he attended 'a very striking service'
for schoolchildren, which made him 'wish for some achievement which
would make it worth the while of Welsh children to sing about & glorify
for generations to come'.[4] At Berne he was pleased to read in *Le Temps*
an account of the British Parliamentary session, in which he was hailed as
'one of the foremost debaters of the epoch'.[5]

In the competition for power the Boer War was an advantage to
Lloyd George, since the views which he expressed, though acceptable only
to a minority in the country, represented for most of the time majority
opinion within the Liberal Party. Among Liberals it was not he, but the
'Liberal Imperialists', who were out on a limb, and the good sectarian
stand which most of them took on the Education Bill did not wholly
rehabilitate them, while at the same time Lloyd George's leadership of the

1. D.L.G. to M.L.G., 12 August 1902 (N.L.W.).
2. D.L.G. to his daughter, Olwen, 22 August 1902 (N.L.W.).
3. D.L.G. to M.L.G., 28 August 1904 (N.L.W.).
4. D.L.G. to M.L.G., 26 August 1904 (N.L.W.).
5. D.L.G. to M.L.G., 18 August 1904 (N.L.W.).

Parliamentary fight against the Bill further strengthened his position. Yet between 1903 and the Liberals' return to power at the end of 1905 Lloyd George was lumbered with the Welsh Revolt and on that account possibly denied his chance of becoming the Party's leading spokesman in a more momentous and truly national controversy, precipitated by Joseph Chamberlain on 15 May 1903, when he expounded the case for Tariff Reform to his West Birmingham constituents.[1]

Chamberlain was still Colonial Secretary when he made the speech. Salisbury's resignation in July of the previous year had resulted, for the Unionists, in a duality of leadership similar to that which afflicted the Liberals after Gladstone. The circumstances and personalities were different, but the consequences equally disastrous.

When Balfour succeeded his uncle as Prime Minister, the most forceful and popular member of the Government – Chamberlain – was passed over in favour of a man twelve years his junior. Yet the appointment was more justifiable than Rosebery's in 1894. Balfour sat in the House of Commons and was leader of the majority party there: Chamberlain, however distinguished in his own right, was merely the leader of a minority group allied to the Conservatives. That was one crucial difference. Another was that personal relations between the two men were almost as good as, between Rosebery and Harcourt, they had been bad. Chamberlain was grateful to Balfour for supporting him with unwavering loyalty throughout the Boer War, and in February 1902 he went out of his way to indicate that he had no designs on the Premiership. Should Salisbury retire he would not, he explained, be willing to serve under *any* successor, but would gladly serve under Balfour.[2] Perhaps he thought he would be able to dominate the new Government as an individual – that with Balfour Prime Minister in name, he would be Prime Minister in fact. If so, he made a fatal miscalculation.

Balfour was not only a much tougher character than Rosebery; he was tougher even than Chamberlain. Though his dialectic was often too subtle for the man in the street, his mind was sharply focussed and he was determined to run his own Government in his own way. His Imperialism was just as strong as Chamberlain's, if less visionary, and he was thoroughly alive to the threat of foreign competition in all fields, including the com-

1. The meeting was for his constituents only, but was held in Birmingham Town Hall, where Lloyd George had so nearly been lynched eighteen months before.
2. Conversation with Balfour's private secretary, J. S. Sandars, 25 February 1902, quoted in Blanche Dugdale, *Arthur James Balfour* (Vol. I, p. 337).

mercial. He had no ideological objection to Tariff Reform and positively favoured the idea of a system of preferential tariffs within the Empire. At the same time he understood, as Chamberlain was temperamentally incapable of understanding – all the more so when he had become, like Gladstone, an 'old man in a hurry' – that the issue had to be broached with extreme caution and care, if it were not to divide the Government's supporters and provoke a disastrous reaction from the public.

It was only half a century since Free Trade had been established as part of the British way of life, but many in all classes had come to regard it as an indispensable condition of peace, prosperity and progress. Agricultural depression had, indeed, revived the temporarily dormant Protectionism of landowners and farmers, and for two decades there had been a movement for limited Tariff Reform – 'Fair Trade' – sponsored by industrialists who wanted to have some weapons to use against the high tariffs of Britain's leading commercial rivals. But agricultural Protectionists and industrial Fair Traders had not hitherto worked together, and in any case belief in the almost mystical virtues of Free Trade was still strong in British industry and among powerful representatives of the landed interest.

As President of the Board of Trade in Gladstone's second Government Chamberlain had, oddly enough, been a scourge of the Fair Traders, but his biographer tells us that this persecution 'proved to be the first step on his journey to Damascus'.[1] Thereafter he gradually became convinced of the supreme necessity for Tariff Reform, partly as the only means of averting Britain's economic decline, partly as a good means of financing social reform, and partly as the best means of promoting Imperial consolidation. In the last matter he was taking his cue from the British self-governing Colonies, more especially Canada which, in 1897, granted a unilateral preference on all imports from the United Kingdom. From the attitude of Canada and the other Colonies it was evident that a system of reciprocal preferences would be welcome to them, but no such system could be brought into being unless and until Britain abandoned Free Trade.

Tariff Reform and Imperial Preference were logically defensible, even noble, aims, but from Balfour's point of view they involved two enormous snags. First, on the question of principle they would divide his own party while uniting the Liberals: secondly, if preferences were to be given on foodstuffs produced in the Colonies, there would have to be a general tariff on food imported from abroad, which would mean, in effect, that

1. Julian Amery, *Joseph Chamberlain and the Tariff Reform Campaign* (Vol. V of the *Life*), p. 210.

the food of the British people would be taxed. Balfour knew that the fiscal changes needed to meet foreign competition, and to enable Britain to join in a preferential system for the whole Empire, could only be introduced by slow degrees and with exquisite political art. He had no desire to shirk the issue, but could see that premature action or rhetoric would damage, if not destroy, the chances of ultimate success.

In the 1902 Budget Sir Michael Hicks-Beach imposed a small duty on imported corn, simply for the purpose of raising revenue to help pay for the Boer War. He was an orthodox Free Trader and the very last thing he intended was that anyone should regard his corn duty as the beginning of a return to Protection. Lloyd George was writing to his wife as the announcement was made, and he appears to have taken it – correctly, so far as Hicks-Beach was concerned – at face-value. 'Aha – a shilling duty on corn & fivepence a hundredweight on all flour imported from abroad. This will help to bring it home to those who cried out for the war.'[1] Balfour, not yet Prime Minister, probably hoped that the duty might be unobtrusively retained after the immediate need for it had passed, but Chamberlain and Sir Wilfred Laurier, Prime Minister of Canada, made no secret of their far-reaching hopes and so alerted the Free Traders. By the time Balfour succeeded his uncle the Government was already viewed with deep distrust by the guardians of fiscal orthodoxy.

Balfour's choice as Chancellor of the Exchequer, in place of Hicks-Beach, was Charles Thomson Ritchie – a distinguished and experienced Minister with a fine record of pragmatic reform.[2] More to the point, he had been an ardent Fair Trader when Chamberlain was on the other side of the argument. Though he was against Imperial Preference, and stressed his opposition to it before agreeing to be Chancellor, Balfour had some reason to hope that his views might not be too inflexible. Unfortunately he turned out to be as bigoted in opposing Imperial Preference as Chamberlain in advocating it. He resolved not only to block Chamberlain's pet scheme, but also to show the whole world that it was being blocked. At first a majority of the Cabinet supported Chamberlain, but between November 1902 and March 1903, when he was out of the country visiting South Africa, the balance of forces swung against him. Ritchie framed a Budget in which the corn duty was to be remitted and on his return

1. D.L.G. to M.L.G., 14 April 1902 (N.L.W. and *Letters*, p. 133).
2. In 1888, as President of the Local Government Board, he brought in the Bill creating county councils, which among other things completed the political revolution in Wales by breaking the local power of the Tory squirearchy.

Chamberlain sadly acquiesced in the proposal. But he did so only because the duty seemed worthless without preferences, and because anyway it was said to be too late to change the Budget. Less than a month later he delivered his bombshell speech at Birmingham.

During the next few months the disagreement in the Cabinet on fiscal policy, which Balfour had hoped either to exorcise or at least to hide from the public, became an irreconcilable conflict out in the open. The Prime Minister then resorted to tactics which were as drastic as they were ruthless. While continuing to move in the direction of Tariff Reform he decided to rid himself of the extremists on both sides. When, in September, Chamberlain offered his resignation so as to be free to campaign for Imperial Preference, Balfour did not immediately reveal the offer, but first obtained, virtually under duress, the resignations of Ritchie and two other Ministers of the opposite faction. He then announced all the resignations simultaneously, so creating in the public mind a strong impression of himself as the moderate leader steering a middle course between extremes. He also published a paper that he had written for the Cabinet advocating retaliatory tariffs, but did not publish another paper in which he had advocated Imperial Preference.

Chamberlain left the Government not as a rebel, but pledging his loyalty to the Prime Minister and with the task of converting public opinion to Imperial Preference if he could. His success would redound to Balfour's advantage, but, if he failed, his failure would be all his own. It was a case of heads Balfour would win, tails Chamberlain would lose. His son, Austen, remained in the Government, promoted to Ritchie's place at the Exchequer. Austen was far less able and dynamic than his father, and above all a natural insider. His filial allegiance would not significantly detract from his allegiance to the Government, and, besides, where could the Chamberlains turn for support if they broke with Balfour? Though Unionist Free Traders tried to make out that he had become the Chamberlains' prisoner, in fact it was the other way round.[1]

1. The best account of Balfour's remarkable political surgery in September 1903 is in A. M. Gollin, *Balfour's Burden*. According to Professor Gollin, 'the quality of Balfour's artifice has seldom been equalled by any Prime Minister, and rarely surpassed, even by Lloyd George'. And he adds: 'The English prefer to believe that Prime Ministers like Disraeli, Lloyd George and Ramsay MacDonald – the upstarts and outsiders – are invariably more devious than the Prime Ministers of Salisbury's or Balfour's calibre . . . So far as the crisis of 1903 is concerned it may be stated at once that Balfour's ingenuity exceeded even Lloyd George's in his most notorious coups as Prime Minister.'

The Duke of Devonshire, stupid but prestigious, was for a short time bamboozled into staying in the Government when the other Free Trade Ministers left it; but he, too, resigned

Ritchie and his associates had a sense of outrage because, had they known that Chamberlain was to resign and that Balfour was no longer pressing for Imperial Preference, they would have been quite willing to remain in the Government. A policy of Retaliation to force foreign Protectionist States to lower their tariffs was quite compatible with Ritchie's idea of Free Trade. But Balfour not only needed to be rid of the anti-Preference men to balance Chamberlain's departure; he also wanted to be free to introduce Preference if Chamberlain were able to demonstrate that the public would accept it, with all the implications. He was himself a sincere believer in the merits of Chamberlain's policy, though sceptical of its practicability, granted the state of British opinion. Ritchie, on the other hand, was opposed in principle to an Empire preferential system, and his presence in the Government would have been an embarrassment if the Tariff Reform campaign had proved a triumphant success.

At first it seemed quite likely to succeed. On the whole the Unionists did better at by-elections during the year following Chamberlain's Tariff Reform challenge than during the year preceding it, when the Education controversy had produced a very marked swing against the Government. Only in the autumn of 1904 did the anti-Government trend become once again consistently adverse, but from then onwards it remained set until the end of the Parliament, with growing evidence that Chamberlain had failed in his central purpose. While fragmenting the Government's forces and cementing the Liberals' unity, he had left a large mass of the British people unconverted to his doctrine.[1]

One reason for his failure was that the economic depression by which Britain was afflicted when the Tariff Reform campaign opened gave way to a period of rapidly reviving prosperity. Industrialists who, in 1903, were full of anxiety were regaining their optimism by the end of 1904, and many unemployed workers were regaining their jobs. Those economic indices which appeared to justify Chamberlain's arguments at the outset appeared

---

at the beginning of October. Balfour's pamphlet advocating Retaliation, *Economic Notes on Insular Free Trade*, was published less than a year after his educational pamphlet replying to Dr Clifford (see p. 37 above).

1. During one by-election that the Unionists lost – at St Albans – Lloyd George was involved in an incident scarcely less dangerous than the Birmingham riot of December 1901, and once again he was saved by the police, though not this time disguised as one of them. After his meeting in the constituency on 6 February 1904, as he was going to the station, a mob rushed on him shouting 'Traitor', 'Pro-Boer', 'Lynch him', 'Kill him'. The public closed round him and eventually he made his escape.

to belie them two years later. But his biggest problem, as Balfour well knew, was how to reconcile any worthwhile scheme of Imperial Preference with the interests and prejudices of the British consumer. Since the Colonies were predominantly food-producing, any preferential system which was to be of substantial benefit to them had to include, on the British side, tariffs on imported food. And such tariffs were described by Alfred Harmsworth – already Britain's most formidable publicist – as 'stomach taxes'. A further difficulty was that home food producers, to whom Chamberlain was also trying to appeal, wanted to be protected against all overseas competition: they had no enthusiasm whatever for a system which would leave the British market open to cheap Canadian wheat.

For two and a half years Balfour hung on to power with a party increasingly weakened and tormented, but never utterly broken, by the fiscal dispute. Chamberlain captured the Liberal Unionist organization for Tariff Reform, and pursued an unrelenting vendetta against Unionist Free Fooders in the constituencies. A handful of Unionists – including young Winston Churchill – crossed the floor to join the Liberals, but most of Balfour's Free Trade supporters did not defect. They were reassured by his pledge that Imperial Preference would not be enacted after the next election, but would have to be approved by a colonial conference and then by the British people at a second general election. Nothing that he could do was capable of bridging the gulf between the Tariff Reform League and the Free Food League, but at least he could not be accused of dividing his Party as Sir Robert Peel had divided it in 1846.

Lloyd George was a convinced, though not a bigoted, Free Trader. In 1896 he had argued in favour of colonial preference on tea, but partly with his tongue in his cheek. (He was, at the time, trying to delay the passage of a Tory Finance Bill.) Unlike some Free Traders he was an out-and-out Imperialist, but experience had made him so suspicious of Chamberlain's form of Imperialism that he was predisposed to find fault with any scheme of Imperial consolidation that bore the Birmingham trademark. Moreover, he believed that there were real flaws in the policy put forward in 1903, and was able to attack it with a clear conscience. As an Imperialist he was necessarily closer to Chamberlain than to Cobden, and he was essentially Chamberlainite as a social reformer. Yet he was Cobdenite in identifying Free Trade with efficiency, prosperity and the cause of international peace. On balance, his instinct and judgment led him to oppose

Chamberlain's tariff policy, just as they would have led him – but for irresistible pressures – to support Balfour's Education policy.

Not that he spurned the purely political bonus which Chamberlain's initiative conferred upon the Liberals. No one was quicker than he to exploit the new situation. On 22 May 1903, a week after the Birmingham speech, he spoke in the House of Commons on Old Age Pensions and reminded Chamberlain of his interest in the subject which, he suggested, was a thing of the past. Chamberlain was stung into replying that Old Age Pensions was not, so far as he was concerned, a dead issue, but that the funds for Pensions would not be available without that review of the fiscal system which he believed to be urgently necessary.[1] By thus reappearing in his old Radical colours he could only create uneasiness among potential supporters of Tariff Reform – as Lloyd George, no doubt, intended.

Within a week he was at it again, and this time elicited a statement which clarified what was to be the vital issue in the controversy. 'We come to this,' said Chamberlain, 'if you are to give a preference to the Colonies – I do not say that you are – you must put a tax on food. I make hon. gentlemen opposite a present of that . . .'[2] Though it is more than likely that Chamberlain would soon have made this 'present' to his opponents in any case, it was Lloyd George who actually brought him to the point of making it.

In the country, as well, Lloyd George was quick to take up the challenge. On May 23rd he said at Cambridge:

We must remember that, in order to protect the Colonies, we must put a tariff upon food and raw material. Protecting manufactured goods doesn't help the Colonies. We must tax corn, wool, cotton, raw material which is used for manufactures . . . It is all very well to talk about our Colonies. Our first duty is to the people at home. The Colonies are looking after their own people first, and perfectly rightly. Let England, at the same time, think of Lancashire and Yorkshire and all those places, as long as we are fair to the Colonies . . . The Colonial trade is only one-quarter of the English trade; three-quarters is with foreign countries . . . Are we going to close our doors against customers numbering 250 millions at least, simply in order to increase the custom of eleven millions of people? It is folly . . . Trade, after all, will follow price

1. Hansard, Fourth Series, Vol. CXXII, cols 1549–53.
2. Hansard, Fourth Series, Vol. CXXIII, col. 185 (28 May 1903).

and quality; it will not follow sentimental considerations. It never does.[1]

In another speech soon afterwards he found a way of attacking, in the same breath, sectarian education, Tariff Reform and Chamberlain's concept of Empire, to which he was able to impute a foreign inspiration. Walter Long had been advising the Tories to take the rust off their weapons and burnish up their armour. But what antiquated armour it was:

> If they rub all the rust off, there will be no armour left. What is their armour? Corn tax and clericalism! They will go into action with the weapons of the Middle Ages, and they will be handsomely beaten . . . Mr Chamberlain fancies himself as a sort of little Bismarck. The notion has turned his head. He is the man who will consolidate the Empire, the man of blood and iron – rather than the man of screws [a reference to Chamberlain's business]; that is all the iron in Mr Chamberlain's Imperialism. After the pattern of Bismarck, he has his social programme and his *Zollverein* . . . but we want no Empire made in Germany. We prefer the British Empire, which has been made by the great men who have built it up, not altogether with blood, but with wisdom and sagacity and statesmanship, with a cement of freedom.[2]

At Oldham in October, soon after Chamberlain had spoken at Glasgow from a platform heavily loaded with patrician supporters, Lloyd George produced one of his happiest images:

> . . . when a statesman of Chamberlain's position comes forward and proposes a return to the old Corn Law days, lords and dukes and earls and squires and baronets are found running and clucking towards him like a flock of fowls when they hear the corn shaken in the tin.

And he developed further his 'more patriotic than thou' line of attack, implying that Chamberlain was denigrating the country's commercial performance and underrating its capacity to hold its own against foreign competition. 'I tell you, I can't stand these people who are always running down their own country.' This remark was greeted with prolonged cheers and a shout from the body of the hall: 'Who are the little Englanders?'[3]

1. Speech at joint annual dinner of the Eights Club and Cambridge University Liberal Club, University Arms, Cambridge, 23 May 1903. His population figures were arrived at by excluding India. 'India practically doesn't count; she isn't a great customer and never will be.'
2. Speech at Abercarn, 5 June 1903.
3. Speech at meeting of Oldham Liberal Union, of which he was hon. president, 10 October 1903.

From the divisive effect of Chamberlain's campaign Lloyd George extracted full polemical advantage. 'Here is a Cabinet,' he said, 'shattered, split – and yet it lives. It is like a worm . . . cut in twain, but both ends wriggle – blindly, I need hardly tell you.'[1] When, at his instigation, Ritchie was given the Freedom of Pwllheli and came to the town to receive it, the new Freeman was fulsomely praised by the local M.P.[2] Above all, Lloyd George's influence helped to secure for the Liberal Party its most important defector from the Government side – Winston Churchill.

The two men had met for the first time after Churchill's maiden speech on 18 February 1901. He had then followed Lloyd George in a debate on South Africa, and later they were introduced to each other at the Bar of the House of Commons. Their brief exchange on that occasion is thus described by Churchill:

> After compliments, he [Lloyd George] said 'Judging from your senti-ments, you are standing against the Light.' I replied 'You take a singu-larly detached view of the British Empire.' Thus began an association which has persisted through many vicissitudes.[3]

It was, perhaps, the most fruitful and momentous association of its kind in British history.

Churchill soon fell under Lloyd George's spell and for the rest of his life never ceased to regard the Welshman as his master. There were twelve years between them, but Lloyd George was never one to stand on seniority. Churchill appealed to him not only as a person, like himself, of sparkling imagination and limited formal education, but also as the son of a politician whom he had much admired in his own youth and by whose political style he had been considerably influenced. He warmed to Churchill's adventurous, agnostic spirit, as Churchill warmed to his. They had both entered Parliament at about the same age, each with the same conviction of his own fitness to rule. Each, in his way, had been a privi-leged child, the member of a self-conscious *élite*. Churchill, however, had been starved of paternal guidance and encouragement. Though not in the strict sense fatherless, as Lloyd George had been, he had a father whom he

1. Speech at annual dinner of the Palmerston Club, Randolph Hotel, Oxford, 13 June 1903. Lloyd George and Hilaire Belloc were the guests of the evening. Chamberlain, said Lloyd George, was ending his career as he began it, with the split of a party.
2. 27 October 1903. Ritchie, said Lloyd George, had given local government to the people and 'they could not realize, probably for many years to come, the great benefits of that measure'. He also said that it was 'the highest form of honouring a man to enrol his name upon the burgess list without placing it upon the rate book'.
3. Winston S. Churchill, *My Early Life*, ch. XXIX.

could only look upon as a remote, unloving, inaccessible god. Lord Randolph had given him none of the devoted attention that Uncle Lloyd had lavished upon Lloyd George throughout his boyhood. As a result Lloyd George came to be more than a political associate and mentor to Churchill; he became, as well, in no small degree a surrogate father or elder brother.

When Churchill crossed the floor on 31 May 1904 he did it in such a way as to give his new relationship with Lloyd George dramatic emphasis:

> ... he entered the Chamber ... stood for a moment at the Bar, looked briefly at both the Government and Opposition benches and strode swiftly up the aisle. He bowed to the Speaker and turned sharply to the right to the Liberal benches. He sat down next to Lloyd George in a seat that his father had occupied when in opposition ...[1]

Actually, Lord Randolph's old place was then occupied by Henry Labouchere. Lloyd George sat immediately behind him – in the corner seat of the second bench below the Gangway – and immediately behind Lloyd George sat Tim Healy. The conscious symbolism of Churchill's choice of place related to the living rather than the dead.

Within a week he and Lloyd George were the opening speakers at the Cobden centenary celebration, when they addressed over ten thousand people under the great glass roof of Alexandra Palace. Already they were being bracketed together.[2] In October Churchill visited Caernarvon and was given a hero's welcome. Repaying the warmth of his reception he described Lloyd George as 'the best fighting general in the Liberal army' and expressed his full support for the Lloyd Georgian policy of Home Rule all Round.[3] Early in their friendship Lloyd George had accompanied Churchill to Blenheim – an extraordinary gesture by one who throughout his career maintained a consistent aversion for the stately homes of England and most of their occupants.

The Blenheim connection and what he knew it meant to Churchill contributed, indeed, to a certain wariness on Lloyd George's part. Much

1. Randolph S. Churchill, *Winston S. Churchill*, Vol. II *Young Statesman*, p. 80.
2. On 1 January 1904 – six months before Churchill formally changed sides – J. L. Wanklyn, a Liberal Unionist M.P., wrote to Lloyd George wishing him a happy New Year and adding:
'How do you like your new stable-companion Winston Churchill? You will make a perfect match-pair, you two, but I should be devilish sorry to try and drive you. Poor Herbert G[ladstone] and poor C.-B. !
You will upset the Radical [next word illegible] between you. Joe is going to win, and at the first time of asking I believe, but personally I shouldn't grudge you a short innings for the fun of it !' (N.L.W.) 3. Speech at the Pavilion, Caernarvon, 18 October 1904.

as he liked his young acolyte he was never wholly convinced that Churchill was, at heart, quite the social radical that he professed to be. But there was another and deeper reason for wariness on both sides. The two men recognized in each other the same quality of ruthless, unlimited, egocentric ambition. This was partly a bond between them, because the mutual recognition was in a sense flattering to the exalted self-esteem which they shared. But inevitably they were also rivals, and when they were together members of the Liberal Government D. R. Daniel noted that the country was talking of their rivalry, 'which must come between them in the future'. It was natural, he thought, to expect that they would 'meet face to face one day on that narrow path which leads to the highest pinnacle of honour'.[1] In fact, they were not competitors at the times – nearly a quarter-century apart – when each in turn was attaining the pinnacle, but at other times their ambitions, as well as their differences of temperament and opinion, brought them into political conflict, though they were never personally estranged for very long.

Granted that each possessed talent of the highest order, commonly known as genius, in what respects did their genius differ? Both had an extraordinary gift for applying their historical knowledge, such as it was, to the problems of the present and future. They looked at politics in a grand perspective and communed with the heroes of former ages as with living contemporaries. But whereas Lloyd George's reflective and imaginative powers were nearly always directly related to immediate practical tasks, Churchill's mind had a brooding, vatic quality which enabled him on occasion to anticipate the future with uncanny accuracy – as in his famous prediction that 'the wars of peoples' would be 'more terrible than those of kings'[2] – but could also lead him into error and folly. If his judgments were sometimes more far-sighted than Lloyd George's, Lloyd George's were often more sensible and realistic.

Another difference was that, while both men were equally self-centred in their fundamental approach to life, Lloyd George was less self-regarding in the ordinary process of living. Both were brilliant talkers, but Lloyd George, unlike Churchill, was also an excellent listener. Lloyd George revelled in the free trade of conversation and discussion, whereas Churchill was addicted to monologue. People would leave Churchill's presence

1. D. R. Daniel, unpublished memoir of David Lloyd George (D. R. Daniel MSS., N.L.W.). Translated from the Welsh by Dr Prys Morgan.
2. Speech in the House of Commons on St John Brodrick's scheme of Army reform, 13 May 1901.

feeling that they had encountered a man of cosmic importance, but they would leave Lloyd George feeling *themselves* more important than when they had arrived. This was part of the secret of his amazing faculty for getting things done, in which he was definitely superior to Churchill. As a speaker, too, he was more effective than Churchill on public platforms and in Parliament: his voice was more musical and his style, because less orotund, appeared more spontaneous. Yet he never mastered the medium of broadcasting, and it was chiefly in that medium that Churchill, during the Second World War, was able to make speeches which had a more profound effect than any others delivered in this century.

It is invidious to compare and contrast the two men with a view to deciding which was the greater. Both were outstanding in their time and even from a distance their stature is not diminished. It was most fortunate for Britain, and very fortunate for the world, that they lived when they did and were willing, for many years, to deploy their phenomenal abilities and energies in concert.

Between 1903 and 1905 Lloyd George spoke repeatedly – and somewhat repetitiously – on the fiscal question, but on that issue he was not Chamberlain's leading Liberal antagonist, as he had been during the Boer War. On Free Trade the running for the Liberals was made by Asquith, whose formidable forensic intellect could master the arguments in spite of his ignorance of economic theory and his total lack of experience in business. It was proof of his political calibre that he managed to hold his own against a self-made industrial magnate who was also a titan of debate; even, many thought, to get the better of him.

Lloyd George had as little knowledge of economics, and almost as little business experience, as Asquith.[1] He also had a less stringently disciplined mind and – with Education claiming so much of his time – less opportunity to study the intricacies of the fiscal question. All the same, his defence of Free Trade was often eloquent, though he tended to use the same illustrations and images over and over again. One favourite peroration, which appeared for the first time towards the end of 1903, did duty on many subsequent occasions:

> Our shipbuilding has grown; our shipping has expanded beyond anything that the dreams of man could have conceived fifty years ago. Our ships sail under every constellation; you will find them trading in every

1. His experience was confined to the promotion of a disastrous Patagonian gold-mining syndicate, which in itself hardly qualified him to lecture his compatriots on commercial policy.

clime; they fill every harbour; they ride on the crest of the wave over the highest tariff walls. There is not a breeze that blows but fills British sails. There is not a storm that sweeps over any corner of the ocean but British seamanship with its stout heart wrestles with it. You find our steamers and our ships plying from one country to the other, laying down invisible cables in the deep which attach nation to nation. And this great humanizing, civilizing enterprise, the splendour and glory of this land, we are asked to give away in order to redeem the credit of a bankrupt Ministry.[1]

The sea had always fascinated him and as a boy he had listened spell-bound to seamen's tales in the harbour at Portmadoc. His rhapsodies on the theme of British shipping came from the heart. And he was no less sincere in identifying Free Trade with liberty, Protection with oppression. 'Germany has two millions of shipping against ten millions of this country, and the great ocean liners of Germany are kept going by the constant stream of emigration from Protectionist countries.' So he commended a Free Trade motion to the Oxford Union – an unfamiliar arena in which he was delighted to excel. 'Last night', he wrote to his wife,

> was a great triumph. Never has the Union been so crowded. 50 extra seats were brought in – a thing never done before – & not only were they full but scores stood at the door & lined the walls. Galleries crowded with ladies & parsons. I dined with the President & Temple (the late Archbishop's son). Spoke for an hour ... They gave me a great ovation when I sat down – & then thronged out to vote ... We carried [the] motion by over 20. A few weeks ago the Union had carried a Chamberlain motion by 80 ... a large number of Tories wouldn't vote at all.
> Met today a retired Colonel who was there & said he knew the young Tory undergrads had come there to scoff but he said 'You made a deep impression on them. You took them the right way.[2]

As usual, he seized upon local examples to bring his argument home:

> I was at the Llanystumdwy smithy yesterday. The blacksmith was placing iron bars on a gate, and I asked him whence the bars came.

1. Speech at Aberdeen, 13 November 1903 – but almost exactly the same words could be quoted from many speeches over the next two years.
2. D.L.G. to M.L.G., from Hertford College, Oxford, 27 November 1903 (N.L.W.). 'Temple ... the late Archbishop's son' was the future Archbishop William Temple. The motion was actually carried by 29 votes in a house of 700.

'Sweden', the smith replied, adding that he had to pay more for Swedish iron than for English iron, but that it answered his purpose better. Mr Chamberlain would make it impossible, under his proposals, for the smith to get Swedish iron . . .[1]

And in one speech, attacking Balfour's policy of Retaliation, he echoed the language with which, in 1898, he had bravely deprecated British jingoism during the Fashoda crisis. Retaliation, he said, was even more dangerous than outright Protection:

> Are we going to start making commercial war on France? After the misunderstandings of a generation, which very nearly precipitated war between two neighbours, between two great democratic countries . . . in the van of human progress . . . and after we have given a friendly handshake to France [the new *Entente Cordiale*] for which civilization is the better . . . are we going to select such a time to declare bitter commercial war against France? What madness![2]

He frequently stressed that the British people were better off under Free Trade than foreigners under Protection. For instance, unemployment in 1900 was at the rate of 5 per cent in Britain, compared with 15 per cent in France and 20 per cent in Germany.[3] Britain sold more than it bought in all but a few countries of the world, but in order to be free to sell it was necessary to be willing to buy. 'Tariff Reformers make one cardinal mistake; they think that our business is to sell and never to buy . . . Trade means buying as well as selling.'[4]

On one occasion he ingeniously wove together into a single passage five colourful strands of political invective:

> You have to go back fifty years to the time when the bread of the people was taxed; eighty years to the time when slavery was rampant in the Empire; one hundred and fifty years to the time when the magistrate's discretion was removed with regard to licences; over four hundred years to the time when the priesthood had a monopoly of the instruction of the people; and over three thousand years to the time when a great Empire was governed by a man called Joseph.[5]

1. Speech at Criccieth, 19 December 1903. It was at the Llanystumdwy smithy that Lloyd George had his first experience of debate, as a member of the informal village debating society.
2. Speech at Manchester Reform Club, 4 November 1904.
3. Speech at Perth, 24 November 1904.
4. Speech at Kingston-on-Thames, 19 October 1905.
5. Speech at Bradford, 2 March 1904.

And soon afterwards he embellished the last point:

> But there is this difference – the ancient Joseph in his dreams made provision for an abundance of corn for the people. The modern Joseph is dreaming about a scarcity of corn.[1]

Such knockabout stuff might not be very fair or substantial, but audiences loved it.

When Lloyd George spoke of 'slavery . . . rampant in the Empire' he was referring to the Chinese indentured labourers who were being shipped to South Africa to work in the Rand gold-mines. Milner's decision to avail himself of this form of labour, endorsed by the home government, was worse than a blunder, because it was clearly wrong to import thousands of coolies[2] to work for very low wages and, when they were not working, to be herded together in all-male compounds. The policy was an offence not only against normal British conceptions of the dignity of labour, but also against normal conceptions of decency. Humanitarian and moral feelings were predictably outraged, since the British collective conscience is always at its most sensitive when reacting against wrongs perpetrated at a distance.

Moreover, righteous indignation was not quite the only emotion aroused by the 'Chinese slavery' issue, and Lloyd George was careful, like Mark Antony, to take rather less noble sentiments into account:

> Do you know that we have an Act of Parliament in South Africa . . . that prevents British workmen from landing unless they have £25 in their pockets? How many British workmen have £25 to spare? But the Chinamen are pouring in in shiploads, without a single cent in their pockets . . . The interests of those who labour are the same the world over.

Milner and the mine-owners, he said, did not want a white proletariat because they would combine and enforce better conditions. The British Government could have insisted that the rich mines should employ British labour and that the deep-level mines, which did not pay so well, should employ black labour. 'After all, the black man is the native of the country

---

1. Speech at Cardiff, 27 May 1904.
2. The total number in South Africa was 20,000 by the end of 1904 and about 50,000 a year later.

and he has as good a right – a better right – than either Dutchmen or British.'[1]

The argument was surely rather confused, because if the native Africans were admitted to have a better right than the British, then why should the best-paid jobs in the Rand mines be reserved for British immigrants? And why, in any case, should there be such discrimination when 'the interests of those who labour' were asserted as being 'the same the world over'? African interests were just as likely to suffer from the large-scale immigration of privileged British labour as from the large-scale importation of cheap Chinese labour.

Balfour's Licensing Bill of 1904 presented the Liberals with another conveniently moral issue. The Bill proposed a new procedure for the renewal or refusal of expiring licences, and a system for compensating publicans whose licences were not renewed. Compensation was to be paid out of a fund raised from a tax on the trade itself. To those who had no strong conscientious objections to the sale of intoxicants, and who recognized the Tory Party's obligations to the brewing interest as a fact of political life, the Bill might seem a reasonable compromise. But Liberals were able to denounce it, with varying degrees of sincerity, as a measure to endow the trade and, therefore, to subsidize sin.

Lloyd George had consistently maintained that the sale of liquor should be subject to local veto, and that publicans should have to take a chance on the annual renewal of their licences. Since the Bill met neither of his requirements he could assail it with a relatively clear conscience, and he did not mince his words. The Bill was 'a party bribe for gross political corruption . . . which Tammany could never exceed',[2] and the drink trade was an abomination.

The cry of the orphan has risen against it, the wild plea of the poor maniac is against it; the moans of the myriads to whom it has brought sorrow and shame have ascended to the Throne against it; the arm of the Most High is uplifted against it; and woe to the Party, woe to the statesman, woe to the Government that intervenes between the recreant and its doom.[3]

Yet he was not a total abstainer and did not advocate total prohibition.
The Bill passed into law and worked, on the whole, quite well. But it

1. Speech at Maidenhead, 26 May 1905.
2. Speech at protest meeting in London, 19 May 1904.
3. Speech at Cardiff, 27 May 1904.

served, along with Education, Tariff Reform and 'Chinese slavery', to solidify the Liberal Party.

There was another issue, possibly more important than the others and certainly more important in the context of Lloyd George's career, on which one would expect him to have spoken strongly as the Liberals were preparing to resume power. This was the broad issue of social reform and, sure enough, he did speak on it very strongly indeed.

That he did not also speak on it very frequently implies no lack of enthusiasm on his part – he had always been a zealot for social reform – but rather that it was an issue of which Liberals knew it would be dangerous to make too much. The British electorate whose support they had to win was by no means the universal electorate of today. Though Disraeli and Gladstone had extended the franchise to include a section of the working class, many of the poorer members of that class were still denied the vote. To be an elector it was necessary to be a ratepayer and millions of working men did not pay rates. In 1900 the electorate still comprised only 58 per cent of the adult male population, and in 1903 G. K. Chesterton could describe the voters as 'some million absolutely distinct individuals, each sitting in his own breakfast room reading his own morning paper'.[1] Such respectable citizens were not likely to welcome too many radical speeches as an accompaniment to their eggs and bacon, and the Liberals had reason to believe that the exceptionally radical programme with which they had gone to the country in 1892 – the so-called Newcastle Programme – had, in fact, deterred some of their potential supporters.

Nevertheless, it would have been against Lloyd George's nature to gag himself completely on what, even before his election to Parliament, he had identified as the outstanding contemporary cause.[2] Now and then he would inject into his speeches passages on general social reform, but it was on 4 April 1903 that he really let himself go in a speech devoted to the subject. And it was certainly no coincidence that he chose to deliver it at Newcastle.

1. G. K. Chesterton, *Robert Browning* ('English Men of Letters', second series, 1903). The voters referred to are definitely those of Chesterton's, not Browning's, day. The total number entitled to vote in 1900 was about 6,750,000 – compared with 21,750,000 in 1919, when women as well as the whole working class were enfranchised.
2. '. . . that vast social question which must be dealt with in the near future. There is a momentous time coming. The dark continent of wrong is being explored, and there is a missionary spirit abroad for its reclamation to the realm of right.' (Speech at Cardiff, 4 February 1890.)

He began with a gesture to old-fashioned Liberalism. The Government, he said, had increased expenditure at the rate of £5 for every household in the country. 'The Prodigal Son isn't in it. Let us say this at least for the Prodigal Son – he spent his own money.' There had been 'too great a disposition to play up to the whims and caprices of what is known as the man in the street':

The man in the street clamours for war, and we all say that war is the right thing. The man in the street says that we must have a big army and we all say 'Right, we must have a formidable army'. The man in the street talks about the expansion of the Empire, and we all garnish our speeches with Imperial allusions. But the man in the street has a relapse. He gets tired, not so much of the pomp of war as of the burden of war, and we all become peaceable. The man in the street then says that it is not an increase of the army that you want, but a small one, and we all say that the army is too big. There is too much disposition to tune our lyre to the sounds that come from the street, instead of standing for the good old principles of Liberalism. Who is the man in the street? . . . [He] is the man who gives neither time nor any serious thought to the study of politics. [A voice: 'Balfour'] No, that is the man on the golf links.

Characteristically, he was humouring his audience in preparation for strong medicine to come. The man, as it were, in the breakfast room would appreciate his derogatory comments on the man in the street, and any uneasiness that his radicalism might cause would be mitigated by his suggestion in advance that it was only an up-to-date version of 'the good old principles of Liberalism'. Having created the right atmosphere, he launched an attack on 'trusts and monopolies', which in Britain were 'part of the social fabric . . . in existence for generations and centuries'. And the first was 'the great land trust'.

There could be no absolute property in land, whether in town or country

The land in London is worth about £500,000,000. It is worth more than all the municipal debt throughout the kingdom – the money which has been sunk in great municipal enterprises, in waterworks, sanitation, lighting, wharves, tramways and roads . . . Who created that wealth? It was not the landlords. London was a swamp, and the landlords did not even create that. All the wealth has been created by the industry, the energy and the enterprise of the people who live in London. Every year the value of that land goes up ten millions . . .

While [the landlords] are going to their race-courses, their property is increasing by this enormous sum . . . The first duty of any reforming, progressive Government is to compel these gentlemen to contribute their fair share.

The same applied, in principle, to any great city or town, or even to villages throughout the country:

It is all very well to produce Housing of the Working Classes Bills. They will never be effective until you tackle the taxation of land values . . . How can you expect a healthy, sound race, with men at the end of their hard day's work going to recruit their strength, consumed in hard toil, in habitations where some of our great landlords would not pen their cattle?

I sat as a member of an Old Age Pensions Committee . . . We drew up a scheme and found that it would cost twelve millions a year. The Government said that it would cost too much and, by way of a diversion, plunged into the South African war as a cheaper business . . .

The Committee had found that large numbers of workmen never reached the age of sixty-five, because of their miserable conditions of life. One-third of the people were living on or about the poverty line:

It is all land. You cannot build houses without land; you cannot lay down trams for the purpose of spreading the population over a wider area, without land. As long as the landlords are allowed to charge prohibitive prices for a bit of land, even waste land, without contributing anything to local resources, so long will this terrible congestion remain in our towns.

Another cause of congestion was that the poor wages paid to agricultural labourers were driving them into towns where, in turn, they had the effect of depressing wages. And the 'martial resources' of the nation were weakened by the drift from the countryside, 'where you develop a robust and strong manhood'.

In every country of Europe except Britain the State had reserved its right over minerals. In France, through the Revolution, they had abolished the private ownership in minerals. 'But we have had no Revolution here.'

Finally, he turned to the 'great monopoly of the governing classes' enshrined in the Constitution itself:

There are about six million electors in this land at the present day, and yet the Government is in the hands of one class. They have so manipulated Parliament that it is all in the hands of that one class . . . It does not matter up to the present which Party is in power, you have practically the same class governing the country.

There is no democratic country in the world where such a state of things exists . . . In this country, the way in which Parliament meets, the burden of expenses for entering Parliament, and the very hours at which they meet, all conspire in the end to keep the Government in the hands of the leisured classes who have nothing else to do except to govern others.

The great weapon for this purpose is the higher Chamber known as the House of Lords. That has got to be dealt with.[1]

In this speech Lloyd George was appealing to the conscience of the better-off, and to their instinct for self-preservation, because he and they knew that his words would carry to the voteless multitude. He was also appealing to bourgeois resentment of the landed aristocracy. Above all, perhaps, he was appealing to organized labour, and in his reply to a resolution of thanks he said that he hoped Liberal and Labour candidates would be returned for Newcastle – then a two-member constituency – at the next election, because he had never been able to see any distinction between them and had found that they worked together very well in the House of Commons.

Two months earlier Newcastle had been the scene of the Labour Representation Committee's annual conference, at which it was decided to raise a fund, from mass contributions of a penny a head, to finance candidates' election campaigns. It was also decided that any successful candidate would, out of the same fund, be paid a salary of £200 a year so long as he obeyed the Labour whip. Thus the Labour movement, with a membership that had increased by 300,000 during the past year to reach a total of 750,000, had found a means of overcoming the financial obstacles to working-class representation in Parliament.

Working-class M.P.s already existed, but they were very thin on the ground. Thomas Burt, a miner's son, had sat for Morpeth since 1874. William Abraham – 'Mabon' – another miner's son, had represented the Rhondda since 1885. They were both 'Lib-Lab' Members, whose class allegiance was to trade unionism but whose political allegiance was to the Liberal Party; and there were several others like them. But in 1892 the

1. Speech at the Palace Theatre, Newcastle-upon-Tyne, 4 April 1903. The audience on this occasion numbered 4,000.

first independent labour M.P.s were returned and a year later the Independent Labour Party was founded. In 1900 the I.L.P. joined with some trade unions, the Social Democratic Federation (S.D.F.) and the Fabian Society to set up the Labour Representation Committee, with James Ramsay MacDonald as its secretary. The L.R.C. was intended to promote the election of Labour M.P.s who would constitute a distinct and independent party, but who would not be committed, as such, to any economic theory.

At the 1900 election the L.R.C. won only two contests and most trade unions were still not affiliated to it. But in 1901 the House of Lords, by its judgment in the Taff Vale case, made trade unions liable for damages resulting from industrial action and so gravely impaired their right to strike. As no remedial steps were taken by the Balfour Government the L.R.C. received a powerful boost. In August 1902, a Labour candidate was returned unopposed for the vacant seat of Clitheroe in Lancashire. And in March 1903 – just after the L.R.C. conference, and a few weeks before Lloyd George's speech at Newcastle – Will Crooks, born in a workhouse, scored a sensational by-election victory at Woolwich.

From its earliest days the Labour movement revealed those fissiparous tendencies which have continued to afflict it throughout its history. The basic division has always been between more or less radical reformism and socialism of one sort or another, and even before the turn of the century the division was manifest in the attitude of John Burns, first towards the S.D.F. and then towards the I.L.P. Burns was a London engineering worker of Scottish descent who began his career as something of a revolutionary – he was known as 'The Man with the Red Flag' – but who gradually moved away from socialism towards cooperation with, and eventually membership of, the Liberal Party. Between him and James Keir Hardie, the Scottish miner who was chairman and moving spirit of the I.L.P., political incompatibility was aggravated by personal rivalry. The two men were first elected to Parliament in 1892, and in 1900 they were the only successful candidates of the L.R.C. But there was never any love lost between them and a few years later Keir Hardie was leader of the Labour M.P.s while Burns was a member of the Liberal Government.

Meanwhile, for electoral purposes, the L.R.C. had entered into a marriage of convenience with the Liberals. In September 1903 a secret pact was made between Ramsay MacDonald and Herbert Gladstone, the Liberal Chief Whip, providing for mutual assistance at the next election. The Liberals were afraid of losing seats to the Tories through a split in the anti-Tory vote, and so far as Labour was concerned the L.R.C.'s poor showing in 1900 would have been motive enough for the arrangement. In addition, Labour was driven towards the Liberals by the Taff Vale decision and, from mid-1903 onwards, by Chamberlain's Tariff Reform campaign. On the whole, the working class was more alarmed at the prospect of dearer food than attracted by the possible benefits of Protection, and even doctrinaire socialists, though opposed to Free Trade as an aspect of the capitalist system, were in sympathy with the internationalism of the Free Traders. Moreover it was evident that the Liberal Party's radical wing was increasingly powerful and likely to wield unprecedented influence in the next Liberal Government. In helping the Liberals, therefore, Labour leaders and trade unionists had reason to believe that they were helping themselves.

To a radical like Lloyd George, who rejected socialist dogmas but was quite willing to contemplate some degree of collectivism, the alliance with Labour seemed the most natural thing in the world, and in the circumstances of the time he was justified in hoping that the Labour movement would go his, rather than the socialists', way. Less justifiable was his slightly patronizing tone when referring to working-class figures. Thus, in support of a 'Lib-Lab' Member in Wales, he could say: 'I have known Mr Brace for many years ... He is the kind of representative of Labour we want in the House of Commons ... There is no better type in the House than the Labour representative – sturdy and honest. No one casts a breath of suspicion on their integrity.'[1] But towards the working class as a political force his attitude was by no means complacent; he could read the message of Labour's by-election victories. 'We have a great Labour Party sprung up. Unless we can prove, as I think we can, that there is no necessity for a separate party to press forward the legitimate claims of Labour, you will find that . . . the Liberal Party will be practically wiped out and that, in its place, you will get a more extreme and revolutionary party . . .'[2]

When he spoke those words Labour still had only a handful of M.P.s and the Liberals were riding high. Yet it was obvious to him that the Liberal Party would be doomed unless it could implement a truly radical programme, so offering Labour an acceptable alternative to socialism.

From the end of the Boer War until the fall of the Balfour Government three and a half years later there was never any serious doubt that Lloyd

1. Speech at Liberal demonstration, Bridgend, 25 May 1904.
2. Speech at National Reform Union meeting, Bacup, 5 November 1904.

George would be in the next Liberal Cabinet. Even before the war he was quite often mentioned as a likely candidate for high office. As one of the most popular and assiduous of Liberal platform speakers ever since he first entered Parliament he was well known to ordinary Liberal Party members in every part of the country, and had special opportunities for knowing, himself, what they were thinking. Unlike most of his colleagues he was nearly always ready to sacrifice his weekends to politics, whether Parliament was sitting or in recess. In the House of Commons he was early recognized as the most effective spokesman for Wales and after Gladstone's retirement in 1894, when the official Liberal leadership was weak and divided, he came to be regarded as an unofficial party leader for general opposition purposes.

It was, however, the Boer War that firmly established his credentials as a politician of unlimited scope and stature. In Parliament he was respected even by those who most strongly resented his opinions, and in the country he was a household name – a good thing for a public man to be, even when in many households his name is anathema. Moreover, one must be careful not to exaggerate the unpopularity of his line on the war. For most of the time he probably had a majority of the country against him, though not an overwhelming majority, and in any case within his own party the view that he held was very definitely the majority view. It was not he, but the so-called Liberal Imperialists, who were out on a limb. By taking the line he did he risked his life – because some of those who hated him for it were prepared to carry their hatred to the point of violence – but as a compensation he undoubtedly improved his standing in the Liberal Party relative to that of Asquith, Grey and other supporters of the war.

The Education controversy at first enhanced his position still further, because he led the attack on Balfour's Bill while the Liberal Imperialists could only take part in the campaign as auxiliaries. Most of them denounced the Bill as heartily as he did, thus regaining much of their lost credit with the Party; but he, at the same time, was adding to the credit which he had already gained at their expense. Before the Bill had become law a socialist organ was commenting on the Liberal revival and asking: 'If the majority of so-called Liberals is elected, who is to be the Premier? Is it to be Rosebery, Bannerman, *or Lloyd-George*?'[1] That Lloyd George should be mentioned at such an early stage as a possible Prime Minister, while Asquith was not mentioned, is truly striking evidence of what the

1. Unsigned note in Keir Hardie's *Labour Leader*, 6 September 1902. (Author's italics.)

Boer War had done to their respective reputations with the political *avant-garde*.

In May 1903, when Lloyd George was visiting Cambridge, a local paper mentioned his growing claims to be a leader of the Liberal Party. 'Sir William Harcourt is away from the House, confined to his bed. Mr John Morley is absorbed in his "Life of Mr Gladstone". Sir Henry Campbell-Bannerman, alone and unsupported, is not able wholly to satisfy even his most faithful supporter, the *Daily News*.'[1] Later in the same year, in an article entitled 'Men who may be Prime Minister', Lloyd George was said to be one of the 'very few young Liberals marked out conspicuously for the highest place'. He was 'already one of the favourite debaters of the Liberal Party' and, when the next Liberal Government was formed, would 'deserve a place in the Cabinet'.[2]

The following March there was a feature on Lloyd George in the *Sketch*, recording that he was usually called whenever he rose to speak in the House, and adding that he was expected to step straight into a Liberal Cabinet, because radicals would enforce his claims as they did Chamberlain's in 1880.[3] At about the same time he had an amiable encounter with King Edward VII at a dinner given in London by Lord Tweedmouth, the former Liberal Chief Whip. The occasion was widely reported, and was interpreted as a clear sign that Lloyd George was now thought fit to be one of the King's Ministers. 'It is an open secret that Mr Lloyd George's personality has a particular attraction for the King, and that the prominent and sensational role which this well-known M.P. has taken on the political stage has made his Majesty very desirous of meeting him. There is no member of the Liberal Party who may be more truthfully described as a coming man.'[4] It was also noted, later in the year, that Lloyd George had won a special title of honour more rare and more to be coveted than any that a king could bestow. He had 'attained the distinction of being always spoken of without the Mister . . . a kind of knighthood which is in the gift of the man in the street [and] much more sparingly distributed than the titular Sir'.[5]

1. *Cambridge Independent Press*, 29 May 1903.
2. Alexander Mackintosh in *Young Man*, September 1903.　　　3. *Sketch*, 2 March 1904.
4. *Daily Illustrated Mirror*, 12 March 1904. Tweedmouth's dinner was the night before and was held at Brook House in Park Lane (which he later sold to the King's friend, Sir Ernest Cassel). It was not only Lloyd George's political activities which might have aroused King Edward's interest. The Mordaunt divorce case (1870), in which as Prince of Wales he had to give evidence, bears some similarity to the Edwards divorce case in which Lloyd George was involved nearly twenty years later.
5. Character-sketch in the *Review of Reviews*, October issue, 1904.

By this time, however, Asquith had reasserted his right to be considered at least the Liberal Party's second-in-command, through his pre-eminent role in the counter-offensive against Chamberlain's Tariff Reform campaign. Any chance that Lloyd George might have had of leading the counter-offensive himself was prejudiced by his tiresomely protracted commitment to the Education struggle in Wales. His role was not much less subsidiary to Asquith's on Tariff Reform than Asquith's was to his on Education. In any case Asquith was ten years his senior in age, and had served as Home Secretary under Gladstone and Rosebery, whereas Lloyd George had not yet held office at all. In Parliamentary experience the two men were more evenly matched, Asquith having been elected to the House of Commons only four years before Lloyd George. But apart from his Boer War deviation Asquith's claim to be the next leader of the Liberal Party would have been incontestable. As it was, his prowess on behalf of Free Trade very largely, though not quite completely, restored the position of heir apparent which had been his before the Boer War broke out.

Meanwhile who was to be Prime Minister when the Liberals returned to power? This question gave rise to much discussion and intrigue in high Liberal circles, and remained an open question almost to the last. In retrospect it may seem that the obvious candidate was Sir Henry Campbell-Bannerman, who led the Party in the House of Commons and who, like Lloyd George, had done himself a lot of good with ordinary rank-and-file Liberals by his forthright opposition to the Boer War. Campbell-Bannerman was certainly much liked and respected in the Party – except by the 'Liberal Imperialists', who could never quite forgive him for his 'methods of barbarism' speech in June 1901. Yet there were others besides the 'Liberal Imperialists' who were doubtful of his fitness for the Premiership. Even those who liked and respected him most had to admit that he had never been a man of dynamic energy, and that he was now approaching seventy. Moreover, until he became Prime Minister he never succeeded in dominating the House of Commons, and there were reasonable fears that he might not stand up too well against a pugnacious Tory opposition led by Balfour.

Since, therefore, Campbell-Bannerman's appointment could by no means be taken for granted, what were the alternatives? The most favoured candidates were, it would seem, two peers – Lords Spencer and Rosebery. Spencer became Liberal leader in the House of Lords in 1902, but he had long been an outstanding member of the party hierarchy. Under Gladstone he was twice Viceroy of Ireland, and he earned his chief's special gratitude by conforming to his policy of Home Rule when other Whig noblemen seceded as Liberal Unionists. Consequently Gladstone would have recommended Spencer as his successor in 1894, if consulted by the Queen, in spite of the acute differences between them over naval estimates when Spencer was First Lord of the Admiralty in his last Cabinet – differences which precipitated the old man's resignation. But the Queen did not seek Gladstone's advice and invited Rosebery, whom he would not have recommended, to form a new Government.

Spencer was a man of dignity and character but very limited intelligence. One day in March 1905, while he was speaking in the House of Lords, Balfour listened to him from the steps of the Throne and then said to Edmund Gosse: 'What an amazing example Spencer is of what can be done in this country by a noble presence and a fine personal record, assisted by no intellectual parts of any kind! It is really very remarkable. Such a sweet, and even such a beautiful character, and no ability at all.' When Gosse admitted that Spencer's mind worked rather slowly, Balfour corrected him: 'It does not work at all. He has no mind. He has character, but no mind. It is only in England that such a man would hold a great position, and' – Balfour wagged his finger at Gosse – 'it is a very good thing for us that it should be so.'[1]

Rosebery was the opposite – a man of brilliant intellect and unstable character. Though more than ten years younger than Spencer or Campbell-Bannerman, he had already held the office of Prime Minister. This gave him prestige, even though his Administration had been very brief and conspicuously unsuccessful. Since 1896, when he had resigned the Liberal leadership, he had been a sort of Liberal king over the water. From some he received homage, to others he was a source of uneasiness; but to all he was mysterious, and mystery never lacks charm. His personality was fascinating, if perverse; his speeches were well turned and oracular. Having the virtues as well as the faults of a *prima donna*, he had a lively theatrical sense and a flair for the poetry of politics. Admiration for him was broad-based and by no means confined to the party of which he was nominally a member. Many Tories admired him, sensing correctly that he had the temperament and opinions of a Disraelian Tory. The 'Liberal Imperialists' looked to him as their leader, though he treated them with scant consideration and gradually forced them to abandon him. Finally, he made

1. Edmund Gosse, unpublished Diary, entry for 9 March 1905. Gosse was Librarian of the House of Lords, 1904–14.

some appeal to Fabians and others on the Left, as a prophet of the fashionable modern cult of national efficiency.

Of the three candidates for Liberal Prime Minister – Campbell-Bannerman, Spencer and Rosebery – there can be no doubt at all that Lloyd George's initial preference was for Rosebery. While he certainly had no sneaking kindness for lords in general, and nothing but contempt for lords of Spencer's type, he did have a sneaking kindness for Rosebery as an individual. And the sentiment was mutual; Rosebery had for some years been cultivating Lloyd George's acquaintance, asking him to *tête-à-tête* lunches in Berkeley Square and taking him for walks in Hyde Park.

The two men were different in many ways, but shared an impatience with the Gladstonian fetish of Irish Home Rule, proclaiming instead the doctrine of Home Rule all Round. Except on the Boer War and a few other issues, Lloyd George largely agreed with Rosebery's Imperial ideas, which were remote from the little Englandism of many Liberals without, he thought, being as crude and arrogant as Chamberlain's Imperialism. Even during the Boer War he put it around that, except on South Africa, he was of Rosebery's school. But there was another, and deeper, affinity. Lloyd George and Rosebery were both at heart dissatisfied with the party system. Both were inclined to feel that party government was inevitably an obstacle to efficiency and that the national interest could only be fully and properly served by a coalition of the best available talent, regardless of party. It was fitting that when, in 1916, Lloyd George was forming his own war-time coalition, he tried to persuade Rosebery to join the War Cabinet.

But though his respect and sympathy for Rosebery were genuine, he was also well aware of the failings which Rosebery had exhibited as Prime Minister, and his interest in promoting a second Rosebery Premiership early in the century could not, therefore, have been wholly altruistic. As we look at the evidence a very strong personal motive appears, which makes sense of what might otherwise be a little puzzling. Lloyd George's desire that Rosebery should be Prime Minister bore less relation to Rosebery's career than to his own.

In May 1903 the leading Irish Nationalist M.P., John Dillon, told Wilfrid Scawen Blunt that Rosebery had been making advances to Lloyd George, 'the most able of the Radicals', to which Lloyd George had responded.[1] This development had already been noted with apprehension by Keir Hardie, who wrote in an open letter to Lloyd George:

1. Wilfrid Scawen Blunt, *My Diaries, Part Two*, entry for 5 May 1903.

Your courageous anti-war attitude, and your really magnificent fight against the Education Bill, have won for you a position of influence with Radicals to which no other politician can lay claim. To what use will you put this great and growing power? Two courses are open to you. You may continue to be a Free Lance or you may accept office and, in course of time, become a Cabinet Minister. Great pressure will be brought to bear upon you to induce you to follow this latter course. Already Lord Rosebery, who loves neither you nor your tenets, has taken to flattering you. You would be an awkward man to have on his flanks were he again to become Premier . . . For over a hundred years the Whigs have played this game of gagging their dangerous rivals.[1]

Dillon and Keir Hardie had a naïve, oversimplified view of the relationship between Lloyd George and Rosebery, Keir Hardie in particular completely misreading the situation. Only a month after his open letter Lloyd George was making the incandescently radical speech at Newcastle which was quoted earlier in this chapter – a speech which hardly suggests that he had been gagged by Rosebery or anybody else. In fact, he was concerned to outbid, simultaneously, the conservatism of the Whigs and the socialism of men like Keir Hardie. And it suited his own book to canvass for a Rosebery Premiership.

At the beginning of 1904 there was an article on Lloyd George in the Imperialist *Sunday Sun*, remarking that he was 'far from irreconcilable to the wider Liberalism of which Lord Rosebery is the representative and leader', and alleging that he had supported Rosebery for the leadership after Gladstone.[2] The day this article appeared Lloyd George was at Fallodon, staying with Edward Grey:

[He] met me at his private station. I had a very long walk with him in the morning & we had a very frank chat about the prospective Liberal Ministry – if it comes off. He says I am certain to have a seat in the Cabinet. Told him I must bargain for Wales.

His ideas are dangerous. Rosebery Premier & Asquith Leader of the House. The former is possible but latter I fear impossible as it means shelving CB & Morley. I told him that could not be done. He is more

1. J. Keir Hardie, Open Letter to Lloyd George M.P., *Labour Leader*, 3 March 1903. Keir Hardie can hardly have been serious in suggesting that Lloyd George would at first receive only minor office in a Liberal Government, since it was the *Labour Leader* which had mentioned him, only a few months earlier, as one of three men who might head such a Government.
2. *Sunday Sun*, 10 January 1904.

bent on an Asquith leadership of the Commons than on a Rosebery Premiership. He would prefer a Spencer Premiership with an Asquith leadership.[1]

This conversation not only shows the lukewarmness of Grey's loyalty to Rosebery; it also provides a significant clue to Lloyd George's attitude. If Grey was above all keen to promote Asquith's leadership of the House of Commons, Lloyd George was above all keen to prevent it. He was unwilling, as yet, to concede to Asquith the position of Liberal heir apparent which would be implicit in his assumption of the Commons leadership. The advantage, from Lloyd George's point of view, of a peer as Prime Minister would be that Campbell-Bannerman would have to remain in the House of Commons as leader. And granted the desirability of a peer as Prime Minister, Lloyd George's choice was naturally Rosebery rather than Spencer.

On the face of it, Grey should have had the same preference in a more marked degree, because he was ostensibly one of Rosebery's closest friends and lieutenants. He had served under Rosebery at the Foreign Office and was, with Asquith, a vice-president of the Liberal League, of which Rosebery was president. Yet we are told that he would have preferred Spencer. Why? Politics has its reasons which the heart does not know, and Grey's political reasons for preferring Spencer were complementary to Lloyd George's for preferring Rosebery. Late in 1904 Lloyd George reported to Herbert Lewis conversations he had had with Rosebery's sister, Lady Leconfield:

> They (Lady L. & G.) discussed the Leadership very frankly and G. put it to her plainly that in relying on the Liberal League to secure the Premiership for him, her brother was leaning on a broken reed. Grey expects the Foreign Office, Asquith the Chancellorship of the Exchequer, and Haldane the Lord Chancellorship, but, said G., is it not obvious that if those three men secure those great offices you must give the Premiership to the other section? If they can secure those offices they will leave Lord Rosebery in the lurch.

Lloyd George also told Herbert Lewis that he had spoken to Morley about the leadership and:

> had urged him to make Lord R. Premier. 'If you do that', he said, 'he will of necessity be bound to give far greater consideration to the other

1. D.L.G. to M.L.G., 11 January 1904 (N.L.W. and *Letters*, p. 140).

section than they would otherwise receive.' But Morley could not see it.[1]

Lloyd George's account of the intended share-out of offices between Grey, Asquith and Haldane anticipates by eight or nine months the compact which the trio entered into at Grey's Highland fishing lodge in September 1905. Under this arrangement – known to history as the Relugas Compact – Campbell-Bannerman was to be allowed the Premiership, but only on condition that he went to the House of Lords. Asquith was to be Chancellor of the Exchequer and Leader of the House of Commons; Grey, Foreign Secretary; Haldane, Lord Chancellor. The three resolved that, unless Campbell-Bannerman could be persuaded to accept their terms, none of them would agree to join his Ministry.

The Relugas scheme almost exactly accords with Lloyd George's inferences and imputations the year before. Rosebery was to be ditched and a Prime Minister was projected who would be both a peer and a member of 'the other section' of the Party. The 'Liberal Imperialists' would thus, it was thought, be able to secure three key offices and control of the House of Commons. The only difference was that, instead of Spencer, the peer in question was to be Campbell-Bannerman translated to the Lords, and the reason for this substitution was that Spencer had developed heart trouble and would clearly not be fit to form a Government.[2] The change was also convenient, in that it provided a decent and dignified way of removing Campbell-Bannerman. To have eliminated him altogether, or even to have left him with nothing more than the Privy Seal or the Presidency of the Council, would have seemed outrageous to many faithful Liberals. By retaining him as Prime Minister in the Lords the conspirators could hope that they would enjoy power without dishonour.

It has been generally assumed that Rosebery's 'friends' were disappointed at his waywardness and forced, reluctantly, to conclude that he was a non-starter for the Premiership. In fact, as Grey's remarks to Lloyd George show, they were not pressing his claims too hard even at the beginning of 1904, and the evidence surely indicates that it was, on the contrary, Lloyd George who was disappointed by Rosebery. Had Rosebery been willing

1. Herbert Lewis diary, entry for 20 December 1904 (N.L.W.). It is impossible to date the reported conversations with Lady Leconfield and Morley, but they were clearly influenced by what Lloyd George had heard from Grey.
2. He was badly shaken by the death of his wife in October 1903, which may have helped to bring on the cardiac illness which began to afflict him the following year. In the autumn of 1905 he had a stroke from which he never recovered, though he lived on until 1910.

to emerge as a straightforward champion of his Party and, consequently, as a powerful, almost irresistible, claimant to the leadership, the 'Rosebery-ites' would have had to pretend to be pleased, but Lloyd George's pleasure would have been genuine. The calculation on both sides would have been that he would necessarily adopt a policy of indemnity for his supposed enemies and oblivion for his supposed friends.

There is one curious document which might, on a superficial view, be taken as evidence that Lloyd George was an accessory to what later became the Relugas plan. In February 1905 Campbell-Bannerman received a letter from Henry Labouchere, in which 'Labby' said:

> Our very opportunist friend Lloyd George was explaining to me a plan for you to go to the Lords – I said to him that as his object was to be in the Cabinet, he would do well to stick to you, as I had gathered from an observation that fell from you that you were for this – It was an invention of my own, but it converted him, for he came to me after-wards and tried to find out what the observation was, but I only replied that it had quite convinced me that he would be in the Cabinet. This is the best plan to deal with these sort of cadgers . . .[1]

What are we to make of this letter? Labouchere says that Lloyd George 'explained' to him the plan for Campbell-Bannerman's removal to the Lords. So, indeed, he may have done, without wishing to identify himself with it or to convey any approval of it. Lloyd George knew very well what was afoot and may have intended, through Labouchere, to alert Campbell-Bannerman to the 'Liberal Imperialist' conspiracy. Or he may simply have been talking about it to an old crony, without suspecting that his words would be twisted or misconstrued.

The innuendo – and it is no more than an innuendo – that he was a party to the conspiracy *must* be false, partly because it contradicts what he said to Grey and is quite contrary to the spirit of what he said to Herbert Lewis, but above all because it was patently against his interest that Campbell-Bannerman should leave the House of Commons in circum-stances which would establish Asquith as the crown prince. Labouchere must either have misunderstood what Lloyd George was saying to him, or have deliberately chosen to misrepresent it.

If the second interpretation is correct, what could have been his motive? At least two good reasons spring to mind. 'Labby' was a born intriguer

1. Labouchere to Campbell-Bannerman, 21 February 1905, quoted in John Wilson, *CB: A Life of Sir Henry Campbell-Bannerman*, p. 426.

and mischief-maker. He had befriended Lloyd George as a young politician, but by 1905 it must have been extremely galling for him that one whom he used to regard as a protégé was now hailed on all sides as a man of the future, while he was himself increasingly written off as a man of the past. Though he had been very ambitious for office it was now clear that he would never obtain it, whereas Lloyd George was poised on the brink of power.

Moreover Labouchere could remember that, after he had been denied a place in Gladstone's last Ministry, ostensibly on account of Queen Victoria's hostility to him, one hope had yet remained – that he might be appointed Ambassador to the United States. And that last hope had been dashed by the personal veto of one man, the Foreign Secretary of the day, *Rosebery*. This alone could explain his malice against Lloyd George in 1905. Anyone who was on good terms with Rosebery could expect to be on bad terms with Labouchere, and the widely bruited fact that Lloyd George had become a Rosebery man would have been quite enough to turn Labouchere against him.

At any rate, we may be sure that Lloyd George did not wish Campbell-Bannerman to go to the Lords, whatever 'Labby's' motive for writing as he did. And we may be equally sure that Lloyd George was not a 'cadger' for office in 1905, though he may well have been interested to know which Cabinet office Campbell-Bannerman had in mind for him. That he would be asked to join the Cabinet in some capacity was as nearly a foregone conclusion as anything could be in politics. Apart from his manifest abilities, he was the acknowledged representative of three major Liberal interest-groups – the Welsh, the Nonconformists and the radicals – which any Liberal Prime Minister would be bound to accommodate. With the possible exception of Herbert Gladstone nobody had less need to cadge for high office than he had, even if cadging had been in his nature, which it was not.

Even Asquith was probably more expendable, and the suspicion that it might be so could account for his failure to stick to the Relugas Compact when it became apparent to him that Campbell-Bannerman would not be pushed into the Upper House. He may have sensed a danger that Campbell-Bannerman might appoint Lloyd George over his head, unless he settled for the Chancellorship of the Exchequer without insisting upon the Relugas conditions. By his splendid showing in the fight against Tariff Reform he had earned the second place in a Liberal Government, and had atoned for his lapse from grace during the Boer War. But his credit would slump again if it became known to the Liberal rank-and-file that he had been engaged, with Grey and Haldane, in a plot to blackmail Campbell-Bannerman. And in that event Lloyd George would be available to fill the gap.[1]

At the end of 1904 Lloyd George left his family, as he quite often did, to spend Christmas and the New Year in the Western Mediterranean. On 16 December he sailed with Herbert Lewis from Plymouth on R.M.S. *Ormuz* of the Orient Pacific Line, and it was during their nine-day voyage to Naples that he spoke to Lewis about his discussions with Lady Leconfield and Morley. All the same, he wrote to Margaret that sea life was boring him so much he was even losing his interest in politics. And he enclosed a 'certificate' written by his friend:

> Know all men by these presents that David Lloyd George of Brynawelon Criccieth in the County of Caernarvon some time Member of His Majesty's Most Honourable Privy Council hath during a voyage from London in the County of Middlesex to Marseilles on the Gulf of Lyons benefited greatly in health and hath likewise conducted himself with the most exemplary propriety As witness my hand this 23rd day of December 1904
>
> Guardian appointed by the
> Lunacy Commissioners   Herbert Lewis[2]

They landed at Naples on Christmas Day and found Frank Edwards there 'beaming as usual'.[3] Staying at Parker's Hotel they spent a week in the city, with sight-seeing expeditions to Puteoli, Cuma, Baiae, Sorrento and Amalfi. From Naples he wrote to Margaret expressing warm approval

1. On 13 November 1905, two months after the Relugas meeting, Campbell-Bannerman saw Asquith – alone – in London, and discussed with him names and places for the Liberal Ministry whose formation by himself appeared to be imminent. He began by suggesting that Asquith should have the Exchequer and then showed that he was well aware of the notion he himself should go to the House of Lords, which he attributed to Haldane, and for which he expressed repugnance. Asquith did not admit that the idea was his as well and said nothing to imply that his own acceptance of the Exchequer would be conditional upon Campbell-Bannerman's elevation. From that moment the Relugas conspiracy was more or less dead so far as Asquith was concerned – though he did not inform his partners.
2. D.L.G. to M.L.G., from the ship, 22 December 1904, and posted next day from Marseilles, with Herbert Lewis's enclosure (N.L.W.). The light-hearted reference to Lloyd George's membership of the Privy Council could accurately and prophetically have read 'some time within the next year'.
3. D.L.G. to M.L.G., 26 December 1904 (N.L.W.).

of the religious revival which was sweeping Wales,[1] and whose political value to his Education campaign has already been explained. He was, no doubt, happy to be able to approve of it from afar.

On 2 January 1905 the three Welsh M.P.s sailed on the German steamer *Preussen* to Genoa, whence they travelled by train, first to Menton, then to stay with Lord Rendel at Cannes. Rendel, formerly chairman of the Welsh Parliamentary group and an admiring patron of Lloyd George, was no longer politically active but still very interested in politics. His butler, accustomed to grand guests, took Lloyd George's name to be 'Lord George' and, to his amusement, called him 'My Lord'. The house was 'like Paradise, especially the garden':

> Groups of stately palms on the lawns shadowing beds of brilliant flowers which they were watering this morning when I looked out . . . The house itself seems to be paved & colonnaded with white marble . . .

And yet, Lloyd George added – not very convincingly – he would have preferred to be with the family at Routh Road.

He had visited Monte Carlo, of whose staple industry he had this to say:

> The Casino haunts you. Men & women recklessly gambling away their whole fortunes. The Grand Duke Sergius, a member of the Russian royal family, throwing hundreds away – walking from table to table having placed a stake of £30 or £40 on each. And this in the very darkest hour of his country's trouble. No wonder Russia is on the brink of revolution.[2]

Lloyd George returned to London during the second week of January.

Nineteen hundred and five was a nerve-racking year for him, with the Welsh controversy at its most difficult stage and a change of Government in the air. When Parliament rose in August he made a brief trip to the Scottish Highlands, staying again with Rendel at another of his many residences. Margaret, though invited, did not accompany her husband.

In late October he travelled to Scotland again, this time on political business. At Kirkcaldy he addressed a great Liberal rally and remarked on the appropriateness of the venue:

> It is fitting that, on the eve of a battle which is to challenge the action of a Government which has attacked Free Trade and has increased the

1. D.L.G. to M.L.G., 27 December 1904 (N.L.W. and *Letters*, p. 141).
2. D.L.G. to M.L.G., from the Château de Thorenc, Cannes, 6 January 1905 (N.L.W. and partly quoted in *Letters*, p. 142).

burdens of taxation, you in Scotland should meet and take counsel in Adam Smith's burgh.

He derided the Government:

> I believe that if you sought the first thirty men you met driving in a morning in Rotten Row – and Rotten Row is the sort of place to go for them – you would get no worse a Government.

Balfour himself was 'not a man but a mannerism', or at best 'an honest man without convictions'.[1]

At Glasgow a few days later Lloyd George supported Asquith for the Lord Rectorship of the University – a gesture of party solidarity which came the more easily to him seeing that Asquith's opponent was a dim Scottish peer. 'I am', he said,

> one of the forty-two millions in this country who had never heard of the Marquess of Linlithgow until recently ... if you had had an examination at Glasgow University six months ago, and if among the questions there had been this: 'Who is the Marquess of Linlithgow?' two-thirds of his present supporters would have been ploughed.[2]

This was Lloyd George's last speech before he became a Minister. His throat had earlier been troubling him and between his two visits to Scotland he had had his tonsils removed. After the operation he had a severe throat haemorrhage which might have proved fatal but for the prompt action of a friend in sending urgently for medical help. The friend in question was his old flame Mrs Timothy Davies – 'Mrs Tim' – in whose company he appears to have been convalescing. Margaret was at Criccieth.

Since he was now advised to give up all work for two months he wrote to his brother William suggesting that, after his speeches at Kirkcaldy and Glasgow which he could not cancel, they should go for a holiday together abroad. William proposed that they should go to Italy, and at his expense. It is interesting that Lloyd George should have turned to his brother at this moment of weakness and nervous expectancy. Though he depended upon William for much practical support, he did not normally seek his company for recreational purposes. Did he perhaps feel a need to recapture the intimacies of his childhood as he prepared for a new and more demanding phase in his career? Or was it simply that others were not free to travel with him at the time?

1. Speech at Kirkcaldy, 27 October 1905. In reality he had the deepest respect for Balfour.
2. Speech in St Andrew's Hall, Glasgow, 1 November 1905.

Whatever the reason, he and William took a ship to Genoa in mid-November. 'Mrs Tim' saw them off on the boat train to Southampton. After reaching Genoa, and staying there a few days, they went on to Florence and Rapallo. At Rapallo – a place of sinister import in Lloyd George's later career – they met an old Liberal who said he had heard Balfour was about to resign and therefore urged Lloyd George to return home without delay. It was decided that William should return first, on the understanding that he would telegraph an agreed code word if he judged it necessary for Lloyd George to follow immediately. On 2 December William arrived back in London and soon made up his mind that the old Liberal's advice was correct. The code message was sent and Lloyd George returned.[1]

Balfour resigned on 4 December, calculating that by resignation rather than dissolution he would expose the Liberals' disunity, which might be such that they would not even be able to form a Government. Many Liberals were equally sceptical, arguing that Balfour should be forced to dissolve. But Campbell-Bannerman did not share their doubts, and it was with him that the decision lay, because Rosebery had put himself finally out of court by a speech at Bodmin at the end of November, in which he dissociated himself from Campbell-Bannerman and the mainstream of Liberalism. On 5 December the King received Campbell-Bannerman and asked him to form a Government. Within a week he had succeeded, and on his own terms. As well as being Prime Minister he remained in the House of Commons as its Leader.

Of the Relugas conspirators only Grey played seriously hard to get, but even he at length agreed to be Foreign Secretary though none of the other Relugas conditions was met. As Campbell-Bannerman had reason to expect, Asquith took the Exchequer without the Leadership of the House, and Haldane had to postpone to a later date his occupancy of the Woolsack, accepting instead – to the nation's boundless benefit – the office of War Minister. Herbert Gladstone went to the Home Office, Morley to the India Office, and John Burns to the Local Government Board. Winston Churchill was appointed Under-Secretary to Lord Elgin at the Colonial Office.

Various posts had in recent years been predicted for Lloyd George, including the one which he was actually offered, but his own preference in the matter is doubtful. According to Loulou Harcourt, he would have

1. William George, *My Brother and I*, pp. 87–9.

liked to be Home Secretary.[1] If so, there was nothing exorbitant or fantastic in the idea. Asquith had been appointed Home Secretary straight from the back benches in 1892, after only six years in Parliament compared with Lloyd George's fifteen. Moreover, since Welsh Disestablishment was a subject for the Home Office, it would have been natural enough for Lloyd George to be sent there. But on Friday 8 December Campbell-Bannerman offered him the Presidency of the Board of Trade, with a seat in the Cabinet, which he did not hesitate to accept.[2]

There is no independent evidence that he bargained for Wales, as he said he would, though Uncle Lloyd was persuaded that he did:

> Had Wales Cause guaranteed before undertaking office, granted him unreservedly. Am so proud of this secured after all his self-spent life of efforts of all kinds on her behalf. Good Providence protect, help and bless my dearest boy, and crown his service to his generation by thy blessing.[3]

What exactly Uncle Lloyd meant by 'Wales Cause' is anybody's guess, but it is most unlikely that Lloyd George demanded, or that Campbell-Bannerman gave, any but the most generalized guarantees, if indeed he gave any guarantees at all. Lloyd George certainly did not stipulate that a new Welsh disestablishment bill should be introduced by a definite date, since he knew very well that there would be no hope of enacting such a measure so long as the House of Lords retained its veto. It is possible that he may have asked Campbell-Bannerman to promise a National Council for Wales, but even that is doubtful. Lloyd George's appointment to the Cabinet was, however, among other things a gesture to Wales, and an earnest of good intentions to the Principality. In addition, Herbert Lewis was appointed a junior Whip.

On 11 December Lloyd George attended at Buckingham Palace the first Privy Council of the new Administration, at which he was one of the new Privy Councillors sworn. Characteristically, he managed to make an instantly favourable impression on the Clerk of the Council, Sir Almeric Fitzroy, who wrote in his diary: 'To Lloyd George I took rather a fancy;

1. Notes in Harcourt's handwriting among Campbell-Bannerman's papers, quoted in John Wilson, *op. cit.*, p. 443.
2. W. Watkin Davies states that he was offered as an alternative the job of Postmaster-General, but 'without hesitation' chose the Board of Trade (*Lloyd George 1863–1914*, p. 241). No evidence is cited for the statement, but Davies may have heard it from Lloyd George himself, who was a friend of his father's.
3. Entry in Richard Lloyd's diary, quoted in William George, *op. cit.*, p. 90.

he is bright, pleasant and courteous.'[1] And Lloyd George himself quite enjoyed the occasion. Though he was the least pompous of men, ceremonial appealed to both his historic and his histrionic sense. 'The ceremony passed off admirably', he wrote to his brother. 'Took only a quarter of an hour in all. King very gracious.'[2]

So, while still only in his forty-third year, he became one of the rulers of the British nation and Empire. To be a member of the British Cabinet is no small responsibility and dignity even now; in 1905 it was to belong, as it were, to the board of directors of the greatest Power on earth. Lloyd George was now to hold high office without a break for nearly seventeen years. During that time Britain and the world would undergo seismic changes, and his own contribution to those changes would be immeasurable. He had already come a long way from the cottage at Llanystumdwy and the solicitors' office at Portmadoc. He had much further to go.

1. Almeric Fitzroy, *Memoirs*, Vol. I, p. 274.
2. D.L.G. to W.G., 11 December 1905, quoted in William George, *op. cit.*, p. 206.

FOUR
Pragmatist Revealed

The Liberals were back in office, but not yet securely in power. Their first requirement was a Parliamentary majority, for which they needed to go to the country without delay. The new Government never met the old Parliament, whose dissolution was announced on 16 December. And on the 21st Campbell-Bannerman set the tone of the Liberal campaign at a great meeting in the Albert Hall.

His speech, ineffably bland and reassuring, was aimed at the electorate rather than at his immediate audience of party enthusiasts. He boasted of the fact that Consols had gone up since his Government was formed. India, he said, would be cautiously governed, and the Colonies would be bound more closely to the mother-country. Foreign policy would be kept steadily on existing lines, there would be less expenditure on armaments, and some tax burdens might be eased. Local authorities would be given more power to improve their own areas and the people would be given more freedom, for instance to control their own schools. Recent judicial decisions affecting the right of combination would be corrected, and there would be some reform of the electoral system. But he said nothing about the House of Lords, nothing about Welsh disestablishment, and nothing about old age pensions. Though he reaffirmed the Liberal commitment to Ireland, he did so rather vaguely and with a vital reservation as to timing. The supreme election issue, so far as he was concerned, was Free Trade, and he insisted that the Tories should not be allowed to pick any other to suit themselves. As he sat down there was a demonstration by suffragettes. but their voices were drowned by the organ striking up 'For He's a Jolly Good Fellow'.

Most of C.-B.'s Cabinet colleagues were on the platform at the Albert Hall, but Lloyd George was not among them. He was at the Guild Hall, Caernarvon, addressing his own constituents – and the Welsh people – on the issues that most concerned *them*. He began in Welsh, and in the tone of a national rather than a party hero:

I have to thank not only Liberals. It is but right and proper that I should thank also many members of the opposite political camp on this first occasion on which I address a meeting in Wales as a Minister of the Crown.[1] Believe me, although I now speak as Minister of the King, I shall not be any the less a Minister of the democracy. It has been said that I am the first Welshman to be a member of the Cabinet since the days of Archbishop Williams. I follow the footsteps of an Archbishop and I am, therefore, in the Apostolic Succession to that extent.

The rest of the speech was largely devoted to the schools question, and included an appeal to 'fair-minded Churchmen', to whom he professed an equal determination to be fair. But he ended – again in Welsh – with a resounding reference to disestablishment and his own unwavering loyalty to the cause:

This I will say – of the nineteen men who constitute the Cabinet, nineteen are in favour of disestablishment . . . When I was first elected by you, I was the youngest Member in the House. Now that others have chosen me, I am the youngest member of the Cabinet. I have accepted that position not to betray, but to serve, my country. If I ever fail to speak for the people, let my tongue cleave to the roof of my mouth!

At those words the whole audience rose and cheered for several minutes. But Lloyd George had, in fact, been no more specific on the timing of Welsh disestablishment than C.-B. on the timing of Irish Home Rule.

In sharp contrast to the previous election it was practically a foregone conclusion that Lloyd George would be returned for the Caernarvon Boroughs. His opponent, R. A. Naylor, was a timber merchant of no political sophistication, and with the added disadvantage of being an Englishman. He did not even have the backing of one of the most prominent local Tories, John E. Greaves, Lord Lieutenant of Caernarvonshire, who as a Free Trader supported Lloyd George and as a slate-quarry owner

1. A week later he said at Conway that he had had almost as many letters of congratulation from political opponents as from his political friends.

refuted the charge that Protection would benefit the slate trade. But Lloyd George's prestige and the general political climate were anyway such that he could safely spend much of the election outside his own constituency, speaking for Liberal or Labour candidates in different parts of the country. He spoke at Fulham (for Timothy Davies, complaisant husband of his friend, 'Mrs Tim') and at Croydon, Darlington, Middlesbrough and Leamington – where, on 11 January 1906, he was denied a hearing in the Winter Hall by an organized gang of roughs whom he described as 'free imports from Birmingham'. The meeting was adjourned to the Liberal Club where he said that the situation reminded him of old times; and after the meeting, which was in the early afternoon, he left by road for Mold in Flintshire, to speak there the same night for Herbert Lewis.

The 1906 election was the first in which the motor-car played an important part, and Lloyd George was obviously excited by his drive from Leamington to Mold, since he drew upon it for oratorical purposes. In his speech on arrival he said that the Welsh had broken the Balfour Government. 'To use a metaphor which is much impressed on my mind after travelling 130 miles in a motor-car, we have punctured them and the huge lumbering thing has been left somewhere on the roadside.' Next day at Denbigh he said that on the same journey there had been difficulty in reading the fingerposts. 'The paint upon them was often obliterated. Sometimes the posts pointed in three or four different directions. It was dark and we lost our way more than once. Now the point is that it is most important for a child on the road of his career that the fingerposts should be perfectly explicit and direct.' In other words, their minds should not be confused by religious instruction at variance from that given to them by their parents. He also prophesied on more than one occasion that, in spite of a late start, Britain would overhaul those countries that had got ahead of her in motor-car production.

Caernarvon Boroughs went to the poll on 20 January and the result was announced shortly after midnight. It was, as expected, a walk-over for Lloyd George:

Lloyd George	3,221
Naylor	1,997

In his four previous elections his largest majority had been 296. Now he had a majority of 1,224. Meanwhile in the country at large, where polling had been going on for over a week, it was already manifest that the Liberals' victory would be of landslide proportions. There were huge swings to them in Lancashire, Yorkshire and London. By the second week of February, when all the results were in, they had a majority of 130 seats over all other parties; and, with their Labour and Irish Nationalist allies, a majority of 356 over the Tories alone. They won every seat in Wales and 58 of the 70 seats in Scotland. Balfour was defeated in East Manchester and only three members of his Cabinet survived. Tories lost heavily even in areas traditionally loyal to them, though Joseph Chamberlain's Unionist redoubt in Birmingham was not engulfed. The political system exaggerated, but did not misrepresent, the popular verdict: there had indeed been a formidable, if temporary, shift of allegiance.

Lloyd George detected in what was happening 'a quiet but certain revolution, as revolutions come in a constitutional country, without overthrowing order, without doing an injustice to anybody, but redressing those injustices from which people suffer'.[1] In the event his words were substantially justified, though a revolution even of the kind referred to was not what the voters necessarily intended. There can be little doubt that their chief motive in voting as they did was conservative – to preserve Free Trade with its allegedly concomitant blessings of prosperity and low food prices. At a time of reviving trade the case for a radical change in the economic system could not be popular, and there are no solid grounds for believing, as Chamberlain's apologists have claimed, that an all-out commitment to Tariff Reform as advocated by him would have produced a more favourable result than an all-out commitment to Balfour's policy of Retaliation. The challenge to Free Trade was itself, in the circumstances, disastrous, but it was inevitably made more so by the divergent forms of it proposed by Chamberlain and Balfour.[2]

Another major cause of revulsion against the Tories was that they had been responsible for involving the country in a long and costly war. This reason has, perhaps, been given less weight than it deserves by historians, who have tended to overlook the fact that after each of Britain's serious wars in the present century the electorate has recorded a decisive vote

1. Speech at Bangor, 19 January 1906.
2. Though Chamberlain's Birmingham base held firm in the election, Unionist candidates there were not immune to considerable swings against them, and in other parts of the country – where personal loyalty to a local hero did not apply – Chamberlainite candidates did no better, on the whole, than Balfourians or Unionist Free Traders. The most detailed analysis of the 1906 election reaches, on this point, the conclusion that 'a strong lead from Chamberlain, and a wholehearted committal of the party to his policy, might have saved more seats than it lost, but so equally would the slower, less crusading, but united evolution of the idea of fiscal reform under Balfour's leadership'. (A. K. Russell, *Liberal Landslide*, p. 181.)

against the party that was in power when the war began. Even in the 'Khaki' election of 1900, when it seemed that the Boer War might be coming to a fairly swift and (for Britain) triumphant conclusion, the mood of the voters was by no means uniformly bellicose. And as the war dragged on, at a heavy cost in lives, money and national reputation, opinion became increasingly disaffected. If the 1906 election was above all a vote for Free Trade, it was surely also to a large extent a retrospective vote against the Boer War.

Yet the familiar view of it as a mandate for sweeping change is not wholly mythical. The return of thirty Labour M.P.s was itself a portent – though not, as many now believe, a portent of inexorable doom for the Liberals. Within the Liberal Party social radicalism was a genuine and powerful current, not merely a response to trade union influence and pressure. Most Liberal candidates were more radical than the electorate, or than their leaders chose to appear. Nearly two out of every three Liberal candidates were explicitly in favour of legislation for old age pensions, on which even Lloyd George – recognized as a protagonist of the measure – was guarded.[1] Over half of those who stood as Liberals went far beyond Campbell-Bannerman in pledging constitutional reforms to give effective power to the poor. All the same, the vast majority of Liberal voters can have neither willed nor imagined the seismic impact of the 1906 Parliament upon the British State and British society. What they accomplished by their votes may have been a rendezvous with Destiny, but it was essentially a blind date.

During the next two and a quarter years Lloyd George successfully performed a dual role that a less talented man could never have pulled off. By his speeches in the country at weekends he sustained his reputation as the Liberal Party's most eloquent and fearless radical. At the same time he devoted himself during the working week to the task of proving that he could run a great department of State, and that in doing so he was no ideologue but a patient, open-minded and resourceful pragmatist. Thus he came very near to making the best of both worlds. His acknowledged competence in office enhanced his value as a spokesman for the New Liberalism, while his vehemence on public platforms made those who had

1. Questioned at Caernarvon on 18 January 1906 he said that the scheme worked out before the Boer War would have been quite practicable, but that now it would be more than the country could afford. The matter must be approached 'gradually', when the national finances had been put 'in spick and span order'.

to deal with him in his official capacity all the more ready to appreciate his moderation as a Minister.

When the new Parliament met his first utterance from the Front Bench was a strictly departmental answer on foreign seamen in British ships (21 February), and in the Debate on the Address he made a very cautious, emollient little speech on coast defence:

> ... this Government ... is in its infancy ... and their money-box is not very full at this moment. We have not the money to spend on all those schemes on which we would like to spend money ... The Government have decided to have an inquiry in the form of a Royal Commission, which will extend not merely to coast defence, but to two or three other kindred subjects – such as waste lands and probably afforestation ... I do not think anything is to be gained by very hasty action. After all, the sea has been at work for a good many centuries ...[1]

The Opposition spokesman who followed could only say: 'I do not think we can complain of the tone which has been taken by the President of the Board of Trade.'

His quickness of repartee soon showed itself at Question Time. Asked by a prominent Tory Protectionist, Sir Howard Vincent, to give the number of British firms forced by foreign tariffs to open works abroad, he replied that the motives for establishing such works could not be ascertained. Then the following exchange occurred:

> *Vincent:* ... Has the right hon. gentleman no list at the Board of Trade of the firms in this country who have established their works in Germany, France, Russia and other foreign countries in consequence of protective tariffs?
>
> *Lloyd George:* Yes, I have one in my pocket now and I will show it behind the Speaker's chair to the hon. Member after Questions.
>
> *Vincent:* But why not give it to the House now? Why should I be preferentially treated or have preferential right of access?
>
> *Lloyd George:* I thought that my hon. friend was a believer in preference.[2]

Such good humour, extending in this case even to describing a political opponent as his 'hon. friend', is what endears a Minister to the House.

The Board of Trade was a key Ministry, though its political head was not a Secretary of State and received a salary of only £2,000 a year,

1. Hansard, Fourth Series, Vol. CLII, cols 873–5, 26 February 1906.
2. Hansard, Fourth Series, Vol. CLII, cols 1307–8, 1 March 1906.

compared with the £5,000 a year drawn by most Cabinet Ministers. Lloyd George had, however, illustrious predecessors in the office, including Huskisson, Gladstone, Cardwell, Bright and Joseph Chamberlain. The department had grown out of the trade committee of the Privy Council and its functions, accumulated over the years, were many and various. So far as the State had any responsibility for industry, transport and labour relations, the Board of Trade was responsible. Under the Free Trade system State intervention and control had been reduced to a minimum, but such powers as were retained to ensure the smooth, orderly working of capitalism were largely exercised by the Board of Trade. Specific matters that came within its purview were company registration, bankruptcy, patents and designs, merchant shipping, railways and other public utilities, trademarks, trade and labour statistics, conciliation in industrial disputes, commercial intelligence and advice to the Foreign Office in commercial negotiations with foreign governments. The Board as such had long since ceased to exist; its powers were concentrated in the person of the President. But in Lloyd George's day appointments of officials and many other departmental acts were still performed at a 'meeting' in the Council Chamber at which he was the only member present.[1]

The building that housed the Council Chamber and Lloyd George's office was in Whitehall Gardens, within a few minutes' walk of the Palace of Westminster.[2] The headquarters staff numbered about 170 officials, and in addition there were two in the legal branch, three on the light railway commission, ten in the standards department, about 70 in the shipping record office, about 90 in the commercial, labour and statistical department, and about 400 in the patent office. The total estimated budget of the Board of Trade was just over £270,000, a sum which was almost exactly balanced by the estimated receipts (£280,000) for patents, designs and trademarks. In a sense, therefore, the Board of Trade could be said to pay for itself.[3]

Lloyd George was always a hard-working Minister, prepared to give any amount of time to what he regarded as really important affairs, but preferring to delegate the more humdrum administrative work to subordinates whom he knew he could trust. In this respect he was well served

1. This harmless charade was discontinued about half a century ago, but the title 'President of the Board of Trade' survived until 1970.
2. The building – it was known as Pembroke House – was demolished in 1938 to make way for the Air Ministry, now the Ministry of Defence. But a saloon from Pembroke House was incorporated in the new building.
3. Board of Trade Estimates (P.R.O.).

at the Board of Trade. His Parliamentary Secretary, Hudson Kearley – the future Lord Devonport – was a self-made businessman six years his senior in age but two years junior to him as an M.P. Kearley had begun his career as a coffee and tea salesman, but had then founded his own business which developed into the famous firm of Kearley and Tonge and International Stores. He was thus a pioneer of the modern chain-store system. His attitude towards Lloyd George was an ideal blend of self-confidence and deference. In the memoir that he wrote years later for private circulation he made this general comment on Lloyd George at the Board of Trade:

> He had no wide knowledge of affairs. He had no knowledge at all of business. He had, as I soon found, a marked dislike of office routine. But he had genius, and having that a man can afford to dispense with a great deal of the equipment that most of us find necessary for a prosperous journey through life . . . In Lloyd George's case it has manifested itself as an extraordinarily quick and subtle understanding of human nature combined with unbounded courage.[1]

Another definition of genius, equally applicable to Lloyd George, is contained in these words by Bernard Shaw: 'A man of genius is not a man who can do more things, or who knows more things, than ordinary men: there has never been a man of genius yet who has not been surpassed in both respects in his own generation by quite a large number of hopeless fools. He is simply a man who sees the importance of things.'[2]

Lloyd George's first Permanent Secretary at the Board of Trade was Sir Francis Hopwood, who had held the post since 1901. But soon after the new Government was formed he was sent on a constitutional mission to South Africa and when he returned was appointed Permanent Under-Secretary at the Colonial Office. In effect, therefore, the leading official with whom Lloyd George had to work throughout his time at the Board of Trade was Hubert Llewellyn Smith, unquestionably one of the great civil servants of his generation. Llewellyn Smith's fine intellect was directed and inspired by a Quaker conscience. Before entering the Board of Trade as Commissioner of Labour in 1893 he lived in the East End of London and gave his support to the dockers' leader, Ben Tillett. One of his friends was Lloyd George's devotee, Harold Spender, with whom he

1. Hudson Kearley, 1st Viscount Devonport, *The Travelled Road* (unpublished).
2. G. B. Shaw, from 'Mr Gilbert Cannan on Samuel Butler', originally published in the *New Statesman* (8 May 1915) then in *Pen Portraits and Reviews*.

wrote a travel book on the Pyrenees, illustrated by himself – for he was also an artist. During the years ahead he would have much to do with the social reforms promoted by Lloyd George, and with his work at the Ministry of Munitions. He would also be Lloyd George's chief economic adviser at the Peace Conference. Meanwhile, at the Board of Trade, he was appointed acting Permanent Secretary in March 1906 and the appointment was confirmed early the following year.

In his private office Lloyd George had one secretary from the ranks of the Civil Service and another recruited by himself in Wales. The former was an Old Etonian, William Clark – clever, humorous and diplomatic. He got on well with the Minister and served him again in the same capacity at the Treasury before joining the Viceroy's Council in 1910. Later he was High Commissioner in Canada and South Africa. His success with Lloyd George was proof of his own talents and of Lloyd George's willingness to work with members of the traditional British *élite*, provided they were efficient and cooperative. Clark was, in that sense, the precursor of Philip Kerr and others.

The Welshman who was brought in was John Rowland. He had come to Lloyd George's notice as secretary of the Cardiff Cymmrodorion Society, and his appointment as assistant private secretary on the Minister's staff, even at the modest salary of £100 a year, was doubtless partly intended as a compliment to Lloyd George's native land, where it could also be taken as evidence that he would not be a prisoner of the alien Whitehall bureaucracy. Yet there was rather more to it than symbolism: Lloyd George always liked to have some Welsh representation in his official 'family', for his own sake as well as for show. With recent experience as a school-teacher Rowland could keep him abreast of Welsh opinion on the Education issue, and it was also helpful that Rowland was from South Wales. He never became a close confidant, but he must have given his master adequate service for he stayed with him until 1912 – the year of Frances Stevenson's advent. Thereafter he had a worthy but unexciting career, ending it, knighted, as chairman of the Welsh Board of Health.

More significant for Lloyd George's future than any of his official aides was the man he had to deal with across the floor of the House of Commons as the principal Opposition spokesman on Trade – Andrew Bonar Law. Law's background, like his own, was neither English nor Anglican. He was born in Canada four years earlier than Lloyd George, his father an Ulster Presbyterian minister, his mother of Glaswegian extraction. At the age of twelve he moved from Canada to Scotland, where he completed his education and where his mother's family was able to give him a flying start in business. By 1900 he was a prosperous banker and iron-master, and in that year was elected to Parliament as a Unionist Tariff Reformer for one of the Glasgow constituencies. His first-hand knowledge of business and a hard, clear technique in debate earned him swift promotion from the back benches to junior office as Parliamentary Secretary to the Board of Trade. In 1906 he lost his seat but within six months was back in Parliament representing Dulwich. Between him and Lloyd George there was always a strong *rapport* in spite of obvious differences of temperament and opinion. They were at one in belonging neither to the hereditary British ruling class nor to the Oxbridge meritocracy. They also respected each other as politicians, each recognizing in the other qualities that he did not himself possess. Circumstances were to make Bonar Law the arbiter of Lloyd George's fate. It was due more to him than to any other individual that Lloyd George became Prime Minister in 1916, and that he fell from power in 1922.

Once installed at the Board of Trade Lloyd George lost no time in bringing forward a major piece of legislation – a Bill to amend the law relating to Merchant Shipping. The repeal of the Navigation Laws in mid-nineteenth century had been followed not by a complete vacuum but by a series of measures to regulate and humanize the new system of Free Trade, for instance by imposing a statutory load-line on British merchant ships, so immortalizing the name of its most passionate advocate, Samuel Plimsoll. The most recent consolidating Act had been passed as recently as 1894, but the need for further reforms was widely recognized and specific proposals had been made in the reports of three committees.[1] The substance of Lloyd George's Bill was, therefore, largely inherited, but he brought to it a genuine enthusiasm for the subject, springing from his early conversations with seamen in the harbour at Portmadoc and since displayed in many florid perorations on the British merchant marine. He also brought to it his own unique qualities as a legislator – his quick grasp of essential points and determination in sticking to them, his infinite flexibility on matters that seemed negotiable, his driving sense of urgency combined with patience and a perpetual willingness to listen to informed

1. The St Helier Committee, the Seaman's Wages Committee and Bonar Law's Foreign Ships (Statutory Requirements) Committee. The first of these reported in 1903, the two last-named in 1905.

opinion, and his unconventional touch in dealing with the House of Commons as well as with interested parties outside. The Bill was already taking shape in his mind during the election campaign, since he promised at Nevin a measure to ensure the safety of all sailors trading with England and to 'put a stop to overloading by foreign ships under the same regulations as British ships'.[1] Soon after Parliament met he announced that his Bill would be introduced 'shortly', and in fact the First and Second Readings were at the end of March.

Undoubtedly the safety and welfare of British seamen were the Bill's prime concerns, but a good additional motive was to reduce foreign competition by forcing other countries to conform to British standards. Opposition spokesmen were thus given an excuse, while welcoming the Bill, to impute Protectionist leanings to its author, though Lloyd George could reasonably draw a distinction between outright Protection and laying down a uniform civilised code for free competition at sea. His original purpose, as proclaimed at Nevin, was to enforce British standards on all ships either in or bound for British ports, but closer study showed him that to assert jurisdiction over foreigners on the high seas would be contrary to international law and that he would have to be content with applying his rules within British territorial waters. This meant that foreign ships when they actually berthed in British ports would be obliged to conform to British standards – or their equivalent – as to load-line, grain stowage, seaworthiness and life-saving appliances. For the British merchant seaman himself the Bill was described as a 'charter', since it made decent conditions of service the general rule instead of dependent upon the goodwill of shipowners. Better food, better ships' cooks, better accommodation, better arrangements in case of illness, easier repatriation, and facilities for the remittance of wages from abroad – all were provided for in the Bill.

Labour prejudice against the employment of foreign seamen was firmly resisted, except where it could be reconciled with considerations of safety. In view of several recent disasters attributable to ignorance of the English language, the Bill ordained that no one without a knowledge of English should be employed unless he were a British subject. The restriction did not, therefore, apply to Lascars, whose employment Lloyd George defended both on economic grounds and on grounds of national honour. 'The Lascar', he said, 'is a Britisher. You cannot make a Britisher of him merely for the sake of bragging of the extent of your dominions, and

1. 23 December 1905.

then the moment he asks for a share of your privileges say "You are a foreigner".' Britain had deprived the Lascars of 'a considerable coasting trade along the coast of India', and in any case the British merchant navy could not do without them.[1] When in Committee an attempt was made to exclude Lascars by a disingenuous amendment ostensibly designed to benefit them, Lloyd George exposed the amendment's hypocrisy and secured its defeat.[2] Though he had plenty of colour prejudice himself his magnanimity could get the better of it, especially when reinforced by practical considerations.

His outstanding success with the Bill was due to careful preparation of a most unorthodox kind. Devonport later described how he set about it:

A Cabinet Committee was appointed to consider the matter, but actually it was left to the Department to work out a scheme. At the very outset Lloyd George did a courageous and unconventional thing. He asked representative shipowners, including Ropner Houston and others who were Members of Parliament, to meet him at the Board of Trade, and received them with a friendly and charming little speech in which he said he thought it only fair that before embarking upon so important a piece of legislation he should have the benefit of the views of those who were most concerned. The shipowners could hardly believe their ears.

1. Speech in the House of Commons introducing the Bill, 20 March 1906 (Hansard, Fourth Series, Vol. CLIV, cols 237–53).
2. It was moved by Havelock Wilson, founder of the Seamen's Union, who sat for Middlesbrough. His demand was that the 120 cubic feet allowed for every white seaman under the Bill should also be the scale of accommodation for Lascars, but only when they were serving in a temperate climate: in the tropics the Bill's space allowance for them of 72 cubic feet per person would, he argued, be tolerable because in hot weather most of them would be sleeping on deck. This proposal, if enacted, would have had a most adverse effect upon the recruitment of Lascars, and that was unquestionably its ulterior object. Trade union restrictiveness, tinged with racialism, was masquerading as concern for human rights. Lloyd George pointed out that it would be absurd to give the Lascars more space in a cooler climate: 'compulsory bronchitis', he called it. He also insisted that the Lascars themselves did not want it 'because they knew that if such an amendment were carried it would exclude them from service on British ships, where they were much better off than they would be at home'. In his speech introducing the Bill he had quoted a petition from them, which must have impressed as well as amused the House: 'We are told that in the Parliament of England sits a gentleman of the name of Havelock Wilson Sahib. He has urged there lately that we should be given more space. We beseech your Lordships to tell him that his benevolence will be our bane; that as we have done him no wrong and if he really wishes us well he will have the mercy to spare us. Should he, however, pursue us with his attentions, we are sure that after this humble representation of ours the other members of the great Assembly will refuse to listen to him'. The amendment was defeated by 248 votes to 105, Bonar Law voting with the majority, Keir Hardie with the minority. (Hansard, Fourth Series, Vol. CLXV, 15 November 1906.)

Hitherto they had never gone to the Board of Trade but hat in hand, humbly craving leave to say a few words . . . Yet here they were now actually being invited to advise the Department! They went out of the conference full of enthusiasm for the new President.

But there was a greater surprise to come. A few weeks later the shipowners were again sent for, and were received in the same genial fashion. Lloyd George produced a bundle of printed papers. 'Here, gentlemen', he said, 'is the draft Bill, upon the general lines of which I have had the benefit of your advice. I am going to give you each a copy so that you may peruse it at leisure, and perhaps you will be good enough to let me have your comments in detail. You understand, of course, that these documents are strictly confidential.' Here were courage and unconventionality with a vengeance. In giving them the draft of the Bill he put himself absolutely at the mercy of anyone who might choose to betray him. But his confidence was rigidly respected. Valuable suggestions were made and in further conference contentious points were easily adjusted in a spirit of give-and-take and mutual goodwill. And let this be noted. By getting on the right side of the owners Lloyd George was able to do a good turn for the men . . .[1]

The net result of Lloyd George's bold and tactful handling of the shipowners was that he was able to present the Merchant Shipping Act (Amendment) Bill to Parliament practically as an agreed measure, which got encomiums from everybody and at a single stroke established his reputation as a Minister.

His admirers at this time included a colleague who was the son of a shipowner – Walter Runciman, junior minister at the Local Government Board under John Burns. On 9 March 1906 Runciman's wife noted in her diary that Asquith, with whom they had been dining, 'thought John [Burns] preferable to Lloyd George to work under – but we don't agree. W[alter] has been helping George a bit with his Merchant Shipping Bill

1. Devonport, *op. cit.* Lloyd George frequently sat on the steps of the Throne in the House of Lords when Bills of his were being debated there, and on 12 December 1906 he wrote to his brother, William: 'Amusing incidents last night on my Merchant Shipping Bill in the House of Lords. The two peers who had undertaken to criticize it and to move amendments primed themselves for the occasion. As it only came on after dinner they overdid it and both got drunk. Lord Balfour of Burleigh managed to get one of them out of the House, but the other stuck to his guns much to the scandal of the Peers . . . The Bill, however, went through flying, or rather reeling. Lord Cawdor was rather ashamed when he saw me looking on at this drunken scene.' (William George, *My Brother and I,* p. 209.) Considering what Lloyd George felt about both drunkenness and the House of Lords, Lord Cawdor was right to feel uneasy at his being a witness of the two combined.

and found him very ready to see a suggestion and easy to work with.'[1] The following year Runciman was moved to the Treasury as Financial Secretary, and so became more closely attached to Asquith. In 1908 Asquith made him President of the Board of Education.

The Merchant Shipping Act was not Lloyd George's only legislative achievement in 1906. Another important measure that year, of which he was to be even more proud, was his Census of Production Act. This was designed to secure accurate statistics of the output of home industries, to supplement those already available for imports and exports. The first census was to be taken at once and managements were required to fill in forms on pain of a £10 fine. When Lloyd George introduced the Bill on 16 May under the Ten Minute Rule nobody opposed it and it was warmly welcomed by Joseph Chamberlain; but it ran into a certain amount of op-position later – Tim Healy, for instance, attacking it on Second Reading as 'a great invasion of public liberty', lending itself 'to oppression of every kind'.[2]

The Bill's progress was not, however, significantly retarded by such frivolities, and as with Merchant Shipping Lloyd George eased its passage by his tactful handling of interested parties. Before the Committee Stage he held a conference with industrialist M.P.s, of which a verbatim record has been preserved.[3] Without making any concessions that would have vitiated the Bill's essential purpose, he showed himself very willing to adopt reasonable suggestions and to go a long way towards removing legitimate fears. In 1907 the first census was taken and another was begun, though not completed, before the outbreak of war in 1914. Further censuses under the Act were taken in 1924, 1930, 1935 and 1949, though Lloyd George's hope that they would become biennial was never realized. His initiative contributed, however, to a heightened awareness of the need for comprehensive and up-to-date statistics as a basis for public policy.

Under both the Merchant Shipping and the Census of Production Acts Lloyd George established advisory committees to ensure that in imple-menting the two measures the Board of Trade would have the benefit of

1. A month later Hilda Runciman wrote in her diary: 'Went out to lunch with the Lloyd Georges at Wandsworth. The *ménage* distinctly homey and not even particularly com-fortable. The eldest daughter an attractive girl. Mrs L. G. a nice simple woman, sensible not intellectual. There were no books about.' (8 April 1906).
2. 1 August 1906 (Hansard, Fourth Series, Vol. CLXII).
3. P.R.O. (BT11/2 C6378/06). The transcript was made from shorthand notes taken by a firm of stenographers, J. Moore & Son, evidently working under contract to the Board of Trade. Such were the makeshift procedures of British official bureaucracy early in the present century.

continuing expert advice and, so far as possible, the goodwill of British citizens and groups principally affected. The Merchant Shipping committee consisted of nineteen members, of whom five were nominated by the shipowners' Parliamentary committee, two were shipbuilders or naval architects, two were representatives of masters and officers, two represented marine engineers, three represented seamen and firemen as nominees of their respective unions, two were underwriters and three were nominated by the Board of Trade. Under the Census of Production Act there was a general advisory committee and further committees to consider how best to apply the Act to particular trades, such as cotton, woollen and worsted, boot and shoe, iron and steel, building, engineering and shipbuilding. In each case the relevant trade associations were invited to put forward names for these committees, whose views were then taken carefully into account before the schedules for the various trades were drafted.

More important, perhaps, than any legislation were the steps that Lloyd George took in 1906 towards providing the country with an adequate system of commercial intelligence. When he came to the Board of Trade Britain had only seven commercial attachés, and reports from British ambassadors, ministers or consuls that might contain information useful to British traders were made exclusively to the Foreign Office, whence the information was transmitted late, if at all, to chambers of commerce. Knowing as he did that German and American traders were much better served by their governments, Lloyd George was quick to promote a scheme under which the commercial work of British missions abroad became more extensive and efficient, while the Board of Trade was able to see to it that their work was not wasted. Instructions to commercial representatives and consuls were in future to be drawn up by the Board of Trade and Foreign Office in concert, and reports on trade matters were to be sent to the commercial intelligence branch of the Board of Trade, by which edited digests of commercial information were to be swiftly circulated. The operation of this system was to be kept under constant review by the Board of Trade's advisory committee on commercial intelligence, which had been in existence since 1900. This met under Lloyd George's chairmanship and its other members were seven officials (from the Board of Trade and the Foreign, Colonial and India Offices), thirteen individuals appointed by the Board of Trade in consultation with the Chambers of Commerce Association, and four representatives of the great self-governing colonies.

Since his visit to Canada in 1899 had left him with a particularly strong impression of Canada's economic potential, it was natural for Lloyd George to send a trade mission to that country in 1906. And he must have been very pleased at the welcome given to this initiative by a Canadian politician of his acquaintance:

My object in writing is to express to you the satisfaction felt by many, including myself, at your action in deciding to appoint commercial agents in Canada. I have urged that some step of this kind should be taken for a number of years. In a foreign country the British manufacturer has a consul to send him information; in a colony there is no one to do this, and while the American consuls serve their country well in business matters, they divert business from the U.K. to the U.S.[1]

After the Colonial Conference of 1907 British trade commissioners were appointed in Canada, Australia, New Zealand and South Africa; and the pattern of formal representation, thus inaugurated, was further developed and expanded after the First World War.

Yet Lloyd George was well aware that even the much-improved flow of commercial intelligence through official channels would never suffice to make British industry as competitive as it ought to be. No less to be desired was a fundamental change in British techniques of salesmanship abroad, which could usefully manifest itself in a greater readiness to learn foreign languages:

Go anywhere and the first man you meet is a German commercial traveller. That is one reason why our trade is going. They take the trouble to learn the language of the people with whom they are dealing. In the Argentine Republic the German speaks Spanish; go to China and he talks Chin-Chin or whatever it is. Go to any part of the world and he talks the language of the people who are his customers. What about the English? Go to any part of the world and the Englishman pushes his goods in broad Scotch. That is where the German has the advantage of us. He learns these languages in the day school. What would be said if the Progressives proposed to teach Spanish and other languages to workmen's sons? These are the people who are learning in Germany and who are beating our travellers. It is not a luxury learning these languages; it is business.[2]

1. F. Carter-Cotton to D.L.G., from the Vancouver Club, 8 August 1906 (Earl Lloyd George collection). Carter-Cotton was Minister of Finance of British Columbia when, in 1899, he showed Lloyd George over the Provincial Parliament buildings in Victoria. In 1906 he was President of the Council.

2. Speech at Free Trade demonstration, Corn Exchange, Rochester, 7 November 1906.

If he had been addressing the Institute of Directors sixty years or more later, these comments would still have been very much to the point.

In 1907 he continued to be active as a legislator, his most significant measure being one to amend patent law for the benefit of British citizens. Under the law as it stood foreigners had been able to abuse the system by taking out British patents and then not working them, or by challenging British inventors in the courts, or by imposing restrictive conditions upon British firms working foreign patents. Of the 14,700 British patents issued in 1906, 6,500 had been issued to foreigners, and experience suggested that a large number of these would be used simply to prevent a competitive process being worked in Britain. Litigation could be abused in two ways. A British patentee with limited financial resources could find himself challenged in the courts by some large foreign firm, and the cost of defending his patent could easily ruin him while at the same time discouraging other British inventors from applying for patents. Alternatively foreign firms could obtain patents drawn in rather wide terms and then use them to resist applications by British inventors. Foreign patents, moreover, could be made to operate in restraint of British trade, when British firms working them were obliged, as a condition of doing so, to forgo for a set period the right to install more up-to-date machinery.

All these abuses Lloyd George was seeking to eliminate or counteract in the Patents and Designs Bill which he introduced on 19 March 1907. Before introducing it he took plenty of advice from experts, particularly from J. M. Astbury K.C., the Liberal M.P. for Southport, who had a large practice in patent litigation.[1] On Second Reading Bonar Law welcomed it for the Opposition as a nakedly Protectionist measure. Lloyd George had described it as being in the interest of Free Trade, and had claimed that a patent was a monopoly granted by the Crown, whose terms Parliament had a right to determine. But Law would allow no logical distinction between the use of such a monopoly and the use of tariffs for national purposes:

> . . . the question is not one of right. We have a right to put on an import duty if we think it to our advantage. It is merely a question of interest. Apply that principle to a patented article. Leave it to the free play of economic forces and what happens? The foreign patentee produces in this country if it pays him, and he produces abroad if it pays him. Let him produce abroad, and let us pay for it by those goods which we

1. In 1913 he became a Chancery judge, and in that capacity delivered a famous judgment during the 1926 strike.

could produce with advantage here . . . If that is sound theory, why compel the foreign patentee to produce here? There can be only one answer – that in the opinion of the right hon. Gentleman it is in the interest of the country that these things should be produced at home . . . If it is right to produce the result by patent laws, it is equally right to produce it by import duties.[1]

This was excellent debating stuff, but not strictly applicable to Lloyd George who was never a doctrinaire Free Trader. He believed that strengthening the patent law would be economically expedient, but that to embark upon a tariff war would be economically disastrous. Though he had to pay lip-service to the principle of Free Trade, his true motive for being on the whole a Free Trader was pragmatic rather than ideological. Pragmatism, however, should not be regarded as the equivalent of opportunism or cynicism, but as itself a valid principle of political conduct.

The Patents Act gave foreign patentees one year in which to begin working their patents in the United Kingdom, and in this respect it was notably effective. Within a year it was reported that a German dyeing syndicate had bought a site on Merseyside, that two other foreign dyeing firms were building works in Cheshire, that a German pottery firm had chosen a site in Kent, that the American Gillette Safety Razor Company had acquired works at Leicester, that the United States Shoe Company had arranged to open a factory in Britain, that a German company manufacturing gas plants was looking for a site in the London area, and that an American machinery firm was also choosing land for a large factory in or near London.[2] The new legal procedure established by Lloyd George for dealing with patent cases has, in essentials, endured to the present day. The key change was that instead of such cases having to be heard by judges with no knowledge of the technicalities, they were in future to be decided by a special Chancery judge appointed to deal with patents and patents alone. Justice for litigants was thus made swifter and surer.

Another piece of legislation sponsored by Lloyd George in 1907 was a Companies Amendment Act, whose effect was to ensure fuller information for shareholders and creditors. This measure was inspired by an expert committee set up in 1905, but without a Minister of Lloyd George's energy and Parliamentary skill it would have taken considerably longer to reach the Statute Book. As he presided over its passage through the

1. Hansard, Fourth Series, Vol. CLXXII, 17 April 1907.
2. *Evening News*, 26 June 1908, quoted in Herbert du Parcq, *op. cit.*, Vol. III, pp. 492–3.

House of Commons his thoughts must have turned now and again to his own ignominious experience as a company promoter at an earlier stage of his career, while he was still on the back benches. It was fortunate for him that so few people knew of the Welsh Patagonian Gold Fields Syndicate Ltd, and that those who did were either personal friends or, at any rate, political supporters. Fuller information about the Syndicate and its supposed gold-mine in Patagonia might have saved quite a number of small Welsh investors from loss.[1]

Notable as were Lloyd George's legislative successes in 1907, his most spectacular coup that year was as a conciliator. Since industrial relations were his responsibility – in so far as Government then accepted any responsibility for them at all – he was the Minister to whom his colleagues and the public looked for therapeutic action when there was deadlock between the railway directors and the Amalgamated Society of Railway Servants, and a national rail stoppage appeared to be imminent. The union was demanding a better deal for its members and, above all, recognition for itself. Though it comprised only 9 per cent of railway workers, those who belonged to it were, in the main, key personnel whose collective withdrawal of labour would have paralysed the railway system. Yet only two of the railway companies – the North-Eastern and the District – recognized the union and the rest were implacably opposed to doing so. After fruitless written exchanges between the parties from January to October, the situation became critical when the A.S.R.S. – and the much smaller General Railway Workers' Union – decided to ballot their members on the question of a strike. Both unions voted overwhelmingly in favour of striking, if necessary, to enforce their demands. The A.S.R.S. announced the result of its poll at a mass rally in the Albert Hall on 3 November.

Meanwhile Lloyd George had been busy. On 21 October he confided to his brother: 'The Railway strike is demanding all my attention. Things are going well so far. Whatever happens I am coming out on top of this

---

1. The story of Lloyd George's Patagonian venture is told in John Grigg, *The Young Lloyd George*, ch. VII. Though the Syndicate had been for all practical purposes defunct since 1900, it was not until 5 November 1907 that notice of its dissolution appeared in the *London Gazette*.

On 20 August 1907 Lloyd George wrote to his wife: '. . . at last by good temper – or rather a mixture of honey & woodworm – I got one Bill through & came to an arrangement with the Tories to give me my Companies Bill in a couple of hours on Wednesday morning. So all my Bills are now assured. The Companies Bill is a huge one & they could easily have killed it had they gone about it in earnest & skilfully.' (N.L.W. and *Letters*, p. 148.) The Bill was passed by the House of Lords on 24 August.

business. I can see my way clear right to the station. Conciliation at first but, failing that, the steam roller. The Companies must give way on that point I am definite.'[1] On 25 October he received seventeen chairmen and twelve general managers of railway companies at the Board of Trade, and we have an eye-witness account of the occasion:

They came – Lord Claud Hamilton [chairman of the Great Eastern], Lord Stalbridge [chairman of the London and North-Western], Mr Alexander Henderson [actually Sir Alexander, chairman of the Great Central] and others, all rather aloof personages of the old-fashioned type of railway magnate. Their bearing, as they assembled in the Conference Room of the Board of Trade, said as plainly as words, 'We have condescended to come, but kindly understand you are wasting your breath and our time.' Sitting on Lloyd George's left I watched them closely, and truly it demanded courage and resource of no common sort to face such an audience with the message Lloyd George had to deliver. He was going to plead for conciliation before men who had expunged the word from their dictionary. When he began they were frigid, indifferent, barely attentive. I could see the little smiles and nudges with which they punctuated his opening sentences. Then came a change. Within a few minutes every man in his audience was following the speaker with rapt attention. Every eye was riveted on him. There were no more nudges and smiles. Never have I seen a projection of personality so rapid, so dramatic, so completely triumphant. When Lloyd George ceased speaking the whole situation had altered. The directors were no longer intransigent. They were almost meek. They were willing there and then to accept Lloyd George's proposals leading to a settlement by negotiation. A half-hearted attempt was made by Lord Stalbridge to raise the question of counter-grievances alleged by the companies against the men, particulars of which were contained in a large and corpulent envelope which he now produced and flourished in our faces. Lloyd George blandly but firmly waved it aside. 'Let us get into conference first', he said, 'and then we can go into everything' . . . Lord Stalbridge put his envelope away again. When the meeting broke up the directors had agreed to nominate six of their number to continue in conference with the Board of Trade with a view to a settlement.[2]

1. D.L.G. to W.G., 21 October 1907. (William George, *My Brother and I*, p. 212).
2. Devonport, *op. cit.* Lloyd George himself gives a brief account of this meeting in a letter to his brother: 'An excellent beginning. They all almost fell on my neck including Lord Claud Hamilton. Old Stalbridge was also very nice. I have won their confidence and that

The railway bosses then adjourned for a working lunch at the Charing Cross Hotel, to discuss what Lloyd George had put to them, and before the day was over one of them, Sir Herbert Maxwell, who was also a former Conservative M.P., was writing to congratulate him on 'the tactful and considerate manner' in which he had handled the morning's conference.[1] Next day another director – this time a sitting Tory M.P., Colonel Mark Lockwood – wrote to him in a similar vein and with useful information about the state of opinion among the directors. Marked 'Very Private', Lockwood's letter read:

My dear George,
This is for yourself alone. We all went to Charing Cross for lunch & discussion, & without being optimistic I can say that the tone of our conversation was hopeful. We all acknowledged that you had put the matter extremely well before us & in a most conciliatory spirit. We (as you know) appt. 6 to deal with you & Granet as sec. – Scotter & Paget & Bonsor & others were distinctly friendly. I think your trouble will be with Allerton. I quite agree with you, that whether you are right in your estimate of the number affected, in case of a strike, or the companies (& my own opinion is & always has been that our figures are fallacious) the inconvenience to put it mildly will be to the Public terrible. Some of our number thought that you wished to drag it on, until Parliament met! I don't. Banbury is following [?] Allerton. Maxwell is with me.

Yours sincerely
M.L.[2]

---

is almost everything. You never saw anything like the change in their demeanour. I have asked them to consider my proposals to appoint six of their number to meet me about them. They consented to do so. I also asked them not to issue manifestos in the meantime. They all promised except poor old Stalbridge whose Board had instructed him to issue one, but he is going to do his best to keep it back. I am sanguine of good results.' (D.L.G. to W.G., 25 October 1907, *My Brother and I*, p. 212.) It would seem that Devonport was incorrect in stating, long after the event, that the directors had agreed to appoint six representatives before the meeting broke up. In fact, they clearly reached the decision to do so at their lunch meeting immediately afterwards.

1. Sir Herbert Maxwell to D.L.G., 25 October 1907 (L.G.P.). Maxwell was Conservative M.P. for Wigtownshire 1880–1906. Though chiefly notable as a scholar – he was F.R.S., LL.D. and President of the Society of Antiquaries of Scotland – in 1907 he was a director of the Glasgow and South-Western Railway.

2. Lieut. Col. the Right Hon. A. R. M. Lockwood to D.L.G., 26 October 1907 (L.G.P.). In spite of the cryptic signature 'M.L.', Lockwood is identifiable from his address, Bishops Hall, Romford, Essex. He was Conservative M.P. for Epping and had become a Privy

To keep up the pressure on the more diehard directors Lloyd George persuaded the *Daily Mail* to publish, on 29 October, an article calling for compulsory arbitration in railway strikes.[1] Possibly at about the same time he heard from George Askwith, head of the Board of Trade's railway department, that Richard Bell, general secretary of the A.S.R.S., would not press for recognition of his union by the employers 'if he obtained a satisfactory method of dealing with grievances . . . and more opportunity for the men to deal with the conditions of their lives, besides the certainty that his union would infallibly be strengthened . . .' Lloyd George may well have heard this earlier, and from Bell direct, because they were Parliamentary colleagues – Bell as Lib-Lab M.P. for Derby. But Askwith claims to have been the intermediary.[2] On the 31st Lloyd George spent all day with the six employers' representatives – who were, in fact, the chairmen of the six principal companies – and, according to his own account, 'had to threaten them'. On 1 November he was able to tell his brother that he had seen them again and that the strike would, he believed, be averted. He sent William in strict confidence a copy of the settlement terms previously agreed.[3]

Thus by the time the A.S.R.S. held its Albert Hall rally Lloyd George had a formula for ending the dispute, which he had reason to hope would be acceptable to both sides. On 2 November, the day before the rally, he wrote to Bell inviting him and his executive committee to a meeting at the Board of Trade four days later. The committee agreed to come and meanwhile deferred strike action.

On 6 November the six chairmen formally presented their scheme to Lloyd George, but – as he told Herbert Lewis three days later at the Lord

---

Councillor in 1905, but it was as a director of the London and North-Western Railway that he was involved in the dispute. In 1917 he became a peer on Lloyd George's recommendation, as Lord Lambourne.

Of the others mentioned in the letter: G. Granet was general manager of the Midland; Sir Charles Scotter, chairman of the London and South-Western; Sir E. Paget, chairman of the Midland; H. Cosmo Bonsor, chairman of the South-Eastern; Lord Allerton, chairman of the Great Northern; and Sir F. Banbury M.P. (Conservative, for the City of London), a director of the Great Northern.

1. D.L.G. to W.G., 29 October 1907 (*op. cit.*, p. 212).
2. Lord Askwith, *Industrial Problems and Disputes*, p. 121. Askwith's book was published long afterwards, in 1920, and perhaps for that reason is maddeningly vague on timing. He confuses the plenary session on 25 October with the subsequent meetings of railway chairmen. All the same, his evidence suggests that Bell's decision not to insist upon recognition was conveyed to Lloyd George *after* the 25th, but while the six chairmen were deliberating.
3. D.L.G. to W.G., 31 October and 1 November 1907 (*op. cit.*, p. 212).

Mayor's banquet – were 'at the last very timid' about signing it, so that he 'had to take them by the scruff of the neck'.

> They wanted to refer the matter back to their shareholders, and declined to sign the agreement until they had had time for consideration, but L.G. pointed out that Bell would have to refer to *his* shareholders (the men), and that delay probably makes an agreement impossible. He insisted upon having the terms ratified there and then and offered to accept the signatures of six of the directors elected by themselves [i.e. the six chairmen].[1]

Having thus secured the employers' agreement to the scheme he lost no time in putting it to the A.S.R.S. committee members, who were meeting in a separate room. They too agreed and the threatened strike was called off. The country breathed a sigh of relief, and in his letter to the King announcing the settlement Campbell-Bannerman said that Britain was 'largely indebted' for it 'to the knowledge, skill, astuteness and tact of the President of the Board of Trade and those around him in his Department'.[2] At the Lord Mayor's banquet on the 9th there was another equally warm, and this time public, tribute by the Prime Minister to Lloyd George, and at Windsor on 12 November he was congratulated by the King and Queen as well as by the German Emperor who was there on a visit.

The following month Runciman wrote to Churchill, who was on a political safari in Africa, that Lloyd George's intervention in the railway dispute had been a dramatic episode, in which 'geniality, finesse & a certain bold art' were the qualities that had brought success.[3]

There have been suggestions that the credit which nearly everybody, high and low, accorded to him at the time was substantially more than he deserved. Lord Askwith, for instance, said in retrospect that he had 'no very difficult task', implying that the vital breakthrough was achieved by himself in negotiation with Bell.[4] But even if Bell's attitude owed everything to Askwith's powers of persuasion, and nothing whatever to Lloyd George's, there was still the task of persuading the employers to accept a scheme of conciliation and arbitration which, to some of them at any rate,

1. Herbert Lewis diary, entry for 9 November 1907 (N.L.W.).
2. Campbell-Bannerman to Edward VII, 8 November 1907 (quoted in J. A. Spender's Life of *Sir Henry Campbell-Bannerman*, Vol. II, p. 370).
3. Runciman to W.S.C., 13 December 1907 (*Churchill* Companion Vol. II, Part 2, p. 722).
4. Askwith, *op. cit.*, p. 121.

was extremely unpalatable. The official historian of the N.U.R., after conceding that Lloyd George 'worked with the greatest energy to achieve a peaceful settlement', goes on to suggest that both the form of the settlement and the fact that it was ever arrived at were only to a very limited extent attributable to his work, since he was in reality little more than a front man in the proceedings. 'As Mr Lloyd George's scheme . . . [it] could be advocated as a brilliant "compromise" imposed on both directors and union officials by a determined and public-spirited President of the Board of Trade.' According to this version, the compromise scheme was largely devised by Sam Fay, general manager of the Great Central Railway, and then – the Askwith version again – endorsed by the railway bosses only because they knew that the union would not press for recognition.[1]

Such worm-eyed disparagement should not go unchallenged because it is surely quite clear from the contemporary evidence that Lloyd George's part in averting the strike was all-important. The strongest evidence is that of the two letters written to him immediately after the 25 October meeting, by railway directors who were also political opponents. They largely bear out Devonport's subsequent, and necessarily sympathetic, account of Lloyd George's personal impact upon the railway bosses who, as even Askwith has to admit, needed someone to force them to see their industry as a whole, and in relation to the national interest. None of their own number was capable of doing this, and no civil servant could have done it unaided. The Askwiths and Fays of this world can achieve little on their own, but with the backing and leadership of a minister of Lloyd George's class their talents are put to good use. Many secondary figures contributed to the settlement, including, no doubt, Askwith and Fay, but also including others such as Llewellyn Smith, who had much to do with the final work of drafting. But when secondary figures have been given their fair share of credit it remains true that Lloyd George alone was indispensable. Without him the strike would almost certainly have occurred.

Next to him the most meritorious figure was Richard Bell, who had the wisdom to postpone insistence upon the formality of recognition in

1. Philip S. Bagwell, *The Railwaymen* (1963), ch. X, pp. 268–70. In 1913 the A.S.R.S. merged with the General Railway Workers' Union (G.R.W.U.) and the United Pointsmen's and Signalmen's Society (U.P.S.S.) to form the National Union of Railwaymen (N.U.R.). Attempts to include the Associated Society of Locomotive Engineers and Firemen (A.S.L.E.F.) in the merger came to nothing.
Mr Bagwell incorrectly describes Fay as general manager of the Great *Eastern* Railway.

return for a compromise which would give his union, still relatively small and struggling, an immediate accession of strength. Disputes were in future to be referred to conciliation boards representing management and men, and ultimately to independent arbitration. Though candidates for the employers' seats on the conciliation boards did not have to be union members, in practice the A.S.R.S. obtained a commanding position on them and non-unionists were 'drawn into the life of the union' through what they saw of its members' work on the boards.[1] This development must have been foreseen by some railway directors, as it was by Bell, and it helps to explain why their agreement to the scheme was hard to win, even when the demand for recognition was withdrawn. It was not Bell's fault that the scheme failed, in the event, to bring peace and contentment to the industry. Nor was it Lloyd George's fault. In 1907 a serious attempt was made to provide the industry with workable machinery for resolving future disputes, and meanwhile the country was spared a most damaging conflict. For this achievement Lloyd George deserves from history very little, if any, less praise than he received from his contemporaries.

As well as intervening to bring peace to the industry, Lloyd George was also well aware of the need to give it a more rational structure. In 1907 he appointed a departmental committee, with himself as chairman, to consider all the workings of the railway system and how they could be improved. J. A. Spender, editor of the *Westminster Gazette*, was asked to join this committee as a lay member and has left us a good impression of Lloyd George's conduct of it:

> He was a first-class chairman, and nothing could have been more skilful than his handling of [the] diverse elements. He always got up his subject beforehand, and though he knew exactly what he was driving at, he generally kept his intention veiled until opponents had been drawn three-quarters of the way he wanted them to go, then he cut off their retreat. He had an almost uncanny way of persuading men in opposite camps that they really meant the same thing – which was the thing he wanted them to mean – and before a few weeks were over, the supposed irreconcilable differences of railways and traders were dissolving into an incredible unity . . . Less than ever did he seem a wild man or zealot of impracticable ideas. I saw him as a man of business, conciliator, moderator, with a touch which made my own modest efforts at smoothing seem crude . . . If this Committee had continued this work and Lloyd

1. Bagwell, *op. cit.*, p. 277.

George had remained President of the Board of Trade, a large part of the reconstruction and amalgamation scheme which followed the war would probably have been anticipated by ten years . . .[1]

This is a striking retrospective tribute from one who was much closer to Asquith than to Lloyd George.

Before leaving the Board of Trade Lloyd George completed the detailed preparation of another major legislative project whose enactment was, however, bequeathed to his successor. This was the Port of London Act, 1908, which established the Port of London Authority.

In 1902 a Royal Commission under the chairmanship of Lord Revelstoke had reported in favour of concentrating in a single authority the powers divided between the Thames Conservancy, the Watermen's Company and Trinity House – so far as they affected the port of London – and of transferring to the new authority the assets and functions of the three London dock companies, London and India, Surrey Commercial and Millwall. The Balfour Government had tried to give effect to these recommendations but the attempt had miscarried, and Lloyd George came to the problem with no illusion that its many intricacies could easily be resolved. Less than a year after taking office he spoke of it at the annual dinner of the *Shipping Gazette*:

> I will venture to tell you that, of all the problems which have ever baffled the head of a poor Minister, nothing has been suggested yet which comes up to the Port of London question . . . I cannot see my way to recommend any scheme yet to Parliament, and I must take at least another year to make up my mind. I quite realize that it is a problem which has to be dealt with, but it is far better that you should take another twelve months . . . to arrive at some sort of common understanding, before you deal with it, than that you should hurriedly plant on the table of the House of Commons an ill-considered scheme which, in the long run, will not only do no good but may do harm.[2]

1. J. A. Spender, *Life, Journalism and Politics*, Vol. I, pp. 157–8. Spender was brother to Lloyd George's faithful acolyte, Harold, by whom he was first introduced to Lloyd George at Etretat in 1902. Of that meeting he writes in the passage quoted above that Lloyd George impressed him as having 'a craftsman's appreciation of good work, whether done by a friend or an opponent; also charm, friendliness, vivacity and a rather deceptive appearance of simplicity'.
2. Trocadero restaurant, 21 November 1906.

It was, in fact, nearly eighteen months before he was ready to introduce a Bill. Meanwhile he exerted himself, as usual, to master the subject and to make sure that all interested parties were properly consulted. In May 1907 he and Kearley went on a tour of inspection of foreign ports, notably Antwerp and Hamburg. In November advance notice of impending legislation was given in the Press, but it was not until 2 April 1908 – ten days before he was appointed Chancellor of the Exchequer – that he was able to present his Bill to the House of Commons.

Though in most respects it followed the Revelstoke report, in several important ways it was different. Instead of a P.L.A. consisting of forty persons, as recommended by Revelstoke, Lloyd George proposed a rather smaller body. 'Good men are rare. I do not know that London could not provide forty, but at any rate it is much more likely to provide twenty-five . . . and I propose therefore that the body shall consist of twenty-five.' Moreover, both the elected and the appointed members of the authority were to be chosen, so far as possible, for their general interest in the river and port, rather than as sectional representatives. The authority was given power to make compulsory purchases of riparian land from Barking Reach downwards, subject to Board of Trade consent after a public inquiry. But there was to be no compulsory purchase of the docks, at a price to be fixed by compulsory arbitration. This was a major distinguishing feature of the Lloyd George scheme, and he appears to have owed it to Kearley's advice, on which he had the intelligence and flair to act.

Here is Kearley's description of how the point was taken:

Compulsory purchases have a way of turning out bad bargains for the public . . . As originally drafted our Bill, like its predecessors, provided that the purchase price should be fixed by arbitration, which sounds all right but in practice means a ridiculous game of 'blind hookey'. The purchaser is committed by the Act of Parliament . . . to buy before he knows the price . . .

This did not seem to trouble Lloyd George and the Board of Trade officials unduly, but to me it was a constant obsession . . . For the dozenth time or so I came out with my slogan, 'If you want to buy the docks you'll buy a white elephant.' Lloyd George lost his temper.

'Yes, I know your views,' he snapped . . .

At the Board of Trade next morning, in accordance with my invariable practice, I looked into the President's room to pass the time of day, on my way to my own room. Lloyd George had just arrived and was in his shirt sleeves washing his hands. He gave me his usual blithe greeting, the petulance in which we had parted the previous day quite forgotten. Then, suddenly turning round with the towel in his hand, 'Look here, Kearley,' he said, 'just imagine you are President of the Board of Trade. How would *you* buy the docks?'

'. . . I would buy the docks in exactly the same way as I have bought many businesses in my time – on the basis of earnings and revealed profits.'

'How could that be done? . . .'

'Insist to the companies that that is the basis – the only basis – on which you are prepared to negotiate a purchase. To effect this, tell them that you must have access to their books by an accountant of repute . . .'

Lloyd George obviously saw the possibilities. He asked me if I knew such an accountant. I mentioned Mr William Plender . . .

. . . He came, and Lloyd George expatiated on the dangers of compulsory purchase which he had suddenly discovered . . .

The next step was to summon the representatives of the three dock companies . . . They asked for a week to consider the proposition. It cannot honestly be said that they were enthusiastic . . . for profits were not their strong point . . . if they had had among them a really bold fighting man they would have called our bluff and insisted upon arbitration. But they had no such person, and the assurance with which we approached them made them uneasy . . . at the end of the week . . . they bowed as gracefully as possible to what they conceived to be the inevitable . . .

. . . the price of the dock undertakings was agreed at a total of Twenty Million Pounds sterling – a very fair figure based on six years' purchase. I think if we had been very keen we could have knocked off another million, but . . . we were not disposed to drive too hard a bargain.[1]

1. Devonport, *op. cit*. The official historian of the Port of London writes of this transaction: '. . . when Mr Lloyd George intimated to the companies his desire to open negotiations they at once responded and allowed Sir [actually at the time Mr] William Plender on behalf of the Board of Trade to examine their books, and Mr Crutwell, an engineer, to survey their properties. When this had been done the question of terms was opened with the London and India Docks Company and the negotiation was settled simply by a private intimation conveyed to Mr Lloyd George of the irreducible minimum which the directors were prepared to recommend their proprietors to take, and by this [his?] prompt acquiescence in the terms suggested. The negotiations with the Millwall and Surrey Companies were not so easily disposed of. The Millwall Company was earning no dividend on its ordinary stock and not likely to do so for many years, but it naturally was not prepared to part with a remote possibility for no consideration whatever. The Surrey Company's future was also

Actually, the total amount of Port stock issued to the holders of dock securities was £22,362,859, and for the purposes of future borrowing the P.L.A. was empowered to issue Port stock for a further £5,000,000. Port rates on goods imported or exported were to be levied by the authority subject to maxima fixed by the Board of Trade, and dues on vessels entering the port were to be levied up to 1s. 6d. per ton, with 2d. per ton rent from the date of entrance. There was to be no subsidy from the London County Council or the City of London as the earlier Conservative Bill had envisaged. The idea of a municipal subsidy had not appealed to the business community, and Lloyd George was wise to leave it out of his scheme.

The Port of London Bill, which was his creature but which he only just had time to introduce, was carried through its later stages by Winston Churchill and received the Royal Assent on 21 December 1908. In March of the following year the new authority took control of the entire port of London, comprising both sides of the river from Teddington to a line drawn from the pilot mark at the entrance of Havengore Creek in Essex to the Lands End at Warden Point in the Isle of Sheppey. It was appropriate that the P.L.A.'s first chairman should be Hudson Kearley, who became Lord Devonport in 1910 and held the chairmanship until 1925.

The toil and strain of office increased rather than diminished Lloyd George's appetite for holidays abroad. In the summer of 1906 Margaret accompanied him on a trip to Lisbon, and during the Christmas holiday he was abroad again, but this time without her. Martin White – a former Liberal M.P. who was a motoring enthusiast – called at the Board of Trade just after the Merchant Shipping Bill was through and offered Lloyd George his car and French chauffeur for a drive across France to Biarritz. The offer was gladly accepted.

In his hotel at Biarritz Lloyd George had the company of five Liberal M.P.s – Herbert Lewis, Frank Edwards, Timothy Davies, Alfred Emmott and the Solicitor-General, Sir William Robson. The weather remained wintry, but Lloyd George did some reading and walking, and plenty of

---

difficult to assess, as the expenditure on their new deep water Greenland Dock had not had time to bear full fruit. Both companies were eventually satisfied, the Surrey Company on the morning of the introduction of the Bill . . .' (Sir Joseph G. Broodbank, *History of the Port of London*, Vol. II, pp. 337–8).

political talking. He was invited to dinner by J. E. C. Bodley, author of a substantial work on the French Republic, who had 'a magnificent villa' at Biarritz; and by George Younger, Tory M.P. for Ayr Burghs and later, as chairman of the Tory Party, a maker and breaker of the post-war Coalition. Staying with Younger was Charles Hobhouse, Liberal M.P. for East Bristol, who before very long would be Lloyd George's junior minister at the Treasury.[1] After attending a Sunday morning mass at Bayonne cathedral Lloyd George wrote:

> Disappointing . . . *Only women – and they old & wilted – in the congregation. The men & the young girls were out on the road. Formal religion has totally lost its influence in France.*[2]

Though it had had very little influence over him since childhood, yet in spite of himself he half wanted it to retain its influence over others.

In September 1907 he took Margaret and the children for a holiday at St Gervais in the French Alps, where he had rented a chalet. Mair, his eldest daughter and favourite child, was now just seventeen. She was intelligent and all who knew her admired her character, but the only surviving report on her from the Clapham High School does not suggest that she was a scholastic high-flyer. In it her progress is described as 'satisfactory', and her conduct as 'very good, but we should like to see a more active part taken in the life of the school'.[3] Perhaps her experience as the child of a public bogeyman during the Boer War had tended to make her a little withdrawn. Beyond doubt she was exceptionally sensitive and sweet-natured. A schoolfellow of hers, destined to play a part in the life of her family that she could not, fortunately, have foreseen, wrote of her long afterwards that 'there was always a certain sadness in her face, & a thoughtfulness beyond her years'.[4] Her father doted on her and she, in her simple devotion to him, was becoming in a sense the youthful and female equivalent of Uncle Lloyd. Not the least of her qualities was that she was musical and able to accompany him on the piano while he sang Welsh songs and hymns.

Quite soon after he became a minister a young boy met him and Mair

1. D.L.G. to M.L.G. from Hotel Continental, Biarritz, dated (in Welsh) (N.L.W.).
2. D.L.G. to M.L.G. from same address, 'Sunday night' (N.L.W.). The words in italics are translated from the Welsh.
3. Report from Clapham High School for Girls, autumn term 1905 (N.L.W.). Mair's name is given as 'Mary Lloyd-George'.
4. Frances Stevenson, *Lloyd George: a Diary*, entry for 10 March 1934, p. 260.

out walking at Criccieth and many years later recorded this impression of the encounter:

> He [the author] was strolling, on a sunny April morning, down the lane which leads from the Criccieth golf links, past the cemetery and the parish church, to the village. Midway he met Lloyd George, attired in a tweed suit, and wearing a broad-brimmed white felt hat, his dark hair falling in waves well over his coat collar, and arm-in-arm with him his eldest daughter, Mair, then in all the fresh loveliness of her sixteen years. A brief stop, a few kindly words, and the smile which has won so many hearts – that was all; but the impression of complete, nay exuberant, felicity has remained graven to this day.[1]

It was the spring-time of Lloyd George's fortunes, and even in adversity he never really lost his exuberance, at any rate until near the end of his life. Yet the perfect happiness that young Watkin Davies thought he saw in him that bright morning in Wales was soon shattered.

When the family returned from their Alpine holiday in the early autumn of 1907 Lloyd George was immediately re-immersed in the work of his department and within weeks was grappling with the railway dispute. But after the settlement he hardly had time to savour his public triumph before the supreme private calamity of his life was upon him. The first intimation was contained in a brief note from his Welsh private secretary, Rowland, dated 25 November, which was presumably left for him on his desk:

> Dear Mr Lloyd George,
>
> Mrs Lloyd George tells me that she is not able to come up to town because Miss Mair Lloyd George came home from school this afternoon not feeling very well.
>
> Yours very respectfully
John Rowland.[2]

'Home' was the Lloyd Georges' house in Routh Road, Wandsworth, and there, five days later, Mair died after an unsuccessful operation for appendicitis, performed in the house. Her last words were 'He is just and merciful'.

No sentiment could have been more remote from Lloyd George's own,

1. W. Watkin Davies, *Lloyd George: 1863–1914*, p. 245. If Mair was, indeed, sixteen at the time the meeting must have been in April 1907, though the context slightly suggests that it was the previous year.
2. L.G.P.

as he reacted to this terrible, unbelievable event. Since at the best of times he had very little faith in the ultimate benignity of Providence, and no faith at all in personal survival after death, he naturally felt the loss of Mair as absolute, and as an act of deliberate divine malice against himself.

> The heartrendings of George were tortured, almost at the edge of madness . . . he obtained not a grain of comfort from the usual springs . . . 'Some hand from the dark' had taken his beloved from his breast. 'Now she is gone' were his words, and he gets no joy from following her on the wings of imagination . . . 'I don't know what it is, and it has come at a time when I have had such curious success in my career . . . when I have been put on a sort of pinnacle, just so that I should become the target for this cruel blow. It's sure to leave a deep mark upon me . . . I'm sure to be much better or much worse than I was. I don't know which yet.'[1]

His brother, William, came up to London from Criccieth, arriving the day Mair died. He and Margaret, knowing that they had to deal with a man almost demented with grief – a man, moreover, who was abnormally squeamish about everything to do with illness and death – conspired that he should be kept away from Routh Road. In old age William recalled the day following his arrival, which was

> spent by Dafydd and myself in rest and contemplation at the Board of Trade offices, it being thought best that my brother should be kept clear of the house whilst certain necessary preparations for the funeral were going on. The most vivid recollection which I still preserve of the long and quiet day spent in a darkened room of that huge building is the skilful and understanding way in which some of the high officials tried to divert my brother's thoughts from his sorrows by relating humorous stories or Lobby gossip about famous politicians, past and present.[2]

Lloyd George had great resilience and a natural disposition to look to the future rather than the past. A. G. Gardiner said of him that he walked out every morning and looked upon a brand-new world, freshly created.[3]

1. D. R. Daniel, op. cit. (N.L.W.).
2. William George, My Brother and I, p. 215. William's future wife, Anita – then a sister at the Royal Northern Hospital – nursed Mair during her last illness.
3. Quoted in D. R. Daniel, op. cit. Many years later a similar observation was made by a close friend of the Lloyd George family of a different generation: '. . . to Lloyd George every morning was not a new day, but a new life and a new chance. That is why the moment he appeared everything became exciting as though an electric switch had been turned on in a dark room.' (Thelma Cazalet-Keir, From the Wings, p. 47.)

From William's account it is clear that even the day after Mair's death he was not entirely deaf to spicy political talk, and Herbert Lewis's account of Mair's funeral at Criccieth on 3 December gives us a similar picture:

> Went to Garthcelyn at 10. Funeral at 11. All very simple. Funeral entirely private, the only mourners in addition to the family being Sir Alfred Thomas, William Jones, Llewelyn Williams, 2 or 3 friends from Criccieth and myself.
>
> In the afternoon Lloyd George, Clark and I went for a 6 mile walk, and the change and exercise seemed to do L.G. good. Spent the evening at Garthcelyn in conversation that sought to divert the current of L.G.'s thoughts. Laughter and tears were very near one another, and in the midst of it he had to leave us for a while. He returned and kept us all amused and interested with a brilliant flow of literary, historical and reminiscent talk.[1]

After the funeral Lloyd George had to go at once to Manchester to attend to a dispute in the cotton industry. His intervention was successful and the quick return to work a welcome distraction. But Christmas was looming up and the prospect of Christmas at Criccieth was, in the circumstances, even more repugnant to him than usual. Moreover his family could see that without a drastic change he might go utterly to pieces. So it was arranged that he should motor to the South of France with Kearley, taking Dick and Gwilym who would have the company of Kearley's two sons, Gerald and Mark. On the Riviera they would stay at the villa La Pastorelle at Nice, lent to them by Lady Nunburnholme.[2]

The party set out on 20 December in Kearley's 60-h.p. Napier. The first night they stayed at Boulogne, the second at Meaux, the third at Lyon. Leaving there in the early morning of Christmas Eve, in dark and drizzly conditions, they narrowly escaped disaster when the car skidded towards a large hay wagon near the Pont des Chataignes. But collision was just avoided and they spent the next night at Aix-en-Provence. Their destination at Nice was safely reached a little after 4 p.m. on Christmas Day.

From nearly every stop on the way Lloyd George wrote to Margaret,

1. Herbert Lewis's diary, entry for 3 December 1907 (N.L.W.). Sir Alfred Thomas was M.P. for East Glamorganshire and chairman of the Welsh group in Parliament. William Jones was M.P. for Arvon (the county division of Caernarvonshire). Llewelyn Williams was M.P. for the Carmarthen Boroughs. Clark was William Clark, Lloyd George's official private secretary. 'Garthcelyn' was William George's house at Criccieth.
2. Widow of the 1st Lord Nunburnholme, a Hull shipowner, formerly a Liberal M.P., who had recently died.

and he wrote to her frequently during the fortnight or so spent in the South of France. A few extracts will show how he passed the time and how his temperament was adjusting itself:

Last night . . . dined with Lord Glantawe in Nice . . . He lost five of his children . . . You may therefore imagine that when a man who had passed through such experiences assured me that time does heal the sore his words carried real consolation to my heart.[1]

Kearley & I & the two small boys are off to lunch with Henniker Heaton. Dick & Gerald are taking the ladies out.

Herbert Lewis coming in tonight . . .

P.S. I hope you have given something to the poor at Criccieth this year. If not I should very much like you to do so New Year's Day – tea or flour. Give more than last year – double it.[2]

[Charles] Henry is extraordinarily kind. He is doing his best to keep me bustling about & he has taken a greater fancy to Gwilym than to any boy he has ever met . . . We may run over to Monte Carlo today for lunch.[3]

Bright day at last. Sun shining brilliantly. Nice is beautiful . . . The palms look in their proper setting & the oranges glow. The hills have also reappeared.[4]

Returned from Lord Rendel's. Very pleased to see me. Poor old Lady Rendel looks very much broken. They both enquired so kindly about you. They would have been so glad had you seen your way to take their villa at Valescure. So would I too cariad [darling] . . . I would rather have you – jealous old Maggie as you sometimes are – I would rather see you near me in trouble than anybody else – you & Uncle Lloyd. You don't mind my bringing him in do you? I was telling Henry about him last night . . .[5]

1. D.L.G. to M.L.G., 26 December 1907 (N.L.W. and *Letters*, p. 150). Lord Glantawe, formerly Sir John Jones Jenkins, was a banker who had been Liberal and Liberal Unionist M.P. for Carmarthen District, and thrice Mayor of Swansea.
2. D.L.G. to M.L.G., 27 December 1907 (N.L.W.). John Henniker Heaton, Tory M.P. for Canterbury, was a passionate and successful lobbyist for cheaper postal rates. He was also highly sociable.
3. D.L.G. to M.L.G., 28 December 1907 (N.L.W.).
4. D.L.G. to M.L.G., 29 December 1907 (N.L.W.).
5. D.L.G. to M.L.G., 5 January 1908 (N.L.W. and *Letters*, p. 150). Lord Rendel, formerly Stuart Rendel, had been chairman of the Welsh group in Parliament when Lloyd George was a young M.P.

I mean to go to the Henry's to stay until Tuesday. It is hardly worth while although an extra four days in this beautiful & balmy climate may be worth something. There will be hard difficult & anxious work awaiting me & I am glad to think that there is . . .

This is going to be a very expensive trip. But if it saves me from a breakdown I think you will consider it cheap won't you darling?[1]

The Henrys were comparatively new figures in Lloyd George's life. Charles Solomon Henry was a millionaire merchant, born in Australia but educated in England and Germany. Since 1906 he had been Liberal M.P. for Wellington in Shropshire. His wife, Julia, was formerly a Miss Lewisohn of New York, and Richard Lloyd George describes her as 'dark, tall and very attractive'.[2] The Henrys had one country house in the constituency and another near Henley-on-Thames. Their London house was at Porchester Gate, Hyde Park, but before long they would be moving to No. 5 Carlton Gardens. Wherever they were they entertained lavishly.

Such a combination of *parvenu* wealth and feminine allure seldom failed to interest Lloyd George, and for the next few years the Henrys were frequent companions of his, jointly and severally. D. R. Daniel has this to say of his 'luxurious nature':

. . . always the best hotels, the best food, the most comfortable seats – whatever the cost this was his motto always, and his weakness was that he never had a sense of delicacy when receiving gifts or favours . . .[3]

'Weakness' is misleading, because it suggests that he was susceptible to political pressure from those whom he chose to befriend. In fact he came nearer to being socially incorruptible than most politicians of his or any other time. It was not only that he eschewed the 'aristocratic embrace': that was fairly easy for him, because a genuine dislike of the atmosphere of old houses reinforced his disinclination to be compromised by too close contact with their inmates. He would not allow himself to be upstaged by members of the traditional ruling class holding court in their natural settings, and he seldom if ever philandered with patrician women. But even those with whom he did associate on familiar terms could expect no tangible rewards from him. Though he looked for friendship and intimate companionship to the world of the self-made, he never felt that his cronies

1. D.L.G. to M.L.G., 10 January 1908 (N.L.W. and part of it appears in *Letters*, p. 151).
2. Richard Lloyd George, *Lloyd George*, p. 107. The author gives her name as 'Lady J.', but it is obvious whom he means.
3. D. R. Daniel, *op. cit.* (N.L.W.).

1a. Lloyd George, with Margaret, Mair and the infant Megan, in the garden of their Wandsworth home

1b. Lloyd George in the same garden, with his dog Peggy

Photographs taken during Lloyd George's drive across France with Hudson Kearley and their sons in December 1907. The car averaged two punctures a day during the trip

2a. (*left*) Lloyd George shopping at Montreuil-sur-mer (later Haig's headquarters for a time during the Great War)

2b. (*centre*) Lloyd George with Hudson Kearley and two of their sons, Gwilym and Mark, outside an inn in the Esterel hills

2c. (*bottom*) Leaving Dijon, watched by an admiring crowd

were putting him under any obligation to promote their interests when he accepted their hospitality. This may have signified a lack of delicacy on his part, but it was not a sign of weakness.[1]

Certainly he liked his comforts, though he was not a sybarite. As Disraeli said, 'there is moderation even in excess', and Lloyd George's self-indulgence was kept under control for the sake of his health and political career. But his tastes were too luxurious to be adequately provided for by his wife, whose standards of domestic comfort were regulated by her puritan convictions and somewhat parsimonious instincts, and who any-way had such an overwhelming preference for Criccieth that she had left him as a young M.P. for long periods on his own in London. During that time he found solace in the well-kept Putney home of Timothy Davies and his pretty, vivacious wife. 'Mrs Tim' accommodated Lloyd George in every way and Davies – a prosperous draper who became an M.P. in 1906 – was a complaisant husband. The Henrys were, in a sense, a more opulent version of the Timothy Davieses. Lloyd George liked being enter-tained by them and no doubt had a bit of an affair with Julia Henry, to which Henry turned a blind eye. But later she became a nuisance to him, presuming too far on a relationship that he never intended to be deeply emotional. Consequently she did not retain his friendship as 'Mrs Tim' did.

Mair's death was a very great shock to Lloyd George and may have extended the range of his sympathy for others in distress. Yet his grief, though intense, did not prostrate him for long and was in the main self-centred. Though his absence from Routh Road the day after Mair died, and from Criccieth over the Christmas holiday, was in accordance with Margaret's wishes – granted her knowledge of his character and state of mind – yet we do not often find him looking at the tragedy from her point of view. In one letter he makes suggestions that must have been bad for her morale, even though the reproach implicit in them is ostensibly directed against himself:

> . . . what about servants? Have you thought that out? Do you mean to have a nurse housemaid who could attend to Megan . . .? We must have

1. As Prime Minister he bestowed offices very largely on merit, regardless of his personal feelings, and his recommendations for honours were made partly on grounds of merit and partly for the time-honoured purpose of replenishing party funds – rarely to reward friends beyond their worth. Henry, for instance, received a baronetcy in 1911, doubtless as a recom-pense for services, including financial contributions, to the Liberal Party. It might just as well have been conferred upon him had he never known Lloyd George, and he received nothing further during the Lloyd George Premiership.

an extra hand that is clear . . . I have made up my mind that your housekeeping allowance must be increased at all hazards to ensure good regular meals to the youngsters when they return from school . . . If in spite of all our precautions the children still get pale & wan in that city then we must make up our minds whatever it costs our feelings to leave them in the country. But I don't think this will be necessary.[1]

He may not have intended to imply that Mair had died because she was underfed and inadequately cared for; but that, surely, is what Margaret must have taken him to mean.

Lloyd George later told Frances Stevenson that he and his wife 'drifted apart' after Mair's death:

> They each had their poignant grief but could not go to each other for sympathy and understanding – there was no sharing of the trouble, both blaming the other, perhaps, for what went wrong, the delay in calling the doctor, the carrying out of an emergency operation without a highly skilled staff and hospital amenities. The gap of incompatibility which had always been there became emphasized and more difficult to bridge.[2]

The truth seems to be that, in the short run, the loss of Mair served much more to reconcile than to divide them. There is no sign of estrangement or recrimination in this letter to Margaret, written from Manchester the day after the funeral:

> I am so pleased to think you are joining me up in town tomorrow night darling. Your placid brave spirit has a soothing effect on my turbulent & emotional nature . . . I have been always disposed towards morbidity. We must help each other not to brood . . . We did our best. It was the decree of fate which millions besides ourselves are now enduring . . .
>
> More than that I have a profound conviction that cruel as the blow may appear & purposeless as it may now seem it will prove to be the greatest blessing that has befallen us & through us multitudes whom God has sent me to give a helping hand to out of misery . . . worse than ours. I can see through the darkness a ray of hope. I am not sure yet what it will reveal but I am certain of its presence & its promise.[3]

1. D.L.G. to M.L.G., 3 January 1908 (N.L.W.).
2. Frances Lloyd George, *The Years that are Past*, p. 49.
3. D.L.G. to M.L.G., 4 December 1907 (N.L.W. and *Letters*, p. 149).

And in the South of France, even while fussing about their way of life, he is urging her to count her blessings and at the same time counting his own:

> No one can cure me except you & your darling children & I think I alone can cure you. There will always be a scar and it will always be tender when . . . memory presses. Still I do not even now despair of life. We have four sweet children & we have each other.[1]

But this recovered sense of solidarity could not restore their marriage to its pristine state, and in their future quarrels the circumstances of Mair's death may have been brought up again and again as a means of hurting each other. All the same, they had drifted some distance apart long before she died, and the immediate effect of her death was to remind them how much they had in common. Even when they drifted apart again there was always a special bond between them, though Lloyd George naturally wished to conceal this from Frances, and she to convince herself that it did not exist.

While he was abroad the Routh Road house was disposed of and the lease of another obtained; No. 5 Cheyne Place, Chelsea. But the Lloyd Georges' stay there was very brief, because within a few months he was in a new job which involved moving to a famous official residence – and which gave him what he felt to be his Providential chance to help the struggling multitudes.

1. D.L.G. to M.L.G., probably 6 January 1908 (N.L.W.).

FIVE

Make-or-Break Promotion

The day before Lloyd George introduced his Port of London Bill the Prime Minister, Sir Henry Campbell-Bannerman, wrote to the King tendering his resignation. Two days later – on 3 April 1908 – it was accepted. Sir Henry's health had been failing for some months and it was evident that there would soon have to be a new Prime Minister. Most people assumed that Sir Henry's successor would be the Chancellor of the Exchequer, H. H. Asquith, and their assumption was correct. On 4 April the King, who was at Biarritz, wrote to Asquith requesting him to form a new government.

Before the Liberals returned to power Lloyd George was concerned, as we saw earlier, that Asquith should not become Leader of the House of Commons and so heir apparent to the Premiership. He must still have hoped at that stage that his own stock would rise, and Asquith's fall, over the next few years to such an extent that the reversion of the Premiership might be his. Certainly his stock had risen in office, but Asquith's had not fallen; as Chancellor he had confirmed the reputation he established as Home Secretary under Gladstone and Rosebery. Consequently it must have been obvious to Lloyd George, in the early months of 1908, that Asquith would succeed the ailing Campbell-Bannerman.

It was not quite so obvious, however, that he would succeed Asquith as Chancellor. Asquith appears to have made him an anticipatory offer of the post on 23 February,[1] but the offer was not made in writing and on 3 March Asquith told the King that he was planning to hold the

1. Herbert Lewis's diary, entry for 23 February 1908 (N.L.W.).

Exchequer himself for a time, together with the Premiership.[1] He prob-ably had two motives for favouring this arrangement. It would have enabled him to carry the Old Age Pensions scheme that he was preparing right through to the Statute Book, and it might also have enabled him, with the authority of an actual rather than prospective Prime Minister, in due course to appoint his friend R. B. Haldane to the Exchequer. But Lloyd George, naturally enough, wanted the second place in the new government for himself, feeling that he had earned it by his work at the Board of Trade and by his general services to the party. Moreover, Haldane's appointment would have been unacceptable to the party's radical wing – though in some respects he was the Government's most radical member – because he, like Asquith, had been on the 'Right' during the Boer War. Morley, as the elder statesman of the 'Left', was as insistent as a man of his vacillating nature could be that the two wings of the party should be properly balanced at the top, and his influence may have helped to change Asquith's mind.

At any rate we know that the Prime Minister designate spent the day following his receipt of the King's letter 'feverishly in interviewing col-leagues and putting last touches to the revised list of Ministers to be submitted to the King',[2] and it must have been then that he made Lloyd George a definite offer of the Exchequer, subject to royal approval. Probably there was also some talk about the junior Treasury appointment and other Ministerial changes. During the evening of 6 April Asquith left for Biarritz where, two days later, he kissed hands and obtained the King's approval of his list. Having done so he lost no time in writing Lloyd George the following letter, marked 'Secret':

My dear Lloyd George,

It gives me great pleasure, with His Majesty's approval, to ask you to accept the office of Chancellor of the Exchequer.

The offer which I am privileged to make is a well-deserved tribute to your long & eminent services to our party, and to the splendid capacity which you have shown in the administration of the Board of Trade.

I know, from experience, both the attractions and the difficulties of the Exchequer. It is at once the most thankless, & the most full of opportunities, in the whole Government.

1. H. H. Asquith to his wife, 4 March 1908, describing conversation with the King after Privy Council the day before. (Quoted in Spender and Asquith, *Life of Lord Oxford and Asquith*, Vol. I, p. 195.)   2. Spender and Asquith, *op. cit.*, Vol. I, p. 197.

The only stipulation that I make is that, following a precedent twice set by Sir Robert Peel, you should leave to me the introduction of the Budget for the present year. The change of government has come at a time when it would not be fair, or even possible, either for you or for me, to follow the ordinary course.

Yours very sincerely
H. H. Asquith.[1]

During Asquith's absence embarrassingly well-informed predictions of the new Ministry had been appearing in the *Daily Chronicle*, and Lloyd George referred to these in his reply, written from Cheyne Place on 11 April – the day after Asquith's return:

Dear Prime Minister,

I thank you for the flattering proposal contained in your letter & even more for the flattering terms in which it is conveyed to me. The condition you impose as to the next Budget relieves me of a great anxiety & I gladly acknowledge its fairness. I shall be proud to serve under your Premiership & no member of the Government will render more loyal service & support to his chief.

Winston told me last night that some of my colleagues had rushed to you immediately on your arrival with the amiable suggestion that I had been responsible for the publication of the Cabinet list. I need hardly tell you that I felt very hurt at the accusation & I think I ought to know who it is amongst my colleagues who deems me capable of what is not merely a gross indiscretion but a downright & discreditable breach of trust. Men whose promotion is not sustained by birth or other favouring conditions are always liable to be assailed with unkind suspicions of this sort. I would ask it therefore as a favour that you should not entertain them without satisfying yourself that they have some basis of truth. In this case there is not a shadow of truth in the insinuation & I am ashamed to think that it should be even necessary to say so.

I should like to put in a formal word about the Financial Secretary unless it be too late. If Kearley is impossible what about Russell Rea? He will guarantee that the Exchequer will remain free from any taint of Protection!

Yours sincerely
D. Lloyd George.[2]

1. 8 April 1908 (N.L.W.).
2. Asquith Papers (Bodleian Library). The word 'formal' in the last paragraph is a further indication that Asquith had discussed the junior Treasury appointment informally with

What was the truth about the Press leak? Lloyd George is so often assumed to have been the culprit in such matters that it is worth examining this particular incident in some detail.

Asquith arrived back from Biarritz at 5.55 p.m. on 10 April and was met at Charing Cross by (among others) his wife, Margot, his new private secretary, Vaughan Nash, and Haldane. These three accompanied him in his carriage first to 10 Downing Street – to ask after Campbell-Bannerman – and then on to the Asquiths' house in Cavendish Square. No sooner were they inside the house than Margot must have sat down and written to Winston Churchill as follows:

Dearest Winston,

I'm told Lloyd George dines with you tonight. I wish you wd speak to him & tell him quite plainly that the staff of Daily Chronicle have given him away to 3 independent people (better praps keep McKenna's name out) Mr Nash & Runciman quite simply told them both that Lloyd George had given them the list. The only man the King resented at all (don't say this to a living soul not even to Henry please) was Lloyd George wh seemed so odd! – Ld Knollys knows it was LG split & he says the King will be furious – Lloyd George's best chance if he is a good fellow wh I take yr word for is not to lie about it when H. speaks heavily to him but to give up his whole Press campaign he will be done as a dog if he goes on – I think you might save him & the Cabinet if you do this courageously. The Editor as well as others told Nash. Do your d—dest. I've just driven H. from the station & he said to me he 'hoped to God' Winston will give it him he is perfectly furious.

Yrs Margot

Burn this[1]

With this highly characteristic letter Margot made her *début* as the most intriguing (in both senses) of British Prime Ministers' wives. It must have been delivered at Churchill's house in Bolton Street just before he dined with Lloyd George, and fortunately he never carried out her final instruction. But he did speak to Lloyd George about the leak and afterwards

---

Lloyd George before he went to France. But he did not take up the suggestion that W. Russell Rea, M.P. for Scarborough, should be Lloyd George's Financial Secretary, and it was not until Lloyd George himself became Prime Minister in 1916 that Rea received office, and then only as a junior unpaid Whip.

1. Margot Asquith to W.S.C., undated, but the date and time are obvious from the reference to driving Asquith from the station.

reported their conversation not, significantly, to Margot, but to Asquith himself:

> I broached the matter to Lloyd George. He denies it utterly. I told him that you had said that you learned that several colleagues thought he was responsible; but that you had of course no knowledge yourself. He intends to speak to you tomorrow on the subject & I have told him he can quote me as having put him the question. It will be a good opportunity for a talk.[1]

Churchill cannot have wished to offend his chief, who had just promoted him to the Cabinet, but we can sense a hint of reproach in the words 'you had of course no knowledge yourself'. It must have seemed very wrong to him that Asquith should have given such a ready ear to gossip, and have allowed his wife to intervene in a matter which ought to have been kept strictly between colleagues. Besides, however keen he may have been to remain in Asquith's good books, he was at least equally keen to do nothing to forfeit Lloyd George's goodwill, since Lloyd George was his closest political ally and the politician he most admired. He may well have shown Lloyd George the letter he had just received from Margot, or at any rate have given him the gist of it. When, therefore, Lloyd George wrote next day to Asquith asking for the names of his accusers, it is quite likely that he was asking for information that he already possessed.

The *Daily Chronicle* revelations did not appear on a single day, but were spread over three days and in the process were significantly developed and changed. The fact that they occurred at all was mainly due to the King, whose refusal to interrupt his holiday at Biarritz meant that there was an unnecessarily long hiatus between Asquith's Cabinet-making activities in London and the publication of his approved list. During that time many politicians knew the posts for which they were or were not destined, and enterprising journalists had every opportunity to work upon, or to be worked upon by, the indiscreet.

On 6 April – even before Asquith left for Biarritz – the *Daily Chronicle* was predicting that Ripon (Lord Privy Seal) and Elgin (Colonial Secretary) would not be members of the new Government, and that Tweedmouth would cease to be First Lord of the Admiralty. A short list was given of Ministers who had 'achieved remarkable success', including among others Grey, Lloyd George, Harcourt, Crewe, Birrell, Burns, Churchill and

---

1. W.S.C. to H.H.A., 10 April 1908, 'midnight' (Asquith Papers, Bodleian Library).

Runciman. It was stated that Lloyd George would 'undoubtedly' succeed Asquith as Chancellor, that succession to the Board of Trade would lie between Harcourt and Runciman, and that Churchill was likely to be the new Colonial Secretary.

Next day – 7 April – there was a further confident forecast that Lloyd George would be Chancellor, since his claim to the post was 'as undeniable as Mr Asquith's to be Prime Minister'. At the same time promotion was anticipated for a Minister whose name had not even been mentioned the day before – McKenna – while the rumour that Harcourt would move to a new post was contradicted. He would, it was said, prefer to remain where he was (at the Office of Works), though at some future time he was 'sure of promotion'; and the report was embellished with a very fulsome account of his supposed merits.

On 8 April all the principal changes were firmly and correctly predicted – Lloyd George to be Chancellor; Tweedmouth, Lord President; Crewe, Colonial Secretary; McKenna, First Lord of the Admiralty; Churchill, President of the Board of Trade; and Runciman, President of the Board of Education. Of McKenna it was said that with his administrative ability he was likely to prove a successful First Lord, and of Churchill that he would 'make an ideal successor' to Lloyd George at the Board of Trade, where there was still plenty of important work to be done. Runciman was referred to in particularly flattering terms: he would 'bring to the Board of Education a fresh mind and a conciliatory temper, together with gifts of industry and concentration of purpose rare in so young a man'. When the official list was eventually published on 11 April the main items in it came as no surprise to readers of the *Daily Chronicle*.

So much for the nature of the leak. The question remains: who was – or were – responsible for it? Apart from Margot's allegation, the evidence does not point to any particular individual, still less to Lloyd George, as the unique source. Anybody reading the successive *Daily Chronicle* reports with an unprejudiced eye would naturally assume that they were based on information from a variety of sources, and indeed there were plenty of people in the know who might have contributed to the paper's evolving story. Lloyd George was by no means reluctant to talk to the Press, but he seldom did so without reason, and in any case there were many other politicians who were equally communicative. The editor of the *Daily Chronicle*, Robert Donald, had many contacts in the Liberal hierarchy. 'More and more', says his biographer, referring specifically to this period, 'Liberal Ministers entrusted him with their confidences, and found in him a well-informed and sagacious adviser.'[1] The *Chronicle's* Parliamentary correspondent, Harry Jones, was also well placed for collecting gossip, and most of the predictions appeared under his by-line.

It is unlikely that Lloyd George was totally innocent. In his letter to Asquith he seems to be protesting too much, and he does not offer what would have been the most convincing defence – that he was ignorant of the principal changes that Asquith was intending to make. So far as his own position was concerned he had a motive for contriving immediate publicity, as a warning to the King in case there were any objections to his appointment from that quarter. On the other hand there were others besides himself who had an interest in ensuring that the Exchequer would not be retained by Asquith or given to another Liberal Leaguer. Moreover, the expectation that he would be Chancellor was not confined to the *Daily Chronicle* and the news that his appointment to that office was imminent was far from being a sensational scoop.

Much less predictable was the news that McKenna would be First Lord of the Admiralty and Runciman President of the Board of Education, and it is rather hard to believe that Lloyd George would have gone out of his way to advertise their prospects. Relations between him and them were still overtly good, but they were more Asquith's *protégés* than his, each in succession having been Asquith's junior Minister at the Treasury. Churchill certainly was close to Lloyd George, but the early report that he would be Colonial Secretary was wide of the mark, as was the report that Harcourt would be moving to another post. Harcourt, by the way, was an inveterate gossip, and the exaggerated praise of him that appeared in the *Chronicle's* 7 April story suggests that he may have been a particularly useful source. In 1908 Lloyd George was still relatively pro-Harcourt, but would hardly have spoken of him in quite such glowing terms in private conversation with a journalist. As for John Burns, who in the initial story was included in the list of most successful and deserving ministers – from which McKenna's name was curiously absent – it is fair to say that there was no member of the Campbell-Bannerman Cabinet of whom Lloyd George had a lower opinion. Finally, it is worth mentioning that the appointment of S. T. Evans as Solicitor-General was not forecast in the *Chronicle*, though it was one about which Lloyd George was most likely to have been informed or consulted in advance.[2]

1. H. A. Taylor, *Robert Donald*, p. 50.
2. One Welshman whose name did appear in the *Chronicle* among possible candidates for junior office was Ellis Griffith. But Lloyd George never thought much of him.

Apart from the evidence reported by Margot, the reasonable assumption would be that Lloyd George was not the only source of the leak, and in spite of what she said that is still the most probable theory, though he may well have given away some information. Margot's story is doubly suspect. She was herself at all times an exceptionally unreliable witness, and the three whom she cites as witnesses in this case were not truly 'independent' even if correctly reported – McKenna and Runciman for the reason already stated, Vaughan Nash for a similar reason. As Asquith's new private secretary, inherited from Campbell-Bannerman, his allegiance was naturally to Asquith, and he must have been very keen to hold the confidence of his new chief. Before entering Campbell-Bannerman's service he had been a journalist on the staff of the *Daily Chronicle*, but had left the paper with Massingham and Harold Spender when its proprietor insisted on support for the war in 1899. That, however, was water under the bridge by 1908, and he was at least as likely as Lloyd George to have spoken unguardedly to acquaintances on the paper, as, indeed, were Runciman and McKenna. For all three of them Lloyd George may have seemed a convenient scapegoat, more especially if they knew that he, too, had talked. But it was not very wise of Asquith to risk a quarrel with a senior colleague so early in his Premiership, and on such dubious evidence.

Up to a point he may have grasped this himself when he read Churchill's letter. At any rate when he replied, on 11 April, to Lloyd George's letter of acceptance, he did not deal 'heavily' with him, as Margot had predicted, but was clearly at some pains to remove ill feeling, while preserving his own dignity:

My dear Lloyd George,

I was very glad to receive your cordial acceptance of my offer, & I reciprocate your wish and belief that our co-operation will always be of the closest.

I confess that I was a good deal annoyed to find, on my way home, that a substantially accurate forecast of the proposed changes in the Cabinet was published in the 'Chronicle' on the very morning on which I was first to submit them to the King.

On my arrival here, I was told by more than one colleague (there is no use in giving names) that it was reported that the Editor of the paper vouched you as the source of his information, & finding from Winston that you were to dine with him last night, I suggested that he should inform you of what was being said. I need not say that I accept without reserve your disclaimer. The press in these days is ubiquitous, difficult to baffle, and ingenious in drawing inferences from silence as well as from speech. I am afraid I cannot get Rea in at this moment but I hope we may include him before long.

Yrs sincerely
H. H. Asquith.[1]

With this letter the incident was closed, though unfortunately it did not altogether cure Asquith and his circle of a tendency to exaggerate Lloyd George's conspiratorial relations with the Press.

The goings-on in London gave Lloyd George a rather spurious excuse for cancelling an engagement in Paris, to attend the British Chamber of Commerce's banquet there on 11 April. His projected visit had been arousing considerable interest in France and he was to have been welcomed by, among others, Georges Clémenceau, then serving his first term as Prime Minister. But the two men did meet quite soon afterwards, when Clémenceau formed a very unfavourable impression of Lloyd George's knowledge of European and American politics.[2]

Campbell-Bannerman did not long survive his resignation. He died at 9.15 a.m. on 22 April and that evening Lloyd George spoke of him at a big meeting in Manchester:

> . . . one of the kindest hearts and one of the wisest heads that ever filled the high position of chief counsellor to his Sovereign in this country. It is only those who have been associated closely with him for years in the great work of Liberalism in this country who can realize what a loss it is to every great cause that he should have passed away. He was a man of deep, tender sympathies, a true friend of the people, a man who, whenever he was in doubt, always dropped on the side of the people. It is a greater loss than the people know, and one that they will realize more and more, that we should have lost his sapient and tender guidance in such a crisis in the history of our cause.

The tribute to Campbell-Bannerman was sincere. Not long before, as a member of his Cabinet, Lloyd George had said to D. R. Daniel:

1. N.L.W.
2. He wrote to a colleague that Lloyd George's ignorance on these subjects, as revealed in five minutes' conversation, was 'phenomenal'. (Clémenceau to Pichon, 21 August 1908, quoted in David Robin Watson, *Georges Clémenceau: A Political Biography*, p. 226 footnote.)

. . . the old chap is the greatest of them by far. He has some common sense that neither education nor anything else can produce. After listening to all of us speaking, he always brings some idea up that is full of cleverness and wisdom . . .[1]

But the Manchester speech could also be read as a rather unflattering comment upon the new Prime Minister who, unlike Lloyd George, had not been 'associated closely' with Campbell-Bannerman during the Boer War, and whose leadership might turn out to be less 'sapient and tender'. Such was the clear implication, and it cannot have been lost upon Asquith.

Lloyd George's promotion involved important changes in his way of life. For one thing, his salary went up from £2,000 to £5,000 a year – a most welcome advance. At the lower figure he was at a serious disadvantage and towards the end of 1907 some of his colleagues approached Campbell-Bannerman with the suggestion that an allowance might be made to his family from privately contributed or party funds. Campbell-Bannerman seems to have favoured the idea, but when Herbert Lewis put it to Lloyd George he expressed 'great doubt' about it. 'He was determined to accept nothing for himself, but he could not decide whether he was justified in refusing a provision for his wife and family. He was anxious to know who was moving in the matter, and was determined not to compromise his independence.'[2] Evidently he soon decided to turn the proposal down flat, because within a few days he was writing to Margaret:

I am not going to accept the charity of the party come what may. I have made up my mind not to. Tom Ellis did it & he was their doormat. I mean to fight my way through myself. This is an offer made to me because they find the jealousies & rivalries are so great that they cannot raise the status of my office & CB wants to do something for me. It is very kind of him but I won't have it. I'll take my chance and I know I can rely on your help.[3]

Lloyd George had been proposing that his office should be made

1. D. R. Daniel, *op. cit.* (N.L.W.).
2. Herbert Lewis's diary, entry for 4 January 1907 (N.L.W.). Lloyd George was seldom reluctant to accept presents from individual friends, but always chary of putting himself under any obligation to a group.
3. D.L.G. to M.L.G., from Nice, 10 January 1907 (N.L.W. and *Letters*, p. 151).

equivalent in all respects to a Secretaryship of State, and the proposal was soon afterwards adopted, though not soon enough to be of benefit to him. As Chancellor, however, he obtained an official salary more than double that which he had been receiving at the Board of Trade.

He also had the very considerable amenity of an official residence within easy walking distance of both the Treasury and Parliament. The outgoing occupant of 11 Downing Street was not the former Chancellor, Asquith, who until he became Premier preferred to live in his own house in Cavendish Square, but the Home Secretary, Herbert Gladstone (whose birthplace it happened, also, to be). No. 11 now became Lloyd George's London home for eight years, until he moved next door to No. 10. He lived there comfortably but unpretentiously with his family. 'So far as the food, service and appointments were concerned', Lord Riddell noted during the War, 'it looked as if a small suburban household were picnicking in Downing Street – the same simple food, the same little domestic servant, the same mixture of tea and dinner.'[1] Lloyd George employed only female, Welsh staff in the house, spoke Welsh – as always – in his domestic circle, and entertained his Welsh friends as freely as English colleagues and journalists. It was at this time that he began inviting people to working breakfasts, at which, as at other meals, his wife and children were normally present. This form of hospitality was not very congenial to some of his guests, but it saved time as well as money.

Margaret, who had left him on his own for long periods when he was a young M.P., did not similarly neglect him during his years of high office. She was with him, as a rule, in Downing Street and her presence there was a great comfort to him, because she understood certain aspects of his nature as no other woman could understand them, and because she shared, in her way, his relish for new-found power and importance, while also sharing his essential simplicity and contempt for smart society. In his extraordinary achievement of remaining true to his cultural origins he never failed to acknowledge her help and support.

Even Frances Stevenson, a necessarily hostile witness, has given us a picture of Margaret as the mistress of Nos. 11 and 10 Downing Street which is full of admiration in spite of itself:

> The visitors to the house in Downing Street were her husband's visitors, sometimes her children's, scarcely ever her own. She was, in effect, a visitor in her husband's house – except at Criccieth, where he was a

1. *Lord Riddell's War Diary*, p. 248.

visitor in hers . . . not that she did not enjoy full sway in both houses, for L.G. was anxious for her to hold with dignity her official position; and this she did. But it was L.G. who gave the real welcome, as it was inevitably he who was the centre of the company . . . she filled her place . . . with natural dignity, and I know of many who went there expecting to find a simple peasant woman being surprised to meet a personality of common sense and humour who, although she would have preferred to greet them in Wales, was perfectly able to make them feel at home in an official residence.[1]

Of the two houses that she successively occupied in Downing Street, No. 11 was the one she preferred, because it was not, like No. 10, an office as well as a dwelling-place, and consequently had, she felt, a more homely atmosphere.

Yet her heart was always at Criccieth, and because of his improved circumstances Lloyd George was able to build for her there the beautifully sited villa which was to remain her true home for the rest of her life. Its design was largely hers, she chose its name – Brynawelon, the Hill of Breezes – and the lovely garden that evolved around it was her creation. The building itself, without being positively ugly, was of no merit whatever and contained at first only two good living-rooms and six bedrooms. Later, it was enlarged to include another living-room and two more bedrooms, but it was never in any sense a grand house – except that it had one of the grandest views in Britain. Like Margaret's childhood home, it looked across the wide expanse of Cardigan Bay and, behind, to the Snowdon massif.

Acquiring the land and building Brynawelon cost the Lloyd Georges £2,000, but this was partly offset by the sale of their old house on the sea-front. Towards the end of 1909 an attempt was made to discredit Lloyd George by suggesting that instead of using Welsh slates for Brynawelon he had roofed the house with cheap slates from abroad. He was able to reply, however, that it was roofed with green slates from Nantlle Vale, Caernarvonshire, even though he could have saved himself a total of £45 by obtaining French slates at one shilling per thousand less – an answer which disposed of the smear while hinting at the virtues of Free Trade.

He did quite a lot of political entertaining at Brynawelon, especially during the summer recess, but the new house did not succeed in reconciling

1. Frances Lloyd George, *The Years that are Past*, pp. 48–9.

him to life at Criccieth. The main reason was that he could have no privacy there. According to one guest:

> Every chick and child in the village knew him and hailed him when he went about . . . every Welshman he had ever known considered that he had a right to call upon him and have an unlimited interview. The result was that his house became a regular centre for tourists, and I hardly ever remember seeing it without one or two peering at him through the trees.[1]

All the same, he enjoyed walks and picnics amid the familiar scenes of his youth, not least when he could show privileged English guests the evidence of his 'humble' background. He also enjoyed playing golf on the Criccieth course, opened in 1906.

But Criccieth was too far to go for weekends, even if he had wanted to go there. It suited him perfectly, therefore, when Lord Rendel lent him a house in Brighton, which he could occupy at weekends during the session. Brighton was a place that had long attracted him. Its invigorating air and exciting atmosphere – reminiscent of the Continent – were just what he liked, and it had the advantage of being within easy reach of London. In 1897 he had tried to persuade Margaret that they should take a flat there, because it was less smoky than London and 'much more sunny and dry than Criccieth'. But nothing had then come of the idea. During his early years at the Treasury – before another friend, Lord Riddell, provided him with a house at Walton Heath – he spent many weekends in Brighton, and on one of these he made his famous remark about the *clientèle* of the Metropole: 'I don't know where they come from; I know very well where they are going to!'[2]

Though he was often prepared to stay in private houses belonging to people of the 'Metropole' type, neither he nor Margaret ever fancied paying visits to stately homes, whose owners knew only too well where they had come from. Visually a Philistine, he was indifferent to the aesthetic appeal of such places, while his hostility to all that they stood for was intense. To oblige Churchill he stayed once or twice at Blenheim, but this was an exception to his normal rule. Spending a weekend there in July 1908, he walked into Woodstock to look for a Nonconformist place of worship – his motive, perhaps, more political than religious – and was eventually directed to a group of Dissenters meeting in a field, who were

1. Lucy Masterman, *C. F. G. Masterman, A Biography*, p. 212.
2. Lucy Masterman, *op. cit.*, p. 137.

pleasantly surprised to find the Chancellor of the Exchequer in their midst.

The Lloyd Georges held aloof not only from country-house parties, but also from fashionable social events in London. Elaborate lunch- and dinner-parties were a feature of the period, but the Lloyd Georges seldom attended and never gave any.

Lloyd George was Chancellor of the Exchequer for a little over seven years, the longest uninterrupted tenure of the office since the younger Pitt's, and a record since unequalled. He was the first Welsh Chancellor since Sir George Cornewall Lewis, who held the post shortly before Lloyd George was born. But Lewis was very anglicized, as was Sir John Aubrey who held it in the eighteenth century. Neither of these predecessors was authentically Welsh in the sense that Lloyd George was.

His place of work, Treasury Chambers, was at the corner of Downing Street and Whitehall, only a stone's-throw from his official home. There he was served by a small group of very able men, mostly drawn from the professional middle class and almost exclusively products of Oxford or Cambridge. In all there were twenty-six of them – a permanent secretary, two assistant secretaries and twenty-three clerks of varying grades. The Treasury consisted of six divisions, through which it kept control over the financial activities of other Government departments, and in which were grouped semi-autonomous departments of the Treasury itself, such as the Board of Inland Revenue. With his handful of potently qualified advisers, the Chancellor had to supervise an administrative empire whose work impinged upon every sphere of government.

Winston Churchill described his father's arrival at the Treasury in 1886 as a shock to the officials, and Lloyd George's arrival undoubtedly had a similar effect. It was not so much that they disapproved of his opinions – though some did – as that they were bewildered by his mental processes and methods of business. They had to keep up as best they might with a darting, challenging mind untouched by the academic disciplines which had formed their own minds, and with a temperament prone to ride roughshod over decorous routines and precedents. Lloyd George could not be bothered to read official minutes; he insisted upon oral advice, and would never allow himself to be bogged down in what seemed to him irrelevant detail. At the Board of Trade he guarded against excessive departmental influence by having a Welsh private secretary, Rowland, brought in from outside, as well as a secretary from the Civil Service, Clark. When he moved to the Treasury he took Rowland and Clark with him, and did not recruit a private secretary from the Treasury establishment.

The head of the official hierarchy when he took over was Sir George Murray. Murray was unusual in being a relic of the pre-meritocratic order in the Civil Service – a kinsman of the Duke of Atholl, who attained only third-class honours at Oxford and was admitted to the Foreign Office under the old system of jobs for the boys. Thence he was transferred to the Treasury and, after serving as private secretary to Gladstone and Rosebery, held a number of senior appointments before becoming, in 1907, sole Permanent Secretary to the Treasury. He was a witty man of the world who, when the Army Council proposed to build a subway under Whitehall for the disposal of War Office archives in the event of invasion, wrote that the application must be refused because 'the last objective of any intelligent invader of this country would be the War Office'.[1] But neither his patrician background nor his strictly Gladstonian views on public finance equipped him to work on close, easy terms with Lloyd George, and there was, indeed, chronic friction between them. Lloyd George suspected, not without reason, that Murray reported on him to Asquith, and Murray for his part resented Lloyd George's habit of by-passing him and seeking advice from other officials, more especially from the chairman of Inland Revenue, Sir Robert Chalmers.

Chalmers was another Scotsman, but from the bourgeoisie, and his rise owed nothing to personal favouritism. He was a scholar at Oxford and graduated from there in classics and natural science, to pass top in the open competitive examination for the Civil Service. As a young Treasury official he spent his leisure doing social work in the East End of London under the aegis of Samuel Barnett. Whereas Murray was an old-fashioned Liberal, Chalmers was an advanced social reformer, naturally in sympathy with Lloyd George's tax and welfare policies. Yet when, in 1911, he succeeded Murray as Permanent Secretary, relations between him and the Chancellor deteriorated. It was he who gave Lloyd George a nickname which stuck – 'the Goat'.

On the political side Lloyd George's first colleague at the Treasury was Charles Hobhouse, whom Asquith appointed Financial Secretary in preference to Russell Rea. The appointment was clearly intended to re-assure traditionalists, since Hobhouse was as unlike Lloyd George as any man could be – an Old Etonian squire, and a strong Churchman, whose recreations were hunting and shooting. He also kept a diary, extracts from

1 H. H. Asquith, *Memories and Reflections*, Vol. I, p. 256.

which have recently been published. They show that he had a grudging admiration for Lloyd George, combined with a laughable belief in his own superior worldly wisdom:

Lloyd George has an extraordinary power of picking up the essential details of a question by conversation. He *refuses* to read any office files or papers, but likes people to come and *talk*. He also possesses a great gift of imposing on people the idea that he sees and agrees with their side of a question to the exclusion of all other aspects.

But his absolute contempt for details and ignorance of common facts of life make him a bad official, and about the end of June Asquith instructed me to come and see him weekly on the financial position, and let him know how things stood.[1]

So he, too, reported to the Prime Minister behind the Chancellor's back.

It is hardly surprising that, while Hobhouse was Financial Secretary, Lloyd George turned increasingly for political advice and assistance to a junior minister at first in another department, Charles Masterman, who became his principal lieutenant, formally or informally, during most of the period of his pre-war Chancellorship.

Intellectual, philanthropist and aesthete, Masterman was, next only to Churchill, the Government's most remarkable young man. In revolt against a puritanical upbringing, he moved through High Anglicanism to free thought, but always with an unwavering Christian dedication to the cause of the poor and oppressed. At Cambridge he obtained Firsts in Natural Science and Moral Science, and was President of the Union. Then he went to live in a tenement flat in a slum quarter of South London, which gave him material for his disturbing books, *From the Abyss* and *In Peril of Change*. He prophesied that the spirit of the future would be nationalistic, but very different 'from those former rallies of a national spirit which . . . identified a nation with a small and limited class, throwing up boundaries around its privileges against a hungry and raging crowd'. In 1903 A. G. Gardiner persuaded him to join the *Daily News* as literary editor, and at the 1906 election he was returned as Liberal M.P. for West Ham (North). At a *Daily News* dinner after the election he reaffirmed his faith as a militant Left-winger: 'I was never more convinced than today that the only real alternative to Protection is a large and vigorous policy of social reform.'[2]

1. *Inside Asquith's Cabinet: From the Diaries of Charles Hobhouse*, edited by Edward David, p. 73.
2. Lucy Masterman, *C. F. G. Masterman; a Biography*, p. 65.

Campbell-Bannerman did not offer him a post, but when Asquith became Prime Minister he was appointed to the Local Government Board under John Burns. At about the same time he married Lucy Lyttelton who belonged, as he did not, to the political ruling class, but who shared his convictions. He was only thirty-four and seemed well embarked upon a long and bright career. But unfortunately it was not to be. His time as a successful politician was destined to be short, though while it lasted he was able to make no small contribution to historic achievements. Apart from the sheer bad luck which later overtook him, his temperament was perhaps rather too nervous and sensitive for politics. In summer he was a martyr to hay fever, and in winter felt the cold to an unusual degree. He also tended to drink too much, which was probably a symptom of inner stress.

Lloyd George's promotion to the Treasury was seen by many as a step which would make or break the Government, as well as himself. He inherited the post at a time of growing difficulty for the Liberals who, by 1908, had lost much of the impetus of their great victory two years before.

To say that they were baulked at every turn by the House of Lords is to falsify the record. The Second Chamber was certainly an Opposition stronghold – since the Home Rule split the anti-Liberal majority there had been overwhelming – but it is not true that the Lords rejected or mangled all the legislation that the Government sent up to them. For two years at least their treatment of the Government's measures was intelligently selective. Reforms that did not challenge any basic Tory interests, or for which there was evidence of strong popular support, were given a fair passage. In particular, no serious resistance was offered to measures beneficial to the working class, because the Tories were fearful of Labour and reluctant to do anything that would consolidate its alliance with the Liberals.

The Government, therefore, got most of its social reform measures through. In 1906 a Workmen's Compensation Act supplemented the pioneering statute of 1897, inspired by Joseph Chamberlain; in 1907 a Factory and Workshops Act provided wide powers for securing the health and safety of workpeople; and in 1908 the principle of an eight hours' working day underground was embodied in the Coal Mines Regulation Act. The Minister responsible for these reforms was the Home Secretary, Herbert Gladstone, whose name is not often included in any roll-call of radicals, but whose radical record is second to none in the Campbell-Bannerman Government. He was, to be sure, no firebrand, but a good party man whose common sense inclined him to be less 'Gladstonian' in the matter of State intervention than his famous father had been. With his able under-secretary, Herbert Samuel, he sponsored no less than thirty-four Acts of Parliament during his time at the Home Office, including measures to transform the administration of justice as it affected young offenders.

For the trade unions the most important Act of all was that which negated the Taff Vale judgment, by restoring the non-liability of unions for damages incurred by their members during industrial disputes. The Trade Disputes Act of 1906 was, in substance, a Labour rather than a Liberal measure. The Government's original Bill, which would have given the unions considerable but not unlimited immunity, was later made to incorporate a Labour Bill which went the whole hog. When the new Bill had its third reading in the House of Commons Balfour did not force a division, and in due course it was also passed without a division in the Lords. Elie Halévy rightly describes its enactment as 'a victory not of the Liberals over the Conservatives, but of the proletariat over the bourgeoisie'.[1]

But while the Government was doing, willy-nilly, quite a lot to satisfy Labour, it was able to do virtually nothing to satisfy the Nonconformist interest, which about 180 Liberal M.P.s represented. The reason was that the Lords felt they could safely obstruct measures dear to the leaders of Nonconformity but of markedly less concern to ordinary voters. This could not fail to be a special embarrassment to Lloyd George. The three Non-conformist issues with which he was inescapably involved were Welsh Disestablishment, Education and Licensing. Though not responsible for them departmentally, he could hardly avoid being held responsible in a general way for whatever was or was not done about them.

The first caused him much trouble, because to the great majority of Welsh Nonconformists the early introduction of a Disestablishment Bill was the touchstone of the Government's and his own sincerity. To him it had long been obvious, however, that the Welsh Church would never be disestablished so long as the House of Lords retained its veto, and he saw no point in wasting good House of Commons time on legislation that was bound to fail. The policy of 'filling up the cup' of Lords iniquity, by sending a succession of measures to that Chamber with no other purpose

1. Elie Halévy, *The Rule of Democracy*, ch. I, Part II, section 12.

than that they should be killed there, always seemed to him rather futile. While, therefore, he was against bringing in a Disestablishment Bill until its passage could be assured, he was well aware that some gesture would have to be made to mollify loyal supporters in Wales, whose sectarian fervour he could understand but not share.

The only available gesture was the all-too-familiar one of appointing a Royal Commission, which Lloyd George justified to Nonconformists as a means of convincing English opinion that the case for Disestablishment was factually sound, while to leading Churchmen he expressed the hope that a more moderate Bill might result from it. The Commission, appointed in May 1906, consisted of four Nonconformists, four Anglicans and a Welsh judge, Lord Justice Vaughan Williams, as chairman. They received their letters of invitation from Lloyd George and he must have hoped that that would be the full extent of his involvement. But before long he was involved in much tedious correspondence with disaffected members of the Commission. The chairman proved incompetent, personal relations deteriorated, and the work of the Commission, which the Government had meant to be protracted, turned out to be acrimonious as well. One of the Anglican representatives, concerning whose appointment Lloyd George had felt strong misgivings, was the very clever, bigoted and cranky Lord Hugh Cecil, who was just the man to make rings round Nonconformist witnesses. Within a year three Nonconformist members of the Commission had resigned, including Lloyd George's former crony, S. T. Evans, who anyway resented not being a Minister. Their places were filled and the Commission remained in being, while Disestablishment was postponed for another year, then for yet another, and while Lloyd George insisted that nothing could be done about it until the House of Lords was tackled. Anyone, he said, who worried the Government while it was 'manœuvring its artillery into position for an attack on the Lords' should be 'put in the guard room'.[1]

His task of keeping Welsh indignation within bounds was facilitated by steady support from most of the Welsh M.P.s, whose chairman, Sir Alfred Thomas, had long been a faithful admirer of his. He was also helped by the

1. Speech at Caernarvon on his forty-fourth birthday, 17 January 1907. A note from the Lord Chancellor, Loreburn, passed to Lloyd George in Cabinet, shows that the Government was content that the Commission 'should be leisurely – not dilatory – and might well last 2 years' (L.G.P.). In the event it lasted four years. A letter from Archbishop Randall Davidson shows that Lord Hugh Cecil was appointed after five other Anglicans had declined to serve; and a letter from the Bishop of St Asaph shows that Lloyd George had been the obstacle to Lord Hugh's appointment (Earl Lloyd George collection).

fact that Disestablishment had become less of a burning popular issue than when he first entered Parliament. But his most valuable asset was the goodwill of his Welsh compatriots, the pride that they felt in his advancement, and the prestige that his talents had won for him. He had a mass following in Wales greater than that of any Nonconformist preacher, and as he became more powerful in the State, so his voice became more authoritative in the Principality.[1] When a convention of Nonconformists was held at Cardiff on 10 October 1907, ostensibly to protest against the Government's betrayal of their cause, he managed to turn it into an overwhelming triumph for himself. Having prepared the ground by meeting some of the leading delegates beforehand, he then made a speech which sent the whole convention into tearful ecstasies:

> Who said I was going to sell Wales? Seven years ago there was a little country, which I never saw, fighting for freedom, fighting for fair play . . . Pardon me for reminding you, I risked my seat: I risked my livelihood – it was leaving me. [A voice: 'You risked your life.'] Yes, I risked my life. [Tremendous cheering, followed by an awed hush.] Am I going to sell the land I love? *Duw a wyr mor anwyl yw Cymru lan i mi!* [God knows how dear to me is my Wales!]

On a less emotional occasion a few months previously he made the telling point that only four of his Welsh Parliamentary colleagues had given first place to Disestablishment in their election addresses, whereas all the rest had mentioned Education first. It was right, therefore, that the Government had given priority to an Education Bill which was also, he suggested, in some ways 'a measure of Disestablishment and Disendowment'.[2]

Birrell's Education Bill, introduced in April 1906, was a deliberate affront to the Established Church. Whereas in urban areas 'extended facilities' for denominational instruction were to be permitted, subject to local authority approval, in country districts there was to be no such teaching in council-controlled schools, even outside school hours. This apparently irrational discrimination had a political logic: the Government wished to penalize Anglicans in the countryside, who voted Tory, without penalizing Roman Catholics in the big cities, who voted Liberal. Lloyd George spoke for the Bill on Second Reading, and began by defending the

---

1. His prestige was further enhanced when he was appointed Chancellor of the Exchequer, and at the same time Asquith shrewdly appointed S. T. Evans Solicitor-General.
2. Speech at Pontypridd, 20 June 1907.

part of it in which he had a special interest. This was Part IV, which incorporated an idea that he had recently put forward – that there should be a national council, representing Welsh counties and county boroughs, to control public education in Wales. The idea had soon afterwards received overwhelming endorsement at an inter-denominational conference in Cardiff, attended (among others) by three of the four Welsh Anglican bishops and most Conservative candidates for Welsh seats. But it later became apparent that their assent to it had been in general terms only. The Opposition quarrelled with Part IV as well as with other provisions of the Bill.[1]

After it had passed the House of Commons, though with less than the Government's normal majority, the Bill was amended out of recognition by the Lords. The Government then had the Lords' amendments rejected *en bloc* by the Commons, the Lords voted for them again, and in consequence just before Christmas the Bill was dropped. It should not be thought that the Lords resisted all educational reform passed by the Commons: in 1906 a Bill went through empowering English education authorities to provide school meals, if necessary at public expense. But the Birrell Bill was a partisan measure, which provoked an even more partisan response. Some of the Lords' amendments went far beyond restoring the 1902 provisions for religious teaching, one even reopening a question settled in 1870. During the two years following the Bill's failure continued efforts were made by moderates on both sides of the sectarian divide to find a workable compromise, but all in vain. The Government introduced two more Bills, but in due course each had to be withdrawn. The second, for which Walter Runciman was responsible, conceded the principle of denominational instruction in school hours, and if this had been done in the Birrell Bill agreement might then have been reached. But by the end of 1908 the Opposition was in no mood to compromise.

The Welsh national council project sank with the Birrell Bill, but in 1907 the Government succeeded in establishing a Welsh education depart-

1. Lloyd George made his national council proposal in a speech to the Cardiff Cymmrodorion Society on 3 March 1906. The inter-denominational conference in the same city was held on 23 March, and Lloyd George's Second Reading speech on the Birrell Bill was on 8 May (Hansard, Fourth Series, Vol. CLVI, col. 1174–88).

In an interview for the *Welsh Review* on 24 July he was reported as saying: 'The Government are in earnest . . . I may tell you that I made it a condition of my joining the Cabinet that a National Council should be set up in Wales.' But three days later he claimed to have deleted the words when correcting the proofs. (Letter to J. Hugh Edwards, dated 27 July 1906, but possibly not sent. Earl Lloyd George collection.)

ment at the Board of Education, with the eminent Welsh scholar and man of letters, Owen M. Edwards, as the first chief inspector of Welsh schools. This did something, though not very much, to satisfy Welsh opinion. Yet the intensity of feeling against the 1902 Act was all the time diminishing in Wales, and the Government was careful not to revive it by applying the previous Government's sanctions to any defaulting Welsh local authority. With the decline of dogmatic religion the sectarian issue was beginning to lose its importance in British politics – a process for which Lloyd George had some reason to be grateful, because a man of his cast of mind could never be entirely at ease as standard-bearer for the chapels militant.

On the subject of Temperance he had fewer inhibitions. He genuinely loathed drunkenness and was aware of its baleful influence upon the lives of the poor. In the autumn of 1906 he described drink as 'the most urgent problem of the hour for our rulers to grapple with', and promised early action by the Government. But though he spoke of drink as the principal cause of poverty in Britain – since it not only impoverished the individual, but diverted earnings from the necessaries of life, whose manufacture would give three times as much employment as the production of drink – he hastened to add that there were other causes:

> There are many thousands of sober, clean-living men and women . . . who today suffer the privations of unmerited poverty. There is more wealth per head of the population here than in any other land in the world. Shame upon rich Britain that she should tolerate so much poverty among her people! The country that spent 250 millions to avenge an insult levelled at her pride by an old Dutch farmer is not ashamed to see her children walking the streets hungry and in rags. There is plenty of wealth in this country to provide for all and to spare. What is wanted is a fairer distribution.[1]

The fate of the Government's Licensing Bill belongs to the next chapter, but meanwhile it is important to note that Lloyd George's attacks on the liquor trade were not simply Nonconformist demagoguery at the expense of a Tory vested interest; they were part of his general indictment of an unjust social system.

To him, the epitome of that system was the House of Lords, in which hereditary economic power and political privilege were concentrated. He objected to the Lords as a Liberal, and even more as a democrat. The

1. Speech at Penrhyndeudrath, 25 September 1906.

Liberal objection was natural enough. When the Tories were in office there was no question of any measure of theirs being rejected or mangled by the Lords. The Second Chamber's veto was used only against Liberal Governments, and any limitation of its use was dictated by the interests of the Tory Party rather than by a sense of fitness or fair play. As Lloyd George put it, the House of Lords was 'petrified Toryism', neither independent nor representative of the nation's multifarious activities.[1] In another speech he varied the metaphor:

> A mastiff? It is the right hon. Gentleman's [Balfour's] poodle. It fetches and carries for him. It barks for him. It bites anybody that he sets it on to.[2]

But he preferred to attack the Lords in the name of democracy. 'If a dissolution comes . . . it will come on an issue of whether this country is to be governed by King and peers or by the King and his people.'[3] Some of his colleagues, including Campbell-Bannerman, regarded his anti-Lords speeches as tactically unwise, but he was convinced that an early showdown was desirable. In after years he used to say that only he and Grey favoured a dissolution when the Lords wrecked the Birrell Bill; and, indeed, that would probably have been the most auspicious time for the Liberals. Their mandate was still relatively fresh and any lack of electoral appeal in the Bill itself might have been more than offset by their general popularity. As it was, the showdown was delayed until the Government had been in office for four years – a period long enough to weaken almost any Government, and to revive almost any Opposition. By 1908 economic conditions, which had helped the Liberals two years before, were working against them; but even if the economy had been healthy – as it became again in the latter part of 1909 – the Government's support would still have been liable to some natural erosion. As early as October 1907 Lloyd

1. Speech at Gloucester, 24 November 1906.
2. Speech in House of Commons on the second day of a debate on the House of Lords, 26 June 1907 (Hansard, Fourth Series, Vol. CLXXVI, cols 1420–35). The idea for this passage seems to have come to Lloyd George in his office, because an undated manuscript note on Board of Trade paper reads: 'Call a thing like that a revising Chamber. It is Balfour's lapdog. Anything he wants it to carry it obediently picks up. Anybody he sets it on to it barks and snarls at and even bites. No wonder he pats it and strokes it so fondly – no wonder he scolds so angrily the naughty boys who throw stones at it. It is his little pet lapdog' (L.G.P.).
3. Speech at the annual 'wine' of the Palmerston Club, Randolph Hotel, Oxford, 1 December 1906. The King, who anyway objected to Lloyd George's attacks on the Lords, was particularly resentful of his name being brought into one, and Campbell-Bannerman 'had to concoct, with Lloyd George's help, a long, soothing reply . . .' (John Wilson, C. B., p. 556).

George had come to believe that an election would deprive the Government of its independent majority.[1]

In spite of his attacks on the House of Lords and other Tory preserves, Lloyd George went to the Treasury enjoying a goodwill that extended far beyond his own party. Bonar Law wrote to congratulate him in strikingly warm terms:

> In one respect at least I am not a Tory (or what is supposed to be a Tory) – it always gives me pleasure to see success attained by merit alone & without any outside aids. Your success has been more rapid even than Mr Chamberlain's & you might now be thinking of the Scriptural warning about those of whom all men think well.[2]

When, shortly before his promotion, Lloyd George received the Freedom of Cardiff, the Lord Mayor said that the council had decided to pay him the compliment, though most of its members were opposed to him politically. And Lloyd George spoke in the same spirit at the official lunch after the ceremony:

> During the time that I have been in politics, no Welshman has been better abused and no Welshman has received more personal kindness. I never know why I am abused, and I cannot say why I have received so much kindness.

Later that day, at an evening meeting of the Cardiff Cymmrodorion Society, he explained his philosophy as a controversialist:

> I recollect what an American soldier once said when he was asked: 'When you aim your rifle at the men on the other side, do you hate them?' . . . His reply was: 'No, I don't fire at anybody. I simply fire at the line of battle.' Really, that is what I have been doing all my life.[3]

He meant what he said. Beneath his polemical ferocity there were no hidden springs of personal malice. He could hate institutions or points of view, but found it very difficult indeed to hate people. Much as he revelled

1. 'During dinner he asked my opinion as to the prospects of the party in case they went to the country on the question of the House of Lords. I sd the party would come back with a majority which would place them at the mercy of a combination of Labour & Irish votes. He then said it was exactly what he had told Herbert Lewis.' (Journal of Ellis W. Davies M.P., entry for 9 October 1907. The dinner took place at Sir Alfred Thomas's house in Cardiff on the eve of the Nonconformist convention referred to above.)
2. Bonar Law to D.L.G., 14 April 1908 (Earl Lloyd George collection).
3. Cardiff, 24 January 1908. On 13 March he received the Freedom of Caernarvon (strange that Cardiff should have honoured him first).

in a good fight, he had far more interest in achieving positive and permanent results. He therefore looked for the sort of victories in which opponents would be not only defeated, but won over; and it followed from this that he was always ready to acknowledge virtue in his opponents. His attitude is well illustrated in two sentences from a speech delivered in Birmingham Town Hall – an evocative setting for him – on 22 October 1906. After praising the people of Birmingham for their loyalty to Joseph Chamberlain, even though it had led them astray, he went on to observe that he had one reason to feel grateful for the Tariff Reform campaign:

> It has focussed the opera-glasses of the rich on the miseries of the poor. Once you do that, there is plenty of kindness in the human heart.

In those words we see the essential Lloyd George – pugnacious but also generous; stinging his adversaries with a deadly phrase ('the opera-glasses of the rich'), but a moment later showing his awareness of their fundamental decency and hinting at the possibility of consensus. Yet, as he approached one of the stormiest periods of his career, he was not only thinking of the ultimate need to reconcile Tories to a programme of social justice, he was also thinking of the immediate need to convince Labour that such a programme could and would be implemented by Liberals. In the speech, already quoted, at Penrhyndeudrath, ten days before his visit to Birmingham, he ended with a solemn warning to his own party:

> . . . I have one word for Liberals. I can tell them what will make this I.L.P. movement a great and sweeping force in this country – a force that will sweep away Liberalism, amongst other things. If at the end of an average term of office it were found that the present Parliament had done nothing to cope seriously with the social condition of the people, to remove the national degradation of slums and widespread poverty and destitution in a land glittering with wealth; if they shrink from attacking boldly the main causes of this wretchedness, notably the drink and this vicious land system; if they do not arrest the waste of our national resources in armaments; if they do not save up, so as to be able, before many years are past, to provide an honourable sustenance for deserving old age; if they tamely allow the House of Lords to extract all the virtue out of their Bills, so that when the Liberal statute-book is produced it is simply a bundle of sapless legislative faggots fit only for the fire – then a real cry will arise in this land for a new party, and many of us here in this room will join in that cry.

Eighteen months later the Liberal statute-book could not in fairness be described as 'simply a bundle of sapless legislative faggots', but the new Chancellor of the Exchequer knew that more, much more, would have to be done if the Liberals were to retain the confidence of the working class. He also knew that it was very largely up to him to take the necessary action and to give the required lead.

SIX

What Sort of Budget?

Asquith's three Budgets show very clearly the tug-of-war in his party, and in himself, between the old Liberalism of Free Trade, small government, strict financial discipline and Parliamentary reform, and the New Liberalism of State intervention and social reform. In some ways he was impeccably Gladstonian, giving satisfaction to those Liberals who felt that they had been elected to check the irresponsibility and profligacy of Tory finance. For instance, between 1906 and 1908 he reduced the national debt by an average of £15,000,000 a year, and, in spite of having a substantial surplus for each year of his Chancellorship, was extremely hesitant and cautious about committing public money to the direct relief of poverty. On the other hand, in his 1907 Budget speech he referred to the 'still unconquered territory of social reform' – rather an understatement – and set aside £1,500,000 towards an undefined measure of old age pensions which, he hoped, it might be possible to introduce the following year. He also announced that for incomes under £2,000 a year a distinction would in future be drawn between earned and unearned income, the former to be taxed at a lower rate; and he imposed a super-tax on the rates of death duty to be levied on estates of £1,000,000 and more. These were important innovations, representing a strong pull towards the New Liberalism.

All the same, the further postponement of old age pensions, and the vagueness of Asquith's language on the subject, annoyed many Liberals and angered Labour. In July 1907 the Government suffered two humiliating by-election defeats, at Jarrow and Colne Valley, in which apparently safe Liberal seats fell in turn to an official Labour candidate and an independent socialist. At the T.U.C.'s annual conference at Bath in early September a resolution was passed, not appealing or urging or even requesting, but demanding, that the Chancellor make provision for old age pensions to take effect from 1 January 1909. These storm-signals could not be ignored, and in the King's Speech at the beginning of 1908 the Government committed itself unequivocally, with the result that Asquith's third budget – introduced, by agreement with Lloyd George, after he had become Prime Minister – contained a definite proposal for old age pensions, which was to be embodied in separate, but immediate, legislation.

Since the Old Age Pensions Bill was given precedence even over the Finance Bill, it was Lloyd George's first major task as Chancellor to pilot it through the House of Commons, and he was well qualified for the task. His personal commitment to old age pensions was of long standing. He came out strongly for them in the general election of 1895, suggesting that the £5,000,000 needed to finance them should be raised by appropriating tithe, by increasing death duties, and by taxing ground-rents and royalties. In 1899 he was a member of the House of Commons Select Committee, whose recommendations showed bi-partisan support for the idea of direct State aid to old people; and according to one source, it was he who converted the chairman, Henry Chaplin, and other Tories on the Committee to the idea. During the Boer War, not the least powerful count in his indictment of the war policy was that it involved the sacrifice of old age pensions, one of which, he said, was carried away by every lyddite shell exploding on the African hills. It was very appropriate, therefore, that he should be the Minister in charge of the Old Age Pensions Bill, and it is not really an historic injustice that he, rather than Asquith, should have received most of the credit for it in the eyes of posterity.

The measure itself was bold only in the principle that it established. In other respects it was a very modest offering. Whereas the T.U.C. had demanded a pension of at least five shillings a week for everybody of sixty or over, the Government's scheme gave five shillings a week to individuals over seventy; and for couples the pension was to be 7s. 6d. Moreover, even among the seventy-year-olds not everyone was to qualify; as well as criminals, lunatics and loafers, people with incomes of more than £26 a year (or £39 a year in the case of couples), and people who would have received poor relief during the year prior to the scheme's coming into effect, were also disqualified. But the example of New Zealand rather than Germany was followed, in that the scheme was non-contributory. A contributory one would have excluded most women, and would also have been beyond the resources of many men, who already had considerable difficulty in setting aside enough money from their wages to guard against the more immediate vicissitudes of life, such as injury, sickness or unemployment. It was felt that the British working class could not be made to insure against a contingency which, for many, was remote in time as well as hypothetical.

In his speech on Second Reading Lloyd George emphasized that the Bill was only a 'first step', hinted that the Government might be willing to agree to a sliding scale instead of the proposed income limit, but warned against opponents of the Bill who were seeking to widen its scope only so that they could make it financially ruinous. The Government's scheme was 'the most liberal' to have been put forward in any country with heavy Defence responsibilities. Yet he had something to say of the much wider projects that were already taking shape in his mind:

> You have never had a scheme of this kind tried in a great country like ours, with its thronging millions, with its rooted complexities; and everyone who has been engaged in any kind of reform knows how difficult it is to make way through the inextricable tangle of an old society like ours. This is, therefore, a great experiment . . . We do not say that it deals with all the problem of unmerited destitution in this country. We do not even contend that it deals with the worst part of that problem. It might be held that many an old man dependent on the charity of the parish was better off than many a young man, broken down in health, or who cannot find a market for his labour. The provision which is made for the sick and unemployment is grossly inadequate in this country, and yet the working classes have done their best during fifty years to make provision without the aid of the State. But it is insufficient. The old man has to bear his own burden, while in the case of a young man, who is broken down and who has a wife and family to maintain, the suffering is increased and multiplied to that extent. These problems of the sick, of the infirm, of the men who cannot find means of earning a livelihood . . . are problems with which it is the business of the State to deal; they are problems which the State has neglected too long . . .[1]

Thus, very early in his Chancellorship, Lloyd George utterly repudiated the Victorian view of poverty and the Gladstonian concept of government. It was clear that, whereas Asquith had been only a half-hearted exponent

1. 15 June 1908 (Hansard, Fourth Series, Vol. CXC, cols 564–86).

3. Friends and rivals: Lloyd George with Winston Churchill at the height of their radical partnership

4a. H. H. Asquith

4b. A. J. Balfour

4c. Sir Henry Campbell-Bannerman

4d. A. Bonar Law

of the New Liberalism, Lloyd George would use the opportunities of his office to promote the sort of comprehensive social reform of which New Liberals had been dreaming.

While the Old Age Pensions Bill was in Committee it was amended in two important ways. First, a sliding scale was substituted for the fixed income limit, as Lloyd George had suggested it might be. Instead of the abrupt cut-off at a permitted maximum of £26 a year, there was to be a scale of pensions descending from five shillings a week for those with incomes of £21 a year to one shilling a week for those with £31 10s. a year. Those in the middle of the scale, who would have been entitled to a full pension under the original scheme, were to receive only three shillings a week – a feature that caused Labour M.P.s to vote against the amendment. But Lloyd George would not incur the extra cost of a sliding scale allowing the full pension to those with £26 a year. The other amendment of note cancelled the lower rate of pension for couples, and made husband and wife (or brother and sister) each qualify for the full rate of pension to which they would otherwise be entitled. This change did add substantially to the cost of the scheme.

In the debate on Report Balfour accepted, by implication, that the Bill was a money Bill which could not be amended by the House of Lords. But, while professing to 'rejoice in a policy of old age pensions', he condemned the Government's scheme on the have-it-both-ways ground that it was financially crippling without meeting the needs of the old. He also evoked the case of an imaginary Irishman from Cork by name of O'Grady who, as an unskilled labourer in London, might announce that his age was seventy and ask for a pension:

> He has no proof. Why should he have a proof? I do not believe I should know my own age if it were not that tactless friends are constantly reminding me of it. Most assuredly a dock labourer who left Cork thirty years ago may very well be excused if he has not proof of his age, since he was born in a country where there was no registration of births at the time when he was presumably born.

In such a case, argued Balfour, there could be no possibility of the legal proof of age which was 'at the very basis of the Bill'.

Lloyd George replied that the vast majority of Irish labourers would belong to trade unions:

> If there is an organization got up for the purpose of fighting anybody, you may rely upon it that an Irish labourer will be somewhere in it.

If he is a member of a trade union, then we can get at his age, for although he may overstate his age when he goes to the pension officer, he is not likely to do it to the trade union.[1]

This was a rather dubious argument, and in any case Balfour had a very good point about Irishmen's ages. Since there had been no official registration of births in Ireland before 1865, there was no hope of enforcing the age-limit there, and the number of Irish old age pensioners soon attained farcical proportions.

Nevertheless the Bill, which became law on 1 August, was on the whole a successful measure. It was certainly very popular, and not only among the Irish. After seeing it through the House of Commons Lloyd George had to dispose of the Finance Bill; but that was quite easily done, because old age pensions had been the most substantial item in the Budget. Once he had completed the business bequeathed to him by his predecessor, he was free to embark upon his own schemes. And since he had made it clear that he intended to use the power of the State to tackle the problems of sickness, infirmity and unemployment, it was hardly surprising that he travelled to the Continent, as soon as Parliament rose, mainly for the purpose of studying at first hand the German system of social welfare. Though he already knew a good deal about it from reports, he always preferred the evidence of his own eyes and ears. Besides, he was invariably glad of any excuse for a trip abroad.

First, he stayed for four or five days in Austria, at Carlsbad, having motored there by way of Amiens, Rheims, Nancy, Strasbourg (then German) and Nuremberg. At Carlsbad he gave an interview to the *Neue Freie Presse* of Vienna, the contents and repercussions of which will be considered in a later chapter. He moved from Carlsbad to Baden-Baden, again for a few days, and then by car to Frankfurt on 20 August. Margaret was not with him: his companions were the Henrys and Harold Spender. But he was at pains to inform Margaret that Julia Henry would soon be leaving the party, and that, moreover, she had 'bought some embroidered handkerchiefs for Megan'.[2] From Frankfurt the three men travelled on to Berlin, where they spent a couple of days. Then, after brief visits to Hamburg and Bremen, they returned to England in a German liner, arriving at Southampton on 26 August.

1. 9 July 1908 (Hansard, Fourth Series, Vol. CXCII: Balfour's and Lloyd George's speeches, cols 175–93).
2. D.L.G. to M.L.G., from Savoy Westend Hotel, Carlsbad, 'Tuesday morning' (N.L.W.).

Lloyd George did not waste his time in Germany. In Berlin, he toured the huge plant of the Allgemeine Electricitäts Gesellschaft, had a long session at the Imperial Old Age and Invalid Insurance offices, and was entertained to dinner by the Imperial Vice-Chancellor, Bethmann Hollweg, who, among other things, was responsible for the insurance system.[1] In Hamburg he talked at length to Herr Krogmann, president of the Seamen's Insurance Organization, whom he already knew, and visited again the harbour and shipyards that he had inspected the year before, when he was deciding what to do about the Port of London. But since he did not wish to hear only the official point of view, he also had a long interview, at Frankfurt, with the general secretary of the Social Democratic trade unions' executive; and in Berlin he talked for three hours to Edouard Bernstein, leader of the 'Revisionist' wing of the Social Democrats. On the train from Southampton to London he gave a Press representative his first reactions to the German social insurance system. He was, he said, 'tremendously impressed with the finished character and perfection of the whole machine'. But he was of opinion that the non-contributory pension was best for old people, and had yet to decide whether or not it would be possible to graft on to the non-contributory system for old age pensions a contributory system for invalidity and sickness.[2]

Within a day or two Lloyd George was in Wales staying, first, with Hudson Kearley and then with Bishop Edwards of St Asaph, for the National Eisteddfod at Llangollen. He was joined by Winston Churchill, who came with a view to discussing future Liberal policy with Lloyd George and also, with the Bishop, arrangements for his forthcoming marriage. On 12 September Churchill and Clementine Hozier were married by Bishop Edwards at St Margaret's, Westminster. Lloyd George signed the register and told a friend soon afterwards that Churchill had talked politics to him in the vestry.[3]

1. At this dinner 'they brought round great foaming glasses of beer in Prussian fashion'. Lloyd George at first looked scared but then 'his face grew resolute'. 'We must show that Great Britain is not to be left behind,' he said. (E. H. Spender, *The Prime Minister*, p. 160.)
2. *The Times*, 27 August 1908.
3. Lord Riddell, *More Pages from My Diary, 1908–1914*, entry for 'October, 1908'. Randolph Churchill has this to say of the choice of Bishop Edwards as the clergyman to marry his parents: 'There is no clue as to why the leading divine in the Church of Wales . . . was invited to perform this task; unless it was on account of the assistance he gave to Lord Randolph Churchill in 1893 when the latter made his last successful speech in the House of Commons on the Welsh Suspensory Bill' (*Young Statesman*, p. 274). Another good reason,

These two men were now entering upon their period of closest collaboration. Shortly before his appointment to the Cabinet, while his departmental sphere was still the Colonial Empire, Churchill had delivered himself – in a letter to Massingham's weekly, the *Nation* – of what amounted to a manifesto in favour of priority for social reform, which he called 'the untrodden field of politics' (as metaphors go, an improvement on Asquith's 'still unconquered territory').[1] Now, at the Board of Trade, he had scope to deploy his talents in home affairs, and his scope was enlarged by the fact that Burns, at the Local Government Board, was strongly opposed to the State interventionism in which Lloyd George believed. It was, therefore, inevitable that Churchill should become Lloyd George's chief lieutenant over the next few years, though equally inevitable that between two men of such originality and ambition there should be a certain mutual wariness and, now and then, irritation on one side or the other. For most of the time, however, they worked very well together, in a spirit of comradeship and shared excitement. Thanking Lloyd George for his wedding present of a silver fruit basket, Churchill wrote: 'It will always be preserved in my family as the gift of a remarkable man & as the symbol of a memorable political association.'[2]

One consequence of Churchill's promotion to the Cabinet had been the loss of his North-West Manchester seat at the required by-election,[3] and his return soon afterwards as one of the two Members for Dundee. His son attributes his defeat at North-West Manchester primarily to the reversion of Unionist Free Traders to their normal allegiance, and in all likelihood that was the main reason. But Manchester was the home territory of a family now increasingly in the public eye – the Pankhursts – and, although the claim of the Women's Social and Political Union to have unseated Churchill was beyond doubt a gross exaggeration, the W.S.P.U.'s hostility

---

surely, was that the Bishop was an old friend of Lloyd George and a strong influence in the Church for compromise over Education. The choice of Lord Hugh Cecil, a Conservative Free Trader, as Churchill's best man had an equally convenient symbolism.

1. *Nation*, 7 March 1908.

2. Churchill to D.L.G., 29 August 1908 (Earl Lloyd George Collection). Unfortunately, the silver basket is not, in fact, preserved in the Churchill family. Though it is impossible to say when or why it disappeared, there was no trace of it in the lists compiled for Probate either at Sir Winston's death or, recently, at Lady Churchill's (private information).

3. Under a law of 1707 those appointed to senior Ministerial posts had to vacate their seats and offer themselves for re-election. In 1919 the obligation was made not to apply within nine months of a general election, and in 1926 was finally abolished.

may, nevertheless, have been a minor contributory factor. In any case, it is important to understand that in the country as a whole the militant women's movement, led by Mrs (Emmeline) Pankhurst and her brilliant daughter, Christabel, was no longer a fringe phenomenon. It was becoming more and more of a threat not only to the Government's dignity and poise, but – more significantly – to the Liberal Party's credentials as the party of progress. In particular, it was challenging Lloyd George's good faith as a radical at the very moment when he was emerging as the supreme champion of radicalism. The challenge was seen most dramatically in an extraordinary incident in October 1908, when Lloyd George – with Herbert Gladstone, the Home Secretary – was subpoena'd to give evidence at Bow Street in a case involving the W.S.P.U. leaders, and was subjected to rigorous questioning by Christabel and Emmeline Pankhurst themselves.

First, a brief look at the background. Women had been voting in local elections for nearly forty years, but repeated attempts to win them the right to vote in Parliamentary elections had been frustrated. Denial of the right had become a manifest hypocrisy, since women were now encouraged to participate in such elections as helpers and canvassers. During the 'eighties the Tory Party began to draw upon their services through the Primrose League, and the Liberals soon followed suit by creating the Women's Liberal Federation. If canvassing for a Parliamentary candidate were not felt to be injurious to women, it was hard to pretend that casting a vote for him would, in Gladstone's words, 'trespass upon their delicacy, their purity, their refinement, the elevation of their whole nature'.[1] By the turn of the century women's suffrage motions were more or less sure to be carried in the House of Commons, but were equally sure to get no further than a symbolic vote. While New Zealand (in 1893) and the Commonwealth of Australia (in 1902) adopted women's suffrage, the mother-country adhered, perversely, to an all-male system at the level of national politics.

Until 1905 women sought the vote by strictly constitutional means, arguing their case with sweet reasonableness and keeping well within the law. But in that year militancy began when Christabel Pankhurst and Annie Kenney courted imprisonment by disorderly behaviour at a meeting

1. Gladstone said this in a letter to Samuel Smith M.P., while using his influence to bring about the defeat of Sir Albert Rollit's suffrage bill in 1892. It was defeated, but by a majority of only 23 – in spite of Gladstone's pressure – and thereafter no women's suffrage bill was defeated in the House of Commons.

in the Free Trade Hall, Manchester, which Sir Edward Grey was addressing.[1] Their action had an electrifying effect upon the public consciousness, and as the W.S.P.U.'s techniques of disruption were more widely and audaciously employed, the cause of women's suffrage became for the first time a live issue in Britain. Moderate suffragists had to admit that what they had failed to achieve in years the suffragettes had achieved within months. Apart from the great gain in publicity, there was also a concrete success when, in 1907, women were made eligible to serve on town and county councils. Yet no progress was made towards the goal of Parliamentary enfranchisement while Campbell-Bannerman was Prime Minister, even though he himself was a convinced suffragist, and even though four hundred members of the 1906 Parliament, belonging to all parties, were pledged to the principle of women's suffrage. Private members' bills were introduced in 1907 and 1908, but without Government help they made no headway.

Christabel Pankhurst had a first-class legal mind at the service of a temperament in some ways akin to that of Joan of Arc. She dominated all around her, including her remarkable mother, and the tactics of W.S.P.U. militancy were pre-eminently hers. Campaigners either had to accept her leadership or leave the W.S.P.U., because within it her authority was virtually dictatorial. In her view the lobbying of backbenchers was a complete waste of time. She had a twofold aim – to make the Government's life a misery, and to capture the imagination of the people. Liberal Cabinet Ministers were to be harried, and she made no distinction in favour of those, like Lloyd George, who were supporters of the women's cause. On the contrary, she regarded them as traitors and backsliders for not insisting upon the introduction of a franchise bill, under threat of resignation.

Asquith at least did not incur that stigma, because he was relentlessly opposed to giving women the vote. Like Gladstone he felt that it would be incompatible with their femininity, maintaining that their 'natural sphere' was 'not the turmoil and dust of politics, but the circle of social and domestic life'.[2] Soon after becoming Prime Minister he told a deputation that his was a minority view in the Cabinet since two-thirds of his

1. 13 October 1905. The two women were sentenced to imprisonment or a fine, and chose to go to prison – Annie Kenney for three days, Christabel for seven. (Annie Kenney was a mill-girl who had joined the W.S.P.U. by way of the I.L.P., becoming one of Christabel's most ardent devotees.)
2. Speech on the Rollit suffrage bill, 27 April 1892 (Hansard, Fourth Series, Vol. III, cols 1510–13).

colleagues were suffragists. The Government, he said, would introduce an electoral reform bill before the end of the Parliament, and would not, as a Government, oppose any women's franchise amendment that might be moved, provided it were on democratic lines and 'had behind it the over-whelming support of the women of the country, no less than the support of men'. Christabel Pankhurst understandably dismissed the offer as valueless, and Asquith himself said a few days later that it related to 'a remote and speculative future'.[1] Militancy continued, and in June a huge demonstration was held in Hyde Park, ostensibly to prove that women in the mass supported the demand for enfranchisement.

Lloyd George, in common with other senior ministers, had to face well-orchestrated heckling whenever he appeared on a platform, and he some-times had difficulty in getting through his speeches. But, given half a chance, he knew how to deal with hecklers. In July he was discoursing on the theme of peace when a woman in the audience shouted: 'Peace must begin at home by giving votes to women.' 'I agree', he replied, 'and I hope that that lady's home is peaceable.'[2] In early October the W.S.P.U. had handbills printed calling upon its supporters, male and female, to 'rush the House of Commons' at 7.30 p.m. on the 13th. When that evening came, about 60,000 people gathered in the neighbourhood of Parliament Square, but the Square itself was cordoned off. About 4,000 special constables were on duty, and there were scuffles as some of the demonstrators tried to break through the police lines. Twenty-four women and thirteen men were arrested, ten people were taken to hospital. One woman, who happened to be Keir Hardie's secretary, managed to reach the floor of the House of Commons, but was removed after uttering a few words.

The demonstration was a fairly quiet affair, by W.S.P.U. standards. Its importance consisted in the sequel. Mrs Pankhurst and Christabel (and another W.S.P.U. leader, Mrs Drummond) were put on trial for incite-ment to riot. On the 14th they appeared at Bow Street, but at their request the hearing of the case was adjourned for a week so that they could procure witnesses. Since it was known to them that Lloyd George and Herbert Gladstone had witnessed part of the demonstration – Lloyd George having walked with Megan from Downing Street to the House of Commons – the two Cabinet Ministers were subpoena'd to appear as witnesses for the

1. The deputation was on 20 May 1908, and the remark, in Parliament, on 26 May 1908 (Hansard, Fourth Series, Vol. CLXXXIX, col. 962).
2. Quoted in Herbert du Parcq, *op. cit.*, Vol. III, p. 596.

defence. This they did on 21 October, and the occasion was later described as 'like a suffrage meeting attended by millions'.[1]

The defendants conducted their own case and examined their own witnesses. Christabel made much of the Crown's apparent desire to deal with them by summary justice, rather than to charge them with unlawful assembly and so entitle them to trial by jury. Questioning Lloyd George, she elicited the fact that he had thought it safe to take his six-year-old daughter with him to the House of Commons, in spite of the alleged danger of a riot. She was less successful in her attempt to show that he had 'set an example of revolt' when, as a young lawyer in Wales, he had advised people to break into a churchyard. Lloyd George was able to reply that in the famous Llanfrothen burial case he 'certainly never incited a crowd to violence' and 'gave advice which was found by the Court of Appeal to be sound legal advice'. But Mrs Pankhurst, who followed her daughter, scored a big point when she led him into an expression of opinion on the nature, or at any rate the motive, of the suffragettes' militancy:

> *Mrs Pankhurst*: I want to ask you whether, in your opinion, the whole of this agitation which women are carrying on, very much against the grain, would not be immediately stopped if women got their constitutional rights . . .?
> *Lloyd George*: I should think that is very likely.
> *Mrs Pankhurst*: I want to ask you whether, in your opinion, the women who are in the dock here today are women who are ordinary law-breakers, or who would have occasion to come into this Court for any other than political reasons?
> *Lloyd George*: No, of course not.[2]

On the face of it the exchange might appear platitudinous, but Lloyd George had, in fact, conceded a point of crucial importance. For a moment he had dropped his guard and allowed himself to go on record as evidently sharing the suffragettes' view that they were political law-breakers. The corollary must have seemed to be that they should be treated as political prisoners – the very issue between them and the Crown which had been the cause of their hunger strikes and resultant forcible feeding. Since their

1. Emmeline Pethick-Lawrence, *My Part in a Changing World*, p. 205.
2. A transcript of the trial, from which the above quotation is taken, was published soon afterwards by the Woman's Press, under the title *The Trial of the Suffragette Leaders* (price one penny).

treatment in prison, more especially the practice of forcible feeding, constituted one of their strongest claims to public sympathy, Lloyd George's admission went some way towards establishing them as innocent martyrs.

The Bow Street hearing was a theatrical masterstroke by the Pankhursts, and no one was better able than Lloyd George to appreciate it as such. Experienced political agitator – and actor – that he was, he must have sensed that he was being upstaged. Yet what could he do? His mind was concentrated upon other matters, which seemed to him to have more immediate relevance to the general cause of radicalism. In 1908 his attitude was comprehensible, but should he not, perhaps, have pressed harder for a women's suffrage bill during Campbell-Bannerman's Premiership, when the Government's only measure of electoral reform was one to remove the comparatively trivial blemish of plural voting? This was rejected by the Lords on the specious but plausible pretext that the franchise should not be reformed piecemeal. But would it have been quite so easy for them to reject a bill to give women the vote? Even if they had rejected it, the Liberals would have gained a very considerable moral advantage.

Women's suffrage was a good Liberal cause,[1] and its electoral significance greater than the all-male character of the electorate may have suggested. After all, suffragettes had fathers, brothers, husbands, sons and fiancés, many of whom shared in some degree the suffragette faith, and all of whom must have been outraged when their womenfolk were maltreated. Apart from those with a direct connection, there was a much wider circle of men who believed that in natural justice women should have the vote, and to whom it must have been apparent that the State was treating the suffragettes more roughly than it had treated male agitators for the franchise. There seemed to be one law for the weaker sex, another for the stronger, and the difference favoured the strong rather than the weak.

Lloyd George cannot escape his share of responsibility for the Liberals' disastrous mishandling of the women's suffrage issue. Though a genuine suffragist, he never gave the issue the very high priority it deserved. There were, indeed, problems and complexities which will be discussed in a later chapter, but they were not of a kind to justify what the Government did and failed to do. It was a tragic irony that, as Lloyd George embarked

1. Though, oddly enough, leaders of the Liberal Party tended to be conservative on the issue, whereas Conservative leaders tended to be liberal. Gladstone and Asquith were opposed to women's suffrage; Disraeli and Balfour favoured it.

upon a momentous radical campaign as the people's champion, half of the people had to be excluded from halls where he was to speak lest they disrupt the proceedings by clamouring for their rights.

That, however, was still in the future. His immediate preoccupation was Budgetary policy for 1909, and while wrestling with a task that was as daunting financially as politically he must have regarded any other issue as a troublesome distraction.

To begin with he had a serious revenue problem. Most of the surplus in Asquith's last Budget was devoted not to building up a fund for old age pensions, as Lloyd George had a right to expect, but rather to reducing the sugar duty – an orthodox Free Trade gesture for which there was no urgent practical need. Apart from the provision of £1·2 millions for financing old age pensions in the last quarter of the financial year 1908–9, Asquith did nothing to help his successor find the money to pay for them, estimated even then at £6 millions, and later increased to £8 millions. The sum of £3·4 millions used to reduce the sugar duty would have gone some way towards paying for old age pensions in 1909–10. The loss of it was all the more acutely felt by Lloyd George since he could not anticipate a revenue surplus such as Asquith had enjoyed throughout his Chancellorship. The trade recession which hit the country in 1908, and made unemployment in that year the worst for more than two decades, was bound to have an adverse effect upon the revenue. Expenditure to which Lloyd George was already committed, without any additions to it for social or other purposes, could be met only by compensating cuts or by higher taxation.

Tariffs, of course, were taboo. It was vital for the Liberals that the problem should be solved within the Free Trade system, more especially at a time when economic conditions were inducing many people to reconsider their objections to Tariff Reform. When Joseph Chamberlain launched his campaign five years earlier he had the misfortune to run into a period of prosperity, which seemed to make a mockery of his argument that Free Trade was ruining the country; while at the same time the Liberals were united and strengthened by his challenge to their most cherished doctrine. Lloyd George himself cherished it with as much warmth as he could feel for any ideology. In his previous post he never ceased to proclaim the virtues of Free Trade, and at the Colonial Conference in the summer of 1907 he and his colleagues maintained their position against a majority of the Colonial Premiers. Yet it was obvious to him that a slump in trade would undermine popular support for Liberal economic policy, and in 1908 the slump occurred, with a corresponding slump in Liberal votes at by-elections. During the year seven seats were lost with an average anti-Liberal swing of more than 10 per cent.

Rising unemployment was by no means the only cause of disaffection with the Government, but it was almost certainly the main cause; and those who were actual or potential victims of it were naturally tempted to believe that dearer food might, after all, be a price worth paying, if there were a reasonable chance that it would help to make jobs more secure. This change of outlook was the biggest threat that Lloyd George, as Chancellor, had to face. Joseph Chamberlain, though allied to the Conservatives, was still the most radical British politician, and his fiscal programme was a truly radical programme. To counteract its appeal Lloyd George had to offer an alternative policy which would be no less radical, and no less inspiring to the masses, but without violating the principles of Free Trade. He had to prove that Liberal economics could be made to serve the contemporary needs of the people better than the economics of Protection and Preference. The challenge was congenial to him, because by temperament and mental disposition he was no less radical than Chamberlain. But unquestionably it was a very tough challenge.

At first his intentions appear to have been more moderate than they later became. Though determined to introduce a programme of wide-ranging social reform, he seems to have been reluctant to reply to the policy of taxing the foreigner (by tariffs) with one of aggressively taxing the native rich. Soon after writing to his brother that it was time the Liberals 'did something that appealed straight to the people . . . to stop the electoral rot',[1] he was telling a Welsh back-bencher of fairly advanced views that he was 'not inclined to increase income tax & death duties in case of rich', and that he thought he could 'carry on without further taxation if economy exercised by various departments'.[2] The departments he must have had chiefly in mind were the Service departments, particularly the Admiralty, and it may have been to them that he was above all referring when, a month later, he made his notorious remark during the Committee Stage of the Old Age Pensions Bill:

> I have no nest eggs at all. I have got to rob somebody's hen roost next year. I am on the look-out which will be the easiest to get and where I shall be least punished, and where I shall get the most eggs, and, not

1. D.L.G. to W. G., 6 May 1908 (*My Brother and I*, p. 220).
2. Journal of Ellis W. Davies M.P., entry for 20 May 1908.

only that, but where they can be most easily spared, which is another important qualification.[1]

There is evidence that in the late summer of 1908 he was planning to take some action against landed property.[2] Landowners as a class were a pet bugbear of his, most of them were Tories, and there was a powerful group lobbying for the taxation of land. Moreover the House of Lords had sabotaged the Government's land legislation for Scotland. But it would seem that Lloyd George was not, as yet, convinced of the necessity to mount a fiscal attack on the propertied classes along a broad front. He was well aware that the Liberal Party had many valuable supporters among the non-territorial rich, and he must also have been aware than an indiscriminate class war between haves and have-nots might play into the hands of the socialists. He was probably hoping, too, that a revival of trade would occur before the spring of 1909, and that one effect would be to swell the revenue from existing taxes.

Circumstances, however, destroyed any hopes he may have had of Budgetary moderation helping to create a large consensus for social reform. The Opposition was in no mood to make life easy for him. In the changed economic climate the Tariff Reformers sniffed victory, and Balfour, lacking the patronage of office, was unable to withstand their influence. Increasingly, Opposition policies and tactics were determined by them. Not that Balfour would have been a tame critic of the Government, in any case. His bantering philosophic manner belied his true nature, which was that of a strong partisan hungry for power. Resenting his defeat in 1906, he was ready to grasp almost any means of avenging it. Towards the end of 1908 he struck a blow, through the House of Lords, which showed unmistakably that all-out partisanship was the order of the day. The Government's Licensing Bill, designed to bring the number of public houses into a fixed relationship to the population of localities, was not, like Birrell's Education Bill, a measure that appealed only to Nonconformists. It would clearly have been more effective in combating an

1. 29 June 1908 (Hansard, Fourth Series, Vol. CXCI, cols 395–6). Lloyd George soon regretted the remark, which was much exploited by his opponents. On 29 January 1909, in a speech to the Law Society, he described it as a bad joke which 'many a dull dog has found . . . his sole substitute for humour'. On the same occasion (marking the presentation of his portrait to the Society) he went on to say: 'If a Chancellor of the Exchequer undertook the framing of a Budget in a retributive or vindictive spirit against any class, against any party, against any section, I say here he is not merely unworthy of his high office, he would not be fit to be appointed an Exciseman in a country village.'
2. See, for instance, Herbert Lewis's diary, entry for 8 September 1908 (N.L.W.).

acknowledged social evil than Balfour's Act of 1904, and when it came to the House of Lords the Church of England bishops voted for it. All the same, it was rejected there on Second Reading, in accordance with a party decision. Though the Tory leadership always had to consider the interests of the liquor trade, on this occasion the motive for what was done was more political than financial. Rejection of the Licensing Bill was a deliberate act of defiance, and was accepted in the same spirit.[1]

Shortly after the Lords' vote Churchill, sitting next to Lucy Masterman at dinner, 'stabbed at his bread, would hardly speak; murmured perorations . . . "We shall send them up such a Budget in June as shall terrify them, they have started the class war, they had better be careful".' And when she asked him how much longer he thought the Government would last, he replied: 'If they thurvive the next Budget, two or three years. That'll be the testh.'[2] Probably he meant no more than that Lloyd George was now intending to circumvent the Second Chamber by taxing liquor as well as land. Two days before Churchill's outburst Riddell was breakfasting with the Chancellor and did not find him 'at all disturbed by the fate of the Licensing Bill'. He said that 'a thanksgiving service would take place in the Treasury . . . as he was looking forward to taxing the trade'. He also 'ridiculed the rumour that the Peers would or could interfere with or reject the Budget'.[3] Next day he wrote to his brother that he was 'thinking out some exquisite plans for outwitting the Lord on Licensing'.[4]

The resolute, but still limited, Budgetary strategy of the Government was indicated by Asquith about a fortnight later in a speech at the National Liberal Club, when he said:

> I invite the Liberal Party . . . to treat the veto of the House of Lords as the dominating issue in politics . . . the Budget of next year will stand in the very centre of our work . . . Finance is an instrument of great

---

1. Commenting on it, Sir Almeric Fitzroy wrote in his diary on 24 November 1908: 'Therein the timidity of property, which is the prevailing characteristic of the House of Lords, expressed itself, as I think, disastrously for the future of that assembly. When sectional fears come to be manipulated for party ends, the claims of the House to the impartiality of a revising Chamber must necessarily be abandoned.' (Fitzroy, *op. cit.*, Vol. I, p. 367.) It was clearly his view that the Tory leadership was exploiting the Lords' veto for general political purposes.

Incidentally, the Bill contained even more stringent provisions for Wales than for England.

2. Lucy Masterman, *op. cit.*, p. 114 (diary entry for 26 November 1908).
3. Riddell, *More Pages from My Diary*, p. 10 (entry for 24 November 1908).
4. William George, *op. cit.*, p. 222.

potency and also of great flexibility . . . it may be found to be, in some directions, at any rate a partial solvent of what, under our existing Constitutional conditions, would otherwise be insoluble problems . . .[1]

Lloyd George, speaking at Liverpool ten days later, echoed the Prime Minister's words in his own more picturesque style:

> We mean to raise the taxes of the – now I am not going to tell any secrets. Yes I will. I will take you into my confidence . . . I mean to raise . . . taxes in a way that will not interfere with any productive industry in this country, and I am not going to butter anybody's bread with taxes . . . if they [the Opposition] want to put the alternative of taxing bread, by all means let them do it.

For good measure he described Tory peers as 'stuff bottled in the Dark Ages . . . not fit to drink, cobwebby, dusty, muddy, sour', and declared that the Government would not 'stand any longer the usurpation of King Lansdowne'. The issue, as he saw it, would be between 'Free institutions and Free Trade' on the one hand, 'Privilege and Protection' on the other.[2]

The aim of these speeches was to intimidate rather than provoke the Opposition, while reassuring the Government's supporters that the Lords' veto over sensitive legislation would no longer be tamely accepted, but would be circumvented by means of the Budget. There is no reason to suppose that the Prime Minister and Chancellor already knew in all essentials what the next year's financial programme would be, and none whatever to suppose that they were deliberately engineering a Constitutional conflict. But Hobhouse's diary shows that some of the proposals were already being discussed at the beginning of December, and his own typical comment is that, 'if propounded to the country, [they] ought to insure [sic] the rejection of the budget by the Lords, enforce a Dissolution, and ensure our irretrievable defeat'.[3]

It was the Board of Admiralty, and public alarm at the growth of German naval power, which finally made it inevitable that the range of taxation in the 1909 Budget should be far wider than Lloyd George initially hoped or desired. Here again he received a *damnosa hereditas* from Asquith. When the Liberals returned to power they were full of pious intentions about cutting arms expenditure and inaugurating a new era of peace. Asquith at the Treasury acted not at all as a Liberal Imperialist, but

1. 11 December 1908.
2. 21 December 1908. Lord Lansdowne was Unionist leader in the Lords.
3. Hobhouse Diaries, entry for 8 December 1908, p. 74.

rather as a Gladstonian 'economist',[1] insisting upon naval cuts. Even in early 1908, when pressure for increased naval estimates was growing, the Admiralty was forced to keep the figure well below what it regarded as necessary. During 1908 the Opposition began to make much of the naval scare, for partisan as well as patriotic reasons. The First Sea Lord, Sir John Fisher, was playing a double game. Nobody was more devoted to the Navy than he was, or had done more to make it efficient, but he had, perhaps, been rather too willing to cooperate with the Liberal economy drive. His instinct warned him against quarrelling with powerful politicians, with whom, moreover, he had considerable sympathy. Yet he was a relentless quarreller within the Service, and his feud with Lord Charles Beresford was one cause of his ambiguous behaviour in 1908.[2] He was in close touch with the Opposition through his friend J. L. Garvin, the formidable editor of Northcliffe's *Observer*, to whom he freely imparted Admiralty secrets.[3] At the same time he did not wish to antagonize Lloyd George.

During the summer of 1908 Slade, Director of Naval Intelligence, noted in his diary:

> It appears according to [Fisher] that the Cabinet is about equally divided, Lloyd George and Churchill standing for a general reduction all round so as to get money for old age pensions; Asquith, Grey and Haldane standing for keeping up our strength . . . I cannot quite understand what part [Fisher] is playing. I rather think he looks on Lloyd George as the coming man, and is inclined to play his games, but at the same time he does not want to break with the others.[4]

Asquith had indeed ceased to be a rigid 'economist' with his departure from the Treasury, and his former Financial Secretary there, McKenna, was now as First Lord a very able spokesman for the Admiralty. Lloyd George and Churchill were certainly the leading exponents of Service

1. In the political idiom of the time, 'economist' meant not a student of economics but a politician disposed to practise economy.
2. Beresford, at the time commander-in-chief of the Channel Fleet, was a menace to Fisher because he combined a following in the Navy with strong social and political connections. Throughout his professional career he was intermittently a Conservative M.P.
3. Garvin, an Irishman born on Merseyside, had exchanged Nationalism for Unionism and become the chief exponent in the Press of Joseph Chamberlain's ideas. He was also, himself, a man of eloquence and originality, whose role in Opposition politics over the next two or three years was almost equivalent to that of a Parliamentary leader.
4. Slade's 1908 diary, entry for 25 July (quoted in Ruddock F. Mackay, *Fisher of Kilverstone*, p. 409).

economy within the Cabinet, though not from the Gladstonian position of 'economists' such as Harcourt, Burns and Morley. There was, therefore, an important shade of difference among the 'economists' themselves. Lloyd George had always believed in a strong Navy and even as Chancellor could be persuaded that higher spending on it was vital for the nation's security. By New Year 1909 the Admiralty's case had been reinforced by the rumour that Germany was accelerating its naval building programme. McKenna was demanding that a minimum of six new Dreadnoughts should be laid down in 1909, and hinting that the number might have to be increased to eight. From Cannes Lloyd George wrote to Churchill: 'I believe the Admirals are procuring false information to frighten us.'[1] But his mind was not, in fact, closed to the Admiralty's arguments, and when in early February he wrote a long letter to Asquith on the naval estimates he suggested – after re-stating the case for economy – that there might be a flexible approach to the building of Dreadnoughts.[2] Towards the end of the month an apparent compromise was reached on very much the lines he had indicated. Four Dreadnoughts were to be laid down immediately, and another four to be added if the need for them were proved. In the event they were added, and anyway, so far as the Budget was concerned, the Admiralty had won.

So far from being able to economize on Defence, Lloyd George had to allow for an extra £3 millions of naval expenditure. This blow to his original intentions was balanced, as he was quick to see, by the advantage that he could accuse the Tories of having forced him to impose heavier taxes on the rich. But he still had to persuade his colleagues to accept his figure for the prospective deficit and to approve his consequent financial proposals. At a Cabinet meeting on 7 April he estimated the deficit at about £16 millions. Runciman afterwards challenged the figure on the ground that it reflected a serious underestimate of the likely revenue from existing taxation, but Lloyd George stuck to his guns and in due course carried the Cabinet with him. Indeed, it was eventually agreed that the deficit to be met should be estimated at about £16½ millions.

Granted the unprecedented scale of the Budget, how was the money to be raised? Lloyd George proposed to levy (in round figures) £13½ millions in new or increased taxation, and to make up the balance by diverting £3 millions from the Sinking Fund. The new taxes were to include a super-

1. D.L.G. to W.S.C., from the Hôtel Prince de Galles, Cannes, 3 January 1909 (quoted in Randolph Churchill, *Churchill*, Vol. II, pp. 516–17).
2. D.L.G. to H.H.A., 2 February 1909 (Asquith Papers).

tax of sixpence in the £ on the amount by which incomes of £5,000 or more exceeded £3,000; a 20 per cent tax on the unearned increment of land values, an annual duty of a halfpenny in the £ on the capital value of undeveloped land, and a 10 per cent reversion duty on benefits to lessors at the termination of leases; motor vehicle taxes varying according to horsepower, and a threepence per gallon tax on petrol; and, finally, a general tax on liquor licences amounting to roughly half the annual proceeds from the sale of drink. Those were the innovations. In addition, income tax was to go up from 1s. to 1s. 2d. in the £ on unearned incomes, and on earned incomes of over £3,000 a year, while estate and stamp duties were to be increased substantially, as were the duties on tobacco and spirits.[1] The tax on licences was to be accompanied by a reform of the licensing system, and the land taxes by a valuation of land, with a view to circumventing the Lords' veto which had recently frustrated Liberal policy in both respects.

It was no easy matter for Lloyd George to win his colleagues' support for the proposals. They were discussed at fourteen Cabinet meetings between mid-March and the last week of April, at one of which Harcourt passed a note to Runciman: 'This Budget will ensure the triumph of Tariff Reform.'[2] Seeing that its purpose was to do exactly the opposite, he could hardly have been more damning. His specific objections were to the levying of super-tax on any part of the first £5,000 of a man's income, and to the proposed scale of duty on settled estates, concerning which he wrote to Asquith: 'I don't feel sure that the Cabinet have realized the savagery of the scale on men of *moderate means*. I hope we may yet be able to reconsider it.'[3] Runciman thought that Lloyd George was making excessive use of direct taxation, and a majority of the Cabinet may have had cold feet about some proposals, including the land taxes. All the same Lloyd George was probably exaggerating his struggle in Cabinet when he told Frances Stevenson long afterwards that it was there he had 'by far the most difficult fight . . . not in the country':

Harcourt was the most inveterate in obstructing his proposals, while posing all the time as an ardent Radical. Crewe, while not liking them,

1. Scope for avoidance of estate duty was, moreover, restricted by the important new provision that gifts would be liable retrospectively if they were made less than five years before a testator's death. In connection with income tax the principle of children's allowances was introduced for parents with incomes of under £500 a year – another novelty.
2. 24 March 1909 (Runciman Papers).
3. 12 April 1909 (Asquith Papers).

said very little, Grey said nothing. But at heart they were all against him.[1]

He admitted, however, that 'Asquith alone was helpful', and this is corroborated by what he wrote at the time to his brother:

> Budgetting all day. Got on extremely well on one point where the Cabinet was very divided, but on which I was very keen. Prime Minister decided in my favour to my delight.[2]

And soon afterwards he told his friend, D. R. Daniel:

> . . . I should say that I have Winston Churchill with me in the Cabinet, and above all the Prime Minister has backed me up through thick and thin with splendid loyalty. I have the deepest respect for him and he has real sympathy for the ordinary and the poor.[3]

Relations between the two men were never more cordial.

How radical were Lloyd George's proposals? Does the 1909 Budget deserve its unique place in history for any other reason than that it precipitated a major constitutional conflict? One historian of the period has described it as 'of the old family of Budgets in its combination of direct and indirect taxation, its gathering of a handful here and a handful there', and has scouted any idea that it was 'revolutionary'.[4] But Elie Halévy calls it a 'new system of taxation',[5] and the historian of British Budgets, contrasting it with Sir William Harcourt's in 1894 – which 'dealt only or mainly with one branch of the revenue, that of the death duties' – points out that it 'not only ranged over the whole field of taxation, but was significant for its abandonment of the older limitations attaching to the raising of revenue and the open and unqualified adoption of the theory that taxation should be used for the purpose of social regeneration'.[6] It was genuinely a people's Budget in that it made far heavier demands upon the

1. Frances Stevenson, *Lloyd George: a Diary*, entry for 30 May 1936 (p. 322).
2. William George, *op. cit.*, quoting letter from D.L.G. dated 6 April 1909 (p. 223). Lloyd George later said that Asquith had decided in his favour on the land taxes, which the Cabinet would have rejected 'by an overwhelming majority' if the matter had been allowed to go to a vote (Lucy Masterman, *op. cit.*, p. 133).
3. D. R. Daniel, *op. cit.*, referring to a conversation on 21 May 1909. Lloyd George was apt at times to suggest that Churchill had been unhappy about some aspects of the Budget, because of his Blenheim connection. But any doubts or regrets he may have felt were very effectively concealed from the public.
4. R. H. Gretton, *A Modern History of the English People, 1880–1922*, p. 761.
5. *The Rule of Democracy*, p. 291.
6. Bernard Mallet, *British Budgets 1887–1913*, pp. 298–9.

rich than upon the poor, for whose benefit, moreover, a large part of the new revenue was to be employed.

Admittedly, as a recent writer has observed, the liquor and tobacco taxes were to yield 'a greater percentage of the total revenue . . . than in any other Budget since the war Budget of 1900'.[1] But Lloyd George was sincere in regarding drink as a menace from which he ought to do all he could to liberate the poor, and he could not regard tobacco as a necessity of life in the sense that food was. For the rest, his taxes bore preponderantly upon those who could best afford to pay. In 1909 only about one million people paid income tax, among whom only a small proportion – the big earners and the non-earners – were affected by his income tax increase. At most 12,000 people would have to pay super-tax, and only about 80,000 were liable to estate duty. Land taxes, stamp duty and the taxes on motorists – then a very small class – had a similarly restricted incidence. The Budget may not have been revolutionary, since it built upon existing foundations as well as adding much that was new. Radical it certainly was.

But was it concocted as a deliberate trap for the Lords? In a book which has had much influence Mr George Dangerfield maintains that it was, drawing upon his rich resources of imagery:

> . . . here was a Budget crying to be vetoed. It was like a kid, which sportsmen tie up to a tree in order to persuade a tiger to its death . . .[2]

Much the same has been implied by several other writers, including at least two of Lloyd George's biographers.[3] Yet the weight of more recent opinion is towards the contrary view. Mr Roy Jenkins suggests that the Chancellor's 'primary object was to circumvent the [Lords'] veto rather than to destroy it';[4] Mr Colin Cross that 'Asquith and Lloyd George intended the Budget to be a means of by-passing the Lords' veto, not of smashing it';[5] and Dr Neal Blewett that it is 'most unlikely that the Cabinet intended to provoke a decisive conflict with the Lords over the Budget'.[6] Dr Bruce Murray, however, hedges his bet with the suggestion

---

1. Samuel J. Hurwitz, *State Intervention in Great Britain*, p. 13.
2. George Dangerfield, *The Strange Death of Liberal England*, p. 20.
3. 'To Lloyd George it was clear that there must be a fight to curb the Lords' power of veto.' (Malcolm Thomson, *David Lloyd George*, p. 178.) 'In this mixed spirit of sincere social crusading and deliberate political provocation, Lloyd George had framed the People's Budget.' (Frank Owen, *Tempestuous Journey*, p. 170.)
4. Roy Jenkins, *Mr Balfour's Poodle*, p. 41.
5. Colin Cross, *The Liberals in Power, 1905–1914*, pp. 101–2.
6. Neal Blewett, *The Peers, the Parties and the People: the General Elections of 1910*, p. 54.

that Lloyd George was hedging his: 'The evidence is . . . that Lloyd George devised his Budget as something of a "catch all" that would serve to promote the Liberal cause irrespective of what happened to his proposals in the Lords.'[1] No doubt he was preparing against all eventualities, but surely his rational hope must have been that the Lords would submit without a fight.

For all his combativeness and brilliance in debate, Lloyd George was above all interested in constructive achievement. He wanted to be remembered for Acts of Parliament rather than perorations; for things done rather than points scored. It would have been quite out of character for him to put together a financial programme as vast and complex as that of the 1909 Budget with no other purpose than that it should be rejected by the Lords. It was the biggest piece of work he had ever attempted and he must naturally have wished to see it through. To jeopardize it gratuitously would have been against all his instincts.

He knew that if the Lords threw it out there would have to be an immediate election, in which the Government might be defeated and his Budget, consequently, lost. Economic conditions were still unfavourable, and it was because he did not count upon their early improvement that he had contested Runciman's optimistic forecast of the revenue from existing taxes. Even if the Government were not actually beaten it could hardly expect to repeat the landslide of 1906, and there was, to say the least, a strong possibility that it would lose its independent majority. Lloyd George could not have relished the thought of being subject to an Irish veto, which was scarcely preferable to that of the House of Lords. He had always been more Chamberlainite than Gladstonian in his view of the Irish question, and was fully conscious of the advantage of not being at the mercy of Irish Nationalist votes in the House of Commons. Resuscitation of the Home Rule issue could only have the effect of antagonizing many people in Britain who might otherwise be attracted by his social policy. The Tories already had a rival popular cause in Tariff Reform; Ireland would give them another. As a constitutional issue, defence of the Union would have far wider mass appeal than defence of the House of Lords, for which, however, it would also serve as a plausible justification.

Lloyd George had to show that the Liberal Government could deliver the goods. He had to revive the enthusiasm of its supporters in the country. He had to hold the confidence of trade unionists and check the emergence

1. Bruce K. Murray, 'The Politics of the "People's Budget"' (article in the *Historical Journal*, XVI, 3, p. 555).

of Labour as a separate political force. The supremacy of the elected Chamber had to be asserted, as it would be if the Lords felt obliged to pass his Finance Bill. Since tradition appeared to put them under an obligation to do so, he had reason to hope that he would recapture the initiative for Liberalism without a premature election, and while the 1906 Parliament still had half its term to run. On the other hand, he knew that the Opposition was in fighting mood, and was ready, if necessary, to go into battle himself. The terrain would be dangerous and the outcome uncertain, but there would also be special scope for a man of his talents, convictions and prejudices.

Before the struggle began, however, he had to face and ward off an attack which, if successful, would have prevented him from introducing his famous first Budget and would, indeed, have put an end to his career. Early in 1909 the *People* newspaper hinted in a series of articles that the Chancellor of the Exchequer was to have been cited as co-respondent in a divorce case, but that the would-be plaintiff had been bought off for £20,000. This was not the first time that Lloyd George had been threatened with similar disgrace. In 1897 he had escaped, in rather mysterious circumstances, from being cited as co-respondent in the divorce action brought by Dr David Edwards, of Cemmaes in Montgomeryshire, against his wife Catherine. At that time he was only a back-bench M.P., whose political fate was of less concern, one way or the other, than it had become by 1909. Even so, if he had been cited and the case had been proved, he would have had to resign his seat in Parliament.

According to the standards of Victorian and Edwardian England, the only breach of sexual morality that a public man had to avoid, if he wished to stay in public life, was any that had the effect of breaking his own, or somebody else's, marriage. Fornication and adultery were not, in themselves, a threat to his career. The Press did not pry into his extramarital affairs, nor did the State treat them as a matter of legitimate public concern. But the institution of marriage was regarded as sacrosanct even by the relatively irreligious, for the sound practical reason that its stability was thought to be vital to the happiness, welfare and proper upbringing of children, and to that extent vital to the stability of society. Public men were therefore required to set an example, and paid the extreme political penalty if they failed to do so. No doubt the system was hypocritical, but surely it was better than one in which those who break marriages suffer no interruption of their careers, whereas those who are exposed by a lubricious Press in casual but compromising situations are as likely as not to be forced to resign.

In 1909 Lloyd George could not afford to have it said of him that he had avoided fatal incrimination only by the payment of hush-money. He sued the *People* for libel and retained the professional services of Rufus Isaacs, Raymond Asquith (the Prime Minister's son), and his friend and political opponent, F. E. Smith. The case was heard on 12 March, when Lloyd George, accompanied by Margaret, appeared in court and testified on oath that there was no truth in the allegations. Counsel for the *People*, Sir Edward Carson, then grovelled on behalf of his clients, and in due course £1,000, voluntarily paid in damages, was used for building a village institute at Llanystumdwy. One writer has suggested that the woman in the alleged affair was a 'musical comedy actress', and that Asquith himself 'personally interceded' with her. But he fails to provide any evidence for the story.[1]

The year before, Lloyd George had survived a less serious defamation, when he sued the owners of the *Bystander* for an item appearing in that paper's issue of 29 July 1908:

> All is not going well with Mr Lloyd George in his new and exalted sphere. Not only is he having a most uncomfortable time of it politically . . . but rumour is now busy as to the existence of embarrassment of another kind, which is even less likely to prove of assistance to his career. Mr George has, of course, been overloaded with flattery of late, especially from the fair sex, which is always difficult for a man of 'temperament' to resist. The matter may, of course, be kept quiet. Also, it may not. 'Nous verrons.'

The case was settled out of court, with the owners agreeing to publish a complete retractation and paying 300 guineas to the Caernarvon Cottage Hospital.

'No smoke without fire' is a normal human suspicion and, where Lloyd George is concerned, particularly hard to resist. But just as witty men tend to be credited with witticisms that are not their own, so men of strong sexual appetite and appeal tend to acquire a reputation far in excess of reality. Lloyd George was too busy with politics – always the dominant passion of his life – to be as busy womanizing as he is generally supposed to have been. All the same it is now possible to show with hard evidence what may have given rise to the *Bystander* story in 1908; also that the *People*

1. Donald McCormick, *The Mask of Merlin*, p. 310.

case was not the only threat to his peace of mind while he **was** preparing the 1909 Budget.

The earlier trouble occurred three months after his appointment as Chancellor, and it may well have been a direct or indirect consequence of a decision to have no more to do with Miss G—— G——. This, at any rate, is the interpretation suggested by a bundle of letters written from her to him at the time of his appointment in April 1908. There are six letters in all, one written on 10 April, two on the 11th, one on the 12th and two on the 13th. They document a silly young woman's attempt, necessarily short-lived, to take possession of Lloyd George and to become his Egeria.[1]

G—— G—— is unknown to history, but her family name was quite well known in Liberal politics. According to herself, she belonged to 'two sets – the smart social set . . . & the smart literary & political'. She read poetry and traded political gossip. Lloyd George seems to have given her some encouragement, though she does not claim that they had yet become lovers. She addresses him, irritatingly, as 'Dear Bird'.

In the first letter she writes:

I was disappointed that the Chancellor could not kiss hands on appointment. I wish you could have contrived to have left a message for me with Mr Clark . . .

Everyone acclaims your supposed appointment . . .

Mamie [a special friend with whom she has been discussing her affairs] . . . couldn't see why I wanted to marry at all, as I had everything I wanted etc. [but] the danger 'would be that when my outlook on life & its demands became different' we would find it impossible to continue our friendship on the purely platonic grounds it is now on. That we had managed so well up to date & no one had heard a whisper (I mean the people who matter). I agreed with her – recognized the danger – hoped nothing would arise – but was prepared quite calmly to face anything that did: & said that it was accepted fact that a statesman might have a married woman to 'run him' as the saying is – & that I meant to be that woman & must be content with that – that my house should become the 'most famous in the whole of Athens' – that anything that I could do to help you & your family, socially – I should do.

She said 'Don't be in a hurry – I *feel* this will come right: & it is so good – it is worth waiting for'.

1. The letters are in Earl Lloyd George's collection.

I said 'It would be so wonderful – that I have little hope; but I shall do nothing [i.e. shall not get married] till the summer . . .'

In the second letter she reports Mamie as being 'frightfully proud' of her (G.'s) success, and as looking forward to the time when she will be able to feel that her best woman friend has 'achieved greatness'. In the third she remarks, part-waspishly, part-wistfully: 'All Liberal statesmen are devoted to their wives & are most domestic'; and she adds the p.s. 'Swinburne has written a fine new poem'.

The next letter, which was the second written on 12 April, carries further her idea of organizing the Lloyd Georges' social life:

Lady Salomons has asked me over on Saturday. They will be going to town after Easter. I will ask her to call on your wife – there is a girl in the family about the age of yours. You see, Bird, the very fact that you don't care whether you become Premier or not will give it to you in all probability – & that is why I want to collect round you and yours the people that I should bring if I could be really with you: & the young people whom I should want your children to be friends with . . . Reginald Salomons I am sure will come in useful: he is an extremely nice fellow.

On the following day she writes about Winston Churchill:

. . . I always hear, that no one can nail Winston down to any particular lady – & that the opinion is that 'he is not a lady's man', though Mamie told me once that he had a rather curious way of looking at a woman . . . The curious fact is that people do not much like a man who doesn't care for someone – & a politician's most valuable asset is: his love for some woman. Best of all – for his wife: & Winston would become a million times more popular if it could be thought that he cared enough for some one woman to risk even a little discomfort for her sake. Perhaps it will come but I doubt it.

This shows her judgment to have been defective; but far more so what follows:

Now: will you tell *all* the Secretaries at the Treasury that 'Miss G.——' is to be treated with consideration & put on to you at once & all that sort of things. Now that I have found my feet I shall drop all concealment and come as Miss G.—— quite simply. There is less likely to be any mystery or ridiculous bother if you leave Mr Clark behind [i.e. if he, whom she already knows, and who knows her, does not accompany Lloyd George to the Treasury]. I shall probably have to get to know one of your new Secretaries – for all our sakes – so as to get him to send me answers to invitations etc. as your manners are past praying for . . .

She says that she will leave '400 Mayfair' – her previous code-name and presumably her address – 'behind with Winston Churchill at the Board of Trade'. Then she loses her balance completely. The other people in the house have gone to church, but

I say, they may win golden crowns in the next world – but I shall have a diamond tiara in this.

I want to go to court with a pretty spiky tiara set far back & my hair waved into little curls all round it.

Diamonds are my birth stone & I love them. If anything untoward happened – to enable me to be with you – we would bust a fair amount of the Chancellor's screw on a gorgeous tiara.

Her last letter, written on the same Sunday, hints that the 'untoward' might, after all be possible:

I am wanting to send you a white rose to celebrate the new appointment . . .

Count Witte [the Russian statesman] married a divorced woman & the English Embassy received her first – & led the way for general reception. So in return England obtained the first concessions. I am hungry for news & have more to give.

And she adds: 'I come up on Wed: 22nd to a flat in the next street to Mamie.'

We may be sure that her visitors there did not include Lloyd George. What could have seemed to him more ghastly than a woman who claimed preferential treatment from his secretaries, who had the effrontery to suggest that she would act as social procuress for him and his family, who dared to imply that she would 'run him', who even hinted at the possibility of marrying him, and who – to cap it all – imagined him buying her a diamond tiara to wear at Court? We do not know how he managed to choke her off, but the fury of a woman scorned (or the gossip of 'Mamie' and other friends) may have had something to do with the *Bystander* item three months later. At all events the correspondence, which seems to have been one-sided, ceased – but he kept her letters.

He also kept two letters written to him nearly a year later by a very different sort of woman, and with far more serious and disturbing subject-matter. They are preserved in a black-edged envelope inscribed, in his hand, 'Private. D.Ll.G.', and they came from a Mrs G——[1] whose address was in the Alexandra Park district of north London.

The first is dated simply 'Monday', but from the precise date of the next one we can tell that it was written on 22 March 1909 – that is to say, ten days after the *People* hearing, and about five weeks before he was due to introduce his Budget. It reads:

Dear Mr George,

I wrote to you on Wednesday to Downing St. [This first letter is missing.] I have no doubt it reached you. I again do so to implore you to accede to my request & also to let me have the two photos of my little son. Surely I am entitled to a reply if it were only in respect to the photos. Must I get a solicitor to write to you before you will reply? Do not think this is a threat far from it, but I want an answer & this I will have but I certainly do not want it through a medium viz a solicitor for your sake I would avoid this. I know it is a critical time with you almost the eve of the Budget, & I am sorry in consequence to trouble you, but my affairs *to me* are equally important & I do now from the bottom of my heart, I appeal to you on my knees to spare me this money [then 'or if' scratched out]. You cannot know what it will mean to me & it will make no difference to you. Or ought I to appeal to Sir G. Lewis [solicitor] & put the facts to him? I ask you as one of your own countrywomen. Do, I beg & beg you to save further annoyance send me a word & dont forget the photos some time please. I must have an answer.

Yours sincerely
M. G——

PS. Do it for my boys' sake please altho' I have never hurt you by word or deed God knows.[2]

Lloyd George evidently answered this letter at once, returning the photographs but not sending any money, because on the 25th Mrs G—— wrote again:

1. Her name also began with G, but she is not to be confused with Miss G—— G—— of the previous correspondence.
2. Earl Lloyd George's collection.

Dear Mr George,

I must write to you in reply to the letter sent with the photos & for which I thank you.

Do you think I would appeal for help did I not need it in the first place it is anything but pleasant to have to ask & the fact that my husband's earnings are 30/– does not make it conclusive that I can do without it, this remark of yours was quite uncalled for.

Had you pondered & considered the case you would have said well the letter states that the boots cost 33/– more than the weekly wage therefore help must be required, instead of which you choose to insult me. The fact that that money has gone to Institutes does not affect me. I again appeal to you to help me & this time I ask you to do it out of your own free will & not to consult others. You know in your heart that to live on 30/– pay, rent, coal, food, clothes & [?] must be a fearful struggle & to add to it a little child under a specialist for years to come. Without the last burden some people who have not been used to better things might be able to do it, supposing you were not in your present position, pause for a moment could you do it? Through the influence of a dear old friend Mrs Guthrie Jones Dolgelly I am able to see the specialist free, but instruments & such like I must pay for. I was for 6 weeks in Liverpool attending the surgery daily. Will it touch some chord of sympathy when I tell you that every day my baby's feet (only about 10 weeks old) were put on blocks & twisted until they bled. [This made her cry so much that she suffered a rupture which entailed more expense. After more medical details] . . . so you see how welcome that £10 would be it would set us up for the year. Mr George let this be the last time I need write to you in this strain. I ask you to spare a few minutes of your valuable time & go back to the time when you first knew me, come along gradually to the present stage. Your verdict will be when you have well weighed the whole facts that you have treated me most unfairly & cruelly. Do you remember that time you asked me down to Wandsworth in reference to a berth for Mr G——, well I spent my last penny in fares & yet you did not as much as ask me if I had enough to take me home. I shall never forget how I felt, brokenhearted hungry & sore. I thought then your colleague would not have dismissed me like that, he has a heart of gold, you know who I mean. I don't want to waste more of your time. I will just wind up by saying that I shall pray to God to open your heart now don't let me lose faith in Him I am asking you as a friend so please don't treat me as the rest that applied to you for charity, it was unkind of you to do so in the first place. You know I do not want to have the feeling that I hate you hate everything in connection with you you'll admit I have good cause so don't dear friend refuse . . . it will be entirely between you & me if you do it . . . Mr George if you have a spark of feeling you will not keep me in suspense Oh do it do it please please. I shall meet you again some day. Things will be different then, in the meantime I do not want to harbour unkind thoughts & I don't want you to do so either. Heaven bless you if you do it.

Yours faithfully
M. G——

These sad letters, in which unction and menace alternate, might appear to convict Lloyd George of terrible heartlessness. But we do not know his side of the story, except in so far it can be deduced from the letters, objectively considered. Moreover, we have to remember that prominent men are natural targets for blackmail, and that unless they stand firm against it they are lost.

What can we deduce from the letters? It seems unlikely that Mr and Mrs G—— were the couple involved in the *People's* allegation, if indeed such a couple existed. But it is, surely, more than likely that Mrs G—— was encouraged by reading about the *People* case in the newspapers to write to Lloyd George reminding him of some past indiscretion, and using it as an excuse for demanding money. It is hard to say whether the photographs referred to were of an older child or of the ailing baby, but in any case there is a distinct innuendo that Lloyd George was the father of the child in the photographs. Since Mr G—— appears to have been a seaman of sorts (for whom Lloyd George may have been able to obtain a berth through his contacts in the merchant shipping world), there could have been opportunities for cuckolding him while he was away at sea.

On the other hand Mrs G—— is not a witness who inspires very much confidence. Her invidious reference to Lloyd George's 'colleague' who, she says, would have treated her so much better than he did, damages her rather more than it damages Lloyd George, because it shows unmistakably the sort of woman she was. She had a grudge against the world as well as against Lloyd George (apparent in her reference to the 'better things' that she has been used to), and she is obviously very ready to find a scapegoat for troubles that she has brought upon herself. It is reasonable to assume that in her original letter (not preserved) she mentioned the damages that

Lloyd George had received from the *People*, suggesting that he ought to spare some of the money for her. This would explain his insistence that it went to charity. We can hardly blame him for not sending her money, when to have done so might have established her claim to further blackmail.

Lloyd George's sexual behaviour may not have been very admirable, but at least he was free from the gravest defect that a glamorous man can have in his dealings with women, that of romanticizing his lust. He did not lead them astray by making them believe that he would sacrifice everything for their sakes. On the contrary, even with the two women whom he really loved he was brutally frank about his priorities, telling Margaret before they married that he would 'thrust even love itself' under the wheels of his 'Juggernaut' if it obstructed his ambition, and explaining to Frances Stevenson that he would have her as his mistress only on strict terms convenient to himself. Any woman who succumbed to him, therefore, had no right to complain that she had been deceived. Whatever else Mrs G—— may have been, she was no Tess of the d'Urbervilles.

Somehow or other she must have been fixed. Perhaps money was paid to her in such a way that it could not be traced to any individual, least of all Lloyd George. (Lord Riddell might have contrived a means of doing it.) Or perhaps no money was paid and she gave up trying to extract any. Whatever happened, Lloyd George remained Chancellor of the Exchequer and completed the preparations for his Budget.

SEVEN
The Road to Limehouse

Budget day was 29 April and Lloyd George introduced his proposals in a speech that lasted four and a half hours, even though he circulated in the morning a paper containing a good deal of background information normally included in a Budget statement. He began his speech with a very long apologia, explaining why the Budget had to be so large and giving a full, reasoned account of its ulterior objectives. After dealing, first, with the naval programme, he turned to social reform and said that the Government was considering how best to provide for 'the most distressing and the most deserving cases of poverty':

> In this country we have already provided for the aged over seventy. We have made pretty complete provision for accidents. All we have now to do to put ourselves on a level with Germany – I hope our competition with Germany will not be in armaments alone – is to make some further provision for the sick, for the invalided, for widows and orphans. In a well-thought-out scheme, involving contributions from the classes directly concerned, the proportion borne by the State need not, in my judgment, be a very heavy one, and is well within the compass of our financial capacity . . . The Government are also pledged to deal on a comprehensive scale with the problem of unemployment.

Trade, he said, had its currents and tides which were beyond human control, but:

> it is poor seamanship that puts out to sea without recognizing its restlessness, and the changefulness of the weather, and the perils and

suffering thus produced. These perils of trade depression come at regular intervals, and every time they arrive they bring with them an enormous amount of distress. It is the business of statesmanship to recognize that fact, and to address itself with courage and resolution to provide against it.

He announced that the scheme of unemployment insurance on which the Board of Trade had been working was already 'far advanced', and that it would be facilitated by the national system of labour exchanges promised in the last King's Speech.

Lloyd George's preliminary survey was not, however, confined to social reform. He also had much to say of development, for it was his view that the country's natural resources were shamefully neglected. There were 'millions of acres . . . more stripped and sterile than they were, and providing a living for fewer people than they did, even a thousand years ago – acres which abroad would either be clad in profitable trees or be brought . . . to a higher state of cultivation'. He gave figures to show how poorly British forestry compared with that of Continental countries. To improve Britain's showing in such matters he proposed to concentrate all the money spent 'in a spasmodic kind of way' on various types of development in a single grant, to the aggregate of which he would add, in the first year, £200,000. Moreover, surpluses accruing either from unexpectedly large revenue or from savings on estimates would in future be channelled into the fund for development rather than into the Sinking Fund.

Road-building was excluded from the scope of the concentrated Development Grant, but not because there was any lack of urgency about the road problem. Though Britain was far ahead of all other European countries in the number of motor vehicles on its roads, the roads themselves were quite inadequate for the new form of traffic they had to bear:

> If there be any truth at all in Ruskin's assertion that 'all social progress resolves itself into the making of new roads', it must be admitted that we have been lamentably deficient. The State has for a very long period done nothing at all for our roads. I believe that no main road has been made out of London for eighty years. We have no central road authority . . . Both the general public and motorists are crying out for something to be done, and we propose to make a real start.

The proceeds of the new taxes on motorists would go into a special Road Fund, which would be used to finance the building of new roads – with compulsory purchase, where necessary – and to subsidize the improvement of existing roads by local authorities. Both functions were to be carried out by a central Road Board. The idea of earmarking particular taxes for particular tasks is incompatible with modern finance, and the Road Fund did not long survive intact. But the 1909 Budget marks the assumption by the State of important new responsibilities for transport, and foreshadows Lloyd George's creation of a Ministry of Transport ten years later.

While disclosing the details of his tax proposals he went out of his way to explain that his imposts on land were aimed at urban and mineral, rather than at agricultural, property. As a back-bencher he had attacked land-owners with indiscriminate gusto, but as Chancellor he was at pains to acknowledge their difficulties in a time of depression, and the amount of money they had put into the land. The value of agricultural land had not, he conceded, risen for twenty or thirty years in most parts of the country, and in some had probably gone down. Yet there had been an enormous increase in the value of urban and mineral property, and the enhanced value of urban land was due, moreover, entirely to 'the enterprise and the energy of the community', while the mineral royalty-owner contributed nothing to a process in which the capitalist risked his money and the miner his life. The proposed land valuation would standardize records, and would distinguish between the inherent value of land and that which was added to it by owners' improvements.

Lloyd George's peroration was brief but telling:

> This is a war Budget. It is for raising money to wage implacable warfare against poverty and squalidness. I cannot help hoping and believing that before this generation has passed away we shall have advanced a great step towards that good time when poverty, and the wretchedness and human degradation which always follow in its camp, will be as remote to the people of this country as the wolves which once infested its forests.[1]

The speech as whole, however, was not an oratorical success. Most accounts describe it as wearisome and the reason is clear. Lloyd George normally learnt his speeches by heart, so that they had the advantage of being carefully prepared without the disadvantage of being read. He would have notes in front of him while speaking, but would refer to them only if he lost the thread of his remarks. Unfortunately a speech as massive and

1. Hansard, Fifth series, Vol. IV, cols. 472–548.

intricate as the Budget speech could not be memorized, and he had to read it from a complete text. Since this was a form of delivery both unfamiliar and uncongenial to him, the result was a poor performance. 'He stumbled over the sentences, rushed past full stops, paused at the commas and altogether gave the impression that at these points he did not himself understand what he was saying.'[1] But Lloyd George felt he had done what he set out to do, which was not, on this occasion, to enthral his audience with the power of the spoken word:

> ... G. said he had determined from the start that he would not aim for *hwyl* and oratory. He had another aim – to set down a manifesto ... the new principles of a country's taxation, something which he hopes will be referred to and quoted whatever the fate of the Budget. 'And it *reads* very well', said G., 'whatever its performance. Mr Gladstone made many masterly speeches, powerful, sweeping ones for his Budgets. But who reads them today?'[2]

Lloyd George was flattering himself if he believed that his speech, apart from the peroration, would be any more widely read than Gladstone's in after years. But he was justified in regarding the contents as vastly more important than the delivery.

When he had been speaking for three hours, from three o'clock to six, there were signs that his voice was failing and Balfour chivalrously moved that the House should adjourn for half-an-hour. No formal question was put. Balfour

> half rose from his seat and bent across the table, his head low, as one not wishing to attract attention. Mr Asquith bowed over to meet him, and the Prime Minister and the ex-Prime Minister talked for a second or two in a whisper.
>
> 'Half an hour, yes, half an hour,' nodded Mr Balfour, raising his whisper. The next minute the great assembly melted away. It seemed as though the House had divined as one man the suggestion made half audibly across the table. The members of the House of Commons adjourned themselves for half an hour ...[3]

During the short break Lloyd George may have fortified himself with a hot drink, because Megan said: 'Mr Balfour gave Daddy a cup of beef

---

1. Austen Chamberlain, *Politics from Inside*, quoting from a letter he wrote on 30 April 1909 (p. 177).
2. D. R. Daniel, *op. cit.*, quoting from conversation with D.L.G. on 21 May 1909.
3. Charles T. King, *The Asquith Parliament*, pp. 306–7.

tea when he was tired.'[1] After the interval he spoke on until eight o'clock. Austen Chamberlain then gave the Opposition's first reaction to the Budget[2] and there was a short debate, which concluded with another speech by Lloyd George. Despite the earlier momentary appearance of fatigue, his stamina was more than equal to the day's exertions. Next morning he played a round of golf at Walton Heath and did the first hole in par.

Austen Chamberlain's speech on Budget day is of the greatest interest, because it contains none of the fire and brimstone that might be expected in view of the line soon to be taken by the Opposition towards the Budget. His first general comment suggests admiration tinged with awe:

> He sketched a Budget not for the year only, but for a series of years; and he not only sketched the Budget for a series of years, but he sketched ... a legislative programme trenching ... upon the province of almost every one of his colleagues – a programme of such magnitude and complexity that it is not a question of one or two years before it can be carried out; it is much more likely to be two or three Parliaments before that vast programme can be achieved. With a good deal of what he said and with a great number of the objects which he set before the House I, for one, heartily sympathize ...

Chamberlain's criticisms of the Budget were mild and measured, but later in the debate John Redmond, the Irish leader, denounced it as a 'very serious injustice' to Ireland and served notice that his Party would 'oppose it on every possible opportunity'. His complaint was that the new indirect taxation, and more especially the whisky tax, would bear unduly hard upon Ireland. Another strong critic was Sir Frederick Banbury, Member for the City of London, who promised 'strenuous opposition to ... the maddest Budget ever introduced in the House of Commons'.

On 3 May Balfour opened a full-dress debate on the Budget resolutions. In spirit, if not in style, his speech was nearer to Banbury's than to Chamberlain's. The rise in taxation of property, both income and capital, was, he said, 'almost dangerously steep'. He defended personal wealth:

> ... what we are suffering from now is not having too many rich men, but having too many poor men. I, at all events, quite clearly take the

1. Herbert du Parcq, *op. cit.*, Vol. III, p. 529.
2. It was not then the custom, as it is now, for the speech immediately following the Budget speech to be made by the Leader of the Opposition. Austen Chamberlain, as the last Chancellor of the Exchequer in the Balfour Administration, was the chief Opposition spokesman on finance.

opinion . . . that the community does not lose by having men of great wealth among it. On the contrary, I think it gains. Of course, if you make poor men less poor by having fewer great fortunes, that is another matter; but I do not think you do. If you do not, nothing whatever is gained by frightening capital, by inducing rich men to accumulate their fortunes and to spend them elsewhere than in this country . . .

He condemned the land taxes as inequitable and inspired by partisan spite, while also questioning their economic value:

This is a Budget for producing willing sellers. How many willing buyers are there going to be to redress the balance? It seems to me the whole idea of taxing these expectations . . . is in itself extremely rash and extremely doubtful. If you are going to do it at all, how can you stop at expectations about land? There are heaps of other expectations in the world which have a market value . . .

And he attacked the liquor duties, with a shrewd appeal to resentment of them in Scotland and Ireland: 'Is he doing it because he wants to get more revenue out of those two parts of the country, or . . . because he wishes to make Scotchmen and Irishmen more sober than they are?'

His final words were blistering:

How different is this finance from that which was proposed to the House of Commons and accepted by the country at the hands of those whom hon. gentlemen opposite, as I think most absurdly, claim as their fiscal ancestors. How widely does it differ from the principle which underlay the Budgets of Sir Robert Peel and Mr Gladstone . . . You have apparently made it your principle to distinguish arbitrarily between one kind of property and another. So blind and ignorant are you of the fact that it is impossible to attack one kind of property . . . without throwing a shade of fear . . . and suspicion over every other class of property. Much of the evil you have done has been done even by the fact of your proposals. Whatever the House may do with them, even the fact that you have proposed them . . . has disturbed the mind of everybody who reflects on the many conditions on which an individualistic society, so long as it lasts, can alone flourish. Your scheme is arbitrary and unjust . . . by the very proposals you have made you have given a shock to confidence and credit, which will take a long time to recover.[1]

1. Hansard, Fifth Series, Vol. IV, cols. 749–773.

Lloyd George used to say of Balfour that he had an eye for the future, and certainly his strictures on the 1909 Budget seem rather more valid in a long perspective than they could have seemed to dispassionate observers at the time, of whom, however, there were extremely few.

No less important than Balfour on the Opposition side was a man who was unable (though still a Member) to speak in Parliament, and who was out of the country when Lloyd George introduced his Budget. In July 1906 Joseph Chamberlain had suffered a stroke which left him a cripple with speech permanently impaired. His mind was still active and alert, but he could communicate his thoughts only in what Garvin called 'smothered words'. At the time of the Budget he was in the South of France, but as soon as news of it reached him he decided to return home immediately. Though he could not campaign against it he was determined to use all his influence and authority to bring about its rejection by the Lords. Like Gladstone twenty years earlier he was an old man in a hurry. He wanted to see the fulfilment of his dream of Tariff Reform and an Empire consolidated by Preference. The Budget was both a mortal threat to his ideas and a glorious opportunity: while destroying his argument that tariffs were the only means of financing social reform, it was itself vulnerable to the charge that it would put the country on the road to socialism. Notwithstanding all that he had said against the House of Lords earlier in his career, he now had no compunction about using the Lords' veto as the only instrument which could force a dissolution and so precipitate, in what appeared to be favourable circumstances, a popular choice between his radical programme and Lloyd George's. While Balfour and Lansdowne still hesitated to risk the Constitution for the chance of regaining power. Chamberlain was resolute. For him it was now or never.

On 3 May the Press reported a statement by Lord Ridley, who was not only a big landowner but also – more to the point – chairman of the Tariff Reform League:

> He did not think any member of the House of Lords ought to say what he thought the House would do with a measure which had not yet come before it, but he was clearly of opinion that they had not only a perfect right to throw it out, but . . . a perfect constitutional right to amend the Budget, and that circumstances might arise in which it would be desirable to assert that right. The mistaken impression of many people that the House of Lords could not touch finance was founded on a

resolution of the House of Commons passed centuries ago. The Lords had hitherto acquiesced in the financial decisions of the House of Commons because the Government had hitherto been conducted by sane men, but there was now a House of Commons controlled by a pack of madmen, and they had to take different measures.[1]

Ridley's statement was followed by speeches at a dinner of the Liberal Union Club, also on 3 May. Lansdowne, proposing the health of the guest of honour, Bonar Law, said that Unionists would fight the Government's 'reckless financial policy' with the policy of Tariff Reform 'which Mr Arthur Balfour has made his own'. And Bonar Law said in his reply that the Government's plans for the House of Lords were 'revolution itself'. If they were adopted the Second Chamber would 'simply exist as a debating society'.[2] Thus within a few days of the Budget the most powerful section of the Opposition was evidently preparing for a fight with no holds barred.

City opinion was hostile from the first, as Banbury's speech on Budget day had indicated it would be. In mid-May the text was published of a letter to the Prime Minister from a number of London merchants, bankers and businessmen. Copies of the letter – a strong attack on the Budget – were left at Martin's Bank for others to sign and over the next week attracted many more signatures.[3] In mid-June the Budget Protest League was started by Walter Long to coordinate opposition to the Budget throughout the country. Shortly afterwards the Liberals responded by founding their Budget League, with Churchill as president, to counteract the work of the Budget Protest League.[4]

On 23 June about a thousand people attended an anti-Budget meeting at the Cannon Street Hotel, in the City of London, under the chairmanship of Lord Rothschild. Next day Asquith and Lloyd George spoke at a lunch at the Holborn Restaurant where, almost exactly eight years before, Campbell-Bannerman denounced 'methods of barbarism' in South Africa. Asquith's speech was by far the longer, but Lloyd George's delighted the audience. He was cheerfully irreverent about the Cannon Street financiers:

> You might have expected in a meeting of that sort to have had . . . some sound financial suggestions. I looked in vain through the reports to find one. You had simply the same old drivel about socialism and, of course,

1. *The Times*, 3 May 1909.   2. *The Times*, 4 May 1909.
3. *The Times*, 15 and 22 May 1909.
4. The Budget Protest League was started on 14 June and the Budget League on 23 June 1909.

the 'thin end of the wedge' – it is becoming very thin indeed by constant use . . . Then of course there was the inevitable Lord Rothschild. He said that the Budget was Socialism and Collectivism. Now I wonder if he knows what Socialism means. I am sure he does not. I suppose it would be too much to ask a financier ruined by the Budget to spend any money on political literature; but I think it would be money very well spent . . . if someone should present him with a sixpenny handbook on Socialism . . .[1]

While the moneyed interest was giving hostages to fortune with its clumsy and ponderous anathemas against the Budget, some representatives of the landed interest were performing in a more burlesque vein. Lord Onslow, for instance, solemnly told his tenants at a lunch to mark the summer rent audit that he would have to sell part of his estate and would probably have to sack all his directly employed labourers, bricklayers, carpenters, sawyers, painters and foresters, putting their work, instead, out to contract.[2] And Lord Sherborne inserted a notice in his local newspaper to the effect that he would have to spend less on the upkeep of his estate in future, because 'super-taxation' necessitated 'super-economy'.[3]

A more sophisticated and resonant voice was added to the chorus of woe when Rosebery issued a statement for general publication.[4] The Budget, he said, was

> not a Budget, but a revolution: a social and political revolution of the first magnitude . . . To say this is not to judge it, still less to condemn it, for there have been several beneficent revolutions.
>
> I am not now concerned with the merits of this one. But the feature of the case which most impresses me is this. It will be effected, if it is effected, without the participation of the country . . . It will be carried out over the heads of the people by a majority in the House of Commons, without the faintest desire or attempt to ascertain the views of the people on the vast changes projected. British citizens will have no more control over them than if they were Tartars or Lapps.
>
> There is no referendum here. A powerful Government does not, naturally, seek a general election . . .

1. A month earlier Ben Tillett, the dockers' leader, had written to *The Times* protesting against descriptions of the Budget as 'socialistic' which, he said, were 'a libel on Socialism'. (*The Times*, 24 May 1909.)
2. *The Times*, 16 June 1909.
3. Notice in *Wiltshire and Gloucestershire Standard*, quoted in *The Times*, 19 June 1909.
4. It appeared on 22 June 1909.

BUDGET – "Did you say that you wouldn't swallow me without mincing?"
LORD LANSDOWNE – "No sir – please, sir – I never said *mincing*, I might have said *wincing*."

2. From *The Westminster Gazette*, 1909

We . . . elect our rulers for six years amid the tumult and confusion of a general election, which usually turns on the demerits of the Government which has been in office during the previous Parliament . . .

Surely the country must begin to see that there are vast flaws in the Constitution, and that the absolute rule of a party in power differs very little from the absolute rule of an individual, which is what we used to call despotism?

If not, the nation must have changed its character, and its former zealous vigilance with regard to its liberties have been replaced by an apathy which is a sinister if not an alarming symptom.

Rosebery's underlying objection to the Budget was the same as that of Onslow, Sherborne, Rothschild and others who had great possessions. As Prime Minister he had done his best to stop Harcourt introducing graduated death duties, and the disingenuousness of suggesting that he did not wish to condemn Lloyd George's tax proposals as such soon became apparent, when he described them as pure socialism, 'the end of all, the negation of faith, of family, of property, of Monarchy, of Empire'.[1] But his initial statement artfully disguised his true motive by carrying the discussion to a high constitutional plane. His intelligence and imagination supplied what the Budget's clodhopping critics would never have found – a means of attacking it in the name of democracy. Tariff Reform gave the Opposition an alternative radical programme, but the only way it could be submitted to the people at an early date was through the antiquated machinery of the Lords' veto. Rosebery's feat was to give the veto a democratic justification and to label the House of Commons as despotic.

His referendum hint was not lost on the Tories and became a key point in their attempt, the following year, to make the hereditary Second Chamber acceptable without restriction of its powers. Meanwhile the Opposition made good selective use of Rosebery's statement, which was all the more embarrassing to the Government coming, as it did, from a Liberal ex-Premier with whom Asquith had been closely associated in the quite recent past. The words 'This is not a Budget, but a revolution' were inscribed on a large banner adorning the peer-laden platform at the Hotel Metropole when, on 29 June, the Anti-Socialist Union of Great Britain held a demonstration there, with the Duke of Devonshire presiding.

At the same hotel, on 16 July, the National Union of Conservative

1. Glasgow, 10 September 1909.

Associations held its annual dinner. Lansdowne spoke at it and in the course of his speech referred in guarded terms to the Lords' prospective treatment of the Finance Bill:

> . . . common caution demands that I should adopt an attitude of reserve as to what may happen to that notorious measure when it comes before us. But if I cannot tell you what the House of Lords will do, I think I may venture to tell you what the House of Lords will not do. I do not think that you will find that . . . the House of Lords is at all likely to proclaim that it has no responsibility at all for the Bill, and that because it is mixed up with the financial affairs of the nation we are obliged to swallow it whole and without hesitation.[1]

He was clearly hinting that the Bill would not be rejected outright, but might be amended. Two nights later, at Edinburgh, Churchill took it upon himself to state that the Government would not tolerate any Lords' amendments:

> . . . when the Finance Bill leaves the House of Commons, I think you will agree with me that it ought to leave the House of Commons in its final form. No amendments, no excision, no modifying or mutilating will be agreed to by us. We will stand no mincing, and unless Lord Lansdowne and his landlordly friends choose to eat their own mince again Parliament will be dissolved and we shall come to you in a moment of high consequence for every cause for which Liberalism has ever fought. See that you do not fail us in that hour.[2]

For speaking thus Churchill was formally rebuked at a Cabinet meeting on 21 July. Asquith's policy was to assume, or at any rate to give the impression of assuming, that the Lords would neither reject nor amend the Finance Bill, and he therefore strongly deprecated the use of threats relating to a hypothetical situation which might never arise. Such tactics seemed to him needlessly provocative, but it was soon brought home to him in the most emphatic manner that his Chancellor of the Exchequer took a different view.

Since introducing the Budget Lloyd George had made only one controversial speech outside Parliament – his light-hearted intervention at the Holborn Restaurant, quoted above. When he spoke at the Bankers'

1. *The Times*, 17 July 1909.
2. Lansdowne had used the word 'mincing' (see also cartoon p. 199).

Dinner on 16 July there were no fireworks, and in the House of Commons he was showing the courteous, often conciliatory, temper that he maintained throughout the Finance Bill's immensely long passage. While Asquith during June and July was making a number of big speeches in support of the Budget, its author was uncharacteristically absent from public platforms.

One reason was the sheer burden of his Parliamentary work. In May the Budget resolutions were debated for a total of thirteen days, and on 26 May the Finance Bill had its First Reading. In early June there was a four-day Second Reading debate. On 21 June the Committee Stage began and with it an endurance test such as no Chancellor, before or since, has had to undergo. This would have been a sufficient excuse for reticence outside Parliament, even if there had been no other. But there was another which probably carried even more weight with Lloyd George. He wanted to have time to judge Opposition and general public reactions to his Budget, before deciding whether or not to bring the big guns of his popular oratory into play. If it seemed to him likely that the Opposition would let the Finance Bill through, however grudgingly, it would be foolish and wrong to indulge in any gratuitous polemics. But if he should feel that the enemy was ready to try conclusions, and with a fair chance of success, then it would be necessary for him to open fire.

The Budget was received with enthusiasm by the Government's own supporters, and its immediate effect was to restore their morale. But Lloyd George knew that demoralization might again set in if the Opposition's fighting spirit appeared to be stronger than the Government's. He also knew that any sign of a loss of nerve by the Government would encourage the Opposition to destroy the Finance Bill. Four by-elections in July showed that the anti-Liberal swing had been reduced to an average of 4·6 per cent, but this was still too much for comfort and could well be increased rather than diminished over the next few months.[1] It must have been obvious to Lloyd George that Balfour, anyway tempted by the prospect of returning to power, was under almost irresistible pressure from the dominant elements on his side to engineer a dissolution of Parliament. Landowners, financiers, brewers and the licensed trade were all up in arms against the Budget, and were therefore more than ever attracted by Tariff

1. The by-elections were at Cleveland, High Peak, Mid-Derby and Dumfries Burghs. The only one that the Unionists hoped to win was High Peak, but their confidence was perhaps rather exaggerated, seeing that the seat had been captured by the Liberals in the 'Khaki election' of 1900.

Reform militancy. Balfour reflected the internal dynamics of Unionism when he spoke to his constituents in the City of London on 27 July, endorsing Tariff Reform and challenging the Government to hold a general election on the rival financial policies offered to the nation.

It was against this background that Lloyd George fulfilled an engagement of nearly a month's standing to address a meeting in the East End of London, organized by the Budget League. On the evening of 30 July he went to the Edinburgh Castle, Limehouse, and there delivered not the best, but the most famous and possibly most effective speech of his life.[1] The occasion itself was marred by rough treatment of male suffragists in the hall and by chanting suffragettes who had installed themselves in neighbouring houses. Since the evening was very hot all the windows in the hall had to be open and the noise could not be kept out. But Lloyd George's words were intended to carry far beyond the immediate audience of four thousand, and carry they certainly did.

He began with a reference to 'Dreadnoughts', for which, he said, the rich had been clamouring but were reluctant to pay:

> We started building; we wanted money to pay for the building; so we sent the hat round. We sent it round amongst workmen . . . they all dropped in their coppers. We went round Belgravia, and there has been such a howl ever since that it has well-nigh deafened us.

Then, after admitting that the security of the country was 'paramount in the minds of all', he spoke of the Budget's social aims:

> . . . provision for the aged and deserving poor – is it not time something was done? It is rather a shame that a rich country like ours . . . should allow those who have toiled all their days to end in penury and possibly starvation. It is rather hard that an old workman should have to find his way to the gates of the tomb, bleeding and footsore, through the brambles and thorns of poverty. We cut a new path for him – an easier one, a pleasanter one, through fields of waving corn . . . There are many in the country blessed by Providence with great wealth, and if there are amongst them men who grudge out of their riches a fair contribution

1. The Edinburgh Castle was originally a pub, and is shown as such in the Post Office London directory for 1870. But in 1873 it is shown as the Edinburgh Castle and Royal Castle music-hall. By 1874 it had ceased to be a pub and had become a working men's club, though still known as the Edinburgh Castle. Soon afterwards a missionary element moved in, because by 1909 the club was known as the Edinburgh Castle Coffee Palace, and the hall attached to it as St Ann's Gospel Hall – a suitable venue for a Liberal meeting.

towards the less fortunate of their fellow-countrymen they are very shabby rich men.

We propose to do more by means of the Budget. We are raising money to provide against the evils and the sufferings that follow from unemployment. We are raising money for the purpose of assisting our great friendly societies to provide for the sick and the widows and orphans. We are providing money to enable us to develop the resources of our own land. I do not believe any fair-minded man would challenge the justice and the fairness of the objects which we have in view in raising this money.

Yet some people were attacking his new taxes, more especially the land taxes, as 'unjust, unfair, unequal, oppressive', and they were attacking 'with a concentrated and sustained ferocity which will not allow even a comma to escape with its life'. For most of the rest of his speech Lloyd George devoted himself to justifying the land taxes and exposing the selfishness of landowners. He did not ask his audience to consider 'merely abstract principles', but focused attention upon 'a number of concrete cases'.

First, he gave an instance relating to the proposed tax on undeveloped land:

Not far from here, not so many years ago, between the Lea and the Thames, you had hundreds of acres of land which was not very useful even for agricultural purposes. In the main it was a sodden marsh. The commerce . . . of London increased under Free Trade, the tonnage of your shipping went up by hundreds of thousands of tons . . . labour was attracted from all parts of the country . . . What happened? There was no housing accommodation. This Port of London became overcrowded and the population overflowed. That was the opportunity for the owners of the marsh. All that land became valuable building land, and land which used to be rented at £2 or £3 an acre has been selling within the last few years at £2,000 an acre, £3,000 an acre, £6,000 an acre, £8,000 an acre. Who created that increment? Who made that golden swamp? Was it the landlord? Was it his energy? Was it his brains? – a very bad look-out for the place if it were . . . It was purely the combined effort of all the people engaged in the trade . . . of the Port of London . . . everybody except the landlord. Now you follow that transaction. Land worth £2 and £3 an acre running up to thousands. During the time it was ripening the landlord was paying his rates and his taxes –

not on £2 or £3 an acre. It was agricultural land, and because it was agricultural land a munificent Tory Government voted a sum of two millions to pay half the rates of those poor distressed landlords, and you and I had to pay taxes in order to enable those landlords to pay half their rates . . . What is going to happen in the future? In future those land-lords will have to contribute to the taxation of the country on the basis of the real value – only one halfpenny in the pound! Only a halfpenny! And that is what all the howling is about.

Then there was the question of unearned increment:

We mean to value all the land in the Kingdom. And here you can draw no distinction between agricultural land and other land, for the simple reason that East and West Ham was agricultural land a few years ago. And if land goes up in future by hundreds and thousands an acre through the efforts of the community, the community will get 20 per cent of that increment.

Among the examples that he gave to illustrate his point he named one individual:

Take the very well-known case of the Duke of Northumberland, when a county council wanted to buy a small plot of land as a site for a school to train the children who in due course would become the men labour-ing on his property. The rent was quite an insignificant thing; his contribution to the rates I think was on the basis of 30s. an acre. What did he demand for a school? £900 an acre. All we say is this – if it is worth £900, let him pay taxes on £900.

Next he turned to the tax on reversions:

You have got a system in this country which is not tolerated in any other country in the world except, I believe, Turkey – a system whereby landlords take advantage of the fact that they have got control over the land to let it for a term of years . . . and at the end of sixty, seventy, eighty or ninety years the whole of it passes away to the pockets of a man who never spent a penny upon it.

In Scotland they had a system of 999-year leases. 'The Scotsmen have a very shrewd idea that at the end of 999 years there will probably be a better land system in existence', so they 'take their chance of the millennium coming round by that time'. In England leases were for shorter periods, and again Lloyd George picked on a duke to show what was vicious in the system:

> The Gorringe case is a very famous case. It was the case of the Duke of Westminster. Oh these dukes – how they harass us! Mr Gorringe had got a lease of the premises at a few hundred pounds a year ground rent. He built up a great business there as a very able business man. When the end of the lease came he went to the Duke of Westminster, and he said 'Will you renew my lease? I want to carry on my business here.' The reply was 'Oh yes, I will; but only on condition that the few hundreds a year you pay for ground rent shall in the future be £4,000 a year.' In addition to that Mr Gorringe had to pay a fine of £50,000, and to build up huge premises at enormous expense, according to plans approved by the Duke of Westminster. All I can say is this – if it is confiscation and robbery for us to say to that duke that, being in need of money for public purposes, we will take 10 per cent of [the reversion value] . . . what would you call *his* taking nine-tenths from Mr Gorringe?

When he came to the tax on minerals Lloyd George was able to draw on his recent experience of visiting the South Wales coalfield:[1]

> I went down to a coalfield the other day, and they pointed out to me many collieries there. They said 'You see that colliery. The first man who went there spent a quarter of a million in sinking shafts, in driving mains and levels. He never got coal, and he lost his quarter of a million. The second man who came spent £100,000 – and he failed. The third man came along and he got the coal.' What was the landlord doing in the meantime? The first man failed; but the landlord got his royalty, the landlord got his dead-rent – and a very good name for it. The second man failed, but the landlord got his royalty.
>
> These capitalists put their money in, and I asked 'When the cash failed, what did the landlord put in?' He simply put in the bailiffs. The capitalist risks, at any rate, the whole of his money; the engineer puts his brains in; the miner risks his life.
>
> Have you been down a coal mine? I went down one the other day. We sank down into a pit half a mile deep. We then walked underneath the mountain, and we had about three-quarters of a mile of rock and shale above us. The earth seemed to be straining – around us and above

1. In early June 1909. He said at the time: 'What I have learned will be most helpful in the forthcoming discussion of the Budget. It will enable me to answer questions that would have floored me before.'

us – to crush us in. You could see the pit-props bent and twisted and sundered, their fibres split in resisting the pressure. Sometimes they give way, and then there is mutilation and death. Often a spark ignites, the whole pit is deluged in fire, and the breath of life is scorched out of hundreds of breasts by the consuming flame . . . yet when the Prime Minister and I knock at the doors of these great landlords, and say to them: 'Here, you know these poor fellows who have been digging up royalties at the risk of their lives, some of them are old, they have survived the perils of their trade, they are broken, they can earn no more. Won't you give something towards keeping them out of the workhouse?' they scowl at us. We say 'Only a halfpenny, just a copper.' They retort 'You thieves!' . . . If this is an indication of the view taken by these great landlords of their responsibility to the people who, at the risk of life, create their wealth, then I say their day of reckoning is at hand.

As he moved into his peroration Lloyd George managed to refer, quite gratuitously, to yet another duke:

I claim that the tax we impose on land is fair, is just, and is moderate. They go on threatening that if we proceed they will cut down their benefactions and discharge labour. What kind of labour? . . . Are they going to threaten to devastate rural England by feeding and dressing themselves? Are they going to reduce their gamekeepers? Ah, that would be sad! The agricultural labourer and the farmer might then have some part of the game that is fattened by their labour. Also what would happen to you in the season? No weekend shooting with the Duke of Norfolk or anyone. But that is not the kind of labour they are going to cut down. They are going to cut down productive labour . . . and they are going to ruin their property so that it shall not be taxed.

The ownership of land was 'not merely an enjoyment', but 'a steward-ship', and if owners ceased 'to discharge their functions in seeing to the security and defence of the country, in looking after the broken in their villages and in their neighbourhoods', the time would come to 'reconsider the conditions' under which land was held. No country, however rich, could 'afford to have quartered upon its revenue' a class which declined to do its duty.

And he ended:

I do not believe in their threats. They have threatened . . . like this before, but in good time they have seen it is not to their interest to carry out their futile menaces. They are now protesting against paying their

fair share of the taxation of the land, and they are doing so by saying:
'You are burdening industry; you are putting burdens upon the people
which they cannot bear'. Ah, they are not thinking of themselves. Noble
souls! It is not the great dukes they are feeling for . . .

We are placing burdens on the broadest shoulders. Why should I put
burdens on the people? I am one of the children of the people. I was
brought up amongst them. I know their trials, and God forbid that I
should add one grain of trouble to the anxieties which they bear with
such patience and fortitude. When the Prime Minister did me the honour
of asking me to take charge of the national Exchequer at a time of great
difficulty, I made up my mind in framing the Budget . . . that at any
rate no cupboard should be barer, no lot should be harder. By that test
I challenge you to judge the Budget.

Speaking immediately afterwards to the overflow meeting in an adjacent
hall, Lloyd George in effect reaffirmed Churchill's statement that no Lords'
amendments to the Finance Bill would be accepted. But he did it in the
form of a rebuke to Curzon, who as an ex-Viceroy of India and a conspicuous grandee was almost the equivalent, for polemical purposes, of a
duke:

Lord Curzon has threatened to amputate the Budget. Well, I don't
mind Lord Curzon so long as he keeps to those bombastic common-
places which have been his stock-in-trade through life; but if he is going
to try here that arrogance which was too much even for the gentle
Hindu, we will just tell him that we will have none of his Oriental
manners . . . I say to you, without you we can do nothing; with your
help we can brush the Lords like chaff before us.

After a weekend's painful digestion of Limehouse Asquith met the King
at Cowes and wrote, on 3 August, the following letter to Lloyd George
from the Admiralty yacht, *Enchantress*:

My dear Ch^r of Ex^r

On my arrival here yesterday, I found the King in a state of great
agitation and annoyance in consequence of your Limehouse speech. I
have never known him more irritated, or more difficult to appease,
though I did my best.

He sees in the general tone, & especially in the concluding parts, of
your speech, a menace to property and a Socialistic spirit, which he
thinks peculiarly inappropriate and unsettling in a holder of your office.

The King, of course lives in an atmosphere which is full of hostility to us and to our proposals; but he is not himself unfriendly, and, so far, he has 'stood' the Budget very well – far better than I expected. It is important, therefore, to avoid raising his apprehensions and alienating his goodwill.

I have communications in the same sense from others – very good Liberals some of them.

I have, as you know, heartily & loyally backed the Budget from the first, and at every stage; and I have done, and shall continue to do, all I can to commend it to the country. But I feel very strongly that at this moment what is needed is reasoned appeal to moderate & reasonable men. There is great & growing popular enthusiasm, but this will not carry us through – if we rouse the suspicions & fears of the middle class, & particularly if we give countenance to the notion that the Budget is conceived in any spirit of vindictiveness.

I am sure you will take what I have written in good part. My sole object is to bring our ship safely into port.

Yours very sincerely
H. H. Asquith.[1]

Lloyd George did not, apparently, send any written reply to the Prime Minister, but on 5 August he wrote to the King:

The Chancellor of the Exchequer, with his humble duty to Your Majesty, has the honour to say that he understands from the Prime Minister with great regret that Your Majesty looks with disapproval on the speech which he delivered on Friday last at Limehouse. The Chancellor of the Exchequer would be grateful if he might be permitted to lay some considerations on the subject before Your Majesty.

It is no doubt within Your Majesty's recollection that when the Chancellor of the Exchequer laid the financial proposals before Your Majesty, prior to the introduction of the Budget, Your Majesty was good enough to listen with consideration, and even on some points with sympathy, to his statement. Since then the country has had full time to consider its proposals, and according to the testimony of *The Times* and other Opposition papers this week, the tide is running in their favour.

The Chancellor of the Exchequer, however, has found himself subjected in connection with these same proposals to a storm of hostile

1. Earl Lloyd George's collection.

criticism, the virulence of which he ventures to think is without parallel in the history of financial legislation in this country. Many and substantial concessions have been granted in order to remove such inequalities and hardships as have been shown to be likely to arise, and the Chancellor thinks he may fairly say that throughout the protracted discussions in the House of Commons he is admitted to have shown a constant moderation and willingness to meet his opponents. But in spite of this attitude on his part, the violence of the attacks to which he has been and is being exposed has been in no way mitigated, and he ventures to submit to Your Majesty that in his recent speech, the first public speech which he has made since the introduction of the Budget, he was justified in retorting upon his opponents in language which fell short of much that has been said and repeated on the other side.

The Chancellor trusts that Your Majesty will excuse the length of this communication. If he might at any future date be honoured with another audience with Your Majesty, he would greatly value the opportunity for a fuller statement of his position, and for learning direct from Your Majesty what are Your Majesty's views.

D. Lloyd George.

It was not strictly true that Limehouse was his first public speech since the Budget, but morally it *was* true, since in neither of the other two speeches had he adopted a seriously offensive tone. His argument to the King could be summed up as 'Cet animal est très méchant – quand on l'attaque il se défend.' Two days later the King replied from the royal yacht *Victoria & Albert*:

The King thanks the Chancellor of the Exchequer for his letter of the 5th instant, and for the explanation which he has given him respecting his recent speech on the Budget at Limehouse.

As regards the Budget itself, the King expresses no opinion, but he was very glad to see the Chancellor of the Exchequer on two occasions concerning it and to have had some interesting conversations with him on various details connected with the Bill.

The points on which he spoke to the Prime Minister on Monday last were those concerning the language used by the Chancellor of the Exchequer, which the King thinks was calculated to set class against class and to inflame the passions of the working and lower orders against people who happened to be owners of property.

The King readily admits that the Chancellor of the Exchequer has been attacked by some members of the Opposition with much violence, and he regrets it, but he must remind him that though those gentlemen may have passed the fair limits of attack, they are private members and do not hold a high office in the Government as is the case with Mr Lloyd George.

If therefore the Chancellor of the Exchequer had been a private member, it certainly would not have been within the King's province to offer any official criticism on his speech; but it is owing to the fact that he holds one of the most important offices under the Crown and is an influential member of the Cabinet, which made him feel it his duty, with much regret, to remonstrate with the Prime Minister against the tone of the Chancellor of the Exchequer's speech, and to express to him his fear that Mr Lloyd George was departing from the best traditions of his high office, traditions that had always been invariably observed by his distinguished predecessors.

The King, in conclusion, must give the Chancellor of the Exchequer every credit for the patience and perfect temper which he has shown, under considerable provocation, during the debates on the Budget.

Edward R. & I.

Cowes, 7 August, 1909[1]

The King was right in saying that no previous Chancellor of the Exchequer had spoken, in office, as Lloyd George had spoken. But the comment must have left Lloyd George totally unmoved, because he never subscribed to the doctrine that Cabinet Ministers should adopt a special, august, 'responsible' style of rhetoric, designed to ensure that they never hurt their opponents' feelings or roused the masses from their torpor. And he saw no reason why the Chancellor of the Exchequer should behave differently, in this respect, from other Cabinet Ministers.

He must have been very pleased, therefore, to receive this letter of support from J. E. C. Bodley, the scholarly political writer whom he had met at Biarritz in the summer of 1906:

Dear Mr Lloyd George,

Will you let me thank you for your speech at Limehouse? It is the first utterance by any member of this government of good intentions which gives a ray of hope that the people will be guided to reject Tariff

1. Lloyd George's letter to the King, and the King's reply, are printed in Frank Owen, *op. cit.*, pp. 180–2.

Reform – although you made but little reference to that subject. It had the effect on me of Gambetta's famous 'Discours de Cherbourg' on disheartened Frenchmen.

Although a Free Trader I write not as a partisan, but as a spectator & a life-student of political questions. Since you came to see me in the S. of France ill-health has rendered my position more detached. But from it I have seen with dismay the chiefs of a vast majority impotent to stem the progress of an economical doctrine fatal to our national interests – for lack of a voice capable of rousing & leading the people.

Some of your ablest colleagues have seemed to me, if I may say so, too fashionably disposed, too disinclined to soil their newly-acquired kid gloves in a popular fray.

But last night (provided you go on) English politics can boast of, once more, a popular leader – for the first time since the defection of Chamberlain, whose strength, before he lost his way, lay in his freedom from subserviency to social influences.

As you have become like me a Brighton resident for part of the year I hope that one day I may see you. One of my Eton boys, whom you saw when they were very small in our Southern home, would be made very happy if he could see you during the holidays, as in spite of the contrary influences of his school he is a keen self-taught Liberal.

Faithfully yours
J. E. C. Bodley[1]

Clearly not all 'moderate and reasonable men' were outraged by his oratorical style.

It is unlikely that the King's reaction to Limehouse caused Lloyd George much surprise or concern, but he must have been quite seriously troubled by Asquith's reaction. If the King's entourage was, as the Prime Minister said, largely hostile to the Liberal Government, Lloyd George knew that on *Enchantress* Asquith was in company largely hostile to himself, since the First Lord, McKenna, was far from being a well-wisher. And who were the 'very good Liberals' who had allegedly been complaining to Asquith about Limehouse? Had good party men been writing to him from different parts of the country, or had he merely been receiving oral 'communications' from Liberal socialites at Cowes? The Prime Minister might be hinting at more disaffection than actually existed, but in any case there could be no mistaking his own attitude. Whereas he had, indeed,

1. The letter is dated 31 July 1909 – the day after the speech (Earl Lloyd George collection).

given Lloyd George's proposals the staunchest backing in Cabinet, it was clear that he was now unwilling to face the sort of tactics that Lloyd George regarded as necessary for success in the country.

What were those tactics? A careful scrutiny of his remarks at Limehouse suggests that he had two principal aims – to demonstrate the justice and fairness of the Budget, and to show the Unionists how vulnerable they would be if they chose to reject it. Unlike Asquith, he doubted the value of sweet reasonableness as an antidote to propaganda working upon self-interest and passion. In his view, mealy-mouthedness would only be interpreted as weakness, by friend and foe alike. If – as he must have considered probable – the Opposition was moving relentlessly towards rejection, a strong statement of the Government's case was already over-due. But if there was still a chance that caution would prevail, it would be salutary for him to bring home to his opponents how savagely he could treat them in the event of its not prevailing. At Limehouse he was giving them a warning similar to the one he had given at Liverpool the previous December, but with this difference, that on the second occasion he had reason to be much less hopeful that it would be heeded.

Was Asquith right to suggest that he was gratuitously alienating the middle class? It was clearly not his intention to do so, since his target at Limehouse was not the bourgeoisie but the landed rich, and more especially those who were also members of the House of Lords. Seeing that the Opposition's weak point was the unnatural alliance between Chamber-lainite radicalism and feudal reaction, he trained his guns upon landowning peers; and, on the principle to which he always adhered of attacking people at the top rather than underlings, he mentioned by name three dukes. Moreover, he contrasted with the idle greed of landlords not only the arduous and perilous toil of coal-miners, but also the skill of engineers and the readiness of entrepreneurs to take risks. In his denunciation of the Duke of Westminster, the Duke's alleged victim was a prosperous businessman, Mr Gorringe.[1] Though Limehouse was certainly calculated to please, above all, the working class, it was also calculated to exploit middle-class resentment of the aristocracy. Lloyd George knew how essential it was to discredit the House of Lords – all the more so now that Rosebery's brilliant sophistry was presenting the Lords' veto in a high and altruistic light.

1. Incidentally, Frank Owen's statement that nobody ever controverted Lloyd George's factual allegations at Limehouse is not correct. The Duke of Westminster defended himself at length, but detailed extenuations were not sufficient to destroy Lloyd George's case.

Ten years later Lloyd George told Frances Stevenson that she could not

> imagine the impression that the Limehouse speech had had not only upon the Tories, but on the Liberals themselves. D.'s [Lloyd George's] colleagues were astounded & afraid at it. He dined with some of them after the speech, & Sydney Buxton sat like a man in a dream, not saying a single word. Some of those so-called Liberals were as Conservative as the worst of the Tories.[1]

They were the sort who got at Asquith.

The immediate effect of Limehouse was to reassure most of the Government's supporters and to demoralize at least some of the Opposition's. On 3 August Lloyd George could write to his brother:

> I hear that reports are coming in to the Tory headquarters from all parts of the country that the Budget is popular. Rutherford, M.P. for Liverpool here now and telling me my Land Clauses were very popular. General feeling here is that they will make a show of fight and then collapse. They are raging over Limehouse, but our fellows most enthusiastic.[2]

And the following day he had even more encouraging news to impart:

> Lord Northcliffe came to see me last night. He is, as you know, the Proprietor of the *Daily Mail* and *Times*. He told me that the Budget has completely destroyed the Tariff Reform propaganda in the country. He said that they had all miscalculated the popularity of the Land Clauses. He wants to trim.[3]

Northcliffe's sensitivity to public opinion was unequalled. Though he and Lloyd George had never met before, they had occasionally exchanged letters, and Lloyd George had only recently made an overture to him which had been politely rebuffed.[4] Now it was the other way round and Lloyd George was not the man to rebuff so important a publicist from the Opposition camp. They talked for about an hour in the Chancellor's room

1. Frances Stevenson, *Lloyd George: A Diary*, edited by A. J. P. Taylor, entry for 17 December 1919, p. 193.
2. William George, *op. cit.*, p. 230.
3. William George, *op. cit.*, p. 230.
4. 'I am sorry I cannot accept the very kind invitation you make because I am one of those people who believe that journalists should be read and not seen.' Northcliffe to D.L.G., 23 June 1909 (Earl Lloyd George collection).

at the House of Commons, and Lloyd George exerted himself to the full – even to the point of giving Northcliffe, who was a keen motorist, a preview of the Development of Roads Bill and authorizing him to publish details of it in the *Daily Mail* before it was submitted to Parliament.[1] The result of this interview was that the Northcliffe dailies, though never converted to support of the Budget, entered a brief period of disorientation during which they printed news reports heartening to the Government. The appearance of such material in *The Times* was opportune for Lloyd George, and he made good use of it in his letter to the King.

Garvin, editor of Northcliffe's Sunday *Observer*, was equally impressed by Limehouse, but did not share his proprietor's momentary disposition to 'trim'. He, like the King and Prime Minister, reflected upon the new situation at Cowes, where he was the guest of Admiral Fisher, and on returning to London communicated his reflections in a long letter to Northcliffe:

> . . . I find a subtle something in the air which thoroughly alarms me.
> I know nothing from any side as yet, but my sixth sense tells me that a Unionist Surrender upon the Budget is much more probable . . .
> The Government is of course less unpopular than last year. If they pass the Budget substantially as it stands they will have secured a Parliamentary triumph as brilliant as any in our recollection . . . That alone will immensely impress democracy, always more attracted by pugilistic force in politics than by anything else . . . Men like Lloyd George and Winston Churchill will do anything to win. Upon the lines of the Budget they will keep on winning if we submit now . . .
> Our Dukes should be warned to keep off the grass. Then the strongest and most audacious policy possible should be adopted . . . In short, my belief is now that *the Budget ought to be rejected*. That was not formerly my opinion . . . but it is my opinion now . . .

He implored Northcliffe 'not to encourage by indirect means . . . thoughts of surrender on the Budget'.[2]

There can be no doubt that Garvin's letter put an end to Northcliffe's post-Limehouse wobble, but any idea that it determined the future course of Unionist policy towards the Finance Bill should be treated with

1. An account of the interview by Northcliffe's brother, Cecil Harmsworth, appears in Tom Clarke, *Northcliffe in History*, pp. 87–8.
2. Garvin to Northcliffe, 4 August 1909; quoted in Alfred M. Gollin, *The Observer and J. L. Garvin*, pp. 109–10.

scepticism. Northcliffe sent a copy of the letter to Balfour, and Balfour must have been delighted to receive it, because the very fact that Northcliffe had sent it was a fair indication that he was now, once again, resolute in his own allegiance. But Balfour did not need Garvin to make up his mind for him. Even before the Budget he had been largely committed to Tariff Reform, and since the Budget he and Lansdowne, whatever their reservations about use of the Lords' veto, had been more than ever identified with Chamberlain's policy. This meant that sooner or later they were virtually bound to decide in favour of rejection, because Chamberlain's intentions in the matter were implacable. He, not Garvin, was the motive force behind Unionist policy. Garvin was no more than his very gifted and eloquent disciple. Granted the Tariff Reformers' power within the Unionist ranks, it was apparent to Balfour that he would divide his party more by allowing the Finance Bill to pass than by using the Lords to reject it. He was, moreover, tempted by the prospect of an election, and may well have hoped what Asquith feared – that Lloyd George's polemics would frighten the middle class. All that we know of Balfour's character and of the circumstances suggests that Garvin's letter served as confirmation and adornment, rather than as determinant, of his own thoughts.

Later it may have suited him to pretend that his decision to have the Finance Bill rejected was provoked by Limehouse, but the evidence is ambiguous and anyway unconvincing. In November 1909 Esher, after lunching with Balfour, recorded that 'from the opening days of the controversy, certainly from the day of Lloyd George's speech at Limehouse, the fate of the Budget was sealed'.[1] And Garvin, in an autobiographical fragment, noted that Balfour's decision was taken after the Limehouse speech 'and perhaps before'.[2] Both statements are significantly hedged. In all probability Balfour was not influenced by Limehouse one way or the other, though it may have been convenient for him to hint that his extremist tactics were dictated by Lloyd George's demagogy.

On 4 August – during Northcliffe's short period of vacillation – The Times said in its Political Notes that a change was occurring 'comparable only to the turn of the tide upon an estuary when the moored boats swing slowly round'. That may be an accurate description of the effect of Limehouse upon public opinion, but almost certainly its effect upon Unionist policy should not be so described. If a fluvial metaphor is to be

1. Esher, Journals, Vol. II, p. 421.
2. Garvin Papers, quoted by Alfred M. Gollin (op. cit., p. 115), who judges that the fragment was written 'probably during World War I'.

used, it seems likely that the stream was flowing strongly, inexorably, towards rejection, and that Limehouse produced no more than an eddy in the current.

EIGHT
Flawed Victory

At Limehouse Lloyd George failed to deter Balfour, but also showed that he was himself undeterred. If the Opposition wanted a fight they could have it, and if any of his colleagues wanted to avoid a fight they were reckoning without him – that was his double-edged message.

Beyond question some members of the Cabinet would have been only too glad to make the avoidance of constitutional strife an excuse for dropping or modifying features of the Budget which they, as much as the Opposition, disliked. Some, moreover, including Asquith himself, favoured the Budget intellectually but shrank from a popular campaign to arouse enthusiasm for it and obloquy for its opponents. Lloyd George was determined to go through with the whole business, and to err neither in underrating the enemy nor adopting too stately an approach to the public.

Yet nobody could accuse him of forsaking Parliament for the platform. Throughout the summer and well into the autumn, with never more than a few days' intermission, he spoke, listened and voted in the House of Commons. It was a matter of pride to him that he was relatively sparing in his use of guillotine procedure during the immensely long Committee Stage of the Finance Bill, though he used ordinary closure quite freely and was particularly tough in dealing with obstruction to the Development Bill, which was a separate, concurrent, measure. There were 554 divisions on the Finance Bill alone – compared, for instance, with 480 on *all* measures during the busy year 1970–1 – and Lloyd George voted in 462 of them. Though he had considerable help at the despatch box from a number of his senior colleagues, as well as from Hobhouse and Masterman, the chief burden of speaking was his and his performance was generally admired. Despite the complexity of the subject-matter he was never seriously at a loss, and despite the length of the session his natural buoyancy never deserted him. Indeed, Masterman recorded that he 'got better and more certain as the Committee went on'.[1]

Apart from the Tory Opposition, he had to face criticism of some aspects of his land tax proposals from a few Liberal back-benchers – known as the 'Dickson-Poynder cave' after Sir John Dickson-Poynder, Wiltshire landowner and Member for Chippenham. But this did not amount to much. The land taxes went through, except that a tax on royalties was substituted for the tax on ungotten minerals. More embarrassing by far was Irish hostility to the Budget, above all to the licence and liquor duties. Whereas in Britain 'the Trade' was a vested interest of the Tories, in Ireland it was a vested interest of the National Party. The Government's majority in the House of Commons was so large that Irish votes could not wreck the Budget, but there was a danger that Irish votes in the country might be lost to the Government at the next general election. Redmond understood Lloyd George to be ready to make a substantial concession at the end of August, but either there was a misunderstanding or the Chancellor changed his mind. If the election had occurred in normal circumstances the cost of this quarrel with the Irish might have been heavy to the Liberals, not least in British constituencies where the Irish element was strong. T. P. O'Connor reported that Cardinal Bourne, Archbishop of Westminster, was 'doing his utmost to get the vote for the Tories'.[2] But Lloyd George could see that if the election were fought on the issue of the Lords' veto, Irish support for the Tories would be out of the question. By late summer, therefore, he had a powerful motive for hoping that the Lords would reject.

This was reinforced by evidence that trade was picking up and unemployment falling. The crucial economic argument against an election was turning into an argument the other way. Lloyd George's instinctive relish at the thought of a struggle with the Lords became, in the months following Limehouse, less and less inhibited by rational calculation, until at length his mind and temperament were at one. Instead of being merely prepared to face a contest if it were thrust upon him, he began to fear that he might be cheated of it.

1. Masterman, *op. cit.*, p. 145.
2. T. P. O'Connor to D.L.G., dated only 'Saturday', but probably late September 1909 – near the end of the Finance Bill's Committee Stage (L.G.P.).

As early as 17 August he wrote to his brother:

> There is undoubtedly a popular rising such as has not been witnessed
> over a generation. What will happen if they throw it out I can conjecture
> and I rejoice at the prospect. Many a rotten institution, system and law
> will be submerged by the deluge. I wonder whether they will be
> such fools. I am almost wishing that they should be stricken with
> blindness.[1]

A fortnight later he told Ellis Davies that he hoped the Lords would throw
the Budget out so that the Liberals could 'smash them'. But he 'seemed to
agree' that the Government would, after the election, be dependent upon
the Irish for a Parliamentary majority.[2] On 8 September he wrote, again
to his brother: 'Cabinet today. Passed off admirably. We discussed the
situation. Very doubtful what the Lords will do. Hope they will throw
it out.'[3] The prospect of destroying the Lords' veto was so congenial that
it seems to have made him rather too ready to accept the prospect of an
Irish veto.

On 31 October Hobhouse wrote in his diary:

> I asked Ll.G. what he really wanted, the Budget to pass, or be rejected,
> and suggested that the author of a successful financial scheme such as
> his was far more likely to go down to posterity than one who was
> Chancellor of the Exchequer merely . . . He agreed but added that he
> might be remembered even better as one who had upset the hereditary
> House of Lords.[4]

This remark in no way weakens the view, expressed earlier, that Lloyd
George's original preference had been that the Lords should accept his
Budget. If possible, he would have been glad not to have to risk his chance
of going down to posterity as 'the author of a successful financial scheme'.
But when it became manifest that the Opposition was bent on rejection,
he naturally fell into a fighting mood, and fell into it wholeheartedly. By
the end of October he was, as will be seen, totally committed to the coming
struggle, and it would have been against his nature to fret about might-

1. William George, *My Brother and I*, p. 230.
2. Ellis Davies journal, entry for 31 August 1909.
3. William George, *op. cit.*, p. 230.
4. Hobhouse, *Diaries*, entry for 31 October 1909, p. 80.

have-beens. When a war was on, his thoughts were of the potential glories of victory rather than of the lost glories of peace.

The Committee Stage of the Finance Bill ended on 6 October, and the following weekend Lloyd George spoke in the country for the first time since Limehouse. Before the weekend Asquith wrote to him nervously from Balmoral:

> The King is making, & will continue to make, every effort that is constitutionally open to him to secure the acceptance of the Budget Bill by the Lords. He is fairly sanguine of success.
> In the circumstances, as you are (I see) speaking in the country on Saturday, I venture to suggest that you should proceed throughout on the assumption that the Lords *will* pass the Bill: and that such a contingency as their rejecting it is, from both a constitutional and an administrative point of view, well-nigh unthinkable.
> The only part of the Budget to wh. the King now takes any serious exception, is the death duties, which he thinks might well be eased down in the case of the more moderate-sized estates. He has nothing to say against the land & mineral taxes, or the licence duties.[1]

Whether or not Lloyd George received this letter before leaving London on the 8th, he was in no mood to act upon Asquith's suggestion. So far as he was concerned the battle was already on and had to be fought to a finish. If aware that his superior officer had hoisted a signal to the contrary, he clearly put a blind eye to his telescope.

Newcastle was his destination and he arrived there on the evening of the 8th.[2] As a convenient prelude to his visit, the Duke of Northumberland had within the past week been ordered by magistrates to close twenty-two cottages belonging to him in the mining village of Walbottle, on the grounds that they were unfit for human habitation and that the death rate in them from TB had been four or five times the district average. Opposing the Government's Housing and Town Planning Bill the Duke had recently stated in the House of Lords that provision of cottages was 'not an urgent

1. Asquith to D.L.G., 7 October 1909 (Earl Lloyd George collection).
2. According to the *Daily News*, Asquith's train from Aberdeen to London was due at Newcastle at 2 a.m. on the 9th and there was 'a probability' that he and Lloyd George might meet. But there is no evidence that they did and it seems unlikely that either of them would have wished to confer at such an hour on Newcastle station. Lloyd George, in any case, had his own good reasons for not wishing to talk to the Prime Minister.

matter', and that it was 'much more important that owners should be safely guarded in the possession of their property'. The issue of 'ducal hovels' was a gift to the Liberals and a source of deep embarrassment to the Tories, all the more so as the Duke was president of the Royal Sanitary Institute, whose health he had proposed at its annual dinner the previous May.

At 2.30 p.m. on Saturday 9 October Lloyd George rose to address an audience of about 5,200 in the Palace Theatre, Newcastle. He began, like Mark Antony, by saying that he would give just 'a plain, straight talk', and by recalling his previous visit to the theatre in April 1903:

> . . . I have some recollection that I then dwelt upon the great burden imposed upon industry by ground landlords and the royalty owners, and I then mildly suggested that it was about time they should contribute something out of their wealth towards the necessities of the State. I come here today, six years afterwards, to tell you it will be done and in a few years.

The chief objection to his Budget, he said, was that it was an attack on industry and an attack on property, but he would demonstrate that it was neither. In refuting the first charge he showed how quick he had been to note the revival of trade since the middle of the year, and how well he understood its supreme political significance:

> It is very remarkable that since this attack on industry was first promulgated in the House of Commons industry has improved. It is beginning to recover from the great crash which first of all came from America, the country of high tariffs, and it has improved steadily. It has not quite recovered . . . but it is better. Industries which were making losses last year are beginning to make profits this year. The imports and the exports have gone up during the last few months by millions. Industrial investments have been steady, and there has been, on the whole, an improvement even in brewery shares.

Lloyd George knew that his audience had come to be entertained as well as instructed, and the reference to brewery shares marked the transition to a fine piece of knockabout:

> Only one stock has gone down badly – there has been a great slump in dukes. They used to stand rather high in the market, especially the Tory market, but the Tory Press has just discovered that they are of no value.

They have been making speeches lately. One especially expensive duke made a speech, and all the Tory Press said 'Well now, really, is that the sort of thing we are spending £250,000 a year upon?' Because a fully-equipped duke costs as much to keep up as two Dreadnoughts – and they are just as great a terror – and they last longer. As long as they were content to be mere idols on their pedestals, preserving that stately silence which became their rank and their intelligence, all went well and the average British citizen rather looked up to them . . . But then came the Budget. They stepped off their perch. They have been scolding like omnibus drivers purely because the Budget cart has knocked a little of the gilt off their old stage coach. Well, we cannot put them back again.

There was no need to name the 'especially expensive duke'. Everybody present knew well enough who he was:

As for property, why should the Liberal Party be against it?
I lay down as a proposition that most of the people who work hard for a living in the country belong to the Liberal Party. I would say, and I think without offence, that most of the people who never worked for a living at all belong to the Tory Party. And whenever . . . you see men building up trade and business, some small, some great, by their industry, by their skill, by their energy, by their enterprise . . . hundreds of thousands of them – not all of them, I do not say that – but hundreds of thousands of them belong to the Liberal Party.

It might be imagined that all the M.P.s who had anything to lose were on the Tory side, and that those who had nothing to lose were on the Liberal side, but in fact the richest men in the House of Commons happened to be Liberals. They were the sort of people who were prepared to make sacrifices for the sake of fairness, but hardly the sort of people 'to engage in a mere wanton war upon industry and upon property'.

The Budget was anathema to the Tariff Reformers, because they knew it would put an end to 'their descried opportunity', and it was anathema to the great landlords of the country, above all because of the proposed land valuation. As at Limehouse, Lloyd George dwelt at length and in detail upon the abuses to which the system of land ownership gave rise, and sought to explain how the Budget would correct them. For tackling these abuses he was vilified as a thief, an attorney and – worst of all – a Welshman:

That always is the crowning epithet. Well, gentlemen, I do not apologize . . . I am proud of the little land among the hills – but there is one thing I should like to say whenever they hurl my nationality at my head. I say to them, You Unionists – Hypocrites! Pharisees! You are the people who in every peroration – well, not in every case, they have only got one – always talk about our being one kith and kin throughout the Empire, from the Old Man of Hoy . . . down to Van Diemen's Land . . . and yet if any man dares to aspire to any position, if he does not belong to the particular nationality which they have dignified by choosing their parents from, they have no use for him. Well, they have got to stand the Welshman this time.

His own peroration was a masterpiece of sustained invective which, though often quoted, must be given yet again in full, because it is an example of Lloyd George at his most witty, brilliant and compelling. It can only have been intended as a direct challenge to the Lords, though it was preceded by a faint suggestion that they might, after all let the Budget through. It was, however, the last words that counted, and they were indeed fighting words:

Who talks about altering and meddling with the Constitution? The Constitutional party – the great Constitutional party. As long as the Constitution gave rank and possession and power to the Lords it was not to be interfered with. As long as it secured even their sports from intrusion and made interference with them a crime; as long as the Constitution enforced royalties and ground rents and fees and premiums and fines, and all the black retinue of exaction; as long as it showered writs and summonses and injunctions and distresses, and warrants to enforce them, then the Constitution was inviolate. It was sacred. It was something that was put in the same category as religion, that no man should with rude hands touch, something that the chivalry of the nation ought to range itself in defence of. But the moment the Constitution looks round; the moment the Constitution begins to discover that there are millions of people outside park gates who need attention, then the Constitution is to be torn to pieces.

Let them realize what they are doing. They are forcing a revolution, and they will get it. The Lords may decree a revolution, but the people will direct it. If they begin, issues will be raised that they little dream of. Questions will be asked which are now whispered in humble voices, and answers will be demanded then with authority. The question will be asked whether five hundred men, ordinary men chosen accidentally from among the unemployed, should override the judgment – the deliberate judgment – of millions of people who are engaged in the industry which makes the wealth of the country.

That is one question. Another will be: Who ordained that a few should have the land of Britain as a perquisite? Who made ten thousand people owners of the soil, and the rest of us trespassers in the land of our birth? Who is it who is responsible for the scheme of things whereby one man is engaged through life in grinding labour to win a bare and precarious subsistence for himself, and when, at the end of his days, he claims at the hands of the community he served a poor pension of eight-pence a day, he can only get it through a revolution, and another man who does not toil receives every hour of the day, every hour of the night, whilst he slumbers, more than his poor neighbour receives in a whole year of toil? Where did the table of that law come from? Whose finger inscribed it? These are the questions that will be asked. The answers are charged with peril for the order of things the peers represent; but they are fraught with rare and refreshing fruit for the parched lips of the multitude who have been treading the dusty road along which the people have marched through the dark ages which are now emerging into the light.

The key phrase was 'five hundred men, ordinary men chosen accidentally from among the unemployed'. Lloyd George had said many rude things about the House of Lords in his time, but never anything so exquisitely insulting or so perfectly calculated to cut that body down to size. The unemployed were a fashionable subject of compassionate, not to say, condescending discussion as the 'poor whites' of Edwardian society. The rich and powerful looked down on them from a great height, often with pity and concern, but never with a sense of personal identification. Their lot was deplorable but remote, and it was still regarded by many – including many peers – as the consequence of fecklessness and moral depravity. Yet here was the Chancellor of the Exchequer saying that the peers themselves were no more than unemployed – that the most august assembly in the land was, according to the moralistic view of unemployment, simply a scratch collection of layabouts. If one phrase could have sufficed to topple the peers from their pedestals, Lloyd George's would have done the trick; and it was, in any case, the most damaging ever used against the House of Lords.

Of course it was not altogether fair, but then politics is neither an exact science nor, even at the best of times, an entirely clean game. As Lloyd George very well knew, not all the peers were idlers or 'ordinary men'. Some were by any standards exceptionally distinguished, and a good number were quite hard-working and meritorious. But as a generalization there was enough truth in the phrase to make it politically deadly.

Throughout his career Lloyd George had spoken eloquently of the appalling disparities of fortune within the richest country on earth. In 1896, for instance, he told an audience in his constituency:

> One man labours and yet starves; another lounges and still feasts. One set of men strive all the days of their lives in the vineyard, and yet, amid the plenty and profusion which they themselves have helped to produce, sink unhonoured into a pauper's grave. Another set of men enter into the precincts of the vineyard only to partake of its most luscious fruit, and they live and die amid the pomp and prodigality of millionaires. This can't go on for ever.[1]

In 1909 he was making the same point at Newcastle, but now the whole nation was listening and he had the power to match his words with deeds.

His speech at the Palace Theatre lasted one hour and thirty-five minutes, but within a quarter of an hour he was addressing another audience of 5,000 at the Drill Hall. In this second speech he made a statement which deserves special attention, though it has been overlooked by historians:

> [The Budget] has got a very dangerous passage still before it is safe. If it does not get through there, it will come to you, and then you will have two questions to settle. One is the Budget; and the next will be the House of Lords. They will both be on the same ballot paper. It will be the last time probably the question will be asked. It is an old question, and it is time it should be answered. Who is to govern this country – the people or the peers?

The important words, surely, are 'They will both be on the same ballot paper.' Did the speaker himself remember them as the crisis unfolded?

Before going to bed on 9 October he was entertained to dinner at the Newcastle Liberal Club where, responding to a toast, he made his third speech of the day. In it he said that he did not think the Lords would reject the Budget. Yet in fact he must have known, or at least hoped, that the

---

1. Bangor, 15 December 1896. Fruity metaphors came naturally to Lloyd George, because he was particularly fond of fresh fruit.

effect of his day's work would be to make rejection even more likely than it was already. At Limehouse he had attacked landlords who were dukes, and had thereby shown how vulnerable the House of Lords would be in an election on the Budget issue. At Newcastle he turned the full force of his artillery on the House of Lords as an institution. For him, clearly, the electoral contest had begun. His aim was no longer to deter the peers, but rather to goad them into an act of self-destructive folly.

Alert readers may have noticed the words 'Well, gentlemen' in one passage quoted from the Palace Theatre speech. Lloyd George could not say 'ladies and gentlemen' because as usual women were excluded from the meeting. Suffragettes were, however, much in evidence during the day, and among those arrested were Emily Davison and Lady Constance Lytton – names famous in W.S.P.U. annals. As the Chancellor left the Palace Theatre two women rushed towards his car, one with 'something in her hand'. And during the meeting itself he was interrupted several times by male suffragists, whom he described, regrettably, as 'hirelings'.[1]

Next day, before leaving the Newcastle area, he and Margaret attended a small Methodist chapel at Spennymoor, where Lloyd George addressed a crowded gathering of Welsh miners – and their womenfolk, who could not very well be excluded from a place of worship. He urged them to keep using their native tongue, as he had done through long years' residence in London. His next public appearance was another supposedly religious occasion, the Welsh Baptist Union's meeting at Treorchy, which on 18 October he attended and addressed as president. Never at his most inspired when giving a political twist to Christianity, he told the Baptists that he could see no hope for the masses but in Jesus Christ, and then urged them to read the history of the French revolution. 'If France had been a pagan nation, and Louis XVI a Roman emperor, the Bastille would not have been taken, the Tuileries would not have fallen, and France would not have been free.'

One Tory newspaper used a French revolutionary analogy to describe Lloyd George after Newcastle. He had, said the *Daily Telegraph* on 11 October, 'definitely left the Girondins to join the Jacobins'. *The Times*'s comment on the same day was that of a disappointed schoolmaster: 'Mr Lloyd George's speeches in Newcastle are entirely in that early manner which the more hopeful observers of his career are now driven to doubt his capacity to outgrow.' And Northcliffe's popular daily, the *Mail*, took the same line: 'Mr Lloyd George has overdone it. His violent and bitter

1. *Daily News*, 11 October 1909.

speech at Newcastle will be read with sorrow and indignation by all right-thinking men.' Asquith's opinion cannot have been very different, and must certainly have been shared by a number of leading Liberals – though there is no evidence of any row. To most Liberals in the country, however, Lloyd George's performance at Newcastle seemed magnificent, and he was himself well pleased with the reactions to it. 'Newcastle was quite unbelievable. They all say that nothing like it has been witnessed since the good Gladstone days, crowds, enthusiasm and all. Never seen the papers so full of anything. They all realize – both sides – that they must fight now or eat humble pie and that will be very difficult for a proud tho' pusil-lanimous aristocracy. I deliberately provoked them to fight. I fear me they will run away in spite of my pains.'[1]

Nineteen hundred and nine was not a year in which Lloyd George had much chance to indulge his taste for foreign travel. He was at Dieppe for a few days shortly before the Budget; he went to Rheims for a day or two towards the end of August; and in October, between his Newcastle weekend and the Baptist meeting at Treorchy, he had a motoring holiday on the Continent – partly, no doubt, to be out of the Prime Minister's way and so to avoid troublesome recriminations. But during the whole year he had no proper holiday, and most of his week-ends were working weekends at Brighton or somewhere else within easy reach of London.

His only visit to Criccieth during the Budget proceedings was for the funeral of his sister Mary in early August. Married to a sea-captain, Philip Davies, she had lived with her brother William and Uncle Lloyd; and when her husband returned from a voyage he would join the family circle at Garthcelyn. She and Lloyd George had never been close, except in the sense that there is inevitably some closeness between a brother and sister brought up together. An austere puritan, she had disapproved, and shown her disapproval, of his many unpuritanical characteristics. But she and Margaret had become friends, and she was a good aunt to his children. Her death from cancer had been expected for some time, but when it happened he was a little moved. The news reached him during a confer-ence on Finance Bill tactics, and after handing the telegram to Masterman he left the room for a few minutes. Later, he took Masterman for a walk and showed him a letter about Mary from William, telling him to expect her death but meanwhile not to interrupt his work 'for the downtrodden

1. D.L.G. to William George, 19 October 1909 (*My Brother and I*, p. 232).

and poor'. Without that letter, he said – and he was in tears as he said it – he could not go back and take the Budget that afternoon. Actually, he took it until four o'clock the following morning, but while sitting on the front bench said to Masterman: 'How death alters things. All this seems to me like the chattering of apes.'[1]

On 29 October the Report Stage of the Finance Bill was completed, and on the same day the Press reported the result of a by-election at Bermondsey, where a Tariff Reformer was elected on a minority vote. The anti-Unionist vote, though in total about the same as the Liberal vote in 1906, was on this occasion split between Liberal and Labour candidates, while the Unionist vote showed a big increase. If the Opposition had needed further encouragement to force a general election, Bermondsey would have provided it. But to a discerning eye there was also some comfort for the Liberals. In a thoroughly working-class constituency Labour had captured only 15·9 per cent of the vote.[2]

The Opposition, in fact, needed no further encouragement. As Lloyd George said in an article published in the *Nation* on 30 October, a constitutional conflict was 'inevitable in the immediate future'. At the end of September Balfour had committed himself irrevocably to Tariff Reform in a speech at Birmingham. In Chamberlain's own city he had made common cause with Chamberlain. And Chamberlain was as determined as ever that there should be an election. On 8 October he wrote to Garvin: 'I do not fear the result . . . I am certain that if we play rightly and with plenty of "go" and ardour we shall win . . .'[3] Even if Balfour had had second thoughts it would have been virtually impossible for him to retreat after his Birmingham speech. But there is no reason to suppose that he did have second thoughts. He shared the view of most Unionists that no position could be worse for them than that which had resulted from the 1906 election. Even if they were not returned to power they could hardly fail to make substantial gains, and the Government, if not defeated, would be weakened. But Balfour, like Chamberlain, was interested above all in the chance of victory, and he was prepared, like Chamberlain, to use the House of Lords as a pawn in his game.

1. Masterman, *op. cit.*, pp. 138–9.
2. John Burns said that the Bermondsey result proved the Tories would 'sweep London', but Churchill said it proved 'parties would be evenly divided' (Ellis Davies journal, entry for 28 October 1909). Churchill comes well out of the exchange.
3. Quoted in Alfred M. Gollin, *The Observer and J. L. Garvin, 1908–14*, p. 123.

If the Tory leader in the Lords had been a more forceful politician than Lansdowne, events might conceivably have taken a different course. But Lansdowne was not really a politician at all. By nature he was a diplomat, as befitted a great-grandson of Talleyrand.[1] The only important practical achievements of his career – his negotiation, as Foreign Secretary, of the Anglo-Japanese Treaty and the *Entente Cordiale* with France – were both essentially diplomatic achievements. For the rest he had been a popular, but necessarily ornamental, Governor-General of the self-governing Dominion of Canada, Viceroy of India during a quiet period, and a conspicuously ineffective War Minister during the first phase of the Boer War. A Whig Liberal Unionist rather than a Tory, he had the prejudices of a large landowner, and more especially of a large Irish landowner. Though not a root-and-branch Tariff Reformer, he admired Chamberlain and recognized the appeal of his fiscal programme. For the party leader he felt more than admiration. At Eton he had been Balfour's fag-master, but in politics the roles were reversed. Lansdowne was undoubtedly aware that outright rejection of the Budget might have disastrous consequences for the House of Lords, and at first hinted, as we have seen, that the Bill might be amended rather than rejected. But it was swiftly made clear, in public statements by Churchill and Lloyd George, that that escape route would not be open to him. Faced with an implacable challenge from the Government that the Budget had to be passed in whole or not at all, and subject to multiple pressures from his own side, he had neither the conviction nor the personality to control events.

It may be asked why the Unionists did not perceive, in the late summer, that the revival of trade was calling into question one of their strongest arguments for an early election. Part of the answer is that very few people, on either side, were as quick as Lloyd George to note the trend or to grasp its significance. But, apart from that, Opposition strategists who were not indifferent to economics were deluded by the hope that unemployment would rise again in mid-winter. Hence their dilatory treatment of the Finance Bill, which in fact turned out to be very much to the Liberals' advantage. There was also a belief among Tariff Reformers that the new register, which was due to come into force in the New Year, would benefit them. Since the Government held the opposite belief, there was a tacit consensus in favour of delay.

The King, who was anxious to avert a conflict, spoke to Balfour and

---

1. His maternal grandfather was the Comte de Flahaut, universally recognized as Talleyrand's natural son.

Lansdowne on 12 October but was wasting his time. The decision to reject, though not yet formally taken by the Unionist peers, had in effect been taken by the leaders.

Third Reading of the Finance Bill was carried on 4 November by a majority of 379–149, the Irish Party abstaining. The following evening Lloyd George celebrated the occasion by giving a dinner for his colleagues. A week later he went to the Savoy Theatre to hear a performance of *The Mountaineers*, a light opera in which two topical songs – 'The Budget' and 'The Chancellor' – were sung by C. H. Workman in the part of Pierre. Suffragettes created pandemonium in the theatre, but the show went on and Lloyd George listened with amusement as Workman sang:

> There's a clever politician who is busily employed
>> In making bloated capital disgorge,
> And though his liberality with labour is alloyed,
>> He's a very clever Minister – by George!
> He's got his party leader in the hollow of his fist,
>> In politics he's playing Box and Cox;
> For though within the Cabinet the goods are Socialist,
>> He keeps the Liberal label on the box.

If the words were brought to Asquith's notice – as they probably were – he must have been rather less amused.

A leisurely three weeks after Third Reading in the House of Commons – on 23 November the House of Lords opened its debate on the Finance Bill, but it was already known that Lansdowne would move 'That this House is not justified in giving its consent to this Bill until it has been submitted to the judgment of the country'. Many wise and many foolish things were said during the debate, which lasted for five Parliamentary days. But the result was hardly in doubt, and at 11.30 p.m. on 30 November the Lansdowne motion was carried by 350 votes to 75. The deed was done, and red rockets flashed the news to 'all important centres of population in London and the provinces'.[1] Lloyd George, who had often listened from the steps of the Throne when Bills of his were being debated in the Lords, ostentatiously absented himself from this debate. He had hoped to be at a theatre when the vote was taken, but the hour of the division defeated him. He was, instead, having supper with Masterman at Frascati's in the Strand, a favourite haunt from his early years in Parliament.

1. This was a stunt organized by the *Daily News*. If the vote had gone against the Lansdowne motion, white rockets would have been fired.

Procedurally, if not in one vital respect politically, the Government was ready for the contest. On 2 December the House of Commons debated, and carried by a majority of 349 votes to 134, a Government resolution that the Lords' action was 'a breach of the Constitution and a usurpation of the rights of the Commons'. Next day Parliament was prorogued.

Since the Finance Bill had not been passed, there was a problem of ensuring that the State would not be starved of funds while the Budget's fate was being decided by the people. This problem had been considered well in advance and the Cabinet's solution was that the payment of new taxes should be voluntary unless and until the disputed Finance Bill was passed by the new Parliament. Meanwhile cash deficiencies would be met by borrowing.

Lloyd George was convinced that the day for first polling should be a Saturday and 15 January was eventually agreed on, though the King was annoyed that the Dissolution Council, originally fixed for 8 January, was consequently changed to the 10th. But if the King was overridden on this very minor procedural matter, he was unfortunately not overridden - indeed, he was not even challenged – on a political matter of the first importance.

It will be remembered that Lloyd George, in the second of his Newcastle speeches on 9 October, had said that both the Budget issue and the House of Lords issue would be 'on the same ballot paper'. On Prorogation day – 3 December – he reiterated and amplified the point:

> For my part, I would not remain a member of a Liberal Cabinet one hour unless I knew that the Cabinet had determined not to hold office after the next General Election unless full powers are accorded to it which would enable it to place on the Statute Book . . . a measure which will ensure that the House of Commons in future can carry, not merely Tory Bills, but Liberal and progressive measures in the course of a single Parliament, either with or without the sanction of the House of Lords.[1]

Apart from the bewildering mixture of tenses, the statement was open to serious objection on grounds of policy, as the future would reveal. But at least it seemed to confirm quite explicitly that the Lords' veto was an election issue – not merely its power to reject a Liberal Budget, but its power to sabotage Liberal legislation in general.

1. Speech at a National Liberal Club lunch, in which he also said that the peers' 'sole qualification' was that they were 'the first-born of persons who had just as little qualification as themselves'.

Even more authoritative confirmation was apparently given when Asquith spoke at the Albert Hall on 10 December. In this speech which, like Campbell-Bannerman's in the same place during the 1906 election was regarded as the touchstone of Liberal policy for the next Parliament, he said:

> I tell you quite plainly, and I tell my fellow-countrymen outside, that neither I nor any other Liberal Minister supported by a majority in the House of Commons is going to submit again to the rebuffs and humiliations of the last four years. We shall not assume office and we shall not hold office unless we can secure the safeguards which experience shows us to be necessary for the legislative utility and honour of the party of progress . . . The will of the people, as deliberately expressed by their elected representatives, must, within the limits of the lifetime of a single Parliament, be made effective.

Asquith certainly meant what he said, but he already knew that there might be some difficulty in implementing the pledge. The will of the Commons could be made to prevail only if the Lords were to renounce their veto or if, failing such renunciation, they were to be deprived of it by law. Yet the required legislation would, in that case, itself have to go through the House of Lords, and it would be necessary either to create, or at least to threaten to create, enough peers to ensure its passage. Since the Crown was the fountain of honour peerages could not be created without the Sovereign's assent, though it was reasonable to regard that assent as formal and automatic, as it was to Parliamentary Bills. King Edward, however, took a different view. On 28 November his private secretary, Lord Knollys, had written to Asquith that 'to create 570 new Peers, which I am told would be the number required . . . would practically be almost an impossibility, and if asked for would place the King in an awkward position'.[1]

This letter was received by Asquith before the Lords' vote on the Finance Bill, and so before the election was an absolute certainty. But when he spoke at the Albert Hall the election was on and it was vital that the issues should be clarified. So far as the Lords' veto was concerned, he did appear to state the Government's policy quite clearly to the immediate audience and to his 'fellow-countrymen outside', and perhaps he hoped that his words would serve as an answer to Knollys and his royal master. If so he was soon disabused of the idea, because five days after the speech

1. Asquith Papers, quoted in Roy Jenkins, *Asquith*, p. 202.

there was a conversation between Knollys and Asquith's private secretary, Vaughan Nash, which showed that the King was prepared to torpedo the policy that the Prime Minister had so recently and unequivocally set before the people.

In his memorandum to Asquith, reporting the conversation, Vaughan Nash said:

> Lord Knollys . . . began by saying that the King had come to the conclusion that he would not be justified in creating new peers (say 300) until after a second general election and that he, Lord K., thought you should know of this now, though for the present he would suggest that what he was telling me should be for your ear only. The King regards the policy of the Government as tantamount to the destruction of the House of Lords and he thinks that before a large creation of Peers is embarked upon or threatened the country should be acquainted with the particular project for accomplishing such destruction as well as with the general line of action as to which the country will be consulted at the forthcoming Elections.

Knollys had added that if the Government's plan for dealing with the veto followed the lines of Campbell-Bannerman's resolution carried by the House of Commons in June 1907, and if it were accompanied by a plan for shorter Parliaments, 'the King would concur, though apparently he would still hesitate to create Peers'. There was also a strong hint that the King's hesitation might be overcome if he were advised to create life peers rather than hereditary peers *en masse*, and there were suggestions by Knollys himself of possible alternative ways of coercing the Lords. Finally, he had said to Nash that it would be useful if Asquith could discuss the matter with the King before the election.[1]

There is no evidence that Asquith made any attempt during the ensuing weeks to resolve the grave issues that Knollys, on behalf of the King, had raised. Though there was evidently room for manœuvre, on the face of it the King was posing a threat to Parliamentary democracy no less serious than the Lords' rejection of the Budget and other Liberal measures. He was stating, quite arbitrarily, that he would not regard the election as decisive in the matter of the Lords' veto, even though it was a cardinal point of Liberal policy that the veto should be dealt with in the next Parliament. He was also suggesting that Asquith should not, for the time being, discuss this extraordinary claim with his colleagues. The Prime

1. The whole memorandum is printed in Spender and Asquith, *op. cit.*, Vol. I, pp. 261–2.

Minister's reaction ought, surely, to have been prompt and firm. He should have asserted, with due courtesy, the Government's right, if re-elected, to carry out their declared policy with the full cooperation of a constitutional monarch. And, if the King's reply had not satisfied him, he should have asserted his right to submit the matter at once to the Cabinet. Unfortunately he left it in abeyance while the election campaign proceeded – an error of baleful import for the future.

Lloyd George's personal campaign began – after his speech at the National Liberal Club – in his own constituency. He returned to London in time to be on the platform for Asquith's Albert Hall speech, and during the following week he made speeches in the London area. On 21 December he spoke three times in Cardiff and once in Swansea, before going on to other places in South Wales. For Christmas he was at Criccieth, and he gave much pleasure to old friends and acquaintances by turning up at the annual *eisteddfod* in Llanystumdwy village on Christmas night. The occasion must have given him some pleasure, too, as he contrasted the obscurity and boredom of his childhood with the excitement, fame and power that he now enjoyed.

On the last night of the year he spoke again in London, and the following night he was at Reading, supporting the candidature of his friend, Rufus Isaacs. Between 4 and 7 January he addressed more meetings in London, and the next weekend he spent in the South-West, at Plymouth, Devonport and Falmouth. Within a few days he was at Stockport on his way to York and Grimsby, and then he returned to Wales, where he spoke at Newtown, Montgomeryshire, on the 18th. Results were already coming in and his own was declared on the 22nd. But still he had electioneering to do in later-polling constituencies, and he ended his campaign in the West Midlands, on Chamberlain's doorstep.

Wherever he went he drew great crowds, but on the whole the meetings were orderly, though he ran into trouble at Grimsby – where exception was taken, apparently, to a Minister speaking in a constituency other than his own on polling day - and at Reading, where suffragettes staged one of their boldest demonstrations. Unquestionably he was the star turn of the election. No one on his own side was his equal in ability to interest, amuse, provoke or – at his best – inspire, and on the Opposition side there was no platform speaker even approximately in his class. Though it is commonly supposed that he spent most of his time bashing the House of Lords, in fact he spent even more time discussing the economic issue – appropriately enough, seeing that he was Chancellor of the Exchequer and his Budget was in contention. He did not, indeed, neglect the theme of 'peers versus people', which he had expounded with such overwhelming force at Newcastle. Yet he showed throughout the campaign his awareness that probably to most electors the most important choice of all was between his own Free Trade radicalism and the Tariff Reform radicalism of Chamberlain.

Chamberlain, he knew, was his arch-opponent – though also, ironically, in many ways his political model and precursor. There was symbolism in the fact that his room at the House of Commons was Chamberlain's old room, with Chamberlain's map still hanging on the wall. One day when the Budget controversy was at its height Lloyd George exclaimed to Masterman:

> This is the old spirit of Radicalism, the spirit that Gladstone killed. Gladstone was no Liberal! He should have made Chamberlain Chancellor after he had won the country for him on the unauthorized programme [in 1885]. If he had done so, we should have solved the land question, we should have got rid of the House of Lords, we should have done with the Licensing question, and we would have got rid of the Church![1]

But Gladstone had driven Chamberlain into alliance with the Tories, and his radicalism, as Lloyd George thought, into the wrong channels. All the same he respected him still, and with good reason. Who is to say what would have happened in the election if Chamberlain had been fit to stump the country? Instead he was a muted cripple, while Lloyd George was at the peak of his powers.

At West Newington Lloyd George said that unemployment at the end of October was down 25 per cent compared with the end of October 1908. But even those still out of work should not be tempted to vote for Tariff Reform. 'If you are going to get unemployment, you had better have it with cheap bread than with dear bread.'[2] At Swansea he said:

> Compare Great Britain with every Protectionist country in Europe, and we beat them all. Are the people mad that they should give all this away? We are not going to surrender a great position. Taxing the foreigner is the greatest rubbish ever talked.[3]

1. Masterman, *op. cit.*, pp. 142–3.   2. 17 December 1909.   3. 21 December 1909.

And in London, at the Queen's Hall, he overreached himself. The Tory managers, he said, had called for an early election, because if they waited another year there would be 'no unemployment, no bad trade'. Technically he was imputing the words to his opponents, but it must have sounded – and have been meant to sound – like a pledge.[1] Nevertheless the trade figures that were published a week before the first polling went far to justify his claim that the economy was returning to health. Whereas in January exports had fallen by nearly £6 millions, in December they had risen by nearly £4·4 millions.

The Reading meeting was the most dramatic of his campaign. It was held in a vast tramcar shed where 7,000 stood to hear him, with many more standing on the tops of cars near its open side. What happened is best described in the words of the *Daily News* reporter:

> Upon the platform were a number of ladies, including Mrs Lloyd George and Mrs Isaacs, but, apart from these, ladies were denied admission. Nevertheless, though precautions which were believed to be of the most thorough character had been taken, two indomitable suffragettes were crouching uncomfortably in the dirt and dark beneath the platform, to appear suddenly, dusty and dishevelled . . . from behind the rough curtain which veiled the space below the platform, and rose by the side of the reporters' tables. 'You're a robber, Mr Lloyd George', cried the first, a frail-looking little woman, catching at a word the Chancellor himself had just used. As stewards rushed forward another woman appeared too dazed, it seems, to say anything, and both were hustled outside without much trouble – except to the reporters, whose tables were upset. A regrettable feature of their expulsion was the behaviour of an excitable old gentleman, who struck at the head of the first woman with his bowler hat, and who put his foot forward to kick the second woman. But the stewards concerned acted with all the restraint possible in the circumstances.[2]

There was also a little male heckling at the meeting. Lloyd George was asked for news of his insurance scheme and of the Government's unemployment scheme. He replied that they were not just vague promises, but that first he needed the money to pay for them. That was what the election was about.

The incident with the suffragettes must have been vividly in his mind

1. 31 December 1909.
2. 4 January 1910.

when he referred to the women's suffrage question two days afterwards in North Kensington. He would, he said, be 'glad to see women get their rights of citizenship' and he urged his audience not to 'allow these wild, hysterical women to affect [their] judgment on a very great issue'. In the same speech he paid a chivalrous tribute to Lord Percy, son and heir of the Duke of Northumberland – and Tory M.P. for South Kensington – who had recently died in Paris.

When he visited his own constituency early in the campaign he had to dispose of a suggestion that he might be accepting a new political base in Cardiff. During the afternoon of 9 December he spoke in Welsh to delegates from all parts of the division, and reaffirmed his loyalty in a simple but most effective way. The proposal had, he admitted, been made that he should represent Cardiff, and Cardiff had shown him great kindness. But 'after all I would rather remain here'. This was greeted with enthusiasm and 'Three cheers for Lloyd George'. Then he said 'I have an attachment for the Boroughs' – and paused, waving his hands in front of him, before adding: 'It is greater than I can say.' With that he sat down. There was a moment of stunned silence, followed by prolonged and heartfelt cheering.

In the evening he addressed an audience of over 7,000 in the Pavilion at Caernarvon. Most of the speech was in English, but first – in Welsh – he explained why. 'I understand that some people on this side and on the other of Offa's Dyke are desirous of reading what I have spoken, and for that reason I am going to deliver my address in English. I have not lost my Welsh yet.' He then spoke for over an hour without saying very much that was worthy of rapt attention on either side of Offa's Dyke. But he reverted to Welsh for his closing words, which must rank among the finest flights of oratory in any language:

Yesterday I visited the old village where I was brought up. I wandered through the woods familiar to my boyhood. There I saw a child gathering sticks for firewood, and I thought of the hours which I spent in the same pleasant and profitable occupation, for I also have been something of a 'backwoodsman'. And there was one experience taught me then which is of some profit to me today. I learnt as a child that it was little use going into the woods after a period of calm and fine weather, for I generally returned empty-handed; but after a great storm I always came back with an armful. We are in for rough weather. We may even be in for a winter of storms which will rock the forest, break many a withered branch and leave many a rotten tree torn up by the roots. But when the weather clears you may depend upon it that there will be something brought within the reach of the people that will give warmth and glow to their grey lives, something that will help to dispel the hunger, the despair, the oppression and the wrong which now chill so many of their hearths.[1]

Even in cold print the passage has an electric quality. What could be more telling than the leap from commonplace to sublime at the words 'We are in for rough weather'? Lloyd George always delighted in storms. They appealed to his imagination and his dynamic nature responded to them. But his taste for political storms was never that of a revolutionary. He wanted to uproot rotten trees, not to destroy the whole forest.

His opponent in the Caernarvon Boroughs was the Mayor of Bangor, H. C. Vincent, and he did slightly better than the Englishman, R. A. Naylor, at the previous election. But Lloyd George was, of course, returned with a comfortable majority. The result was:

Lloyd George	3,183
Vincent	2,105
Majority	1,078

In Wales as a whole the results were excellent for the Administration. Only two border seats were lost and 'in twenty-three seats the Liberal or Labour majority was the highest ever, higher even than in 1906'.[2]

But the national result was a very different story. Whereas at the

1. For Welsh-readers here are his words in the original:
'Ddoe ymwelais a'r hen bentref lle'm dygwyd i fyny. Crwydrais trwy y coedwigoedd y gwyddwn yn dda amdanynt yn fy machgendod. Gwelais yno blentyn yn casglu tanwydd a meddyliais am yr oriau a dreuliais i gyda'r un gwaith. Dysgais un profiad yr adeg hon oedd o wasanaeth imi. Dysgais, fel plentyn, nad oedd o fawr ddiben myned i'r goedwig ar ôl tymor tawel, oblegid fe ddychwelwn adref yn gyffredin yn waglaw ond dychwelwn yn llwythog bob amser ar ôl ystorm fawr. Yr ydym wedi dechreu ar dywydd garw. Gallwn fod i mewn am auaf o ystormydd a ysgydwa y fforest gan dorri llawer o ganghenau gwywedig a gadael llawer coeden bydredig wedi ei rhwygo yn y gwreiddiau. Ond wedi i'r hin glirio gallwn ddibynnu y bydd i rywbeth gael ei ddwyn o fewn cyrhaedd y bobl a rydd gynhesrwydd a sirioldeb i'w bywydau, rhywbeth a rydd help i ymlid y newyn, yr anobaith, y gormes a'r camwri sy'n achosi y fath fferdod ar lawer o'u haelwydydd.'
In contemporary Welsh newpaper reports the passage is printed in the third person, but here it has been rendered back into the first person by Mr David Jenkins, C.B.E., Wales's National Librarian.
2. Kenneth O. Morgan, *Wales in British Politics, 1868–1922*, p. 249.

Dissolution the Liberals still had an overall majority of 76 – in spite of by-election losses since 1906 – after the last votes had been counted in early February 1910 the Liberals had only two seats more than the Unionists – 275 to 273 – and the Government would have a working majority in Parliament only with Irish Nationalist support. Labour won forty seats, compared with thirty at the previous election, but the increase was largely due to the fact that mining M.P.s were now affiliated to the Labour Party. The average swing to the Unionists in Great Britain was 4·3 per cent.

It is hard to say whether or not Lloyd George was prepared for the result; the evidence is conflicting. Probably in the heat of the campaign his hopes surpassed his rational expectations. In any case, he made the best of things in his public statements as the result emerged. At his own eve-of-poll meeting he said: 'I feel not merely gratified but I feel elated at the results which up to the present have come and the results which I can see coming over the horizon.'[1] And at Droitwich a few days' later he rebutted Tory claims that the Government would lose its mandate:

> Thirty would have been quite enough for them to reject the Budget; it would have been quite enough for them to set up Protection in this country and tax the food of the people. They admit that we shall probably get a majority of 120, and say a majority of thirty would be more than sufficient for them but that four times thirty is not enough for us. That is, if the rival team score thirty over and above ours, they have won. If our cricket team scores 120 over theirs, we have lost. That is not cricket. Although it is not cricket, it is Toryism.[2]

He was right to claim a victory, because the Opposition would remain in opposition and the Government would continue to govern. But in his heart he must have known that it was a flawed victory.

Why did 'the people' fail to give sweeping, massive endorsement to 'the People's Budget'? Why did so many of them decide, apparently, to vote against themselves in the struggle of 'peers versus people'?

First, it must be remembered that the electorate in 1910 was by no means representative of the whole British nation. Only 58 per cent of adult males had the vote, and it is a fair assumption that the remaining 42 per cent would, if enfranchized, have voted in very large numbers for Liberal or Labour candidates. In what was still a disproportionately middle-class

1. 21 January 1910. 2. 25 January 1910.

electorate the fear of Socialism was strong, and many voters were susceptible to the argument that the Budget was a first instalment of Socialism.

This was particularly true in the South of England, where radical tendencies are at all times less pronounced than in the North of England and the Celtic fringe. Liberal gains in the South at the previous election would scarcely have been possible, even with so many other factors favouring the Liberals, if their economic policy had been as radical as the Newcastle programme of 1892. In fact, their economic policy in 1906 had been conspicuously moderate, even conservative. They had offered sound finance in exchange for Tory waste, and the traditional policy of Free Trade in preference to the dangerous innovation of Tariff Reform. While in 1910, the recent slump made voters take a more sceptical view of Free Trade than in 1906 – in spite of the apparent trade revival – and a less jaundiced view of Tariff Reform, those who had voted for sound finance were unlikely to feel much enthusiasm for the Lloyd George Budget. It was hardly surprising that the South of England reverted solidly to its normal Tory allegiance.

Another very important difference between 1906 and 1910 was that in the earlier election Irish Home Rule was not much of an issue, because it was widely believed that the Liberal Government would not bring in a Home Rule Bill in the next Parliament, whereas Asquith in his Albert Hall speech gave an explicit Home Rule pledge – received, incidentally, with marked coldness by his otherwise rapturous audience. This was a gift to the Unionists, because opinion in Great Britain remained as strongly pro-Unionist, in that sense, as it had ever been. The Opposition also clearly succeeded in extracting very considerable value from the Defence issue – fear of Germany and alarmism about relative naval strengths. It was noteworthy that dockyard seats at Chatham, Portsmouth and Devonport fell to the Tories. Finally, the Liberals suffered heavy losses in county seats, especially in the Southern counties. The Tory Party was able to establish itself, once and for all, as the defender of rural England against the supposedly hostile forces of industrialism and urban collectivism.

How much was Lloyd George responsible for the Liberal setback? Certainly he must have contributed to the alienation of voters in the countryside. Though in his Budget speech he had been at pains to discriminate between urban and rural landowners, stressing the latter's virtues, he could not for long disguise his prejudice against landlords in general. His attitude towards them was conditioned by his experience in Wales, where landowners were anglicized and therefore, as a rule, resented by Welsh tenants and farm-workers. But in England the situation was different. Feudal or quasi-feudal sentiments were still very powerful and not offset, as in Wales, by cultural antagonism. Lloyd George was not biased against the land and in favour of urban industry – quite the reverse – but he wanted to see the existing hierarchy in English country life replaced by an emancipated yeomanry. He was hostile not to the interests of countrymen as opposed to townsmen, but simply to the landed interest in its existing form. Yet such was the solidarity of rural communities over large areas of England that in being hostile to landlords he appeared to be hostile to the land. English country people of all classes tended to feel that their way of life was menaced by what he represented.

Yet without him the Liberals would probably not have won the election at all. For any damage that he may have done to Liberal chances in the countryside or elsewhere, there were more than compensating gains. The radicalism of the Budget, which doubtless lost the party some of its 1906 support, was also the means whereby Liberal morale was rekindled and a disastrous drift towards Labour arrested. Moreover his attack on the House of Lords was on the whole popular, as the second 1910 election would presently demonstrate.

Of course his enemies tried to make out that his rabble-rousing had denied the Liberals the more decisive victory that would otherwise have been theirs. Harcourt, for instance, wrote to Asquith of his alleged experience at Rossendale in Lancashire: 'I was surprised to find how little real *anger* there was about the H. of Lords: all my people wanted to know was that we "meant business" and were not in for a compromise or sham fight, but they have no conception of a constitutional question.' And he added that Lloyd George's and Churchill's speeches had done the party 'much harm even with advanced men of the *lower* middle class'.[1] But Harcourt's evidence is suspect because he was himself opposed to much of the Budget, and because the election results in Lancashire do not bear it out. The Liberals, in fact, did strikingly well in that part of England. But in any case it was surely Lloyd George, above all, who had shown the country that the Government 'meant business' and was 'not in for a compromise or sham fight'.

In 1910 he was, indeed, the people's champion. Even though not all of them may have appreciated what he was trying to do for them, and even though millions were debarred from voting for him, the cause that he championed did up to a point prevail.

1. L. Harcourt to Asquith, 26 January 1910 (Asquith Papers).

NINE
Coalitionist Revealed

Before the last results were in, but with the pattern of the new Parliament no longer in doubt, Asquith and Lloyd George met at 10 Downing Street on 26 January. There is no record of their discussion, which lasted several hours, but it is unlikely that they applied their minds to the future with much clarity or conclusiveness. Both men were tired – Lloyd George especially – and both felt the need for a little respite. Asquith went straight to the South of France, forgetting an engagement to dine and sleep at Windsor, and thus compounding his difficulties with the King. Lloyd George also went to the South of France a few days later, but first spent a long weekend with the Mastermans at Folkestone, where he was joined by Margaret and, for a time, by Churchill.

Lucy Masterman gives us a vivid picture of him that weekend. It was very cold and there was snow on the ground. In Canterbury Cathedral he showed the somewhat resentful uneasiness that he never ceased to feel for the stately or sacred monuments of traditional England. He took no part in the service that was going on, but was pleased when Masterman told him as they left that it had included the words 'He filleth the hungry with good things and the rich he hath sent empty away.'

After asking to borrow a cheque he was unable to remember the name of his own bank, until he found it on an envelope in his pocket. Then it occurred to him that the 'chaps' in question had signed the City petition against his Budget, and he vowed to withdraw his money from them, adding with a wink that he wished it were more. To Lucy Masterman he seemed 'incredibly without vanity'. Though he had a natural liking for praise, he was 'extraordinarily clear-sighted about himself and his own capacities'.

Margaret did not accompany him to the South of France, but Masterman did. They stayed for a week at Nice, where Charles Henry – and probably also Julia Henry – were staying. The Chancellor attended an unexpurgated performance of *The Merry Widow*, but was careful not to enter the Casino at Monte Carlo. He read, and was 'stimulated by', Masterman's copy of Kropotkin on the French Revolution. He motored, played golf, and seems to have been uncharacteristically reluctant to talk politics. But in the second week of February he was back in London, as the Liberal Government faced a crisis which brought it near to disintegration.[1]

Ministers had a majority in the new Parliament, but a majority for what? Unionist leaders were ready to acknowledge that the electorate had decided in favour of the Budget, but not that it had decided anything about the House of Lords. Yet an indispensable section of the Government majority held exactly the opposite view. Irish Nationalists had no love for the Budget and could argue that Ireland had not voted for it; but they were determined that Home Rule, now once again firmly promised, should not be blocked by the House of Lords, and they could very plausibly claim that the Government had a mandate for abolishing the Lords' veto.

Unfortunately abolition of the veto required legislation, which meant that the bill to give effect to it would have to be passed by the House of Lords itself. And since it was Unionist policy to deny the existence of any electoral mandate for such a bill, there could be no question of its being passed by a House still virtually monopolized by the Unionists. It would be necessary for peers to be created in adequate numbers to carry the bill, and this would require use of the Royal Prerogative.

Government supporters in the country assumed from what Asquith had said in his Albert Hall speech that the King had promised to use his Prerogative to enforce the will of the people. The Prime Minister had said that he would not hold office without the necessary safeguards, and a similar pledge had been given by Lloyd George. Indeed, he had been even more explicit than Asquith, stating at Newcastle that the Budget and the House of Lords would 'both be on the same ballot paper', and then at the National Liberal Club that he would 'not remain a member of a Liberal

1. Lucy Masterman's diary dictated in February 1910, and Masterman's letters to her from the South of France (Masterman *op. cit.*, pp. 151–7).

Cabinet one hour' unless he knew it had 'full powers' to remove the Lords' veto. It was almost certainly not until after the election – perhaps at their meeting on 26 January – that he received from Asquith some inkling of the King's views on the subject, which had been allowed to go unchallenged, because in the last days of the election, when polling had already begun, he still felt able to say: 'It must be made perfectly clear that if the Lords reject a bill sent up by the Commons a second time the measure will be sent straight through to the Throne.'[1] Evidently he was still campaigning in the belief that removal of the veto was high on the Liberal agenda for the next Parliament.

Yet at about the same time he confessed privately that the House of Lords was 'a most difficult question'.[2] It seems that he may already have been feeling some doubt about the veto policy. Was it, after all, the best way to tackle the problem of the Lords? In common with the Liberal Party as a whole he had spent years of his life denouncing the second chamber, but had never given much thought to the practical implications of having to deal with it. Nor, in any case, was there much of the political philosopher in his make-up. Having a genius for action, he could be highly original and resourceful in improvising change on the executive side of the Constitution. But Parliament interested him far less than the machinery of government. In so far as he had any idea how he would like to reform Parliament it was not, apparently, on bicameral lines. 'I am a single chamber man,' he told Herbert Lewis at breakfast on 19 February, 'but nobody wants a single chamber now.' Yet he added: 'It might be accepted if the plan were daring enough to attract the Labour and Irishmen.'[3]

It was certainly true that none of his Cabinet colleagues wanted a single-chamber Parliament. To that extent the Cabinet knew what it did not want, but there was acute division among its members on what positively to do about the House of Lords. A strong faction, including Grey, Haldane, Crewe, Runciman and Samuel, pressed for discarding the Campbell-Bannerman veto policy in favour of a policy of Lords' reform. Their objection to limiting the veto in the manner outlined in 1907 was that it could easily be represented as tantamount to single-chamber rule. Harcourt on the other hand argued that the party had a clear mandate to end the veto but none whatever to reform the Lords. Both points of view were influenced, though in different ways, by hostility to Lloyd George. Some

1. Speech at Newtown, Montgomeryshire, 18 January 1910.
2. Talking to Ellis Davies at Criccieth, 23 January 1910 (Ellis Davies Journal).
3. Herbert Lewis diary, entry for 19 February 1910 (N.L.W.).

of the reformers believed that a viable second chamber would be the most effective barrier against unduly radical change, while Harcourt perceived, and was glad to perceive, that the Campbell-Bannerman formula would by no means reduce the existing second chamber to impotence.

Churchill put forward a scheme in which reform and veto limitation were combined. In a memorandum to Asquith he advocated abolition of the House of Lords as such and its replacement by an elected second chamber with no power to touch money bills. He shrewdly remarked that whatever might be done by way of tinkering with the Lords would leave the Unionists in ultimate control. But there was one serious weakness in his scheme: it was not to be implemented at once, but was to be submitted to the people at a further general election.

The Prime Minister, who should have been giving the Cabinet a firm lead, drifted for several weeks in a state of almost cataleptic indecision, summed up in the notorious phrase 'We had better wait and see.'[1] In 1907 he had accepted the idea of a limited suspensory veto, but without much enthusiasm and only after toying with the idea of a referendum to resolve differences between the two Houses. Campbell-Bannerman had secured the Cabinet's agreement to his veto plan, but neither at the time nor subsequently was it ever given the critical examination it deserved. Thus in February 1910 Asquith was ill prepared for the urgent, practical problem that he had to face. The Opposition, reinforced by the election, was in no mood to ease his task, and the problem was further complicated by the King's reluctance to create peers. Temperamentally Asquith shrank from the prospect of a constitutional struggle which might involve the Monarchy as well as the House of Lords. From the first he had hoped to avoid a head-on clash, and now that the nightmare seemed imminent his one thought was to find some way of escaping from it.

For a time reform may have seemed to him a possible way out. His closest colleagues were eagerly recommending it and he shared their interest in spiking Lloyd George's guns. Yet it must soon have been apparent to him that reform alone, without definite steps towards curbing the Lord's powers, would be wholly unacceptable not only to Irish and Labour Members, but also to a large number of his own back-benchers.

There was, no doubt, a temptation to believe that the Irish and Labour

1. First used on 3 March 1910, in answer to a question in the House of Commons about the timing of the Budget's reintroduction. Roy Jenkins argues that he used it at the time 'as a threat', but admits that in February he 'exhibited less sureness of touch than at any other stage in the long constitutional struggle'. (*Asquith*, pp. 204–8.)

might be bluffing because they had nowhere else to go, but the argument was unsound. By voting with the Unionists the Irish could not hope to obtain Home Rule – at least so long as Balfour was leader of the Unionist Party – but they could give themselves the satisfaction of wreaking vengeance upon the party that had promised and failed to deliver it. And Asquith was not so ignorant of them as to be unaware that blind vindictiveness was a passion by which they were capable of being moved. As for Labour, their big new grievance was the Osborne judgment of July 1908, which had made the trade union political levy illegal. But the Unionists might have the intelligence to see that facilitating Labour's political advance would damage them less than it would damage the Liberals. In any case, quite apart from what his allies might or might not do, Asquith had good reason to fear that many Liberals would become mutinous if limitation of the Lords' veto were postponed. Nevertheless he was very slow to allow his feelings to be overruled by the logic of the situation.

What was Lloyd George's attitude through the period when the Cabinet was at sixes and sevens? It is often alleged that he made matters worse by temporarily throwing in his lot with the reformers, but this is to misunderstand his conduct. Unlike most of the reformers he was determined to establish the supremacy of the House of Commons, but he was equally determined that the substance of his Budget should not be lost through inflexibility on his own part or disingenuousness on the part of others. Thus he was willing to make some Budgetary concessions to the Irish, and to entertain the idea of 'mending' the Lords if, but only if, his colleagues would accept the necessity for 'ending' the veto. The Campbell-Bannerman plan was no more sacrosanct to him than any other political device, and he could see at least one of the flaws in it, that it left the hereditary composition of the Lords intact. To that extent reform of almost any kind was an improvement on the Campbell-Bannerman plan, but Lloyd George would never have favoured reform as a substitute for restricting the Lords' powers. Reform-plus-restriction was as far as he could be expected to depart from the single-chamber solution that he would ideally have preferred.

His temporary espousal of reform was, therefore, similar to Churchill's, and probably the details of the Churchill scheme were evolved by the two men in collusion. But first Lloyd George seems to have tried to persuade the Cabinet to tackle the veto at once, without any concurrent proposals for reform. On 12 February Redmond wrote to his colleague, John Dillon, that Lloyd George had been pressing for a time-table with the following order of priorities:

1. Whole time up to Easter to be devoted to necessary supply. Debate on the Address etc. etc. etc.
2. Immediately after Easter Recess first business to be introduction of Veto Bill.
3. Interval between 1st and 2nd reading of Veto Bill, a budget to be introduced in which very substantial concessions on whiskey duty etc. to be made to Ireland. The old budget would thus disappear altogether. It would be a budget for 1910–11.
4. Veto and new budget to run *pari passu*, but *Veto* bill to go first to Lords.
5. On rejection of Veto Bill by Lords, but not till then, the King to be asked to appoint peers. On his refusal (which is taken for granted) Parliament to be dissolved – about July . . .[1]

This proposed time-table indicates that Lloyd George, accepting the regrettable fact that Asquith had obtained no guarantees from the King before the January election, was now prepared to force a midsummer election in which his fiscal programme and ending the Lords' veto would definitely be on the same ballot paper. Moreover the Royal Prerogative itself would be an issue, since the King's refusal to act on the advice of his Ministers would be the precipitating cause of the new election. It was characteristic of Lloyd George to suggest that his 1909 Budget should be formally dropped and reintroduced as the Budget for 1910. He was never a stickler for form. All that mattered to him was that the substance of his programme should be enacted, and as it would now have to be enacted in 1910 he had no objection to its being called the 1910 Budget.

Similarly, he felt that he could afford to meet the Irish grievance on spirits, because during the past year there had been an astounding drop in consumption, even in Ireland. The increased duty – levied provisionally under the authority from the Budget resolutions – had produced so much less than the estimated revenue that he had decided, in October 1909, to take £500,000 more from the Sinking Fund. Now it seemed to him that he could safely make a concession to the Irish without defeating the social purpose of his liquor and licensing duties, which over the country as a whole had already succeeded far beyond expectation. His colleagues,

1. Quoted in F. S. L. Lyons, *John Dillon: a Biography*, p. 314.

however, were most reluctant to concede anything to the Irish under what would appear to be duress, and the Irish for their part wanted an immediate and unequivocal statement on the veto.[1] So Lloyd George had to concentrate upon persuading the Cabinet 'reformers' to agree to such a statement, and his instinct told him that he would have a better chance of persuading them if they no longer had to regard him as an implacable opponent of Lords' reform.

But they were not easily won over and when the new Parliament met the Cabinet was still hopelessly divided. The King's Speech on 21 February reflected the division:

Recent experience has disclosed serious difficulties due to recurring differences of strong opinion between the two branches of the Legislature. Proposals will be laid before you, with convenient speed, to define the relations between the Houses of Parliament, so as to secure the undivided authority of the House of Commons over finance and its predominance in legislation. These measures, in the opinion of my advisers, should provide that [the House of Lords] should be so constituted and empowered as to exercise impartially, in regard to proposed legislation, the functions of initiation, revision and, subject to proper safeguards, of delay.

Veto limitation was clearly to be given no priority over reform, and the whole package was to be introduced, not immediately, but 'with all convenient speed' – a disquietingly vague phrase. And later in the day, speaking on the Address, Asquith confessed to his outraged supporters that he had neither asked nor received any guarantees from the King.

At this stage the Cabinet's plan of business was, first, to obtain necessary supply and then to table, but not discuss, resolutions on the Lords simultaneously with reintroducing the Budget.[2] Lloyd George seems to have gone along with this plan, but no doubt he only did so because he was confident that it would soon have to be abandoned. He was facing a critical dilemma in his own career. His attempts to persuade the 'reformers' to agree to immediate limitation of the second chamber's powers had so far met with no success, and he knew that unless he could soon convert

1. Redmond, though leader of the great majority of Irish Nationalist M.P.s, was subject to very strong pressure from opinion in Ireland and from the independent group of Nationalists, in which William O'Brien and Tim Healy were the leading figures. Their hostility to the Budget was extreme.
2. Runciman's pencilled note of report to Cabinet by Lloyd George and Birrell, after meeting Redmond and Dillon, 17 February 1910 (Runciman Papers).

them his position would be fatally compromised. Once the non-existence of guarantees became known to the Party at large, his pledge that he would not remain 'one hour' in a Liberal Cabinet without 'full powers' to get rid of the veto was bound to be a grave embarrassment to him. Inevitably he thought of resigning and it was in these circumstances that he spoke to his old and intimate friend, Herbert Lewis, of the possibility of winning Irish and Labour support for a 'daring' plan to abolish the House of Lords and dispense with any kind of second chamber.

Why did he not, after all, break away as leader of a Left-wing alliance? Reflection must have convinced him that there was no future in it, and we can guess at his reasoning. The Irish would be very dubious allies: on most issues he and they were out of sympathy, and their radicalism was largely confined to making the Constitution safe for Home Rule. Labour, too, was an uncertain quantity. It was one thing to secure working-class support as a leader of the preponderant Liberal Party, but it would be quite another to deal with Labour if he had only the Liberal radicals behind him. Socialism would be much harder to resist and the trade unions very difficult to control.

Moreover how would he acquire an organization of his own, and how finance it? The only political machine that might serve his turn was the Budget League, which had the right sort of membership and the necessary funds. But the Budget League was run by Churchill, without whose cooperation its resources might not be available.[1] In any case, unless Churchill were prepared to resign with him his chances of survival as an independent Left-wing leader would be slight. Apart from the Budget League, the importance of Churchill was that he was universally recognized as Lloyd George's radical partner in the Cabinet. If the two men failed to move together, radicals throughout the country would be perplexed and confused. But would Churchill risk everything for the privilege of being Lloyd George's lieutenant on what might be a long march through the wilderness? He had just been appointed, at his own request, to the Home Office, the senior Secretaryship of State, of which he was the

1. On 2 December 1909 Ellis Davies recorded in his diary a heated exchange between Lloyd George and the Chief Whip, J. A. Pease, at a meeting of the Budget League Executive, with Churchill in the chair. The point at issue was whether or not a cheque for £14,000, just received by Lloyd George for the League, was given in expectation of a title. But Ellis Davies added the comment: 'The flare-up with Pease rather indicated strained relations between him and G[eorge] possibly because the Budget League in possession of great funds will be an effective rival to the party organization in case of a break-up of the Liberal Party' (Ellis Davies Journal).

youngest holder since Peel. Asquith had first tried to move him to the Irish Office, which would have been one way of weakening the radical partnership, since his energies would have become absorbed in the complex affairs of Ireland. But faced with his demand for a loftier post at the centre of the stage, the Prime Minister may have consoled himself with the thought that by putting him roughly on a par with Lloyd George some tension might be created between the two men. Beyond question the appointment made it less likely that Churchill would resign with Lloyd George, and therefore unlikely that Lloyd George himself would resign.

During the period of malaise before the Cabinet crisis was finally resolved he spoke on one occasion of 're-forming a Government in which he would be Prime Minister, playing with the idea of having it composed of business men, Sir Christopher Furness, Alfred Mond and such, which would carry enormous weight in the country'.[1] 'Playing' is the operative word. Lloyd George was allowing his fancy to wander. At the time he knew very well that there was no chance whatever of his being empowered to form such an administration. It was simply not within the realm of practical politics – as a Leftward resignation, however perilous, undoubtedly was. Yet his mention of the idea, even in airy conversation with a friend, is significant as evidence of his hankering for efficient government, and of his growing distaste for the party game. These tendencies were soon to have a more serious manifestation.

Lloyd George was not the only member of the Cabinet who thought of resigning in February. Grey was another, and after the fiasco of the King's Speech and Asquith's statement some Ministers felt that it would be best for the Government as a whole to resign. But this would have meant handing the initiative and the choice of a time for dissolution to Balfour, so repeating the mistake that he himself made at the end of 1905. Common sense prevailed and the defeatist mood passed, to the accompaniment of an unmistakable, if artfully camouflaged, victory for the radicals. On 28 February Asquith announced that the Government would take all Parliamentary time until Easter (the end of March), and that the time would mainly be used for obtaining supply. Immediately after Easter veto resolutions would be introduced, embodying the principles of a bill. Only

1. Masterman, *op. cit.*, p. 160. Lloyd George was talking to Masterman on a park bench. No exact date is given for the conversation, but from internal evidence it was probably Monday 11 April 1910.

when these resolutions had been carried would the Budget be brought on again.

The new time-table left most of the Cabinet's disagreements formally unresolved, but in reality signified defeat for the 'reformers'. By postponing the ultimate crisis, and by deciding to carry veto resolutions rather than a veto bill in advance of the Budget, the Cabinet could persuade itself that it was not acting under dictation from the Irish–Labour–radical front. But it was tolerably clear that pressure from the rank-and-file had forced Ministers to think again more urgently of the veto than of reform, and consequently the time-table was accepted.

By Easter Lloyd George had regularized the financial position – by means of a temporary borrowing measure and a vote on account for six weeks – while the Cabinet had reached agreement on the terms of its veto resolutions. These contained no reference to Lords' reform, but when Asquith introduced them on 29 March he said that the ensuing legislation would 'contemplate in a subsequent year' replacing the hereditary second chamber by one that was democratically based. Such was the meagre sop with which the 'reformers' had to be content.

The resolutions bore a close resemblance to the 1907 Campbell-Bannerman plan, though there were several important differences. Campbell-Bannerman, assuming that the Lords would never tamper with a Finance Bill, had devised a system applicable to all legislation. Any measure passed three times by the House of Commons would be treated as if it had been passed by both Houses, and would receive the Royal Assent. Since this procedure was obviously too slow and cumbersome for a Finance Bill, the Asquith Government fell into the trap of distinguishing between 'money bills' and 'bills other than money bills'. The House of Lords was to be shorn absolutely of power to delay the passage of any measure certified by the Speaker of the House of Commons as a money bill, but was to retain the power to delay any other measure for a period of not less than two years. The period of delay for such measures was, in effect, somewhat longer under the Asquith plan than that allowed for all measures under the Campbell-Bannerman plan, though Asquith's had the merit that the period could overlap from one Parliament to another.

Another difference was that, whereas Campbell-Bannerman had envisaged consultation between representatives of both Houses when a bill was obstructed by the Lords, the Asquith scheme did not provide for any such joint consultation. Finally, the last of Asquith's three resolutions concerned the statutory life of a Parliament, proposing that it should be reduced from seven to five years. This was relevant to the issue of Lords versus Commons only in the sense that more frequent elections would enhance the Commons' moral authority. It became, however, the one unquestionably good feature of the eventual Parliament Act.

The veto resolutions were carried by good majorities and in mid-April the Parliament Bill had its First Reading. Shortly beforehand the Cabinet reached agreement on the next stage of its programme, thus ensuring its survival. But things were touch-and-go at its meeting on 13 April. The two questions to be decided were what concessions, if any, should be made on the Budget, and whether or not the King should be asked for contingent guarantees to ensure passage of the Parliament Bill after the next election. Even the veteran Morley was threatening to resign if it were decided to recommend use of the Prerogative to coerce the Lords, and there was also very strong feeling in the Cabinet against making any fiscal concession to the Irish. Lloyd George sensed that if he dropped his idea of cutting the whisky tax the right atmosphere would be created for others to drop their objection to the request for guarantees. And so it proved. There were no resignations and the lesser Irish grievance was sacrificed to the greater; or, to put it another way, the Cabinet strained at a gnat while swallowing a camel.

An hour before midnight on 14 April Asquith spoke on the adjournment, amid great excitement in the House of Commons. He said that if the Lords and, by implication, the King were to obstruct the veto policy endorsed by the Commons, the Government would either resign or ask for a dissolution; and that if there had to be another appeal to the country it would make sure in advance that 'the judgment of the people, as expressed in the election, [would] be carried into law'. The statement was not quite all that radicals could have desired. There must have been some uneasiness at the hint of possible resignation, as well as justifiable annoyance that there would probably have to be another election to settle a matter which most of the Government's supporters believed to have been settled at the last. All the same the Prime Minister's words brought, on the whole, relief and encouragement to his own side. The internal party crisis was over.

Lloyd George cannot escape his share of blame for the Government's near-fatal ineptitude on the constitutional issue in late 1909 and early 1910. Though his responsibility was obviously much less than Asquith's, and though he had the excuse of very heavy work in his own departmental sphere, he should not have talked as much as he did about the second chamber without clarifying his thoughts on its future, nor should he have given the pledges that he gave during the election without being sure that they would be honoured. Moreover he seems to have been not quite sufficiently aware of the need for rapid decisions after the election. With whatever misgivings, he acquiesced in a process of argument and manœuvre which lasted for weeks running into months, while the Government's credit sank to a dangerously low level and the chance was forfeited of pursuing Liberal policy on the House of Lords without seeming to be driven to it by the Irish.

On the other hand it must be said in his favour that he played a key part in holding the Cabinet together. But for him the 'reformers' might never have been reconciled to the indefinite postponement of their own policy or the acceptance of one that they detested. Haldane later acknowledged that Lloyd George was 'very good' in Cabinet, though he was critical of Asquith's chairmanship and very critical of Churchill's long-windedness.[1] According to Masterman, Lloyd George's supreme feat during the Cabinet crisis was establishing a good personal *rapport* with Grey, who had been strongly prejudiced against him.[2] It was also very important that he judged correctly when to give way on the Budget, and that he did so with such telling effect. His negotiations with the Irish were neither discreditable nor a waste of time; it was right that he should explore all ways of getting his Budget through, and if the Cabinet had remained weak and divided on the veto, fiscal concessions to the Irish would have been the only hope. But in the end the concessions were valuable for a different reason; by waiving them he salved his colleagues' pride and so induced them to give way on a much larger issue.

It was now possible to dispose of the Budget and this was swiftly done under guillotine procedure, with amendments allowed only where the Bill had been changed since it first passed the House of Commons. Discussion of it occupied less than five days of the Commons' time and on 27 April it received its Third Reading by 324 to 231, with most of the Irish Nationalists voting in the majority. Before it left the Commons Asquith paid tribute to Lloyd George's 'genius, tact, patience and courage', and said that he was proud to be associated with 'this great financial scheme'. Next day the Bill passed through all its stages in the House of Lords, and in the evening Lloyd George gave a celebration dinner at the Savoy Hotel – perhaps a slightly incongruous place to celebrate the 'People's Budget'. On

1. R. B. Haldane, *An Autobiography*, p. 217.
2. Masterman, *op. cit.*, pp. 160–1.

THE LITTLE DOTARD.

REGISTRAR JOHN BULL (*to bearer of venerable infant*). "Well, what can I do for it – birth certificate or old-age pension?"

3. 'The Little Dotard', *Punch*, 20 April 1910

29 April it received the Royal Assent, a year to the day after its first introduction.

All the signs now pointed to the summer election that Lloyd George had envisaged back in February. The Parliament Bill – in substance a veto bill, though with a vague preamble to satisfy the 'reformers' – was before the House of Commons and would be carried there by large majorities. The House of Lords would certainly reject it, and the King would presumably continue to insist that there should be another election before he would consider using his Prerogative to force the Bill through. In these circumstances Asquith would surely advise an immediate dissolution, and if the King refused to grant him contingent guarantees the Monarchy itself would be dragged into the campaign. Nothing could be more distasteful to Asquith, but what were the alternatives?

Reform was out of the question, at any rate as a substitute for curbing the existing Lords' powers. The Government's supporters had shown that they would not tolerate a policy that seemed to involve indefinite postponement of action to end the veto. Besides, there was very little evidence that the Lords would agree to any serious reform of their chamber. Even those who favoured reform in principle differed widely on the form that it should take, and many were adamantly opposed to it. In mid-March Rosebery carried three resolutions of a general character, including one that hereditary peers should no longer have the automatic right to sit and vote in Parliament; but he felt obliged to shelve two further resolutions, in which details of a reform scheme were spelled out. Balfour and Lansdowne were, to say the least, unenthusiastic about reform, and any encouragement that they may have conveyed to Liberal reformers was solely for the purpose of weakening and dividing the Government.

One theoretically possible means of resolving deadlock between the two Houses of Parliament was the device of a referendum. This had been mentioned the previous year by Rosebery, and was now attractive to the Unionist leaders as a way of improving their democratic credentials without touching the hereditary composition of the Lords. Asquith, too, was attracted by it. In 1907 he had fancied the idea, among others, before giving his reluctant assent to the Campbell-Bannerman formula, and recently, on 13 April, had raised it again in a letter to the King. If the Lords tried to block the veto policy it would, he said, be the Cabinet's duty 'at once to tender advice to the Crown as to the necessary steps – whether by exercising the Royal Prerogative, or by a Referendum *ad hoc*, or otherwise . . .'

In his statement next day to the House of Commons he was silent on the referendum, taking refuge in the doctrine that it would not be right for him to divulge in advance 'the precise terms' of his advice to the Crown. But rumours must have been going around, because Ramsay MacDonald had already commented on the subject in an article written, surprisingly, for the ultra-Unionist *National Review*:

> A proposal has been made that at the point when the Premier has to approach the King a referendum might be taken on the Commons resolutions. This is quite unnecessary. It is a method of reference foreign to our British habits, and great risks would be run of an unsatisfactory poll and inconclusive results. It would entail almost the cost of an election . . .[1]

Most of Asquith's colleagues seem to have shared this view, because a very short time after his letter to the King the referendum idea was quietly dropped by the Cabinet – though it lived on in the minds of the Opposition.

Would Asquith, then, have resigned, as in his 14 April statement he hinted that he might? It is unlikely that he would have done so from motives of escapism. The tenacity with which he clung to office later in his Premiership strongly suggests that he would not have yielded to any political death-wish in 1910. If he had resigned merely to avoid embarrassing the King a large section of the majority alliance would probably have dissociated itself from his decision, and there might well have been a move to make Lloyd George leader in his place. According to one source Asquith told the King that, if he were forced to resign, Lloyd George would have to be sent for.[2] His intention, no doubt, was to alarm the King into making life less difficult for the existing Prime Minister. When, six and a half years later, he eventually resigned his office, he took the step for purely tactical reasons, not at all meaning to go and still less to be succeeded by Lloyd George. If that was his attitude in 1916, how much more so in 1910, when he was still a comparative newcomer to the Premiership and his vital energies were relatively unimpaired.

There was, however, one situation in which he would have been almost bound to resign, and that situation was by no means remote. At a meeting on 27 April at Lambeth Palace, Balfour told the Archbishop of Canterbury,

1. 'The Tactics of the Present Crisis', *National Review*, April issue 1910.
2. Wilfrid Scawen Blunt, *My Diaries*, Part Two, entry for 13 May 1910, but referring to events of the previous weeks.

Esher and the King's private secretary, Knollys, that in his view the King could not only safely refuse to create peers before another election, but could also refuse to grant a dissolution with contingent guarantees, provided the refusal were carefully worded. In either event he, Balfour, would be willing to form a government, though in the first there would, presumably, be no need for Asquith to resign. Only if the King refused the alternative request – for a dissolution with guarantees – would the Prime Minister's resignation be more or less inevitable. Balfour must have been tempted by the prospect of becoming Prime Minister and then immediately holding an election, as Campbell-Bannerman had done so successfully at his expense. But the circumstances now were different and Balfour's chances of scoring a tit-for-tat against the Liberals very dubious. It was, however, certain that if the King were to act on Balfour's advice the Monarchy itself would be dragged into partisan controversy.

Would the King have acted thus? Probably his worldly wisdom and constitutional sense would have restrained him. But we shall never know, because on 6 May – while Parliament was in recess and the Prime Minister out of the country – King Edward died. From early March until the end of April he was at Biarritz, but on the day of the Lambeth meeting, and only a few minutes after it ended, he arrived back in London. The following evening he gave his last audience to Asquith, who 'found him most reasonable'.[1] Immediately afterwards the Prime Minister attended Lloyd George's celebration dinner at the Savoy, which he left early to motor to Portsmouth and join the *Enchantress* for a southerly cruise. Approaching Gibraltar he heard that the King was critically ill, and soon afterwards news of his death reached the yacht as it steamed for home.

To Asquith, the news must have been just as shocking and bewildering as he later said it was. At a most delicate moment in the struggle between Lords and Commons he now had to deal with an inexperienced sovereign who, moreover, lacked his father's breadth of outlook. Though certainly no radical, Edward VII had a number of liberal-minded friends and his native realism was a good working substitute for liberalism. Even his faults were of value to him as a constitutional monarch, since they tended to make the company that he kept more diverse, and his sympathies more catholic, than they would otherwise have been. Besides, there was a streak of generosity in him which was preferable to his son's rectitude, politically if not morally. Strict notions of right and wrong may keep a man from

1. Margot Asquith, *Autobiography*, Vol. II, p. 135.

behaving badly, but they are also apt to keep him from behaving un-predictably well. George V was a prince who never did less than his duty, but was incapable of doing very much more. His father devoted most of his life to wasteful self-indulgence, but could make a magnanimous gesture far beyond the line of duty. For instance, when the virulent anti-monarchist Keir Hardie was recovering, in 1903, from an operation for appendicitis, he received a letter of sympathy from the King, who had recently nearly died of the same illness. 'What could be nicer?' was Hardie's comment, and it must be history's as well.[1]

Lloyd George was no less disconcerted than the Prime Minister by this sudden twist of fate. 'I do not quite know what to think about this catastrophe. It never entered our calculations. What insolent creatures we all are. We reckoned without taking the Great Ruler into account.'[2] He had no sentimental illusions about Edward VII, but paid him the great compliment of thinking he would have made his way in the world even if he had not been born in the purple. The old King was 'rather an able man' who 'could have earned his living in the City' whereas his son was 'a much smaller man'.[3] Lloyd George had to admit, however, that the new King was very friendly when receiving him in audience for the first time on 9 May. By and large the two men got on surprisingly well during the twelve years of their association as monarch and minister.

At their first official meeting the King told Lloyd George that he meant 'to try his hand at conciliation'.[4] The idea of conciliation was already in the air, since the day before, 8 May, Garvin had written a famous editorial in the *Observer*, in which he said:

> If King Edward upon his deathbed could have sent a last message to his people, he would have asked us to lay party passion aside, to sign a truce of God over his grave, to seek . . . some fair means of making a common effort for our common country . . . Let conference take place before conflict is irrevocably joined . . .

Nor was this the first intimation of this idea to King George. At the end of March it had been suggested to him that there should be a royal initiative to promote such a conference, and this suggestion was made by none other than the Liberal Chief Whip, Alexander Murray, Master of Elibank.

1. Kenneth O. Morgan, *Keir Hardie: Radical and Socialist*, p. 137.
2. D.L.G. to M.L.G., 8 May 1910 (N.L.W. and *Letters*, p. 152).
3. D. R. Daniel, *op. cit.*
4. D.L.G. to M.L.G., 9 May 1910 (N.L.W. and *Letters*, p. 152).

Garvin had thus raised publicly an idea which had already found favour with the King when put to him, privately and unofficially, by a member of the Government.

It was only in February that Murray had succeeded Pease as Chief Whip. Now, and until his resignation two years later, he was a crucial figure in a period of intense political activity. 'The Master' had a gift for behind-the-scenes negotiation and intrigue, which owed much to his natural bon-homie. He was a tough but also a genial operator, well liked by politicians of all parties and factions, and able to be a crony of Lloyd George while retaining Asquith's full confidence. Margot described him as a 'rare combination of grit and honey', and J. A. Spender gives us this picture of him:

> His ample figure and full-moon face, with its fringe of curls, were always a pleasant vision, and he had a persuasive manner that was hard to resist. He was in some ways *the* character of these times, and his chronic good humour soothed many savage breasts . . . He knew exactly what to say to Redmond, and when to say it; he kept Lloyd George from boiling over, and raised Asquith's temperature when it seemed to be falling. He soothed the rich Liberals who were uneasy about Limehouse, and got large cheques out of them to be used for their own despoiling. When two people quarrelled, he was at infinite pains to bring them together again, and could make each of them seriously believe that the other was pining for reconciliation. It was pleasant to be in his company, if only to realize for the first time in one's life what charming things other people, who were very disagreeable to one's face, were saying about one behind one's back.[1]

As well as being on excellent terms with his fellow-politicians, Murray was liked and trusted by the new King and his two private secretaries, Knollys and Sir Arthur Bigge (Stamfordham), who disagreed with each other on the constitutional issue.

Garvin's article expressed a view for which there was strong support among the general public, but not among committed partisans on either side. The conference proposal was equally denounced by the *Morning Post* and the *Daily News*, with the result that even those party leaders who saw its advantages had to move very warily. Lloyd George, above all, had to move with extreme discretion, not to say deception, because if he were to show too obvious an enthusiasm for a party truce his reputation as hero

1. Spender, *Life, Journalism and Politics*, Vol. 1, p. 235.

of the Liberal Left would be blasted. While, therefore, he conveyed his approval of the idea to Garvin through an intermediary, he was careful not to give it any countenance in public, and seems either to have opposed it in Cabinet or to have acquiesced in it only as a tactical manœuvre. But he could do so with impunity, because after much discussion the Cabinet as a whole decided in its favour.

On the Opposition side Garvin used all his personal influence to persuade Balfour and Joseph Chamberlain. On 24 May he wrote to Balfour's aide, J. S. Sandars:

> What I hate is the thought of our having to drag the new King into the fiercest of party battles. We might win – I think we would; but the ultimate results would not be good for the Crown nor for us. Anything worse than a small majority for a Unionist party compelled to tackle Lords reform and tariff reform cannot be conceived.

This may have helped to overcome Balfour's misgivings, because by the beginning of June he was ready, at least, to respond to an invitation from the Crown. At the same time Garvin was 'largely' converting Chamberlain, who had just returned from the South of France 'flatly against the conference policy'.[1] So, when Parliament reassembled on 9 June, and Asquith, with the King's blessing, wrote to Balfour formally proposing a conference, Balfour agreed. The Truce of God (or Garvin) was now in being. It was to last for five months.

In the spirit of conciliation, as well as for good practical reasons, Lloyd George's second Budget, introduced on 25 June, contained no proposals for new taxation. The Chancellor pointed with satisfaction to the effectiveness of his increased liquor duty, evident in rapidly falling consumption and fewer convictions for drunkenness. He also referred to the 'great national scheme of insurance against unemployment and against invalidity' which he was now planning to bring in the following year. In making a correct forecast that the general revenue would expand, he went on the assumption that trade would continue to improve. Opposition criticism was muted, though the Government's decision to postpone consideration of the Finance Bill until November, after carrying only the Budget resolutions, was condemned as a 'dangerous novelty'.

In the spring or early summer of 1910 Uncle Lloyd paid his first visit to 11 Downing Street. D. R. Daniel found him drinking tea at the far end

1. Garvin to Northcliffe, 13 June 1910. Garvin's proselytising efforts with Chamberlain had been at lunch on 1 June.

of the dining-room table, and was welcomed 'gaily, politely, kindly'. They spoke of Gladstone, a former occupant of the house, and of Herbert Gladstone who was born there. 'I am very sorry', said Uncle Lloyd, 'that he has allowed the title of Lord to be attached to that famous old name.' Daniel was moved by the spectacle of 'this famous, honest craftsman from the little countryside of distant Eifionydd, the most Nonconformist preacher in Wales, sitting in the rooms of his old hero, Gladstone, the highest of churchmen'. And he recorded that Uncle Lloyd himself was moved by 'the simplicity of No. 11 – the plain and beautiful oak'. The two men also spoke of Lloyd George's father and Uncle Lloyd remarked that he was shorter and more lightly built than his son, who was 'heavier by now, for there is a tendency on our side to fatten'.[1]

Uncle Lloyd had stayed before with the Lloyd Georges in London but never before in the Chancellor's official residence. Now, at the heart of the British political world, he must have experienced a sense of glorious fulfilment as he witnessed the buzz and bustle around his favourite nephew, to whose education he had applied himself with such hopeful zeal. In David he could see his own desires and aspirations realized, for he was not only a genuinely good and godly man, but also something of a frustrated politician. What he could never have hoped to achieve himself he could now feel he was achieving, vicariously, through Lloyd George. And this illusion was sustained by Lloyd George's affectionate flattery, making out that he set great store by his uncle's political opinions and so repaying him for years of never-failing worship and praise.

Ostensibly the six months of party truce were devoted to meetings of the eight politicians who together formed the Constitutional Conference. Each side was represented by four of its leaders, the Prime Minister, Lloyd George, Crewe and Birrell for the Government, Balfour, Lansdowne, Austen Chamberlain and Cawdor for the Opposition. There was no official representative of the Irish Nationalists or of Labour, but the inclusion of Birrell, Chief Secretary for Ireland, was presumably meant to show that Irish interests would never be forgotten, while Lloyd George's presence was no doubt relied upon to give adequate reassurance to the Left. In the Opposition team Austen Chamberlain was the natural spokes-

1. D. R. Daniel, *op. cit*. Daniel gives the date as 22 April 1910, but there is evidence in a letter from Lloyd George to his wife that Uncle Lloyd was at 11 Downing Street at the end of July. Perhaps his visit was prolonged. Herbert Gladstone had become a viscount on his departure from the Cabinet to take up the post of Governor-General of South Africa.

man for Liberal Unionism, and the majority in the House of Lords had the satisfaction of seeing two of its members among the Tory negotiators. (Cawdor, least well known of the eight to his contemporaries – and to history – had been First Lord of the Admiralty in 1905. He had large estates in Wales as well as Scotland, and before succeeding to the peerage had sat in the House of Commons as M.P. for Caernarvonshire. He had also been chairman of the Great Western Railway.)

The Constitutional Conference met for the first time on 17 June and held eleven more meetings until it adjourned for a summer holiday on 29 July. There were further meetings in mid-October and a final series in early November. In all there were twenty-one sessions, but the parties never came really close to agreement. The Conservatives tried to establish a distinction not only between ordinary and financial legislation – which the Government had already, mistakenly, admitted – but also between ordinary and constitutional legislation. Finance bills, they conceded, would have to be passed by the Lords, provided they were strictly for the purpose of raising revenue and had no far-reaching 'social or political consequences'. Ordinary bills, in cases of dispute between the Houses, would be referred to a joint sitting whose decision would be accepted as binding, but disputed constitutional proposals would have to be referred to a plebiscite of the whole nation.

The joint sittings idea revived one originally put forward by a Cabinet committee in early 1907, and actually accepted by the Cabinet, only to be reconsidered soon afterwards by Campbell-Bannerman (who disliked it from the first) and then superseded by his scheme based on the idea of a suspensory veto, in which, however, joint sittings also featured. The earlier scheme was known as the Ripon plan, though in fact it was largely the work of Crewe and Asquith.[1] In 1910 the Unionists were quite ready to accept a version of this plan, but the conditions that they attached to it made agreement impossible.

Both the size of Lords' representation at joint sittings and the definition of constitutional legislation presented insuperable difficulties. The Government, naturally enough, was determined that Liberal measures should not be exposed to automatic defeat at a joint sitting, where even a comparatively small Tory majority would be a sufficient veto. Yet the Tories, in

1. The genesis of the 'Ripon' plan, and its revival in 1910, are very fully discussed in Corinne Comstock Weston, 'The Liberal Leadership and the Lords Veto, 1907–1910' (*The Historical Journal*, XI, 3, pp. 508–37). The author believes that Lloyd George was a member of the Cabinet committee which produced it, but the only evidence is that a copy of the committee's report is among the Lloyd George Papers.

effect, were not prepared to make an absolute surrender of their right to pick and choose which Liberal measures to let through. They rejected the Government's proposal that, at joint sittings, Tory peers should out-number Liberal peers by forty-five, even though it meant that a Liberal Government with a majority of less than fifty in the House of Commons would be virtually at their mercy. The Government could not have gone any further to meet them and should probably not have gone as far as it did.

On the question of 'organic' or constitutional legislation the principal stumbling-block was Ireland, though Asquith maintained that this cate-gory, as defined by the Tories, could include electoral reform bills as well. He was not, like many of his colleagues and supporters, inflexibly opposed to direct consultation of the voters on particular issues. In 1907 he had preferred it to joint sittings as a means of resolving deadlock between the Houses, and in his last letter to King Edward had suggested a referendum as an alternative to exercise of the Royal Prerogative. But it was Irish Home Rule that the Tories had chiefly in mind when they insisted upon special procedure for 'organic' legislation, and the Government could in no circumstances agree to a referendum on Home Rule, for which, it well knew, there was no popular majority in the United Kingdom as a whole.

The Conference was, therefore, an essentially futile exercise, tediously prolonged and more or less doomed to fail. But it was neither the only nor, indeed, the most significant political activity during the truce. There was a far more interesting 'play within a play', initiated by Lloyd George.

After the first series of meetings it was clear to him that there could be no agreement on the constitutional issue taken in isolation. The only hope lay in a much wider and more ambitious project. Bored, anyway, by mere constitution-mongering, and increasingly alarmed at the effect of un-bridled partisanship upon the nation's capacity to tackle a whole range of desperately urgent problems, he became convinced of the necessity for a coalition government with an agreed programme. His ideas on the subject were committed to writing in a memorandum dated 17 August.[1]

The case for a temporary coalition was stated in the preamble. Britain, he said, had 'gained a good deal' from party conflict in the past, and could gain more from it in the future, but the country's immediate need was to bring 'the resources of the two Parties into joint stock in order to liquidate arrears which, if much longer neglected', might 'end in national im-

1. The full text of this remarkable document is given as an Appendix, pp. 362–8.

poverishment, if not insolvency'. The rest of the memorandum consisted of twelve sections relating to specific areas of policy – housing, drink, insurance, unemployment, the Poor Law, national reorganization, national defence, local government, trade, the land, Imperial problems and foreign policy.

The most striking passages were those in which the author hinted at resolution by compromise of the fiscal and Home Rule issues. Under 'trade' he said that the various problems connected with State assistance to it 'could be enquired into with some approach to intelligent and judicial impartiality if Party rivalries were eliminated', and he did not hesitate to mention tariffs as one of the problems requiring such impartial scrutiny. Under 'Imperial problems' he said that the Irish question might be dealt with more effectively by statesmen of both parties if they were no longer 'subject to the embarrassing dictation of extreme partisans, whether . . . Nationalists or Orangemen'. Under 'national defence' he suggested that 'even the question of compulsory training should not be shirked', citing the example of Switzerland.

Lloyd George did not rush into action to promote his scheme. Excelling, as he always did, at persuasion through the spoken word, he must have felt that it would be better to wait until his colleagues and leading opponents were back from their holiday haunts. Postal exchanges on matters of high policy were not in his style, and his memorandum was never intended to be a circular, but rather to serve as a basis for discussion in face-to-face encounters.

It was written in London – not, as often stated, at Criccieth – and on the same day he wrote to Margaret, who was in Wales: 'My holiday is truncated. Today a message came from the King inviting me to be Minister in attendance at Balmoral from the 5th to the 12th Sept. I must go of course.'[1] Before his visit to Balmoral he travelled on the Continent with Masterman. At Oberammergau he witnessed the passion play, without emotion. Near Treviso, on the way to Venice, he had a very lucky escape when the car in which he was travelling crashed into a peasant's cart at 60 m.p.h. The only victim, providentially, was a horse. While in Venice he went to the Lido and bathed in the Adriatic, but paid little attention to churches, palaces or pictures. Visually he was responsive to natural, but hardly at all to man-made, beauty. Though Bologna, Lucca and Florence were also included in the trip, it was not, for him, a cultural pilgrimage.

1. D.L.G. to M.L.G., 17 August 1910 (N.L.W.). The royal invitation was not a spontaneous gesture but was engineered by Crewe in collusion with Knollys.

On 4 September he took the night train to Scotland. At Aberdeen and at Ballater he was greeted by enthusiastic crowds in which, he believed, there were 'some Tories' – a good augury for coalition. During his time at Balmoral the King and Queen were extremely friendly, but he found them 'simple, very, very ordinary people', which was, perhaps, 'how it should be'. The Prince of Wales seemed to him 'quite a nice little fellow' and he was touched when Queen Alexandra, arriving for her first visit to the castle since King Edward's death, gave him 'a warm handshake' with 'tears in her eyes'. His bedroom and bathroom were adorned with portraits of illustrious statesmen, ranging from Wellington to Disraeli, Gladstone and Salisbury. He did not accompany the King on his grouse-shooting expeditions, but had plenty of other opportunities to talk to him and may have mentioned the coalition project in general terms. If so, the King's reaction is likely to have been sympathetic, because, as later events were to prove, he was by nature coalition-minded.[1]

After a brief interlude of work in London he went, at last, to Criccieth and there entertained the Churchills at the end of September. During their stay Lloyd George's plan was definitely expounded and discussed, and in his bread-and-butter letter Churchill afterwards wrote:

> My own opinion has not departed from our conversations. It is not for me to take the lead. I cannot tell how such an arrangement might ultimately affect democratic political organizations. But if we stood together we ought to be strong enough either to impart a progressive character to policy, or by withdrawal to terminate an administration which had failed in its purpose.[2]

In other words, he was in favour of a coalition provided he were himself a member of it, and provided it did not involve too many concessions to the Right, with permanent alienation of the radical element in Liberalism. If Lloyd George had failed to enlist Churchill's support he could have proceeded no further with his plan, because it would have been fatal for him to move towards the Centre while a man of Churchill's talents remained on the Left, in a position to do to him what Disraeli did to Peel.

The next question was how to approach the Opposition, and he decided

1. Lloyd George wrote nine letters to his wife while he was at Balmoral, using Welsh far more than usual. (Nos. 1333 to 1340B in the N.L.W. collection. Parts of Nos. 1336 and 1340 are reproduced in *Letters*, p. 153.)
2. W.S.C. to D.L.G., 6 October 1910 (L.G.P. and printed in *Winston S. Churchill* Companion Vol. II, Part 2, pp. 1024–5).

that the first Tory politician to be contacted should be F. E. Smith. This was a logical choice, because Smith was the Tory back-bencher best able to 'do a Disraeli' to Balfour, having the necessary ambition, unscrupulousness and brilliance in debate. Though he had made his name as an intensely militant partisan, Lloyd George knew that he was, in reality, an undogmatic progressive like himself, who for one thing had regarded the Lords' rejection of the 1909 Budget as folly. He, Churchill and Lloyd George were kindred spirits. As for Balfour, though he had no fondness for Smith, he would all the same be sure to appreciate the value of a coalition proposal brought to him, and commended, by such an intermediary.

Early in October, therefore, Lloyd George showed Smith his memorandum at 11 Downing Street, and he had not misjudged his man. Smith reacted with enthusiasm and hastened to inform Balfour, who soon afterwards lunched or dined with Lloyd George to discuss the project. In many ways it must have appealed to the Tory leader, whose subtle intellect was impatient of party slogans and shibboleths, who was deeply concerned about domestic and foreign threats to Britain's power in the world, and who had every reason to welcome the chance of ending the fiscal controversy that had plagued him since 1903. It must also have been a relief to him that Lloyd George was showing such a marked preference for the politics of consensus over those of demagogic agitation. Whatever his precise motives, he did not reject Lloyd George's idea out of hand, but asked for permission to discuss it with his senior colleagues.

Over the next two or three weeks there was a genuine, if faint, chance that the idea would prevail. Austen Chamberlain was keenly interested when Lloyd George – putting a very bold gloss on his memorandum – suggested to him, through Smith and Bonar Law, that the Tariff issue might be referred to an impartial body which should report within six months, and whose verdict would be accepted by the Government. Garvin was taken into confidence and through him the backing of the Northcliffe Press secured. Lloyd George's project seemed a heaven-sent realization of the dream which had inspired Garvin when he called for the party truce, and he exerted himself above all to make the proposed federal solution for Ireland acceptable to Unionists.

Meanwhile Lloyd George was also working on his colleagues. After Churchill the first to be told was probably the Master of Elibank, but it was not long before Asquith was shown the memorandum. At his request copies were then sent to Crewe and Grey, who both wrote to the Prime Minister indicating general support. In their view the Liberal Government had achieved just about all that it could achieve on its own, and Grey even predicted the break-up of the Liberal Party if the truce had no constructive outcome. Haldane and Birrell were also approached at some stage, and are said to have reacted favourably. Another Minister in the know was Masterman, but the circle on both sides was severely restricted.

In mid-October Lloyd George cancelled a routine party speech but kept an engagement to speak at the City Temple to the Liberal Christian League, a supposedly non-political body. This speech, one of the best of his career, was in some ways no less inflammatory than Limehouse or Newcastle. It contained some of his most telling invective against landlords and the idle rich. The theme of the speech was social waste, and he identified one of the causes of it as the vast area of the country given over to sport:

> In all, you have millions of acres exclusively devoted to game . . . A good deal of it is well adapted for agriculture and afforestation. In addition to these great preserves, in some of the most fertile parts of this country you will find hundreds of thousands of acres where the crops are injured and their value damaged by game preservation. When you come to the land around the towns, here the grievance is of a different character. Some may have a greater waste in parsimony than in prodigality. That is the way the land around our towns is wasted . . . Amongst the many contrasts which a rich country like ours presents between the condition of rich and poor there is none more striking than the profligate extravagance with which land by the square mile is thrown away upon stags and pheasants and partridges, as compared with the miserly greed with which it is doled out for the habitations of men, women and children . . . The greatest asset of a country is a virile and contented population. This you will never get until the land in the neighbourhood of our great towns is measured out on a more generous scale for the homes of our people. They want, as a necessity of life, plenty of light, plenty of air, plenty of garden space, which provides the healthiest and the most productive form of recreation which any man can enjoy. I am not against sport; I only want to extend the area of its enjoyment. A small number of people like to take their sport in the form of destroying something; the vast majority prefer cultivation to destruction. Some like blood; others prefer bloom. The former is considered a more high-class taste; but so few of us can afford to belong to that exalted order – they must be content with such pleasures as flower gardens and vegetable patches and fruit bushes can afford them.

Unemployment was another conspicuous source of waste, and he was glad to say that unemployment among the working classes was at last receiving a good deal of attention. But

absolutely no thought has been given to unemployment amongst the upper classes. This is just as grave as the other, and is a prolific cause of unemployment amongst the workmen. A number of men and women are given the best training that money can afford, their physique is developed, their brains are strengthened and disciplined by the best education, and then, after they have spent the first twenty years, the first third of their lives, in preparing and equipping themselves for work, they devote themselves to a life of idleness. It is a scandalous and stupid waste of first-class material; and the worst of it is, the system requires that they should choose some of the best men whom wealth can buy to assist them in leading this life of indolence . . . It is a common but shallow fallacy that, inasmuch as these rich find employment for and pay good wages to those who personally minister to their comfort, to that extent they are rendering a service to the community. Quite the reverse. They are withdrawing a large number of capable men and women from useful and productive work.

The man who spoke those words could hardly be suspected of contemplating any deviation to the Right. Yet the speech as a whole was admired and praised across party lines. One reason was its emphasis upon social reform as the only alternative to social revolution, and upon the necessity to mobilize the nation's strength. These were both themes that appealed to intelligent, patriotic Tories, and Lloyd George had never doubted that there were many Tories, as there were many rich Liberals, prepared to subordinate their own class interests to what they saw as a higher cause, or at least to act from the motive of enlightened self-interest.

But the most significant part of the speech was an elaborate tribute to Joseph Chamberlain and an explicit recognition that his Tariff Reform campaign had been more than a threat to the people's cheap loaf:

I am not a Tariff Reformer; all the same I recognize that Mr Chamberlain's historic agitation has rendered one outstanding service to the cause of the masses. It has helped to call attention to a number of real crying evils festering amongst us, the existence of which the governing classes in this country are ignorant of or had overlooked. We had all got into the habit of passing by on the other side. You will only have to look at the five or six main propositions which underlie Mr Chamberlain's great appeal in order to realize that nothing can quite remain the same once [they] are thoroughly accepted by a great political party. What is the first proposition? That this is the most powerful Empire under the sun. What is the second? That Great Britain is the heart of this Empire; strong, powerful, rich enough to send even more of its blood to the remotest member of this huge body, for he would tax us even further for the enrichment of the Colonies . . . But what is the third proposition? That in the affluent centre of this potent Empire there is a vast multitude of industrious men, women and children for whom the earning of a comfortable living, and often of a bare subsistence, is difficult and precarious. What is the fourth? That to alter this state of things needs drastic and far-reaching changes . . . What are the fifth and sixth? They are so important, when you come to consider remedies, that I invite your special notice to [them]. The fifth is that the fact of such a sweeping change, involving losses and injury to the fortune of individuals, ought to be no barrier to its immediate adoption, since the well-being of the majority of the people would thereby be secured . . . The sixth proposition is that the time has come for seeking a remedy, not in voluntary effort, but in bold and comprehensive action on the part of the State.[1]

Thus did Lloyd George offer a glistening olive-branch to the man who, in spite of all appearances to the contrary, had been the prime inspiration of his radical thinking, and whom – but for the perverse allegiance of Welsh Liberalism to Gladstone – he would have cheerfully followed in 1886. It was unfortunate that his conciliatory message could not be delivered in person, but Chamberlain might not have been willing to receive one who had damaged his credit and impugned his honour during the Boer War. Close as the two men were in political outlook, circumstances had driven them into opposing camps and into conflict which had left unhealed wounds. Another obstacle to their meeting in 1910 may have been Lloyd George's fear of illness. Throughout his life

1. City Temple, 17 October 1910. Such was his desire for a settlement that at about this time he joined with his colleagues at the Constitutional Conference in agreeing that taxation should not be exclusively the business of the House of Commons if it 'would effect important social or political changes through expropriation or differentiation against any class of owners or property'. When the Conference broke down the Liberals opposed any public statement 'largely on the ground that it would make known their attitude on finance'. If he had not been so hopeful of achieving comprehensive progress by means of a coalition, Lloyd George would surely never have agreed to such a restrictive formula. (Weston, op. cit.)

disease and infirmity of any kind had filled him with revulsion, and he would probably have shrunk from visiting a Chamberlain chair-ridden and slurred in speech, remembering the erect, incisive gladiator with whom he had done battle in the past.

Certainly the prospects for coalition would have been immeasurably brighter if Joseph Chamberlain could have been persuaded to give the idea his blessing. Even without it, Lloyd George was slow to give up hope, and at the end of October he produced a second memorandum in which he was more specific than in August about the Irish question. It was to be settled 'on some such lines as were sketched by Mr Chamberlain in his speech on the First Reading of the Home Rule Bill of 1886', and this settlement 'might form a nucleus for the Federation of the Empire at some future date'. But whether or not Lloyd George could have brought his own colleagues to agree to virtually total repudiation of Gladstonian Home Rule – for that is what his formula implied – has to remain a matter of speculation, because Balfour rejected it from the opposite standpoint and so, in effect, torpedoed the Chancellor's initiative.

Garvin's eloquent pleading failed to convince Balfour that federalism within the United Kingdom was either desirable or practicable, and he gave his reasons in a long letter to Garvin which remains of topical as well as historical interest nearly seventy years later. He saw no permanence in any limited measure of devolution:

> Is it not true that such force as lies behind 'Home Rule all round' . . . is
> . . . based, not upon administrative advantages, but upon historical
> sentiment? And is it not in the nature of things that in such cases in-
> complete concessions (and provincial powers are necessarily incomplete)
> only increase the appetites they are intended to satisfy, while they
> provide new instruments for extorting more?

He also put his finger on the crucial, perennial Irish difficulty:

> Is Ireland to form one province or two. If you prefer the latter, will
> any nationalist, of any type, accept this administrative solution? and if
> not, why not?[1]

Balfour was willing enough to compromise on tariffs, or temperance or the Welsh church or social reform, but he would not compromise on the Union.

1. Balfour to Garvin, 22 October 1910 (quoted substantially in Gollin, *The Observer and J. L. Garvin*, pp. 215–18).

This was the reason why, at the beginning of November, he politely disengaged from the unofficial negotiations. And on 10 November the Constitutional Conference itself met for the last time. The truce had failed to produce a settlement and normal party hostilities were promptly resumed.

Lloyd George believed that Balfour's decision was dictated by Akers-Douglas, the Unionist Chief Whip, and this, apparently, is what Balfour gave him to understand. But in reality his coalition plan, like the Constitutional Conference, foundered on the issue of Ireland. Balfour's Unionism was more fundamentalist than Chamberlain's, which was much the same as Lloyd George's 'Home Rule all Round'. Lloyd George was the prisoner of Gladstone's commitment to Irish Home Rule, which he had always regarded as a catastrophic error. As a young politician he had felt obliged, for the sake of his career, to conform to the Gladstonian doctrine which was more or less *de rigueur* among Welsh Liberals. But he had done his best to escape from it through the ingenious, if superficial, conception of all-round federalism. He could go no further to meet Balfour if he wished to retain any semblance of Liberal orthodoxy; and Balfour, on Ireland, would make no move at all to meet him.

Lloyd George's abortive attempt to break out of the party straitjacket in 1910 is one of the most important incidents in his life, revealing to us, as it revealed to a few of his leading contemporaries – and perhaps even to himself – what he really felt about the British political system. He was a good patriot, but not a good party man. Much as he relished controversy, and superbly gifted though he was as a destructive critic, his strongest impulse was towards creative action. The more he looked at the nation's problems, the more acutely aware he became of things needing to be done. He could also see that they needed to be done urgently and by the best available people. Why, then, should so much time be wasted in fruitless and largely artificial conflict between men of first-class ability on both sides, who together might be running the country as it ought to be run?

Party government involved the distribution of many key offices to 'duffers', and grossly excessive attention to party 'principles' which were, in his view, mere 'fads'. In Parliament, the clash of Government and Opposition was a faithful reflection of courtroom battles in which counsel for the prosecution and counsel for the defence would belabour each other and each other's witnesses. But, he might have argued, the function of an ordinary court of law was essentially different from that of the High Court of Parliament. Ordinary courts had to apply and interpret the laws, but Parliament had to make them. Moreover, the function of any barrister was simply to state his own, and demolish his opponent's, case, the power of decision resting with judge or jury; whereas in Parliament the leading advocates on either side were liable to become the nation's rulers, with a duty to propose legislation and to take all manner of executive decisions.

Since it did not, of course, follow that someone with a gift for political advocacy would also have it in him to be a dynamic man of action, the alternation of parties in office tended to produce relatively inefficient government, which was made even more inefficient by the demands of party ideologies. Parliament had assumed nearly all the prerogatives of monarchy while ensuring that it would nearly always have to behave as a weak, capricious and confused monarch. This was bad enough when the country was enjoying effortless superiority in the world and a measure of social equipoise at home. By the end of the first decade of the twentieth century it was no longer tolerable, at least to a man of Lloyd George's energy and vision.

The constitutional crisis occasioned by his 1909 Budget seemed to him far more than a showdown between the two Houses of Parliament; it was a challenge to the British political system in all its aspects, a crisis of the regime. Since his mind was not of the philosophic sort, he did not develop his intuition and perception into a theory of government. But it is clear from what he attempted in 1910, and from what he later did as Prime Minister, that he wished to change the system radically, in particular to strengthen the executive. After the January 1910 election he first considered, and for various good reasons rejected, the possibility of trying to achieve his ends through leadership of a Left-wing-cum-Nationalist alliance. Then we find him speaking to Masterman of the attractions of forming a government of businessmen. When the Constitutional Conference began his options were still open, but after the first round of meetings he became convinced that limited agreement on the Lords' powers was out of the question, and that only a much wider agreement, with a coalition of the nation's ablest men to implement it, would serve the needs of the hour.

Was he wrong to try, and did he set about it the wrong way? The second question can be answered quite briefly. Though it would be absurd to suggest that his tactics were flawless, it is most unlikely that anyone else could have made the progress that he did, or that even he could have succeeded by using other methods. He was quite right to approach Churchill first on his own side, and probably right to tackle Smith first on the Opposition side. During the negotiations he stretched and adapted his proposals to suit the different susceptibilities with which he had to deal, and so to improve the chances of a decision in principle to cooperate – after which, he hoped, conflicting interests would gradually be reconciled. This, surely, was diplomacy rather than duplicity. He knew very well that everyone would soon be in a position to compare notes, but trusted that the benefits of his activity would then be so apparent that his sleight of hand would be forgiven. Even though he failed, none of the participants seems, in retrospect, to have resented or condemned the efforts that he made.

But was the whole experiment a predictable waste of time? Many would say that it was, quoting with uncritical reverence Disraeli's axiom that 'England does not love coalitions'. It is manifestly true that the English (and others) sooner or later fall out of love with governments of any kind. But does the evidence prove that they are more swiftly disenchanted with coalitions than with party governments? Disraeli's long exclusion from office during the middle years of the nineteenth century bears witness to the fact that coalitions of Whigs and Peelites were, on the whole, far more popular than his Tory Party. And the coalition of Tories and Liberal Unionists that held office from 1895 to 1905 clearly had a more durable basis of public support than the ensuing purely Liberal Government, which lost its independent majority in 1910. In the twentieth century. Lloyd George's peace-time coalition certainly did not retain the people's love, though it was brought down by the defection of its major constituent party rather than by popular vote. On the other hand, the 1931 coalition has to be regarded as the best-loved government of the inter-war years, since it won two successive elections with thumping majorities.

Disraeli is not, therefore, a sufficient answer to Lloyd George. In fairness, one should say that most of the coalitions so far referred to were not of the 'grand' variety, that is to say coalitions involving leaders of both, or all, the main parties – and that the government Lloyd George was proposing in 1910 would have been such a coalition. The undeniable snag in such cases is that only inexperienced, fringe politicians are left to carry on the vital function of opposition, and that there is no obvious or satisfactory alternative to the people in power. But this may be a price worth paying for effective action to tide the country over exceptional difficulties, more especially as 'grand' coalitions are unlikely to hold together for long.

That the difficulties and dangers facing the country in 1910 were of no ordinary kind is even clearer to us now than it was to most of Lloyd George's contemporaries. In an atmosphere supercharged with partisan feeling, and with no decisive majority for either of the major parties, the auspices for party government could hardly have been worse; and the events of the next few years provide the strongest possible vindication of Lloyd George's arguments for coalition. No doubt he later exaggerated the extent to which he was moved by the threat of war and his sense of the nation's unpreparedness, but these were unquestionably among his motives. He was not out for himself. By acting as he did he risked his own position for what he believed to be the highest national interests. It was not good for his career to propose a coalition in 1910, but if the proposal had been adopted Britain might have been spared many calamities.

Balfour's attitude was equally disinterested, but less far-sighted. He sacrificed all the potential benefits of coalition in 1910 to his view, probably in itself justified, on the single issue of 'Home Rule all Round'. Yet in 1921 he was a member of the Lloyd George Coalition which signed the Irish Treaty, accepting then an imperfect and impermanent, but realistic, settlement of the Irish question. If he could have shown as much adaptability eleven years earlier he would have stood to obtain far greater advantages in exchange for whatever damage might have been done to the Union.

It must not be assumed, however, that if Balfour's attitude had been different Lloyd George's scheme would have worked. It is very far from certain that anything like the proposed package could have been sold to the Liberal Party. Apart from the ideological concessions required, there would also have been acute personal complications. Whereas Unionists had the incentive of office, Liberal Ministers would have known that some of them would be deprived of their posts. It is not natural for a party in power to show such a spirit of self-denial unless it feels that the only alternative is utter catastrophe. Could Lloyd George and Asquith have made their followers see the 1910 situation in that light?

Whatever might or might not have been, the reality is that Lloyd George tried and failed to institutionalize the truce, and that in the attempt he both revealed what he was and foreshadowed what he would become. He never had any intention of moving to the Right, though inevitably those who believed him to be on the far Left would so interpret his coalitionist tendencies. Throughout his life he was a Centre radical, opposed alike to doctrinaire capitalism and doctrinaire socialism, to the old establishment of hereditary privilege and to the rising menace of politically motivated trade unions. But the system favoured a perpetual contest between parties rooted in powerful interest-groups and therefore committed, at least in theory, to rival philosophies. Until 1910 Lloyd George seemed to all but the most discerning an outstanding exponent of the system. After 1910 the truth became increasingly apparent, in spite of his enforced reversion to the role of party gladiator during the next four years. The war gave him his opportunity and as Prime Minister he was able to put many of his ideas into practice, including the recruitment of Ministers from outside politics. But the system itself proved too strong for him, and while endeavouring to destroy it he was himself destroyed.

TEN

The Liberals' Dilemma

The ending of the party truce marked the beginning of a bad time for the Liberals. Asquith had agreed to the Constitutional Conference partly to avoid embarrassing the new King, but also partly because he hoped that it might relieve him of the necessity to coerce the Lords. Like Gladstone, he was politically a moderate progressive but socially a traditionalist. He very much disliked having to ask the King for a guarantee that the House of Lords would be swamped with new creations if the Liberals' just demands were not met, and this reluctance had already cost his party dear. As for the prospect that the threat of mass creations might actually have to be carried out, it appalled him scarcely less than it appalled Balfour or Lansdowne.

Once again the Liberals had lost momentum. Nearly a year had gone by since the Lords' rejection of the 1909 Budget, and apart from getting the Budget through nothing of substance had been achieved. With the failure of Lloyd George's attempt to negotiate a grand coalition the Government was thrown back upon its own small coalition, and so was open again to the charge that it was under dictation from the Irish.

Another general election was clearly inevitable at an early date. But how early? It would be more democratic to delay voting until January, when a new register was due to come into force; and there were some who argued that the new voters would, on balance, favour the Liberals. But the Master of Elibank pointed to the result of a by-election at Walthamstow on 1 November, which had shown a slight swing to the Liberals, and after discussion the Cabinet decided that polling should be before Christmas. On 18 November Asquith announced that Parliament would be dissolved ten days later and that the first constituencies would go to the poll on 3 December. The shortness of the interval between announcement and election was a record in British history.

The King, meanwhile, had been prevailed upon to give a secret guarantee that he would, if necessary, create enough peers to ensure passage of the Parliament Bill, but once again this important matter was mishandled by Asquith. Visiting the King at Sandringham on 11–12 November he seems to have been unable to bring himself to mention the Government's desire for a contingent guarantee, with the result that the King was outraged when Knollys reported to him, a few days later, that the Prime Minister actually wanted an immediate guarantee for the next Parliament. Only after Asquith had seen him again, fortified by the presence of Crewe and an explicit demand from the Cabinet, did the King finally acquiesce; and even then he may have done so because Knollys judiciously withheld the information that Balfour would be willing to form a Government if he refused.

It seems very curious, in retrospect, that his freedom to act or not to act upon Ministerial advice in what was, after all, a strictly political matter, was never questioned by the Government. The Labour M.P. George Barnes called for an immediate creation of peers instead of an election, adding – in an echo of Lloyd George at Newcastle – that 'plenty of unemployed would be glad of the job'. But Asquith was committed to the second election, and the validity of the King's independent prerogative to create peers was taken for granted.

During the brief session of Parliament before the Dissolution Lloyd George carried a shortened version of his Finance Bill which had been given its First Reading on 25 July. The significant new feature was a supplementary estimate of £500,000 to enable pensions to be paid to nearly 200,000 old people, who had hitherto been disqualified because they were receiving Poor Law relief. This Bill passed the House of Lords without debate on 27 November, but some parts of the original Bill had to be held over for the next Parliament.[1]

The main concern, however, of Liberals and Unionists alike was to establish the policies on which they would fight the election. For the Government the prime issue was, of course, its policy for curbing the Lords' veto, and the policy was unfortunately defined as that of the Parliament Bill by the introduction of that measure in the House of Lords

---

1. Legislation to give effect to them was introduced soon after it met and received the Royal Assent on 31 March 1911 – the last day of the financial year.

on 16 November. In addition, the Liberals' commitment to Irish Home Rule was reasserted, and there was a pledge that facilities would be provided for a Women's Suffrage bill in the new Parliament, though without any indication of its place in the legislative time-table. For Labour's benefit, at least one of the grievances caused by the Osborne Judgment was met by a pledge that there would be legislation for the payment of M.P.s; and it was also stated that trade unions were to be not only permitted, but obliged, to have political funds, though contributions to them were to be voluntary.

The Unionists' programme turned out to be rather more surprising. Faced with an election in which the Lords' veto was undeniably the paramount issue, even the more obtuse and cautious of the Tory peers could see that something had to be done about their Chamber. The veto on its own would clearly be an electoral liability. Ignoring the Parliament Bill, the Lords therefore applied themselves to a feverish display of self-reforming zeal. One of Rosebery's resolutions that had not been proceeded with in April was moved and carried within a few hours. This was to the effect that the House should in future consist of Lords of Parliament, some chosen by the whole body of hereditary peers from among themselves, some chosen from outside, some sitting *ex officio* and some nominated by the Crown.

Lansdowne then followed with resolutions of his own concerning the procedure for resolving disputes between Lords and Commons. The House of Lords would abandon its right to amend or reject bills 'of a purely financial character', and the right to determine what was or was not a money bill would be exercised by a joint committee, with the Speaker presiding and having the casting vote. Most other bills were to be referred, in cases of dispute 'persisting for over a year', to a joint sitting whose composition was not defined, but when there was dispute on 'a matter of great gravity which had not been adequately submitted to the judgment of the people' this issue was to be decided by a national referendum. These resolutions were carried without a division.

Needless to say, the Lords were making gestures rather than substantive changes. The Rosebery resolution was no more than a declaration of intent, and even if it were to be translated into fact the House would remain basically hereditary and, in all probability, overwhelmingly Unionist. There was no guarantee that the Unionists would not have a majority in the proposed joint sittings, and no definition of the matters 'of great gravity' which were to be decided by referendum. All the same, the

Lords' cosmetic operation, undertaken at the last minute, was of incalculable value to the Unionists, since it enabled them to give a spuriously democratic twist to their defence of the veto. In the referendum proposal, however, there was a trap for them which they did not at first perceive.

Shortly before the election campaign Redmond returned from a fund-raising tour in Canada and the United States. On arrival at Cork he announced that he had raised the largest sum 'ever subscribed for Irish political purposes', and this boast was eagerly exploited by the Unionists. Garvin thundered in the *Observer*:

> He comes with the money of America to wipe England out. He comes with the money of Protected millionaires . . . He comes with subscriptions from the country which has the strongest Constitutional safeguards in the world. . . . Above all he comes with his Republican cash to extort from the British Crown his guarantees . . .[1]

The Government was described as a 'kept Ministry', and its subservience to the 'dollar dictator' immediately became the favourite theme of Unionist speakers, leader-writers and cartoonists.

Lloyd George counter-attacked strongly in his first speech of the campaign. At Mile End – where he began with a pregnant reminder that he had not spoken in East London since Limehouse – he turned the dollar argument against Tory peers. In twenty years eighty million dollars had passed from America to Ireland, and this money had helped Irish peasants to pay rent to their landlords, including Lord Lansdowne. Moreover, since when had the British aristocracy despised the financial aid which an American heiress might bring? Dollars had 'underpinned many a tottering noble house'.

The Tories always had to have an election bogey and this time it was a 'gilt-edged' Irishman. But Ireland was not the real issue. 'We are fighting a British quarrel . . as much a British one as the old fight between the Commons and the King.' How could anyone defend the Constitution in its present form?

> No country in the world would look at our system – no free country, I mean . . . France has a Senate, the United States has a Senate, the Colonies have Senates, but they are all chosen either directly or indirectly by the people.

1. 13 November 1910.

Lord Curzon had said 'with that modesty that perfumes all his utterances' that 'the best work in the world was always done by members of the aristocracy'. An Australian, 'very much impressed with that portentous truth', might ask them what Australia should do to be saved. How could Australia get an aristocracy? And a Briton would reply:

> Nothing easier in the world. I will tell you how we got ours. I will give you our oldest and most ancient stock, and consequently our best, because aristocracy is like cheese. The older it is (A Voice: 'The more it stinks') the higher it becomes.

British aristocrats were, in fact, the ultimate issue of Norman plunder, Reformation pillage and royal indiscretion.

The speech was not all knockabout. There was also a serious defence of the 1909 Budget, both for the revenue it had produced and for the good social use that the money was being put to. Moreover, the dire warnings of its effect upon trade had been completely falsified:

> Before the Budget trade was depressed; we were down in the trough of the wave. Since then the good old ship has been rising and rising and rising, and we are not yet on the crest.[1]

As in the January election, Lloyd George could see that the general state of the economy was a vital asset to the Government.

At St Pancras two evenings later he asked a very pointed question:

> Will [Lord Lansdowne] have a referendum which will submit Tariff Reform? . . . I am asking that question and I am entitled to demand an answer. If not what is the point of talking about referendums? A referendum which does not refer all questions is purely a one-sided party dodge.

And he challenged the concept of the peerage as a separate, privileged estate of the realm:

> They seem to assume that the peers are one party and the nation another, and that they are on equal terms with the nation. But if there is a dispute between the nation and themselves, well it is to be settled by some extraneous means. What business have they to set themselves up as equals of the whole nation?[2]

1. Speech at the Paragon Theatre, Mile End, on 21 November 1910. Lloyd George was addressing an audience of about 5,000, and his speech was interrupted by suffragists.
2. Speech at the St Pancras Baths, 23 November 1910.

The challenge to submit Tariff Reform to a referendum was exceedingly awkward for the Unionists. Balfour had reaffirmed their total loyalty to the Tariff Reform programme, including food taxes, in his opening speech of the campaign on 17 November; and it had been assumed by dedicated Tariff Reformers that the programme would be put through as part of a Unionist Budget, without any delay or impediment. But the referendum challenge made that assumption morally untenable and gave Unionist candidates who were anyway opposed to food taxes, or who were sensitive to their immediate influence in the constituencies, a good excuse for pressing Balfour to modify his stand. Even Bonar Law, a strong Tariff Reformer – who had left Dulwich to fight a Manchester seat in the crucial north-west – wrote to Balfour suggesting that he would on the whole favour acceptance of a referendum for Tariff Reform. Others conveyed the same message, without qualification, and it was one to which Balfour himself was naturally amenable. On 29 November, without consulting his Shadow Cabinet formally or informally, and in spite of Austen Chamberlain's known hostility, he declared at the Albert Hall that he had 'not the least objection' to submitting 'the principles of Tariff Reform to referendum'. He did not even make the pledge conditional upon an undertaking from the Liberals that they would agree to a referendum for Home Rule. No single act of Balfour's did more to weaken his position as leader of the Unionist Party, once it became apparent that this gamble had failed.

Lloyd George did not confine himself to demanding that the referendum should be applied to Tariff Reform. He also drew attention to its cost, which he estimated at about $£1\frac{1}{2}$ million a time, and argued that it would be 'a prohibitive tariff against Liberalism', because it was only when the Liberals were in office that disputes arose between the Commons and the Lords. Most peers, he said, were out of touch with ordinary life. 'The brilliance of the sunshine of their lives blinds them to the squalor around them.' And he ridiculed the idea that property rights were seriously in danger. 'Taxes on property are not the real dangers of civilization ... You are building up ramparts against dangers that do not exist. You might as well repair Hadrian's Wall in order to defend the people of the South against the raids of the Picts and the Scots. Those are past perils. Civilization has no perils for property; it is not property that stands in need of defence, but poverty.'

These remarks were made in the King's Theatre, Edinburgh, on 26 November. 20,000 people applied for tickets to hear him, though the theatre could only hold 4,000. After his main speech he addressed an overflow meeting for half an hour, and then left for a tour through Midlothian, Peebles and Selkirk, during which he made many short speeches. At Loanhead, a village in the Pentland Hills, the *Daily News* reporter noted that his voice was showing signs of strain.

Another affliction soon came his way in the form of a letter from Margot Asquith, dated 29 November:

Dear Mr Lloyd George

I am sure you are as generous as you are impulsive. I am going to make a political appeal to you . . . Dont when you speak on platforms arouse what is low and sordid and violent in yr. audience; it hurts those members of it that are fighting these elections with the noblest desire to see fair play; men animated by no desire to punch anyones head; men of disinterested emotion able to pity and heal their fellow man whether a lord or a sweep. I xpect the cool-blooded class hatred shown for some years in the corporate counsels of the House of Lords has driven you into saying that lords are high like cheese etc. etc. etc.

If yr. speeches only hurt and alienated lords it wd. not perhaps so much matter – but they hurt & offend not only the King and men of high estate but quite poor men, Liberals of all sorts – They lose us votes. If a wave of caution and irritation bursts over England we shall have a tremendous beating in the next three weeks – dont let anyone say your speeches helped to set this wave in motion. You are a great artist: with a little more political prevision and less self-indulgence you cd. draw to yourself in public as you do in private not merely the feverish curiosity the gloomy fervour of a clammering [sic] crowd but the growing confidence and enduring interest of the best kind of Liberalism.

Yrs. in affectionate sincerity

Margot Asquith.

This letter infuriated Lloyd George, and the Master of Elibank had to use all his conciliatory art to make peace between the Downing Street neighbours. Remembering Asquith's letter to him after Limehouse, Lloyd George must have suspected that the Prime Minister was behind Margot's outburst, but 'The Master' wrote on 30 November: 'The P.M. knows nothing about it . . . and I do hope you will banish it all from your mind.' He also enclosed an apologetic letter from Margot, with the assurance that it was written without any prompting from him. It was dated 30 November 7.30 p.m., and was by no means a total recantation. She had always defended his Budget, she said, but could not defend his 'Limehouse

& Newcastle & Mile End speeches', though she liked his recent Edinburgh speech. She begged him not to be vexed with her. 'I can't bear this; may I run in and see you (if only for 5 seconds) so that you may know by my face and my hand shake that I am genuinely sorry.'[1] With or without this affecting scene, the row seems to have blown over.

A few days after his Midlothian campaign he was touring in Wales, and on 2 December addressed two meetings at Ipswich. But the following evening he had to miss a big meeting at Nottingham, pleading loss of voice, and for the rest of the campaign his speeches tended to be shorter and more perfunctory. At Bangor, indeed, on 9 December he answered written questions handed up to him, instead of making a set speech. At East Ham on 15 December he touched, almost casually, upon what should have been the Liberals' policy for the House of Lords.

> Mr Balfour has talked of the Veto Resolutions as if they are the end of the Government's programme; they are the beginning. When the Veto Resolutions are carried there will still be inequality. The Veto Resolutions will stop Liberal legislation for two years (A Voice: 'Shame!') I agree. They will not stop Tory legislation at all. That is inequality. We must proceed to reform the Constitution in such a way as to extend equal treatment to both sides, and it has always been our intention to do so.

But for the next Parliament it was not the Government's policy to end the Lords' veto except in the matter of finance, strictly interpreted. In other respects the veto would merely be limited. The Parliament Bill was not designed 'to extend equal treatment to both sides', and whatever Lloyd George might say it was on the Parliament Bill that the election was being fought.

By the time he spoke at East Ham it was, in fact, nearly over. Polling had been going on for twelve days and it was already clear that the national result would be much the same as before. In his own constituency, fighting a new candidate – A. L. Jones – Lloyd George increased his majority to only sixteen votes short of his 1906 record. But in the country at large there was no such swing to the Liberals. When all the votes were counted the two main parties had 272 seats each, while the Irish Nationalists had 84 and Labour 42. The aggregate poll was down by a million and one-third, but this was not, as used to be believed, an indication of public apathy. The fall in the vote was due very largely to a substantial increase

1. The letters are preserved in Earl Lloyd George's collection.

in the number of seats that were not contested, and to the fact that the second election of 1910 was fought – except in Scotland – on a stale register.[1]

Shortly after the election Lloyd George gave an interview to Jean Longuet, a grandson of Karl Marx, which was published in Jaurès' paper *L'Humanité*. Longuet was brought to breakfast with Lloyd George by Ramsay MacDonald and he described the Chancellor as 'without anything of the Anglo-Saxon about him – in fact, a man who could be taken in the streets of Paris as a quintessential Frenchman'. In the interview Lloyd George was reported as saying that the Unionists should no longer be regarded as the natural party of Government, and that there would be 'great social transformations' in Britain over the next five years, provided there were no 'external difficulties'. At about the same time he was pleased to hear from M. E. J. Dillon, the *Daily Telegraph*'s eminent Russian correspondent, that he had taken Gladstone's place on the Continent of Europe, that his was the best-known British name in all European countries, and that Count Witte (ex-Premier of Russia and a close friend of Dillon's) was anxious to meet him.[2]

His throat, however, was still giving him trouble and on 16 December his London doctor, G. W. F. Macnaughton, told him that he must 'stop talking and smoking for some weeks'. On 20 December he left for the South of France accompanied by Margaret, Megan and Rowland, his Welsh private secretary. It turned out to be partly a working holiday, as we shall see, and his throat was no better when he got back. On 20 January 1911 Macnaughton found it still inflamed and recommended a few weeks' complete rest. This was impossible for a man of Lloyd George's temperament with urgent work to do, but he was seriously worried about his health and feared for a time that he might have cancer. He was lent a house in Kent – Beachborough, near Shorncliffe – by Arthur Markham, the Liberal M.P. and coal-owner, and spent a fair amount of time there in the early spring. According to Harold Spender, he was 'driven back on reading as his sole diversion . . . rambled widely through literature and read a great deal of history'.[3] He also had treatment in London from a 'voice-restorer' called Miss Hicks, in whom he had great faith and who was credited, in the family, with having cured him. By May he was distinctly better,

1. Even Elie Halévy fell into the trap of mistaking the lower poll for a relative decline in the will to vote. It was Dr Neal Blewett who set the record straight (*op. cit.*, pp. 379–80).
2. D.L.G. to M.L.G., 15 December 1910 (N.L.W. and *Letters*, p. 154).
3. E. H. Spender, *The Prime Minister*, p. 173.

though his voice continued to give him some trouble for the rest of the year.

Was it purely physical, or may it have been partly a nervous reaction to the frustrating experiences of 1910? Throughout his life he was prone to sneezing fits, in summer as well as winter, and was always afraid that he might be seized by one while making a speech (though apparently this seldom, if ever, happened). He also had a marked streak of hypochondria: if anything was wrong with him he would naturally assume the worst. But whatever the precise pathology of his throat trouble during and after the December election, it has a very apt symbolism, because it was fitting that he should lose his voice in the process of reverting, against his will, to the wasteful and destructive inter-party slanging-match, from which he had sought in vain to find a means of escape.

When the new Parliament met in February the Parliament Bill was reintroduced, in exactly the same form as before, immediately after the debate on the Address. Asquith conceded that the suspensory veto embodied in it would be exercised only against the Liberals, and that the system would not be fair until the House of Lords was reformed. But meanwhile, he argued, something had to be done to mitigate the evil. Balfour did not deny the need for Lords' reform, but discussed the idea of an elective second chamber as incompatible with the dominant role of the Commons. He also indicated very clearly that the Opposition did not regard the election result as a mandate for Home Rule.

Despite the use of 'kangaroo' closure the Bill did not leave the House of Commons until 15 May, and by then the Government had allowed a significant amendment, that the two years' delay for non-money bills should date from Second Reading rather than from introduction. Lloyd George took no active part in these proceedings. The state of his voice would anyway have made it impossible for him to speak in the debates, even if he had not been deeply involved in preparing his own National Health Insurance scheme. In his absence, Asquith's chief lieutenant during the Parliament Bill's passage was Churchill, whose attitude was notably more militant than the Prime Minister's. Whereas Asquith shrank from swamping the House of Lords with new peers, Churchill had no such inhibitions. Early in the New Year he wrote a long letter in which he urged Asquith to push the Parliament Bill through before the King's Coronation in June, without fearing, if necessary, to 'clink the coronets in their scabbards'. A mass creation of peers would, he said, be advantageous to the Liberal Party, which would gain at a stroke 'a great addition of influence in the country'.[1] Unfortunately the Cabinet as a whole did not share his robust sentiments.

While the Bill was in the Commons the Lords discussed, but did not proceed with, a referendum Bill introduced by Lord Balfour of Burleigh, and then turned their attention to a reform Bill introduced by Lansdowne himself, which received its Second Reading on the same day that the Parliament Bill received its Third in the Commons. There was very little enthusiasm in any quarter for the Lansdowne proposals. Limiting the number of hereditary peers entitled to sit in the House of Lords did not appeal to many of his own supporters, while to Liberals it was inadmissible that the House should retain its hereditary character and an automatic, if much reduced, Tory majority. On 29 May the Parliament Bill was given a Second Reading in the Lords without a division, but Lansdowne warned that it would be heavily amended in Committee. Parliament then rose for a Whitsun recess that was prolonged to include the Coronation, with nothing yet said by Asquith about the King's undertaking to create peers.[2]

After the Coronation the Lords returned to the Bill and by mid-July had amended it out of recognition. In particular, they had inserted a provision that measures of 'grave importance', among which Home Rule was specifically listed, should be referred to a direct vote of the people. Asquith therefore wrote a formal letter to Balfour on 20 July, which was published in the Press two days later, stating that he would call for rejection of the Lords' amendments by the Commons, and ending with the highly charged words:

> In the circumstances, should the necessity arise, the Government will advise the King to exercise his prerogative to secure the passing into law of the Bill in substantially the same form in which it left the House of Commons, and His Majesty has been pleased to signify that he will consider it his duty to accept and act on that advice.

1. Winston S. Churchill to H. H. Asquith, 3 January 1911 (*Winston S. Churchill*, Companion Vol. II, Part 2, pp. 1030–3).
2. The Coronation was on 22 June, and in the festive atmosphere leading politicians were able to joke about the constitutional crisis. Lord and Lady Desborough started early for Westminster Abbey and 'waited for a long time in the Annexe, where the processions were formed, with Lord Milner, George Curzon, Lord Rosebery and Lord Morley. When the Guard came clanking in, Lord Rosebery said to Lord Morley: 'Are these the men you are going to use to turn us out of the House of Lords next month?''' (*Pages from a Family Journal*, compiled by Lord Desborough from Lady Desborough's diary, privately printed.)

Lansdowne, Balfour and most intelligent Unionists in and out of Parliament saw now that the game was up and favoured submission to the Commons as the only alternative to mass dilution of the Lords and destruction of the Unionist majority there. But during the months since the election diehard opinion had been gathering strength. Peers ready to die in the last ditch, nicknamed 'Ditchers', were threatening to overwhelm the more rational but less heroic 'Hedgers', and the spirit of all-out resistance was also being shown, with varying degrees of sincerity, by irresponsible elements in the House of Commons. On 24 July, when Asquith made his first appearance there after the publication of his letter to Balfour, he was howled down by Unionist M.P.s after trying for half an hour to get a hearing. One of the leaders of this ugly demonstration was F. E. Smith who, mindful of his recent coalitioneering and of having received a privy councillorship in the Coronation honours on Asquith's recommendation, no doubt felt obliged to go to exaggerated lengths to prove that he was still on side.

All the same, when at long last the issue was brought to a decisive vote in the House of Lords, the Government narrowly won. On 10 August the proposal that Lansdowne's major wrecking amendment should not be insisted upon was carried by a majority of seventeen. Most of the 'Hedgers' followed Lansdowne in abstaining, but thirty-seven Unionists and thirteen bishops voted with the Government. On 18 August the Parliament Bill, which owed its passage to the reluctant use of a royal threat, finally became law with the Royal Assent.

One early and obvious victim of the Act and of the course of events preceding it was the Leader of the Opposition. Balfour had led his party to three consecutive electoral defeats; he had tried to kill a Liberal budget and to bring about a change of government by invoking the power of the Lords, and the stroke had miscarried; he had betrayed the cause of Tariff Reform by announcing, without adequate consultation, that it would be subject to referendum; and he had eventually shown no stomach for the fight between Lords and Commons which he had initiated. He was, in fact, as ill qualified to lead a party as he was well qualified to govern a country. A shrewd observer once wrote of him:

The very qualities which made his mind so fine and percipient when dealing with the abstract were exactly those which militated against his power for political leadership. He brought no passion to it: he was literally unable to bang the drum or thump the tub or inspire enthusiasm

5. Lloyd George speaking in the Pavilion at Caernarvon, 9 December 1909–the 'firewood' speech (see p. 238)

6a. (*left*) Christabel Pankhurst

6b. (*centre left*) W. J. Braithwaite

6c. (*centre right*) Sir Robert Morant

6d. (*bottom left*) J. Ramsay MacDonald

6e. (*bottom right*) F. E. Smith

in others by being carried away by his own, nor could he mock and execrate the convictions of those with whom (on the whole) he did not agree. He was too subtle for such rough work and also too fair-minded, and while fair-mindedness is essential to a philosopher, it is a handicap to the militant politician... Nobody was further from being a dilettante, as is sometimes urged against him, than he; all the energies of his mind were concentrated on his work . . .[1]

The work that most attracted him was, undoubtedly, that of government, and he brought to it a mind no less realistic than speculative. But he disliked, and was bad at, the task of running a democratic opposition.

In September 1911 Leo Maxse coined the famous B.M.G. ('Balfour Must Go') slogan, and on 8 November Balfour announced his resignation to his City of London constituents, remarking afterwards, typically: 'I really think I must ask Leo Maxse to dinner tonight, for we are probably the two happiest men in London.' His successor was Bonar Law, who had neither his talents nor his defects but who shared his admiration and liking for Lloyd George.

Apart from what it did to Balfour, the Parliament Act was far less damaging to the Unionists than to the Liberals. From their point of view it was a singularly misconceived piece of legislation, and many of the troubles that beset them over the next three years were directly due to it. The basic error was to differentiate between money and non-money bills, and so to invite Lords' obstruction of measures falling into the second category. Unless and until the Second Chamber was reformed, this meant in effect – as Lloyd George said at East Ham – that a two-year veto could operate against many Liberal measures. Without the Parliament Act to define and legitimize their delaying power, the Lords might have been a little chary of risking further conflicts with the people's elect. But with the sanction of a new law they could do so cheerfully. The Act added nothing to the fear of popular wrath which had often restrained them before 1909, and which was bound in any case to become more acute after their Budget fiasco. But it did give them licence to frustrate the will of the Commons on most issues for a specific period, while it established a procedure for certifying bills as money bills which seemed to endorse the Tory view that Budgets should not be used for general purposes of social reform. If the procedure had existed in 1909 Lloyd George's great Budget would have been disallowed, and in 1914 he was, in fact, tripped up by it. Why, since

1. E. F. Benson, *As We Were*, pp. 218–19.

the Government rightly maintained that no distinction should be drawn between ordinary and constitutional bills, did it admit a distinction between money and non-money bills? It is hard to understand.

Before very long the House of Lords, though still unreformed, was reduced to near-impotence by the advent of universal suffrage and of Labour as a party of government. In theory the Parliament Act has remained in force, and even after the Second World War the theoretical delaying power of the Lords was only modified, not abolished. But in practice the suspensory veto was virtually a dead letter for more than half a century. Until recently, at any rate, there has been a tacit recognition that the Lords' legislative function is to suggest amendments to bills sent up by the Commons, rather than to hinder or hamper the Commons' work. Until 1914, however, the Parliament Act served as a most effective check, not upon the power of the Lords, but upon the power of the Liberal Government.

Even by his own standards May 1911 was an extraordinarily busy month for Lloyd George. On the 4th he introduced his National Insurance Bill, the vast, complex and historic measure whose vicissitudes will be described in the next chapter. On the 16th he brought in his Budget for the year, which attracted relatively little attention but was, of course, no light matter for the Chancellor. He was able to announce that the revenue had exceeded his estimate of its growth by more than £4 million, and he predicted another 'sunny year' for British trade. Consequently he again left the 1909 fiscal pattern undisturbed, with only marginal adjustments. The Finance Bill had its Second Reading a week after the Budget statement but the Committee Stage, held over until the autumn session, was not begun until 11 December. Though the Bill eventually went to the Lords without a certificate from the Speaker that it was a money bill, it passed there without debate.

One interesting feature of the Budget was the provision of £250,000 for M.P.s' salaries, and on 10 August – the day of the Lords' surrender on the Parliament Bill – the House of Commons decided by a simple financial resolution that its Members should be paid at the rate of £400 a year. This reform had been promised by the Liberals as a gesture to Labour necessitated by the Osborne Judgment, but Lloyd George favoured it on other grounds. In his view it was not only desirable that poor men should be free to sit in Parliament, but also undesirable that they should have to sit there as the paid representatives of sectional bodies, such as trade unions.

Since justice required that there should be payment of Members, it was right that they should be paid by the State, which was impartial. No doubt he hoped that the change would actually benefit the Liberals at Labour's expense, by helping to emancipate working-class politicians from trade union control. Among Labour leaders Keir Hardie was alone in perceiving the danger, arguing that payment of Members would encourage men to enter Parliament 'under the auspices of all parties'. But his argument was rejected by most trade unionists.[1]

The chief working-class grievance at the time was not, in any case, a product of the Osborne Judgment, nor capable of being met by political concessions to the Labour Party. It was that wages were failing to keep pace with the cost of living. Despite the national prosperity of which Lloyd George could justly boast, real wages were going down, and in such circumstances trade unions turned to industrial action, which was facilitated by the Trade Disputes Act of 1906 and stimulated by syndicalist ideas imported from the Continent. In 1905 the number of workers involved in strikes was 67,653; in 1910 it was 385,085. And in November 1910 the veteran Ben Tillett and Tom Mann, both recently returned from Australia, formed a National Transport Workers' Federation comprising (among others) seamen and dockers – thirty-six unions in all.

During the sweltering summer of 1911 organized labour seemed, for a time, to be threatening revolution. Trouble began when the seamen came out on strike in June, with the backing of other unions in the Federation. Rioting and arson occurred in several large ports and frightened employers conceded wage increases. But soon after a general settlement appeared to have been reached at the end of July, even worse trouble broke out. Dockers in the Port of London struck for the second time, and this strike was the signal for action by the railwaymen. The conciliation machinery established by Lloyd George in 1907 had not been allowed to work properly, and the men were thoroughly dissatisfied with it. Richard Bell, blamed for its failure, had been replaced by a new general secretary and the rank-and-file were in fighting mood.

The first action by railwaymen was at Liverpool. A thousand of them stopped work there, and the Liverpool dockers came out in sympathy. On 13–14 August there were grave disorders in the city. Many people were injured in riots and at one point troops opened fire, killing two. On 15 August representatives of the four railwaymen's unions met at Liverpool, protested against the authorities' violence, and issued

1. Kenneth O. Morgan, *Keir Hardie: Radical and Socialist*, p. 238.

an ultimatum to the employers. Either they must enter into negotiation with the unions within twenty-four hours or there would be a general strike on the railways.

This formidable challenge sent tremors through the whole community. Without essential supplies that could only be transported by rail the British people would soon be reduced to starvation. Moreover, those who had shares in railway companies were more numerous than the railway workers, and the boards of their companies consequently felt that they had to stand firm. They refused to talk under duress and it was clear that only a swift and forceful move by the Government could avert the threatened stoppage. On 17 August the Prime Minister and Sydney Buxton, Churchill's successor as President of the Board of Trade, met the union leaders in London. It was not Asquith's day: his handling of the meeting could hardly have been worse. While offering the unions a Royal Commission to investigate their grievances, he spoke of the Government's determination to keep the railways working if the offer were rejected. In fact, the Government could do nothing of the kind, granted that the engine-drivers were willing to participate in the strike. The union leaders knew that Asquith could not give effect to his brave words, even if he himself believed that he could. After considering his offer they told him that they saw no reason to postpone the strike, and he then provoked them still further by saying, as he left, that they would be responsible for whatever might befall. Quite apart from the disastrous tone of his remarks, he had made the mistake of trying to coerce the unions when he should have been exerting pressure on the employers.

At this point Lloyd George was called in to save the situation, and though it was too late for him to prevent the strike he managed to bring it to an end within forty-eight hours. Working from his old office at the Board of Trade he reopened talks with the union leaders and assured them that the proposed Royal Commission would report quickly. He also persuaded the employers to reinstate all the men who were on strike, and to meet the union secretaries at once in what might appear to be a gesture of recognition. There is some evidence that he appealed to both sides to show patriotic restraint in view of the international crisis over Morocco, then at its height. However it was done, he succeeded, and though the settlement again proved disappointing in the longer run, it was accepted at the time and the railwaymen immediately went back to work. Lloyd George's peace-making efforts were not helped by Churchill's distinctly militaristic approach to his duties as the guardian of law and order, which included claiming the right to send troops into any area without a prior request from the local authority. But in spite of this and all the other adverse circumstances, the magic of 1907 was repeated.

Asquith, who had withdrawn to the country after his own meeting with the railwaymen, acknowledged his indebtedness in a letter which the recipient was happy to quote in later years:

My dear Ch^r of Ex^r,

I cannot sufficiently express to you how strongly I feel the debt of obligation which I myself, and all our colleagues, owe to you for the indomitable purpose, the untiring energy, and the matchless skill with which you have brought to a settlement one of the most formidable problems which we have had, as a Government, to confront.

It is the latest, but by no means the least, of the loyal and invaluable services which you have rendered since I came to the head of the Government 3½ years ago.

> Always
> Yours very sincerely
> H. H. Asquith.[1]

And it is evident that a young member of the Prime Minister's family also wrote Lloyd George a fan letter at this time, because we have a copy of his interesting reply:

Dear Miss Elizabeth,

It is is so charming of you to have written to me.

The Prime Minister has also written me a letter which I shall treasure to the end of my days. I cannot tell you how proud I am of it. What a fine fellow he is to serve under, generous and chivalrous and so far above the pettiness which spoils most of us public men.

I am delighted the struggle is over. I was genuinely afraid of the 'river of blood' between Liberalism and Labour. We ought to thank God that Labour had no daring leader otherwise British Liberalism could have become what Continental Liberalism now is – a respectable middle-class affair – futile and impotent.

> Many thanks to you.
> Ever sincerely,
> D. Lloyd George.[2]

1. Lloyd George Papers. The letter was written on 20 August 1911, after Asquith's return to Downing Street.
2. Presumably written to the fourteen-year-old Elizabeth Asquith, 22 August 1911. (The copy is preserved in Mr William Lloyd-George's collection.)

This letter vividly illustrates Lloyd George's awareness of the Liberal Party's need to retain working-class support, and of the ever-present danger that the Labour Party might usurp its position. During the two elections of 1910 Labour had been most successfully contained. In January attacks on Liberal territory had nearly all been beaten off, with the result that in December Labour attempted less than a dozen challenges, most of which again failed. For holding the electoral line against Labour most of the credit is surely due to Lloyd George – to his polemics no less than to his policies. Had he refrained altogether from oratorical aggression, to suit Elizabeth's mother and 'respectable' Liberals at every level of society, a great many working-class voters would probably have been alienated. If the Liberal Party ceased to interest them they had somewhere else to go, and Lloyd George, knowing that their allegiance could not easily be held, both did and said what was necessary to hold it.

Then, in the summer of 1911, he proved equally alive to the significance of trade union direct action, and equally sensitive in his response to that threat. Against syndicalism he could count on discreet support from most Labour Parliamentarians, and Ramsay MacDonald, in fact, gave him some tangible assistance towards ending the railwaymen's strike. Perhaps a more 'daring' Labour leader would have exploited the industrial crisis instead of helping a Liberal Minister to reach a settlement.

As the century entered its second decade the Liberals faced an increasingly stark dilemma. Their traditional interests and beliefs were growing ever harder to reconcile with new forces in Britain and the outside world, and there were also many signs of tension within the party itself.

One crucial aspect of the dilemma was what to do about the Parliamentary franchise. 'Reform' – meaning, above all, Parliamentary reform – had been an essential feature of the old Liberalism, but it had rested upon the tacit assumption that most new voters would be Liberal voters. In practice, however, the last major extensions of the franchise had not prevented long periods of Tory rule, and even the Liberals' glorious victory in 1906 had been slightly clouded by the fivefold increase in Labour's vote. Evidently the party would in future have to contend with powerful enemies on two fronts, and there was good reason to fear that a truly democratic franchise would mean an enormous addition of strength to Labour. Yet how could 'the party of progress' tolerate an electoral system which still effectively denied the vote to about 40 per cent of the male population?

And what of the women? The question of female suffrage was more urgent than that of extending the vote to unenfranchised males, because women were on the warpath and making politicians' lives a misery. Besides, it was clearly even more unjust that no women at all should have the Parliamentary vote than that only 60 per cent of the men should have it. Nevertheless, Liberals were divided on the principle of votes for women, with Asquith himself on the conservative side of the argument.

The most that he would concede, at the outset of his Premiership, was that an electoral reform bill would be introduced before the end of the then current Parliament, and that he would not object to the moving of a women's suffrage amendment to the bill, provided the amendment was on democratic lines and 'had behind it the overwhelming support of the women of the country, no less than the support of men'.[1] There was no question of including women's suffrage in the original bill, or of Government sponsorship for the amendment; and it was clear, moreover, that Asquith's conditions for its mere introduction were such that he might well find an excuse for official opposition to it when the time came.

Lloyd George was a convinced suffragist, but while preparing his great Budget for 1909 he was ready enough to fall in with Asquith's delaying tactics. On 5 December 1908 he sought to persuade the Women's Liberal Federation, at the Albert Hall, that suffrage should await the settling of more urgent accounts and should then be brought in as part of a general measure of electoral reform. His speech took two hours, instead of twenty minutes, to deliver because of interruptions by members of the W.S.P.U., some of whom occupied front-row seats and one of whom kept stewards at bay with a dog-whip. It was to avoid such scenes that women were later excluded from meetings addressed by Liberal leaders, but their exclusion failed to ensure peace at the meetings while making the party seem anything but liberal.

By the summer of 1909 it had become normal for suffragettes in prison to go on hunger strike, and in September the Government responded by instituting the process of forcible feeding. This could only have the effect of placing the suffragettes in a more heroic, and the Government in a more odious, light. The Cabinet however supported the Home Secretary's refusal of privileged prison status for suffragettes – a disastrous mistake for which all its members must share responsibility. All the same, at least fifteen of them were disposed to favour the women's cause, against at most four who opposed it, and Herbert Gladstone, the Home Secretary, was himself among the sympathizers. Liberal opinion on the back benches

1. 20 May 1908. Asquith was speaking to a delegation of sixty Liberal M.P.s.

and outside Parliament was probably divided in very similar proportions. Undoubtedly there was strong support for suffrage at every level in the party. Yet in the first election of 1910 the Government was merely committed to extending Asquith's 1908 pledge into the new Parliament, not to any bolder or more generous policy.

After that election the W.S.P.U., claiming that its militancy had contributed to the Government's loss of seats, declared a truce which lasted for the best part of two years. During the truce a Parliamentary 'Conciliation Committee', with all-party membership, devoted itself to the task of suffrage legislation. The first Conciliation Bill proposed only that the vote should be given to women who were £10 householders, with the further restriction that married women could not qualify in respect of the same property as their husbands. This Bill was welcomed by the suffrage societies as a step in the right direction, and it was particularly welcome to Tories, male and female, as a means of strengthening the anti-radical vote in the country. But for the same reason it was opposed by Churchill and Lloyd George, who both voted against it on Second Reading. Though it secured a majority at that stage, it was immediately referred to a committee of the whole House and made no further progress.

The suffragette truce had meanwhile been overtaken by the Truce of God, but when the parties returned to battle towards the end of the year there was also a brief resumption of the sex war. On 18 November, while Asquith was speaking in the House of Commons and announcing its imminent dissolution, the W.S.P.U. was holding a meeting at the nearby Caxton Hall; and when reports of Asquith's speech reached their meeting there was anger that he had not mentioned the Conciliation Bill's future.

Over three hundred women then marched, in detachments of twelve, from Caxton Hall to Parliament Square and tried to gain access to the Palace of Westminster. A large force of policemen, hastily assembled, acted on the understanding that the women had to be kept out but as few as possible arrested. Consequently a battle developed and lasted for nearly six hours, during which the police were increasingly goaded into rough, even in some cases obscene, treatment of the suffragettes. Ordinary human exasperation was doubtless compounded with some degree of male chauvinism and even of class feeling, because most of the suffragettes were well-to-do and many of the police came from the East End. 'Black Friday', as it became known, was one of the nastiest episodes in the whole history of the women's movement. Churchill, now Home Secretary, tried to minimise its baleful effects by immediately releasing those whom the police had, willy-nilly, arrested, and by claiming that his orders had been misunderstood. But damage to the Government's credit was lasting.

Before the suffragettes reverted to quiescence for another year there were further violent scenes. On 22 November Asquith had to be spirited away in a taxi when his car and many windows were smashed in the so-called 'Battle of Downing Street'. His colleague, Augustine Birrell, was less fortunate. Caught by a group of twenty suffragettes approaching Downing Street from the Horse Guards side, he was kicked and jostled and, while struggling to escape, injured the cartilage of his left knee. Next day a further march to Parliament Square resulted in eighteen arrests.

When the new Parliament met, in February 1911, there was no reference to women's suffrage legislation in the King's Speech. But it was not long before another Conciliation Bill was introduced by a private Member. This Bill was rather less restrictive than the first, in that it proposed the enfranchisement of female householders without the £10 limit. Moreover its title implied that it was open to free amendment, though this was a more questionable advantage, since amendments could be of a wrecking character. The Bill had many friends, and the W.S.P.U. had good reason to hope that the Government would allow it to pass. But Lloyd George was no friend to it, though he felt obliged to vote for it in May and was more actively concerned than ever before to win the vote for women. In the late summer of 1911, amid all his National Health preoccupations, he found time to apply his mind to the question of electoral reform, including women's suffrage, with a new sense of urgency.

Instead of the piecemeal policy favoured by many of his colleagues – a measure to end plural voting, amendment of the registration laws, and facilities for the Conciliation Bill – he set out to promote a comprehensive reform of the franchise on lines outlined in a letter to the Master of Elibank dated 5 September 1911:

> I am very concerned about next year's Registration Bill. As you know, I proposed to the Cabinet . . . to drop the idea of introducing a mere Plural Voting Bill and to immediately press forward a measure for simplification and extension of the franchise. To this they agreed. Unless it is introduced and sent up to the Lords next year it will not be available for the next General Election. Now, as you know, I am rather keen that you should circularize all your leading agents, with a view to ascertaining from them . . . what the effect would be in their districts of a simple,

residential qualification. In this connection I am very concerned about our pledges on the Female Suffrage question. We seem to be playing straight into the hands of the enemy. The Conciliation Bill could, on balance, add hundreds of thousands of votes throughout the country to the strength of the Tory Party . . . We have never really faced the situation manfully and courageously. I think the Liberal Party ought to make up its mind as a whole that it will either have an extended franchise which would put working men's wives on to the Register, as well as spinsters and widows, or that it will have no female franchise at all . . . We are likely to find ourselves in the position of putting this wretched Conciliation Bill through the House of Commons, sending it to the Lords, and eventually getting it through. Say what you will, that spells disaster for Liberalism . . .[1]

Lloyd George's arguments evidently swayed his colleagues, because on 7 November Asquith told a deputation of the People's Suffrage Federation that the Government planned to bring forward in the next session a bill extending the franchise to all *bona fide* male residents, that is to say to nearly all adult males, and with scope for amendment in the interests of women's suffrage. This announcement provoked a return to militancy by the W.S.P.U., and Christabel Pankhurst's fury was directed, above all, at Lloyd George. On 10 November she wrote in her paper, *Votes for Women*:

The Government's latest attempt to cheat women of the vote is, of course, inspired by Mr Lloyd George. The whole crooked and discreditable scheme is characteristic of the man and of the methods he has from the first employed against the Suffrage cause.

H. N. Brailsford, secretary of the Conciliation Committee, had already told C. P. Scott – who reported it to Lloyd George – that Christabel 'envisaged the whole suffrage movement . . . as a gigantic duel between herself and Lloyd George whom she designed to destroy'.[2] Her motives are only partly comprehensible. It is true that the Conciliation Bill had a good chance of being enacted swiftly, because there was all-party support for it, whereas the wider measure would become a bone of contention between parties and would, therefore, call for use of the slow-motion Parliament Act procedure. On the other hand Lloyd George's objection to the Conciliation Bill, even in its revised form, was perfectly rational,

1. Murray of Elibank Papers (National Library of Scotland).
2. *The Political Diaries of C. P. Scott, 1911–1928*, edited by Trevor Wilson, p. 57.

and his insistence upon a democratic franchise neither 'crooked' nor 'discreditable'. Christabel was an extreme radical in her feminism but not, like her sisters Sylvia and Adela, a social radical. Lloyd George may have been right in regarding her as an enemy to his form of Liberalism, though her personal hositility to him may also have had springs in her own rather mysterious psyche.

On 21 November there was another W.S.P.U. deputation from Caxton Hall to Parliament Square, but this was only a blind. In the evening suffragettes met at the Women's Press Offices in Charing Cross Road and then set off, singly, armed with hammers and bags of stones, to break a large number of windows at the Treasury, the Home Office and other Government buildings, various shops, two hotels, two newspaper offices and two clubs, including the National Liberal Club. When, therefore, Lloyd George travelled to Bath three days later, to address a meeting of the National Liberal Federation, he knew that he was in for trouble.

The meeting was held at the Skating Rink and the attendance was about five thousand. Lloyd George began his speech by proposing that there should be a truce until the end of the meeting, when he would try to answer any questions. But those who had come to demonstrate were unmoved by his offer. Within five minutes he was forced to stop speaking by a male interrupter, who was ejected with some difficulty, and similar scenes were repeated at intervals throughout the speech. *The Times* commented next day that a Cabinet Minister 'had seldom been subjected to a more deliberate attempt to break up a meeting'. Yet he managed to say what he had to say, and it was well worth saying.

Before turning to the question of women's suffrage, he attacked the existing male franchise with its gross anomalies and deficiencies:

> At the last General Election there were over forty seats whose fate was determined by those who had more than one vote, who had several votes in many cases. If in a commercial enterprise anybody reckons his assets three times over – well, he is guilty of fraud. And I say that if a man votes three times over, by this process he is guilty of a fraud on the democracy.

He was scathing about the university seats:

> Now what is the idea of university representation? The idea is this; that by this means you get a specimen of the cultured, impartial, calm, judicial, fair-minded sort of person – a kind of super-man; somebody

who is above the rancour and the excitement of party. That is the ideal. (A Voice: 'Lord Hugh Cecil!') That is it; that is the reality; a sort of male suffragist who howls down the Prime Minister in a fit of hysteria because he does not approve of his policy.

And he summarized his indictment of the still far from democratic electoral system:

All the dodges and devices which you have on the register – the university representation, the plural voting, and kind of lodger franchise which puts on a young man who has never earned sixpence in his life and never will, and keeps off the register the young artisan who before he reaches the age of twenty-one has been earning his living for years – all these dodges have just one basis, and that is a fundamental distrust of the people.

Then he came to a theme on which, he said, he did not anticipate the same unanimity. But he asked the audience to listen carefully and his words reverberated, in fact, throughout the country:

Liberalism stands above all for fair play . . . Don't you be misled by these exhibitions. They only emanate from a small and infinitesimally small proportion of the women of this country . . . This movement that interrupts meetings . . . is much less pro-Suffrage than it is anti-Liberal. I want to give you one or two reasons for that, because it is an important accusation. They interrupted Liberal meetings when the Liberal Party was in opposition. They never went to Tory Ministers, although they were in power at the time . . . They interrupted Sir Edward Grey who has always been in favour of the suffrage . . . Now let me give you another fact about it. They have opposed Liberal candidates at elections when they were in favour of the suffrage, and supported Tory candidates who were against the suffrage. And I will give you another reason. Did you notice that they smashed the windows of the National Liberal Club, although nine-tenths of its members are in favour of the suffrage. And I will give you a last reason . . . Why are they angry now? They ran the Conciliation Bill, a measure of limited suffrage which, in my judgment, would have been grossly unfair to Liberalism. Now that Bill has been torpedoed and the way is clear for a broad and democratic amendment of the suffrage for women . . . Now we have a chance . . . for the insertion in the Government bill of an amendment which will enfranchise not a limited class of women chosen just to suit the Tory canvasser, but for the insertion of an amendment which would include the working man's wife. That explains the fury of these anti-Liberal women . . .

It was right that women in general should now be enfranchised:

Laws affect the interests of women just as deeply as they do the interests of men. Some laws, many laws, affect them more gravely. There has been a fundamental change during the last generation or two . . . You constantly hear that Liberals are interfering with business and with the homes . . . As long as Government was confined to invading the rights of others or defending rights against invasion . . . to tracking and backing marauders, so long as the instruments of government were the sword, the battle-axe, the pillory, the rack, the dungeon and the gallows, women were better out of it.[1]

But now government had other instruments, to match its more humane concerns.

Lloyd George's unequivocal statement that the Conciliation Bill had been 'torpedoed' sent the W.S.P.U. into fresh transports of rage, and disconcerted even moderate suffragists who had assumed that the Government, in spite of its commitment to a wider measure, would still make time available for the Conciliation Bill. In the event both bills came to grief, though in different ways. The revised Conciliation Bill, which had secured a large majority in 1911, was brought in again in March 1912 and defeated, then, by fourteen votes. The Government's own Bill seemed to be making good progress until, at the beginning of 1913, the Speaker (Lowther) ruled that certain proposed amendments to it, including three alternative women's suffrage amendments, would so change the character of the Bill that he would be obliged to insist on its withdrawal. This strange ruling came as a boon to opponents of suffrage as well as to all who, secretly or overtly, were opposed to full democratization of the franchise. In consequence the Bill was abandoned and there was no reform of the system, nor any Parliamentary enfranchisement of women, until 1918 when Lloyd George was Prime Minister.

Why was his earlier effort frustrated? One reason was the campaign of vandalism wantonly promoted by Christabel Pankhurst. Another was the Irish Nationalists' dislike of a measure which would necessarily compete with the Home Rule Bill for Parliamentary time. But the chief reason was,

1. Bath, 24 November 1911.

beyond doubt, the Government's lack of solidarity and collective resolution. Even among Liberals in the country there were confused feelings and opinions. Plural voting was thoroughly unpopular with them, and there is evidence to suggest that they shared Lloyd George's hostility to the Conciliation Bills. But much proselytisation was needed if they were to be brought to rally enthusiastically in support of his comprehensive programme.

According to one writer, the clue to his failure is the loss of influence that he suffered in 1912–13 through involvement in the Marconi scandal:

> At a time when the Government was pressing a Franchise Bill and was split on Suffrage, the only man with political force enough to secure the inclusion of suffrage, and prevent the break-up of the Government, was being embarrassed by charges of corruption . . . At the very time when his political instincts told him that the Liberals must break out of the sterility of coercion on Suffrage, he was a captive of the chief architect of that policy – the Prime Minister . . . The Marconi affair is the crucial backcloth to the struggle that, at least in public, went on to amend the Government's Franchise Bill . . .[1]

This is a good point, affording at least a partial explanation of what happened. But surely there was another and even more crucial weakness in Lloyd George's position, which was cramping his style long before Marconi. On the franchise issue he lost the support of Churchill, ostensibly his radical brother-in-arms but now also, increasingly, his rival. And this gave Asquith a decisive advantage.

Churchill's argument was that Asquith could not be expected to use the Parliament Act to bring about a constitutional change which, in his view, would be disastrous. Moreover, 'Votes for Women' was not a vote-winning cause with the existing electorate. To press for enfranchising eight million women would lead to the loss of by-elections and ship-wreck for the Government's other policies. The right course would be to hold a referendum to discover if women really wanted the vote, and then to submit the question to the men. Naturally enough, Lloyd George was appalled at Churchill's referendum proposal, seeing that at the previous election Ministers had been denouncing referenda as subversive of the Constitution. He and Grey – who remained a staunch suffragist – arrived at a compromise with Churchill, under which the democratic suffrage amendment to the Franchise Bill was to be moved without a prior

1. David Morgan, *Suffragists and Liberals*, pp. 108–9.

referendum, but which envisaged a subsequent 'referendum or initiative' – if the amendment were carried – to determine whether or not the newly registered female voters wished to exercise their rights. In reporting this absurd scheme to Asquith, Churchill was careful to say that it was not a 'fixed agreement', and that in any case it would 'probably get smashed' if any attempt were made to give effect to it.[1] A cynic might observe that Churchill, having used his alliance with Lloyd George to secure from Asquith a position of near parity in the Government, was now seeking a 'favourite son' relationship with the Prime Minister by working with him against Lloyd George.

During the summer of 1911 Lloyd George cut a figure in what Bagehot called the 'dignified' sector of the Constitution, as distinct from the 'efficient' sector which was his normal sphere of interest. Since 1908 he had been Constable of Caernarvon Castle, succeeding his old political opponent, Sir John Puleston; and when in 1910 another old political opponent, the Bishop of St Asaph, suggested that the Prince of Wales should be invested at a ceremony in the castle, he was quick to respond to the idea. The Bishop and he had long been personal friends, and they shared a desire to settle the Welsh Church question on mutually saleable terms. In his memoirs the Bishop thus described how Lloyd George reacted to his suggestion:

> It seemed a wild venture. I had never asked him a personal favour. But I knew his character well and could trust him. He has the gift of chivalry . . . and in victory is a generous opponent. Above all else for my purpose, he has imagination, which the slow-witted interpret as want of principle. The interview brought instant approval and action.[2]

The idea appealed to Lloyd George's political sense no less than to his imagination. He saw that it would enable him to gratify Welsh national pride and, at the same time, to reassure traditionalists in every part of the Kingdom. By stage-managing the Investiture he could make a harmless

---

1. W.S.C. to H.H.A., 21 December 1911 (quoted in *Winston S. Churchill*, Companion Vol. II, Part 3, pp. 1475–6). What was meant by 'initiative', as an alternative to referendum, was not explained.

2. A. G. Edwards, *Memories*, p. 245. The idea of reviving the ceremony of investiture at Caernarvon, in abeyance for three hundred years, was not Bishop Edwards' own. It was suggested to him by Queen Victoria's eldest daughter, the Empress Frederick, when he was on a visit to Windsor Castle in 1893.

gesture to those elements in society which had been most affronted by his words and deeds. The King, when approached, was glad enough to cooperate, because from his point of view the ceremony would be a gesture to his Welsh subjects, which might also facilitate 'his dealings with the difficult Mr Lloyd George'.[1]

Great pains were taken to ensure its success. An architect, Frank Baines, was seconded from the Office of Works to give the ruined Castle a face-lift in the manner of Viollet-le-Duc, using stone from the original quarries, and beams of Canadian oak. For the Prince's regalia gold was taken from the mountains of Merionethshire, and for the few words of Welsh that he was to utter when presented to the crowd at Queen Eleanor's gate he received tuition from Lloyd George himself. But the local hero was content to go through the ceremony without a speaking role, even letting Churchill have the privilege of proclaiming the Prince's titles. An eye-witness has given this description of the scene on 13 July:

> The day was intensely hot, and from early dawn the little town was full to overflowing. Drapery embroidered with the Royal Arms, and with the Feathers of the Prince of Wales, covered the ancient grey walls of the castle, while Union Jacks and Welsh Dragons hung from every staff, and waved from every window. Within there had assembled all that was brilliant and representative of Welsh life; while accompanying the Royal Family came a crowd of their most distinguished servants – Mr Asquith . . . Mr Churchill . . . Mr Balfour . . . and, of course, the Constable of the Castle. Lloyd George was then at the summit of his marvellous popularity in Wales . . . He knew perfectly well that, were he to appear in one hall, and the Royal Family in another, the vast majority of the people would be with him. And for that reason, in order that the King, the Queen and the Prince might have the whole stage to themselves on that day, he was careful to keep himself well in the background. He performed the Constable's duty of receiving the King at the gate, and of handing him the Key of the Castle; but beyond that he played no part in the ceremony, and gave no opportunity to the crowd to acclaim him when it was more fitting that they should acclaim their King and their Prince. The great moment of a particularly fine ceremony was that in which the Prince greeted the Welsh people in their own language.[2]

1. The Duke of Windsor, *A King's Story*, p. 81.
2. W. Watkin Davies, *op. cit.*, pp. 381–2.

The occasion was not without its under current of political muttering. The night before the Investiture Sir Samuel Evans – formerly a crony of Lloyd George and until the previous year Solicitor-General, but now a High Court Judge – told Ellis Davies about Lloyd George's coalition project, of which he had received some account 'from a member of the Cabinet . . . confirmed indirectly by another'. And on the day of the Investiture Davies ran into Lord St Davids who quoted 'a lady in high position' as saying 'that Lloyd George will join their [Tory] party soon and *that* on the Veto Bill'. But St Davids added that he did not for a moment believe it.[1]

Lloyd George went to Balmoral again in September 1911 and found the King obtuse about working-class grievances. 'He is a very very small man and all his sympathy is with the rich – very little pity for the poor.' Towards the end of his short visit he wrote to Margaret that he was looking forward to his next destination, Skibo, where he would be staying with an old friend and admirer, Andrew Carnegie:

> I am not cut out for Court life. I can see some of them revel in it. I detest it. The whole atmosphere reeks with Toryism . . . Everybody very civil to me as they would be to a dangerous wild animal . . . The King is hostile to the bone to all who are working to lift the workmen out of the mire. So is the Queen . . .[2]

Anyone who thought that Lloyd George had sold out to the 'establishment' was misjudging him. But the more he appeared in his true colours, as a patriotic radical of the Left Centre, the more he was bound to be misjudged; and events were conspiring to make his true colours increasingly apparent.

Industrial unrest was not the only important topic discussed while he was at Balmoral. Another was the crisis over Morocco which was threatening the peace of Europe. Among his fellow-guests were Balfour, still Leader of the Opposition, and Count Benckendorff, the Russian ambassador. With them, as with the King, he discussed the international crisis at length.

By then it was known to the whole world that he was no pacifist or Little Englander. The illusion that he was either, deriving from a

1. Journal of Ellis W. Davies, M.P., entries for 12 and 13 July 1911.
2 D.L.G. to M.L.G., 13 September 1911 (N.L.W.) and 16 September (N.L.W. and *Letters*, pp. 158–9).

misapprehension of his stand against the Boer War, had been shattered by his famous speech at the Mansion House two months previously. Why he made that speech, and the reasons for his changing attitude towards Germany, must now be explained.

Temperamentally he had far more in common with the French than with the Germans. He loved visiting France, and Frances Stevenson, whose mother was half-French, later said of him that in character he was even more like a Frenchman than a Welshman. During the Fashoda crisis in 1898 he had taken the highly independent and unfashionable line that it would be crazy for Britain to go to war with the only other liberal democracy in Europe. Yet when he was first a Minister he certainly did not regard the *Entente Cordiale* as a defensive alliance against Germany. At that stage he believed in keeping the peace through all-round appeasement and was not unduly concerned about the German danger, though he reacted sharply when, at the time of his appointment as Chancellor and consequent cancellation of an official visit to Paris, Northcliffe suggested that the French might suspect him and the Liberal Government of being pro-German:

> I am genuinely surprised at what you say as to our being suspect by the French for pro-German tendencies. The only real pro-German whom I know of on the Liberal side of politics is Rosebery, and I sometimes wonder whether he is even a Liberal at all! Haldane, of course, from education and intellectual bent, is in sympathy with German ideas, but there is really nothing else on which to base a suspicion that we are inclined to a pro-German policy at the expense of the entente with France. Still, if such a feeling exists, it makes me all the more sorry that I am unable to go to Paris . . .[1]

Before Lloyd George's visit to Germany in August 1908 Grey arranged for him to meet Count Wolff-Metternich, the German ambassador. On 14 July Grey had Metternich to lunch to meet him, and a fortnight later he lunched with Metternich alone. At both meetings he explained that naval supremacy was vital to Britain and that any apparent threat to it could only result in tension and a continuing arms race. He suggested that the German navy should be limited to a 2 : 3 ratio, as compared with the British. The ambassador did not exclude possible future discussion of curtailing naval armaments, but when he reported to Berlin the Kaiser's angry comment was that such a possibility should not have

1. D.L.G. to Northcliffe, 9 April 1908.

been mentioned, because he (the Kaiser) did '*not* wish a good under-standing with England at the expense of the extension of the German fleet'.[1]

At Carlsbad soon afterwards Lloyd George made a public statement on Anglo-German relations to a correspondent of the Vienna *Neue Freie Presse*. In the interview he expressed his desire to see 'an *entente* between England and Germany', so that the two countries would be able to devote themselves 'wholly to the tasks of peace, of progress and of social reform'. But he insisted that without an end of naval rivalry there could be no hope of such an *entente*, and he stressed Britain's determination to maintain her supremacy at sea. Later in the journey, at Frankfurt, he allowed Harold Spender to speak on his behalf to a local journalist representing the *Daily Mail*. Spender's remarks added nothing of substance to what Lloyd George had said to the *Neue Freie Presse*, but taken in conjunction with a speech by Churchill at Swansea – in which he deprecated talk of inevitable conflict between Britain and Germany – they were interpreted as evidence of an attempt by the two radical Ministers to run a foreign policy of their own, different from Grey's. Actually, Lloyd George had done Grey a service by showing publicly that he was as firm as anyone in resisting German naval pretensions.

Long afterwards he described incidents during the visit which had aroused his fears,[2] but no letter or other contemporary document so far published contains any reference to the incidents. This does not mean that they were invented, but merely that the details of them, and his account of their effect upon him at the time, should be treated with a little caution. Yet there is no reason to doubt that, with his exceptional sensitivity to atmosphere, he became aware in Germany of a degree of nationalistic fervour and latent hostility to Britain which he had not previously suspected.

Over the next two years, while immersed in the 1909 Budget and its consequences, he gave only fitful attention to foreign affairs. But his approach remained the same – that bilateral *ententes* should be sought or upheld as a reinforcement to, though never as a substitute for, the Concert of Europe. His desire for an *entente* with Germany was viewed with disquiet by the French who misread it as Germanophilia, and by the

---

1. The Kaiser's comment (on Metternich's report of the 14 August meeting) was not of course made public until after the war. Lloyd George quoted it in his *War Memoirs* (Vol. I, p. 22).
2. D. Lloyd George, *War Memoirs*, Vol. I, pp. 28–32.

Foreign Office whose prevalent philosophy was that safety depended upon a balance of power, with Britain, France and Russia forming a counterpoise to the Triple Alliance of Germany, Austria and Italy. But he stuck to his belief that an accommodation with Germany could and should be reached, and early in 1911 he joined a Cabinet Committee to explore the possibilities.

Nothing, unfortunately, came of the Committee's work, and in the summer of 1911 a major international crisis began when France sent an expedition to Fez and Germany sent a small warship, the *Panther*, to the Moroccan Atlantic port of Agadir. The complex background to these events has no place in a study of Lloyd George, except in the briefest outline. In 1905, while cruising in the Mediterranean, the Kaiser had gone ashore for a couple of hours at Tangier and claimed melodramatically to be the Sultan of Morocco's protector. His purpose had been to humiliate the French and to prove to them and others the ineffectiveness of the recently formed *Entente Cordiale*. But the stroke miscarried, and after the resulting conference at Algeciras France was well on the way to converting Morocco into a French protectorate, having benefited from steady British support throughout the crisis.

Agadir in 1911 was, in a sense, a repeat performance of Tangier in 1905. Once again Germany was trying to divide France and Britain, while extending her own influence; and once again the attempt failed, despite a considerable readiness on the part of the French Prime Minister, Joseph Caillaux, to settle the affair in direct negotiation with Germany, without reference to Britain. In Grey's view, Britain had both a legal and a moral right to be involved, and within a few days of receiving news of the *Panther*'s arrival at Agadir he told Metternich, with full authority from the Cabinet, that Britain would not allow the future of Morocco to be settled behind her back.

That was on 4 July, and more than two weeks then passed without any reaction from the German Government. On 21 July Lloyd George was due to speak at the annual bankers' dinner at the Mansion House, and by agreement with Grey and Asquith he used the occasion for a statement on the Moroccan crisis, which made a profound impact:

> ... I am also bound to say this – that I believe it is essential in the highest interests, not merely of this country, but of the world, that Britain should at all hazards maintain her place and her prestige amongst the Great Powers of the world. Her potent influence has many a time been

in the past, and may yet be in the future, invaluable to the cause of human liberty. It has more than once in the past redeemed continental nations, who are sometimes too apt to forget that service, from overwhelming disaster, and even from national extinction. I would make great sacrifices to preserve peace. I conceive that nothing could justify a disturbance of international goodwill except questions of the gravest national moment. But if a situation were to be forced upon us in which peace could only be preserved by the surrender of the great and beneficent position Britain has won by centuries of heroism and achievement, by allowing Britain to be treated, where her interests were vitally affected, as if she were of no account in the Cabinet of Nations, then I say emphatically that peace at that price would be a humiliation intolerable for a great country like ours to endure. National honour is no party question. The peace of the world is much more likely to be secured if all nations realize fully what the conditions of peace must be. . . .

Some historians have taken the view that Lloyd George's warning was meant for France rather than for Germany, and it is certainly true that Caillaux was prepared to leave Britain out of the negotiations for a Moroccan settlement. But is it necessary to choose between the two explanations? The Cabinet was, beyond question, alarmed at the prospect of a German naval base in Morocco, threatening British trade routes, and there is no reason to suspect Lloyd George of deception in stressing this aspect of the matter to C. P. Scott the day after the Mansion House speech.[1] Exaggerated though the fear may have been, it was real. Moreover, it was a fair calculation that if Britain did not make a stand over Agadir the Germans would be tempted to go to all lengths in their challenge to British sea power. In the circumstances there was much to be said for a gesture which might simultaneously deter Germany as a potential enemy and remind France of her obligations to a friend.

Lloyd George's words represented no change of outlook on his part, but they astonished all those, at home and abroad, who had mistakenly supposed him to be a pacifist and anti-Imperialist. The mistake derived principally from his opposition to the Boer War, which had been very widely misunderstood. If the Boers had been threatening Britain's maritime supremacy, Lloyd George would have been a whole-hearted supporter of the Boer War. His statement on Agadir should have been no surprise

1. *The Political Diaries of C. P. Scott, 1911–1928*, edited by Trevor Wilson, entry for 22 July 1911, pp. 46–9.

to Metternich or the German Government or, indeed, to attentive readers of his *Neue Freie Presse* interview in 1908. But in fact it created a sensation and, in Germany, intense resentment.

What, if anything, did it achieve? Certainly it must have helped Caillaux to negotiate a settlement which, on the whole, was favourable to France and of small advantage to Germany. The threat of a German naval base in Morocco was removed, if it ever seriously existed. But for several months Europe trembled on the brink of war, and the eventual avoidance of it cannot be attributed solely, or even chiefly, to Lloyd George's intervention. In early August it did seem to have done the trick and Churchill wrote to his wife: 'They [the Germans] sent their *Panther* to Agadir and we sent out little Panther to the Mansion House: with the best results.'[1] But later in the month, and again at the beginning of September, war seemed to be imminent. Lloyd George at that time was not only ready for a showdown with Germany but, it would appear, disposed to feel that the moment and occasion for it were as propitious as they would ever be. He was also convinced that Britain could not fight the war purely at sea but would have to send troops to the Continent. When there was a row in the Cabinet over Anglo-French staff talks – of which the Cabinet as such had not previously been informed – he was one of only four Ministers who supported Haldane and the War Office on that issue. The others were Grey, Churchill and Asquith himself. But in November, for a variety of reasons, the crisis was over. Germany accepted another humiliation and the showdown was postponed.

There are some who believe that Lloyd George's speech, far from preventing war, was a contributory cause of the terrible conflict which broke out in 1914. The evidence gives little support to this view, though of course it is always easy to describe the alternative to appeasement as warmongering. A famous British historian has written thus of the pre-1914 period:

> As to the Balance of Power, it would be truer to say that the war was caused by its breakdown rather than by its existence. There had been a real European Balance in the first decade of the Franco-Russian alliance . . . The Balance broke down when Russia was weakened by the war with Japan; and Germany got in the habit of trying to get her way by threats . . . In fact, peace must have brought Germany the mastery of Europe within a few years. This was prevented by the habit of her

1. 6 August 1911 (Randolph S. Churchill, *Winston S. Churchill*, Vol. II, p. 529).

diplomacy and, still more, by the mental outlook of her people. They had trained themselves psychologically for aggression.[1]

And an eminent German historian, admitting that Germany's ulterior aim in the Agadir crisis was, indeed, to break or at least weaken the *Entente Cordiale*, and that it was 'parried' by Lloyd George's Mansion House speech, has further commented:

> Up to 1911 Germany had not succeeded in adopting Britain's policy of concluding compromises with her competitors, for she had equated moderation with an inferiority incompatible with the world power status which was her aim. Such a policy [i.e. a policy of moderation and compromise] was inevitably rejected by a generation of politicians who had grown up in revolt against Bismarck's doctrine that Germany was a 'saturated power', regarded the expansion of Germany as the supreme object of their policy, and were now occupying the leading positions in the imperial Chancellery, the Foreign Ministry and the Prussian ministries.

In the author's judgment, Germany's aims and methods made war sooner or later 'inevitable'.[2]

Foreign affairs and defence represented the Liberal Party's most cruel dilemma. So long as other nations accepted British maritime supremacy as the price of free entry into British markets, Liberals could afford the policy of Peace and Retrenchment. But Germany was now, in effect, repudiating the tacit bargain upon which their traditional policy was based. They could justifiably claim to have resisted strong pressure to abandon their Free Trade principles under the impact of competition from Protectionist countries such as Germany. But how could they be expected to stand idly by while the largest Continental nation built up a fleet that might, before long, be a match for the Royal Navy? It was not simply a question of safeguarding British commerce, but of defending Britain itself against invasion. To their chagrin Liberal Ministers were forced to spend far more, rather than less, upon armaments, and some of them began to see that increased involvement with foreign countries was inescapable. The new trend of policy was to prove fatal to their party in the long run, but any other might have been fatal to Britain.

Lloyd George's attitude towards Germany was that of a reluctant realist.

1. A. J. P. Taylor, *The Struggle for Mastery in Europe, 1848–1918*, p. 528.
2. Fritz Fischer, *Germany's Aims in the First World War*, p. 24.

Though military history and tactics had always interested him, he had no romantic illusions about modern war and no aspiration to be the great war leader that he was destined to become. His tough talk in 1911 was not the product of hot-headedness, but reflected his growing belief that the German challenge had to be faced. Perhaps he was unduly reassured by the outcome of Agadir, so that he was less quick, three years later, to perceive the implications of Sarajevo. At any rate, it is surely easier to criticize his Hamlet-like indecision on the second occasion than his clear-sighted audacity on the first.

ELEVEN
Ambulance Man

At the beginning of his 1909 Budget speech Lloyd George had referred to the Government's ambitious plans for further social reform, which the Budget was designed to facilitate. In particular he spoke of a 'well-thought-out scheme' to provide 'for the sick, for the invalided, for widows and orphans', and to the Government's pledge 'to deal on a comprehensive scale with the problem of unemployment'. What was the background to this confident assertion of the New Liberalism, and how far was he able to give effect to it?

He had always believed in social reform; that is to say, in the duty of the State to remedy injustices with which do-gooders could, at best, only tinker. During his early years as a politician he had frequently denounced the social order, and attacks such as he then made were beginning to stir not only the compassion but also the enlightened self-interest of the rich. Most politicians, Liberal and Tory, were men of ample means, and even the electorate was still predominantly bourgeois. But among the 'haves' there was a growing recognition that society would have to be modified if its essential features were to be preserved, and at the same time patriots were becoming aware that something had to be done about the waste of human resources, and consequent damage to the nation, that poverty entailed.

The first major step towards the so-called Welfare State was the Old Age Pensions Act, which Asquith planned and Lloyd George piloted to the Statute Book in 1908. While it was going through, Government spokesmen emphasized that it was only a first step, and in his Second Reading speech Lloyd George mentioned other problems which it was 'the business of the State' to tackle and which it had 'neglected too long'. The next problems to be attended to were unemployment and invalidity, and it was to study the German way of dealing with them that Lloyd George visited Germany in the summer of 1908. He returned favouring, for these problems, the method of contributory insurance which had not been applied in the old age pensions scheme. And it was a great encouragement to him that four trade union leaders who went to Germany in the autumn reported afterwards that State insurance would have no injurious effect upon trade unionism.

In 1908 the number of trade unionists out of work had risen to 7·8 per cent, from 3·6 per cent in 1906. The level of unemployment was higher than at any time since 1886, when one result had been the Trafalgar Square riot in London, whose effect upon the governing and propertied classes had been traumatic. It was clearly an urgent necessity to take action to mitigate the evil of unemployment, and Churchill at the Board of Trade was able to bring in the first practical measure, his scheme for a national system of labour exchanges, which came into operation in February 1910.

This scheme was largely uncontroversial, and Parliamentary discussion of it was upstaged by the great Budget row. For the planning and administration of it Churchill turned to the young William Beveridge, who was recommended to him by the Webbs and who, like the Board of Trade's Permanent Secretary, Hubert Llewellyn Smith, had worked at Toynbee Hall. Labour exchanges already existed in Britain, but only under private or municipal auspices. As a result of Churchill's measure the State took over sixty-one existing exchanges and established many new ones, so that by the end of 1913 there were 430 labour exchanges in the United Kingdom, as well as upward of a thousand small branch offices in rural districts. The function of the exchanges was to notify unemployed workers of suitable jobs vacant in different parts of the country and, if required, to lend money for travelling expenses. Trade union rights were safeguarded by permission to workers to refuse jobs for which the pay was below union rates, and by denial of labour exchange services to employers in search of blackleg labour during industrial disputes.

But it was stressed that the scheme was only a prelude to, and had to be complemented by, a scheme of unemployment insurance. Lloyd George claimed that the idea for such a scheme was his, and always intended that it should be combined with health insurance in a single measure. But rather to his annoyance Churchill took the matter into his own hands and planned a separate Bill during 1909. In the event Lloyd George got his way, because when Parliament was dissolved after the Lords rejected the Budget, Churchill's old Bill was abandoned; and the substance of it was later carried as Part II of Lloyd George's National Insurance Act.

By contrast with Part I it had a fairly easy passage and its main features should now be summarized. Unemployment insurance was made compulsory, but limited to trades in which unemployment was cyclical rather than chronic – trades such as shipbuilding, mechanical engineering, iron-founding, vehicle manufacture and the construction industry. This excluded some of the nation's most important industries and the total number of workers insured was only about two and a quarter million. The scheme was based upon contributions of $2\frac{1}{2}$d. per week each from employer and employed, to which was added an Exchequer subsidy of 2d. per week for each insured person. And the State further undertook to provide up to £3 million in case the insurance fund was unable to meet all the demands upon it. The rate of benefit was eventually fixed at 7s. per week for a maximum of fifteen weeks within any twelve-month period. Trade unions were encouraged to participate in the scheme and to offer benefits larger than those offered by the State. They could act as administrators on behalf of the Government and would be re-imbursed three-quarters of whatever amount they paid out in benefits.

The Churchill–Lloyd George system of unemployment insurance was never properly tested, because the recession in which and for which it was designed gave way to several years of prosperity before the outbreak of war in 1914. It is likely, however, that it would have proved equal to the needs of 1908, or to unemployment of comparable dimensions in the post-war period. But after 1918 the scale of the problem became so much vaster that the insurance principle had to be discarded in favour of means-tested unemployment relief. Later still, during the Second World War, the mature Beveridge sought to reinstate insurance in his famous Report, but only on the assumption that 'full' employment would be maintained.

By far the more difficult and complicated part of Lloyd George's insurance legislation was evolved through his own efforts, and that was the part dealing with invalidity. Among the victims of social hardship, he sympathized most of all with sick or disabled breadwinners and their dependants. Public health, as such, interested him rather less, and personal illness repelled him. But he cared very much about poverty, of which sickness and disablement were evidently prime causes. His aim in promoting health insurance was 'to replace lost income, not to cure sickness',[1] though the system that he brought into being had important consequences for the development of therapeutic medicine in Britain.

Before he entered the field there was no national system for combating the hazard of ill-health as it affected working-class families. There were plenty of doctors, but of course their quality varied and many of them had little to do with the poor. It would not, however, be true to say that the poor were completely neglected. For those who lived in big cities excellent treatment was often available, at little or no cost, in the voluntary hospitals, and a much larger number of poor people received medical attention in the Poor Law infirmaries, or in provident dispensaries run by a variety of charitable organizations. But these forms of medical relief for the poor were viewed with suspicion by many doctors, who felt that free treatment was too often given to patients who could afford to pay. And there was a strong repugnance for the Poor Law among a majority of the working class, but more especially, of course, in that section of it which set most store by independence and respectability.

These 'aristocrats of labour' were the natural *clientèle* of the friendly societies, institutions which embodied the Victorian ideal of self-help while also appealing to the traditional British taste for social exclusiveness. By the end of the nineteenth century there were many thousands of them, predominantly in the Midlands and North of England, with a total membership of about four and a quarter millions. Their names – such as Hearts of Oak or the Ancient Order of Foresters – might be evocative of the pre-industrial past, yet they ministered to the needs of skilled industrial workers, including the need for some collective insurance against the hazards of life. In return for a contribution of between 4d. and 8d. a week, a member might expect to receive about 10s. a week when he was ill, medical attention from a doctor under contract to his society, and a sum of up to £15 to give him a decent funeral when he died. A doctor working for a friendly society was paid a salary or capitation fee, and the relationship between him and his patients was not that normally approved by the medical profession; he did not choose them, nor they him. But the society wanted to be able to control the doctor, because his certificate determined the payment of sickness benefit and any system that gave him too much freedom might encourage malingering. However objectionable to the B.M.A., a friendly society contract was a coveted prize to many struggling

1. Bentley B. Gilbert, *The Evolution of National Insurance in Great Britain*, p. 314.

doctors: so much so that the disposal of it was not always free from corruption.

When Lloyd George turned his mind to social insurance the friendly societies were still very powerful, and not least in Liberal politics. But their finances had run into serious trouble. More and more of their members were living on into old age, while the declining birth-rate was a blow to recruitment. There were too many societies chasing too few potential members and finding their actual members an increasing burden. Yet their whole ethos was so opposed to State action that they were hostile, at first, to the Government's old age pensions scheme, even though it brought relief to their funds; and when Lloyd George approached them about his wider project, their initial reaction was suspicious. All the same, after several meetings with their representatives at the end of 1908, he managed to secure their qualified cooperation and a preliminary plan was submitted to a committee of actuaries. This plan was designed to make State insurance compulsory for all working men who could not be better provided for by friendly societies, but in no way to compete with the societies. It was to cover sickness, disability, maternity and widowhood.

During 1909 Lloyd George was preoccupied with the Budget, and in any case the actuarial report was not presented to the Government until March 1910. Then he began to talk again to the friendly society leaders, though a further delay occurred during the summer and autumn, when the constitutional conference was meeting and when he was making his private attempt to bring the parties together in a coalition. After the breakdown of the talks, the year's second election campaign followed.

Meanwhile he had become aware that he had to deal with another interest-group even more formidable than the friendly societies when, probably in early August, he met representatives of the industrial insurance industry. The components of this industry were, for the most part, limited companies operating largely for the benefit of their stockholders and travelling salesmen. There were also the so-called collecting friendly societies – not to be confused with proper friendly societies – which differed from the companies only in having no stockholders and being run, therefore, exclusively for the benefit of their agents. Industrial insurance was very big business indeed. The most important of the companies, the Prudential, was the country's largest owner of freehold private property, as it was also of Bank of England stock and Imperial government bonds. The twelve principal institutions sold between them nearly ten million new policies a year, for a sum equivalent to roughly half the total national budget. The Big Twelve included three collecting friendly societies – the Liverpool Victoria, the Royal Liver and the Scottish Legal – as well as the 'Pru', the Pearl and seven other limited companies.

So far as the working class was concerned, industrial insurance was aimed at those who lacked the means, or at any rate the temperament, to join friendly societies, and it exploited to the full the desire of even the poorest Englishman to be 'pompous in the grave'. As a rule industrial insurance policies provided only funeral benefit. For a penny a week a man of twenty (or his wife) might, for instance, buy a policy worth £8. 10s. after six months. The value of policies varied according to the ages of the persons insured, but only proof of age was required; there was no need for any medical examination. The job of selling and collecting was done by an army of agents, 70,000 or more, who earned commissions amounting to over 22 per cent of each institution's annual income, compared with an average of no more than 37 per cent paid to beneficiaries. The insurance salesman was a figure that no politician of the period could afford to ignore:

> Like the patent non-crushable, non-stainable, detachable collar he wore, or the Coventry bicycle he rode, [he] was a product of the mature, late-Victorian British industrial society. His equipment was a board school education and the ambition to get on. The sale of funeral policies offered the sharp, unabashed, clever young man from the slums a quick way to the £3 or £4 per week income enjoyed by only one person in six before World War I . . . He was likely to be a radical Liberal in politics and, scorning the commodity he himself sold, a member of a friendly society. The agents had no particular love for the companies that employed them, and were well organized in the National Union of Insurance Agents.[1]

Above all, these men had the political influence which came from being regular visitors to most British working-class homes. To ordinary people 'the man from the Prudential' might be a music-hall joke, but his views and interests had to be taken very seriously by a Liberal Chancellor of the Exchequer.

The industrial insurance lobby would have been powerful enough in any case, but it gained an incalculable addition of strength in the man retained as its principal lobbyist and tactician. Howard Kingsley Wood was, in 1910–11, a solicitor in his thirtieth year, with a good City practice

1. Bentley B. Gilbert, *op. cit.*, p. 320.

4. A Liberal poster showing the benefits of Lloyd George's Health Insurance scheme

A HITHERTO UNDISCLOSED INTEREST.

Mr. Balfour: *My dear Lloyd George, I am so dreadfully anxious about these dear Trade Unions! I do hope you won't do anything to destroy them!*

("He believed it would be the last thing the Government desired to destroy what was good in either of these great Institutions (Trade Unions and Friendly Societies), but he was not sure that they were not doing it." – Mr. Balfour on the Insurance Bill, October 7, 1911.)

5. 'A Hitherto Undisclosed Interest', 10 October 1911

and burgeoning political ambitions. (He was elected to the London County Council as a Municipal Reformer in the course of 1911.) Already known in the industrial insurance world as the legal representative of two of its larger units, he was then appointed salaried adviser to the whole 'Combine', in which capacity he achieved very important results for his clients without, however, wrecking Lloyd George's scheme as many of them would have wished. Later, as Sir Kingsley Wood – the name by which he is known to history – he collaborated with Neville Chamberlain at the Ministry of Health in building substantially upon the foundations that Lloyd George had laid. Later still, he played a part second only to that of Adolf Hitler in bringing Winston Churchill to the Premiership in 1940.[1]

After meeting the insurance men Lloyd George could see that he would not be able to work his scheme through the friendly societies alone, as he had originally hoped. He could also see that one at least of the benefits that he was intending to provide would probably have to be scrapped, for even the absence of funeral benefit from his scheme would not satisfy the insurance men; they were also implacably opposed to widows' and orphans' pensions, which in their view would remove much of the attraction of their own funeral policies. Lloyd George's first thought was to buy the agents out, but it soon became apparent to him that the sum involved would be too vast. In his ensuing attempt, earlier described, to find a basis for coalition government, one of his motives was undoubtedly to deal with the insurance problem without the aggravation of party politics. The paragraph on insurance is, in fact, the longest in his memorandum of 17 August 1910, but this does not mean that the new-found threat to his insurance scheme was the principal, still less that it was the only, cause of his decision to propose a coalition. Among the many contributory causes it was by no means the greatest, but it did have a special urgency and the details of the subject were increasingly in his mind as he wrote the memorandum.

In the first election of 1910 Liberal candidates were pestered by the friendly societies; in the second they were got at even more effectively by the industrial insurance lobby, as were the candidates of other parties, with the result that 490 members of the new Parliament were pledged 'to oppose any measure of State Insurance . . . likely prejudicially to affect the

1. After the famous Norway debate he quietly withdrew his allegiance from Chamberlain and transferred it to Churchill, whom most other leading politicians at the time – Labour as well as Conservative – did not favour for the succession. He advised Churchill not to agree to serve under Halifax, who might otherwise have become Prime Minister. For his unique service he was appointed Chancellor of the Exchequer, despite his appeasement record.

7a. Joseph Chamberlain during the 1906 election campaign

7b. Charles Masterman arriving at the House of Commons

8. The Lloyd Georges, with Megan, at 11 Downing Street

interest' of the collecting companies. On 1 December Lloyd George himself issued a letter confirming that the benefits envisaged in his scheme did
not include 'a funeral benefit or any immediate money payment on the
death of a contributor or his relatives', and pledging the Government to
submit no measure to the House of Commons dealing with sickness or
invalidity 'until all societies having any interest in the matter' had been
'consulted'. He did not yet commit himself to abandoning widows'
pensions, though he cannot have had much hope of being able to salvage
them. At all events he entered the New Year determined to enact a substantial measure of State insurance, yet fully conscious of the difficulty of
squaring both the friendly societies and the 'Combine'. He did not at this
stage look for any serious trouble from the doctors.

With the New Year a period of intensive preparation began. On the
ministerial side his chief aides were Masterman and another friend, Rufus
Isaacs – whose friendship was before long to prove costly to him, but whose
suavity and quick wits were meanwhile of great value to the matter in
hand. Isaacs had been promoted Attorney-General in October. Some
assistance was also given by a senior colleague, McKenna, and by a young
Whip, ardent for social reform, William Wedgwood Benn. On the official
side Lloyd George's Welsh private secretary, Rowland, was active, but
far more important was the work of three Treasury civil servants, R. G.
Hawtrey, J. S. Bradbury and, above all, W. J. Braithwaite. Hawtrey had
recently become the Chancellor's official private secretary. Like his predecessor, Clark, he was a product of Eton and Trinity College, Cambridge,
but unlike Clark he had the advantage of being a mathematician. Later,
he acquired some eminence as an economist. Bradbury had been head of
one of the divisions in the Treasury since Lloyd George became Chancellor. His family background was North-country and mercantile; he was
educated at Manchester Grammar School and Brasenose College, Oxford,
where he obtained firsts in Greats and Modern History. At the outbreak of
war in 1914, when he was joint permanent secretary of the Treasury, the
new pound notes became known as 'Bradburys' because they bore his
signature. A witty, sardonic man, he brought to the big work of 1911
plenty of intellect and ingenuity, but little or no idealism.

Braithwaite, on the other hand, was idealistic to a fault, with a high-
mindedness sometimes verging on self-righteousness. A parson's son from
Suffolk, he was a Wykehamist not only in the strict sense of being educated
at Winchester and New College – where he took the traditional course of
Mods. and Greats with high honours – but also in the rather pejorative

sense in which the term is too often indiscriminately used. After joining the Civil Service he went to live at Toynbee Hall in the East End of London, and for the rest of his life took an enthusiastic interest in boys' clubs and the provision of playing fields. He also had first-hand knowledge of the working of friendly societies, and a deep understanding of their ethos. Lloyd George found him useful when the 1909 Budget was being prepared and at the end of 1910 sent him to Germany to make a rapid, up-to-date study of the State insurance system there. Thus began a period of close and fruitful collaboration, of which Braithwaite's memoirs, largely based on diary entries and therefore unaffected by his subsequent bitterness against Lloyd George, give an artlessly vivid account.[1]

When Braithwaite got back from Germany he was almost immediately summoned to the South of France, where Lloyd George was staying, with the Mastermans, Isaacs, Bradbury and Rowland already in attendance. During the early evening of 3 January there was an informal conference on the pier at Nice:

> It was crowded. [Lloyd George] found a quiet and sheltered corner where he could not hear the band too clearly. He arranged a circle of chairs or got others to arrange it, fussing about over it all . . . ordered drinks all round, put me on a chair in the middle – a straight stiff one I remember with a table against it on which I spread out a wallet – full of notes and papers – and when everyone was settled down in their lounge chairs – L.G. just opposite to me – with their drinks, he said: 'Now then, tell us all about it.'

One of the questions that arose during the conference on the pier was whether British national insurance should work, like the German system, on the 'dividing-out' principle, or should follow the example of private insurance in accumulating a large reserve. Lloyd George instinctively favoured the first method, but Braithwaite was dedicated to the second. On his own admission, his attitude was that of the typical insurance man:

> If a fund divides out, it is a 'state club', and not an insurance. It has no continuity – no scientific basis – it lives from day to day. It is all very well when it is young and sickness is low. But as its age increases sickness increases, and the young men can go elsewhere for a cheaper insurance.

1. *Lloyd George's Ambulance Wagon*, the memoirs of William J. Braithwaite, 1911–1912, edited, with an introduction, by Sir Henry N. Bunbury, and with a commentary by Richard Titmuss (1957). Braithwaite also visited Germany – and Switzerland – a little earlier in 1910, to study the operation of local income tax in those countries.

All this is the commonplace of insurance, but, said L.G., quite acutely, 'how does it apply to compulsory insurance? If everyone has to belong, you can average your risks, and the young man can't go elsewhere.'

And he advanced further arguments.

Why accumulate a fund? The State could not manage property or invest with wisdom. It would be very bad for politics if the State owned a huge fund. The proper course for the Chancellor of the Exchequer was to let money fructify in the pockets of the people, and take it only when he wanted it.[1]

The argument continued, on and off, until the middle of March, when Lloyd George gave way in characteristic style. He was staying at Arthur Markham's house in Kent, Beachborough, for the sake of his throat, and was joined there by Braithwaite. After a day of golf:

Just before dinner L.G. said to me, 'Really, Braithwaite, we ought to do some work.' I had been wondering when we would, and I had carried all day in my golf coat with the golf balls a piece of paper with some boiled down figures showing the effect of interest on accumulative insurance . . . So we went into the library. There L.G. said he had read my paper and did not understand it, nor the necessity for interest . . . I managed to convince him that one way or another it was, and had to be paid. It was at any rate an extra payment which young contributors could properly demand, and the State contribution must at least make it up to them if their contributions were to be taken off and used by the older people. After about half an hour's talk he went upstairs to dress for dinner, saying over the banisters: 'I am inclined after all to be virtuous.'

'Dividing-out' was dead! I did not know it for certain at the moment, but he never after this came back to it.[2]

It was not virtue, or Braithwaite's figures, that changed his mind, but rather a sense of political expediency. He needed the cooperation of those to whom the accumulative principle was almost sacred, and he wanted as much general, inter-party support for his scheme as he could possibly secure. Though it could not be a coalition measure, at least it could be – and he hoped it would be – essentially non-controversial. In this spirit he

1. Braithwaite, *op. cit.*, pp. 84–5 and 88.
2. Braithwaite, *op. cit.*, pp. 126–7.

organized a badger hunt while he was at Beachborough, and afterwards entertained the local gentry:

> The East Kent Hunt, a body of hard Tories, were in the hall of the house enjoying drinks and on terms of great amity with the Radical Chancellor of the Exchequer. He was thoroughly enjoying himself, and a great deal of merry chaff about digging out the old badger was flying about.[1]

His conviviality was genuine, but the form that it took on this occasion was calculated. To the Tories, and indeed to many Liberals, the dividing-out principle was suspect, whereas accumulation seemed responsible and sound. Since his aim was to win conservative endorsement of a radical measure, he felt obliged to accept a method of insurance which his private judgment rejected; and for the same reason he went out of his way to be friendly to natural opponents.

Apart from the political motive, there was, perhaps, one other consideration which helped to reconcile him to the accumulative principle. Despite his remark at Nice that the State could never invest with wisdom, he may have been tempted by the prospect of using the insurance reserve to underwrite other programmes of social betterment. But if this could be described as a virtuous motive, it was making a virtue of necessity, because there is no reason to doubt that he would have preferred to divide the money out in benefits, other things being equal.

By the process of adaptation and improvisation for which he was uniquely gifted, Lloyd George's scheme was gradually taking shape. Its name had been changed, at Braithwaite's suggestion, from invalidity insurance to health insurance – a change very much for the better. And there were other more important changes. Under Kingsley Wood's influence, the 'Combine' had asked to join in the scheme and to have, in its operation, the same approved status that was already promised to the friendly societies. This point was conceded in principle, though Braithwaite still hoped that the rules governing approved societies would, by stipulating a democratic structure, exclude the industrial insurance companies. Another gesture to the 'Combine' was that widows' and orphans' pensions were definitely dropped, though Lloyd George used this as an excuse for doubling the proposed sickness benefit. In doing so he upset the friendly societies, because the State scheme thus ceased to be an extension

1. Braithwaite, *op. cit.*, p. 134.

of friendly society welfare and became, instead, 'a full-fledged and competing State programme, which any group of men who cared to form themselves into an insurance society would be permitted to administer'.[1] But the friendly societies were kept in line by an opportune bribe – a financial arrangement which, for many of them, was the only alternative to bankruptcy. The societies were to be allowed to keep the sums of money released by the State's assumption of responsibility for paying minimum benefits to their elderly members, and were given grounds for hoping that eventually they would receive the equivalent of minimum benefits for all their members, young and old. The arrangement was, in effect, a massive subsidy to friendly society reserves, and it did the trick so far as Lloyd George was concerned. Ailing societies could not resist the proffered blood transfusion, and even those which were in relatively good health were attracted by the thought of being able to pay extra benefits to their members out of the large additional funds that would be coming to them. Lloyd George thus gained the qualified support of the 'Combine' without losing that of the friendly societies, and without altering his scheme out of recognition.

By the beginning of April it was ready for submission to the Cabinet, and he asked his colleagues to approve it in the following form. Insurance was to be made compulsory for all regularly employed workers over the age of sixteen and with incomes below the level – £160 a year – of liability for income tax; also for all manual labourers, whatever their income. The rates of contribution would be 4d. a week from a man, and 3d. a week from a woman; 3d. a week from his or her employer; and 2d. a week from the State. These contributions would together add up to 9d. a week for a man, of which he himself would be paying only 4d. – hence Lloyd George's famous phrase 'ninepence for fourpence'. In addition, workers not obliged to insure would be free to do so under the scheme, but would have to pay the employer's contribution as well as their own. It was estimated that about fifteen million people would come within the ambit of national insurance.

Benefits would be wide-ranging. There would be sick pay of 10s. a week for men, and 7s. 6d. a week for women, from the fourth day of illness for a period of thirteen weeks; and for the next thirteen weeks, 5s. a week for both sexes. Thereafter the sick person would receive disability benefit of 5s. a week, which might continue indefinitely. There was also to be medical benefit – the right to attention from a G.P., with the

1. Bentley B. Gilbert, *op. cit.*, p. 340.

appropriate treatment and medicines – and a specific right to treatment for tuberculosis in a sanatorium. Finally, there would be maternity benefit of 30s. paid direct to the insured man's wife, or £3 if both husband and wife were insured. The expected cost of the scheme in the first year would be £20 millions for health insurance alone, or £24½ millions for the whole project including the building of new sanatoria and the unemployment scheme (outlined earlier in this chapter) which was to form Part II of the Bill.

Health insurance was to be administered mainly by existing private bodies which, on compliance with certain conditions, would become 'approved societies' empowered to manage the funds, pay most of the benefits and control the doctors. Any workers who did not wish to join a society, or who for any reason did not qualify for admission to one, would have to insure through the Post Office and would receive a lower scale of benefits. In every county or county borough there was to be a committee of between nine and eighteen members, one-third appointed by the approved societies, one-third by the local authority and one-third by the Post Office depositors. These committees were to be responsible, initially, for administering the sanatorium benefit. At the centre there was to be an Insurance Commission with the task of enforcing the new law, interpreting it and even amending it by administrative regulation.

Such were the basic elements of the scheme that Lloyd George put to the Cabinet. It also contained, of course, many intricacies and special provisions for special cases, but only the essentials need concern us. On 5 April the Cabinet gave its approval and Braithwaite recorded this striking tribute to Lloyd George:

> Looking back on these three and a half months I am more and more impressed with the Chancellor's curious genius, his capacity to listen, judge if a thing is practicable, deal with the immediate point, deferring all unnecessary decision and keeping every road open till he sees which is really the best. Working for any other man I must inevitably have acquiesced in some scheme which would not have been as good as this one, and I am very glad now that he tore up so many proposals of my own and other people which were put forward as solutions, and which at the time we had persuaded ourselves into thinking possible. It will be an enormous misfortune if this man by any accident should be lost to politics.[1]

1. Braithwaite, *op. cit.*, p. 143.

On 4 May details of the scheme at last became public knowledge, when Lloyd George introduced the National Insurance Bill in the House of Commons.[1]

He began by referring to the state of his voice and appealing to the House for its indulgence. Then he struck what he hoped would be the dominant note in the Bill's passage through Parliament. 'I think it must be a relief . . . to turn from controversial questions for a moment to a question which, at any rate, has never been the subject of controversy between the parties in the State. I believe there is a general agreement as to its urgency, and I think I can go beyond that and say there is a general agreement as to the main proposals upon which the remedy ought to be based.'

He explained the need for compulsory insurance:

It is no use shirking the fact that a proportion of workmen with good wages spend them in other ways, and therefore have nothing to spare with which to pay premiums to friendly societies. It has come to my notice, in many of these cases, that the women of the family make most heroic efforts to keep up the premiums to the friendly societies, and the officers of friendly societies, whom I have seen, have amazed me by telling the proportion of premiums of this kind paid by women out of the very wretched allowance given them to keep the household together.

Workmen had been driven, 'sometimes by their own habits', but more often by circumstances over which they had no control, to abandon their policies. As a result less than half of them had any provision for sickness, and less than one-tenth of them for unemployment.

The Government had decided to have a uniform rate of contributions, so that the initial loss could be wiped out in about fifteen years and so that younger contributors could, in due course, be rewarded for their (obligatory) thrift by larger benefits. Employers should find that they were repaid for their contributions by a more efficient and contented work-force.

The working men whom I met . . . told me that many a time they used to go on working at their business because they dared not give it up, as they could not afford to, and it would have been better for them to

1. Its imminence had been known since it was promised in the King's Speech on 6 February, but despite all the discussions with interested parties the actual proposals had been a surprisingly well-kept secret.

have been in the doctor's hands. This procedure generally brings about a very bad breakdown, and not only that, when a man is below par neither the quantity nor the quality of his work is very good.

The State equally stood to gain from the physical welfare of the people, and Lloyd George next spoke of the State's proposed contribution, comparing it favourably with that of the German State, which was paying only £2½ millions a year towards a scheme that included old age pensions. The British State was already carrying a burden of £13 millions a year for old age pensions, and if it were not doing so the benefits offered under the new scheme would have to be much less than they were, or he would have to propose 'very much dearer and sterner terms both for the employer and the employed'. By this argument he justified the State's relatively modest contribution towards the new scheme.

On the subject of medical relief he said:

> There is no doubt that there is great reluctance on the part of workmen to resort to the Poor Law medical officer . . . He has to prove destitution, and although there is a liberal interpretation placed on that by boards of guardians, still it is a humiliation which a man does not care to bear among his neighbours. What generally happens is this. When a workman falls ill, if he has no provision made for him, he hangs on as long as he can and until he gets very much worse. Then he goes to another doctor [i.e. not to the Poor Law doctor] and runs up a bill, and when he gets well he does his very best to pay that and the other bills. He very often fails to do so. I have met many doctors who have told me that they have hundreds of pounds of bad debts of this kind which they could not think of pressing for payment of, and what really is done now is that hundreds of thousands – I am not sure that I am not right in saying millions – of men, women and children get the services of such doctors. The heads of families get those services at the expense of the food of their children, or at the expense of good-natured doctors.

The Government was, therefore, proposing that virtually every industrial worker would be able to command the services of a competent doctor in the knowledge that he could pay, and with the doctor also knowing that he would be paid.

This brought Lloyd George to the 'delicate' subject of doctors' remuneration on which, he said, the profession and the friendly societies were at variance. The yearly rate paid to doctors ranged from 2s. 6d. a head in some districts to 6s. a head in others, but the average seemed to be 4s. a head. The doctors said this was too little, and he was 'inclined to agree with them'. In the first place he would tackle the problem of relieving them of the burden of paying for the medicines they prescribed out of their capitation fees. It was anyway desirable 'to separate the drugs from the doctors, because a patient, so long as he gets something discoloured and really nasty, is perfectly convinced that it must be a very good medicine'. There ought to be 'no inducement for underpaid doctors to take it out in drugs'.

Maternity benefit, the Chancellor said, was of great importance in the fight against infant mortality and childhood diseases, as well as for the mother's own sake. Death and 'a good deal of anaemic and rickety disease among the poorer class of children' was very often due to 'neglect in motherhood'. He was proposing that the benefit should be paid only on condition that a mother who was in a job should not return to it for four weeks after the birth of her child, because he had heard that mill-girls, for instance, often worked up to the last moment and returned to work 'in a comparatively few days'.

His most eloquent passage was on the scourge of tuberculosis:

> There are forty-three counties and towns in Great Britain with a population of 75,000, and there are 75,000 deaths each year from this disease. If a single one of those counties or towns were devastated by plague so that everybody, man, woman and child, were destroyed there and the place were left desolate, and the same thing happened a second year, I do not think we would wait a single Session to take action. All the resources of this country would be placed at the disposal of science to crush out this disease.

He did not suggest that it could be eliminated, but doctors and researchers were 'full of bright hopes' of what they could achieve if only they had the means. In Germany there were sanatoria all over the country, and the number of cures effected was very large. But in Britain there were only 2,000 beds for tubercular patients:

> I really think it is about time that the nation as a whole, that the State, should take the matter in hand, because the State has suffered.

After describing the machinery by which his scheme would be worked, and discussing other particular aspects of it, Lloyd George summed up his case for the reform while emphasizing that it would leave much still to be done, and while invoking on its behalf the patriotism of Coronation year:

> I do not pretend that this is a complete remedy. Before you get a complete remedy for these social evils you will have to cut in deeper. But I think it is partly a remedy. I think it does more. It lays bare a good many of those social evils, and forces the State, as a State, to pay attention to them. It does more than that . . . till the advent of a complete remedy, this scheme does alleviate an immense mass of human suffering, and I am going to appeal, not merely to those who support the Government in this House, but to the House as a whole, to the men of all parties, to assist us . . . I appeal to the House of Commons to help the Government not merely to carry this Bill through but to fashion it; to strengthen it where it is weak, to improve it where it is faulty. I am sure if this is done we shall have achieved something which will be worthy of our labours. Here we are in the year of the crowning of the King. We have got men from all parts of this great Empire coming not merely to celebrate the present splendour of the Empire, but also to take counsel together as to the best means of promoting its future welfare. I think that now would be a very opportune moment for us in the Homeland to carry through a measure that will relieve untold misery in myriads of homes – misery that is undeserved; that will help to prevent a good deal of wretchedness, and which will arm the nation to fight until it conquers 'the pestilence that walketh in darkness, and the destruction that wasteth at noonday'.

Despite his throat he had spoken for over two hours.[1]

Austen Chamberlain responded warmly from the Opposition front bench, assuring the Chancellor that every party wished to see his measure successfully carried, and promising his own and his colleagues' help. In a family letter the following day he wrote:

> . . . the Sickness-Invalidity scheme is bold, sound and comprehensive and in many respects original. This is Lloyd George's part. The Unemployment scheme is, I think, hazardous, tentative, incomplete and probably bad, but it is Llewellyn Smith's and not Ll. George's and I believe L.G. not only knows little about it but thinks ill of it.

And on 7 May:

1. Hansard, Fifth Series, Vol. XXV, cols 609–44.

Confound Ll. George. He has strengthened the Government again. His Sickness scheme is a good one and he is the on right lines this time. I must say I envy him the opportunity and I must admit that he has made good use of it.[1]

John Redmond, who spoke after Chamberlain, welcomed the scheme as 'great', 'comprehensive', 'noble', 'magnificent' and 'merciful', while entering a routine caveat that the needs and interests of Ireland would have to be taken fully into account.

Ramsay MacDonald was scarcely less generous, complimenting the Chancellor on having tackled the problem 'not in a small and niggling way, but in a large way', and making only two reservations: that the workers' contributions seemed proportionately too high, and that the position of the trade unions might need to be safeguarded. His speech, however, did not express the united view of Labour. Among his colleagues in Parliament, and in the Labour movement outside, there were many who shared the Webbs' objection to any sort of contributory scheme, holding that it was for the State to protect and care for the poor, using taxpayers' money alone. To MacDonald this was 'national charity of the most vicious kind, which would adversely affect wages and would not help the Socialist spirit'.[2] The trade unions, on the whole, were nearer to MacDonald's view than to that of the Fabians and the I.L.P. Though unhappy about some features of Lloyd George's scheme, they did not oppose the principle of contributory insurance.

The almost unmitigated goodwill lavished upon the Bill at its First Reading proved ephemeral, mainly because one powerful and indispensable group reacted strongly against it. The doctors had been taken too much for granted by Lloyd George. Since they already disliked the system of contract practice imposed upon them by the friendly societies, they were naturally even more resentful at the prospect of its being confirmed and extended under the auspices of the State. Money was another grievance. From Lloyd George's speech they gathered that doctors working for approved societies would receive only 4s. a year for each patient, and this seemed to them quite inadequate even excluding the cost of medicines. To mobilize the profession for battle the B.M.A. called a special conference to meet in London at the end of the month.

Lloyd George saw at once that the situation demanded flexibility and

1. Austen Chamberlain, *Politics from Inside*, pp. 336–7 and 338.
2. Writing in *Socialist Review*, June 1911: quoted in David Marquand, *Ramsay MacDonald*, p. 139.

tactical adroitness. As between the doctors and the friendly societies, there could be no question which was the more dangerous enemy. The societies were so dependent upon his scheme financially that their threats to with-draw or rebel could for practical purposes be ignored. If necessary he could call their bluff and threaten to run the scheme without them. But he could hardly expect to launch a successful health insurance scheme in the teeth of genuine, mutinous opposition by the type of doctor who ministered to the poor. Earlier, he had fought shy of meeting medical deputations, because he found that they always consisted of 'swell' doctors and did not seem to represent 'slum' doctors. But in May 1911 he sensed, as he did not before and would not again the following year, that the slum doctors whose cooperation he needed were truly aroused. So he asked to be allowed to speak to the B.M.A. conference, and decided to use the occasion to play the doctors off against the friendly societies.

His speech, on 1 June, was a personal triumph. One of the doctors present wrote that the 'bright-eyed, alert, popular politician, courageous, ready and good-humoured, was a glorified example of the witty, business-like market practitioner compelling his wares on a circle of admiring but doubting critics'.[1] The Chancellor told his audience that he would be happy for the administration of medical benefit to be transferred from the approved societies to the local committees that would be established under the Act, but that it was up to them – the doctors – to persuade Parliament to make the change. In the event, the Bill was so amended on 1 August, with Lloyd George voting among the majority. The objection-able system of contract practice came, as a result, to be replaced by the panel system, under which local insurance committees drew up panels of doctors from which patients could make their own choice. The doctors' contention that the relationship between them and the people they served should be free on both sides was thus met. The financial problem re-mained, and was not so easily removed; but at least the doctors were prevented from opting out of the scheme on principle within weeks of its introduction.

Ten days after his speech to the doctors in London Lloyd George addressed a large public meeting in Birmingham – in the Town Hall, which had already contributed in no small way to his fame. It was his hope, he said, that his Bill would become law within the next three months; but he wanted it to be properly discussed. He spoke of the evils that it was designed to combat, and of the gap that it had to fill:

1. Quoted in Bentley B. Gilbert, *op. cit.*, p. 366.

You may say there is the Poor Law. Ah! Let me say this to the honour of the workers of this country, the last thing they pawn is their pride. There is no greater heroism in history, and you find in the humble annals of those who fight through life against odds to maintain their self-respect and independence they will suffer the last privation before they pin the badge of pauperism over their hearts, and certainly before they will put it on the breast of their children ... A struggle is made to keep up contributions so as to avoid the charity of the parish and keep up the honour and pride of the family; family pride is not in the rent-book, and you will find it amongst names that have never yet appeared in Dod, Burke or Kelly.

He made shrewd, apposite reference to statements by Joseph Chamberlain and another local notability, Dr Baxter Wilson. Then he pointed out that a brewer's horse was rested and cared for when it was ill, and a machine oiled and overhauled as a precaution against breakdown. But human beings were not so fortunate:

How much better is man than a machine! He may be better, but he is not better off, poor fellow. I will tell you the trouble; there is no one there who has a sense of responsibility to look after him. It is nobody's concern to see that that wonderfully delicate piece of machinery is all right, is fit. A man owns the machine, he owns the horse; if they break down they are costly to replace. I will tell you what is wanted in this country and in many others; you want to cultivate in the State a sense of proprietorship over these workers. They are the greatest asset of any land. When you reckon up the national wealth and begin to talk about imports and exports – when you add up our bank balances and the value of our railways, our house property and our investments – I have never seen a balance-sheet of that kind up to the present that did not omit the greatest asset of all, and that is the men, the women and the children of the land.

With cheerful audacity, he defended himself against the charge that he was offering the doctors too little money:

... I am warned that there are gentlemen of the medical profession present; I know there are gentlemen representing friendly societies; I hope they are not on the same side of the hall. There has been a good deal of discussion as to what they ought to be paid ... I had two hours discussion with the medical men themselves the other day. I do not think there has been anything like it since the days when Daniel went into the lions' den . . . but I can assure you they treated me with the same civility as the lions treated my illustrious predecessor . . . I cannot say that I care very much for this wrangle in the sick-room; it is unpleasant and may well become unseemly; all the same, it has got to be settled. For the moment I am the buffer state. The doctors say to me 6s. is not enough, and they cuff me on one side of the head. [He gave the figure of 6s., which was a capitation fee of 4s. plus the amount to be paid separately for medicines, 2s.] The friendly societies say, 'How dare you give as much?' and I get another cuff this side of the head, and between them I can only receive it with that Christian meekness which characterises politicians. The only comment I would make is this. When one set of people say you are paying too little and another set of people say you are paying too much, it rather means that you are somewhere about right.

Describing his principle of insurance, he used phraseology that only he, perhaps, could have found to irrigate a dry subject:

I am going to start everybody as if he were sixteen years of age for this purpose. I am going to make everybody young, to renew their youth, financially. I start everybody with this scheme at the rate which he would have to pay if he were a young man. Well now, that costs money; it means a great deficiency. The man of forty-five and of fifty will be a loss, so I have to make provision for wiping out that loss, and that is where the money of the State comes in. The State comes and puts its strong shoulder under that burden and carries it.

After giving many instances of how the scheme would work – how it would affect individuals and how it would be administered – he came to one of his most powerful perorations:

The protection of property in this country is the most perfect machine ever devised by the human brain. The guardians of property patrol every street, and if the transgressor eludes their vigilance he is pursued to the ends of the earth. Continents cannot hide him, the waves of the ocean cannot cover his tracks . . . But you compare that with the way in which the Public Health Acts, the Housing Acts, are administered in this country. We have had Public Health Acts in this country for years and years . . . and yet there is no city or town, not a village, in which you have not got the reek of insanitary property. I want to see the law protecting property, yes. But I also want to see it protecting the worker's home. I would treat the man who receives rents or ground-rents from insanitary dwellings, which kill little children – I would treat him as I would the receiver of stolen property . . . Look at the minuteness with which the most insignificant property is protected. Take the game of the land. Why should not life, health, be protected with the same ruthlessness, with the same remorselessness, with the same care? . . .

I never said this Bill was a final solution. I am not putting it forward as a complete remedy. It is one of a series. We are advancing on the road, but it is an essential part of the journey. I have been now some years in politics, and I have had, I think, as large a share of contention and strife and warfare as any man in British politics today. This year, this Session, I have joined the Red Cross. I am in the ambulance corps. I am engaged to drive a wagon through the twistings and turnings and ruts of the Parliamentary road. There are men who tell me I have overloaded that wagon. I have taken three years to pack it carefully. I cannot spare a single parcel, for the suffering is very great. There are those who say my wagon is half empty. I say it is as much as I can carry. Now there are some who say I am in a great hurry. I *am* rather in a hurry, for I can hear the moanings of the wounded, and I want to carry relief to them in the alleys, the homes where they lie stricken, and I ask you – and through you I ask millions of good-hearted men and women who constitute the majority of the people of this land – I ask you to help me to set aside hindrances, to overcome obstacles, to avoid the pitfalls that beset my difficult path.[1]

The Parliamentary road along which his ambulance had to be driven was even longer and more twisty than he reckoned it would be in June. His hope of getting the Bill through before the summer recess proved vain, and it was necessary to return to it in an exhausting autumn session. The doctors, though no longer rejecting the scheme on principle, were busy drawing Parliamentary and public attention to their outstanding grievances. The industrial insurance Combine was seizing its chance to improve on the advantages it had already gained, and the Labour Party, divided on

1. The meeting was organized by the Midland Liberal Federation and the Birmingham Liberal Association. 3,000 people attended, out of 70,000 who applied for tickets. As well as representatives of the various interest-groups concerned with insurance, there were also a few women in the audience.

the principle of the Bill, was more or less united in promoting the interests of the trade unions. Moreover, the initial benevolence of the Conservatives did not survive the intensification of party feeling during the last stages of the Parliamentary Bill, which was combined with a realization that the Government was more vulnerable on the National Insurance Bill than might at first have been expected. The attitude of Tory M.P.s at the time was later recalled by one who took his seat on the day that Lloyd George introduced the Bill, and who described his speech as 'masterly both in its exposition of a complicated subject and in its human persuasiveness'. As time went on it was seen that:

> the Bill offered a wide field and a wonderful opportunity for us back-benchers. A natural leader in this task emerged in L. [afterwards Sir Laming] Worthington-Evans, a city solicitor with wide friendly society experience, and a shrewd debater . . . He at once began to get together a small committee, what would now be called a 'brains trust', to study every aspect of the Bill . . . We worked indefatigably and, I think, very much surprised Lloyd George by our mastery of the subject when the Bill reached Committee. We certainly played a useful part in improving the Bill. But, as an Opposition, we were naturally no less concerned to emphasise features likely to be unpopular . . .[1]

Lloyd George could hardly complain of such conduct, after his own treatment of Balfour's Education Bill.

His performance in Committee was, as usual, a marvel to friend and foe alike, and perhaps even more to the officials watching from their box. Though he also had the Finance Bill on his hands, he made speech after speech during the Committee Stage of the Insurance Bill, often in the small or not-so-small hours of the morning, while continuing to negotiate tirelessly with the interested parties outside. Braithwaite, for instance, gives an admiring account of his handling of a Labour move on 19 July to reject Clause 11 of the Bill, which was designed to avoid duplication of benefit in workmen's compensation cases:

> Labour party broke loose on Clause 11 and went on till 5 a.m.! Rufus and McKenna did not manage very well; shortly before breaking up the Chancellor took the House in hand again. It was a thoroughly sulky House, everybody angry, Labour Party annoying and aggressive. He started with irrelevancies, and trapped Stephen Walsh into allowing a

1. L. S. Amery, *My Political Life*, Vol. I, pp. 373-4.

joke to be made at his expense, which brought everybody quickly into a good humour. He then spoke as he felt for the first time about the bill, the Press being absent and the Tory party away asleep. His speech is worth reading. It was the first time that he had used the argument about organizing the working classes, which I have been so keen on all along. It was just like him to use it where and when it would be most effective for immediate purposes.[1]

The speech is indeed worth reading, even now. Though the joke at Walsh's expense seems a little tame in cold print (and is not worth reproducing), the passage on working-class organization loses none of its impact:

Mr Lloyd George: . . . Here is another thing that I want to put to my hon. Friends. We are only at the eleventh Clause. They can put it, if they like, that they have wrung concessions out of the Exchequer.
Mr James Thomas: That is a way a man talks when he is beaten.
Mr Lloyd George: I have been beaten sometimes, but I have sometimes beaten off the attack. That is the fortune of war and I am quite ready to take it. Hon. Members are entitled to say that they have wrung considerable concessions out of an obstinate, stubborn, hard-hearted Treasury. They cannot have it all their own way in this world. Let them be satisfied with what they have got. They are entitled to say that this is not a perfect Bill, but then this is not a perfect world. Do let them be fair . . . I think they are right in fighting for organizations which have achieved great things for the working classes. I am not at all surprised that they regard them with reverence. I would not do anything which would impair their position. Because in my heart I believe that the Bill will strengthen their power is one of the reasons why I am in favour of this Bill. In Germany, the trade union movement was a poor, miserable, wretched thing some years ago. Insurance has done more to teach the working classes the value of organization than any single thing . . . You cannot get a Socialist leader in Germany today to do anything to get rid of that Bill, and I think . . . many Socialist leaders in Germany will say that they would rather have our Bill than their own Bill. This Bill marks an enormous advance. If hon. Members reject the Bill it will be a very serious responsibility. I do not think it is one for which the labouring classes would thank them. They are right in fighting for their trade unions. They represent, on the whole, the best stock of the working

1. Braithwaite, *op. cit.*, p. 192.

LG—L*

classes. I would remind them that this Bill benefits the poorer classes and that it will do greater things for them than any Bill introduced for a great many years in this House. It will remove anxiety as to distress, it will heal, it will lift them up, and it will give them a new hope. It will do more than that, because it will give them a new weapon which will enable them to organize, and the most valuable and vital thing is that the working classes will be organized – 15,000,000 of them – for the first time for their own purposes.[1]

Strictly, it was disingenuous to treat the attempt to get rid of one clause as an attempt to sabotage the whole Bill, but it was important for Lloyd George to remind Labour M.P.s that he was a true champion of the people they represented, and that consequently he deserved their support even on some details that they might not like. He had the art, indispensable to a minister in charge of a bill, of seeming always to be in control of the situation, whatever the mood of the House and however awkward or arcane the subject-matter of debate. Another civil servant of the period, writing long afterwards, could recall 'Lloyd George rising to reply, knowing practically nothing when he rose about the particular facts, briefed as he went along by little scraps of paper passed along the bench from the officials' box, and yet leaving the impression that he had a more complete mastery of every detail than his critic'.[2]

After his summer labours, which had included his Agadir speech, introducing the proposal for payment of Members, and settling the railway strike, in addition to the constant, grinding toil at the Finance and Insurance Bills, Lloyd George had three weeks' holiday at Criccieth before returning to London and then going to Balmoral (for the visit recorded in the last chapter). At Criccieth he was joined by, among others, the Mastermans, Braithwaite and a painter, Christopher Williams, who was doing a portrait of him. He was in high spirits, and his guests 'had a perfectly delightful time – a very simple country life, with picnics, bathing and such like entertainments'. He showed them the scenes of his childhood, and one day they

passed by a cottage where an oldish, grey-haired woman was standing at the door. George greeted her in a friendly manner. 'I kissed that

1. Hansard, Fifth Series, Vol. XXVIII, cols 1237–9.
2. Arthur Salter, *Memoirs of a Public Servant*, p. 61.

woman when I was young,' he remarked. 'I wonder if she remembers?' 'Yes, they were great girls, and great rosy apples too,' he went on. 'My mouth waters when I remember them. But I would not have my youth again.'

It was true that he would not have wished to experience again the boredom of his early years in Llanystumdwy, Criccieth and Portmadoc. But in another sense he was feeling and regretting the loss of his youth, and trying to recapture it – as middle-aged men often try to do, even when they are far less dynamic than Lloyd George. This was evident when the party went for a picnic beside a river, on the edge of which there was a large tree:

George (who had been bathing) announced his intention of climbing this. He vanished into the leaves and swarmed up the tree, reappearing at the top . . . his face flushed, his hair on end, and shouting and cheering . . . When he was back on the ground his collar was off, his tie crooked, his hair pointing to all the ends of Heaven, and he shouted and sang at the top of his voice.[1]

Such behaviour suggests a man who is trying to prove something to himself, or who is under a compulsion to show off. And in fact the motive for showing off existed, though Lloyd George was probably not yet conscious of it himself. The motive was supplied by a young woman who was spending the summer at Brynawelon as holiday governess to Megan. Her name was Frances Louise Stevenson.

She was the child of a Lowland Scottish father and a mother of mixed French and Italian extraction, and her parents had sent her to Clapham High School, where in the fifth form she had made friends with Mair. Later she read classics at Holloway College, and then became a teacher at a girls' boarding school in Wimbledon. In 1911 Lloyd George asked Mair's old headmistress to recommend someone to coach Megan during the holidays. The first girl recommended had already made her plans for the summer, so Frances Stevenson was asked, as second choice, to go for an interview at 11 Downing Street at the end of July. She got the job, and with it a niche in history.

In her autobiography, written more than half a century later, she

1. Masterman, *op. cit.*, pp. 209–10 and 212.

conveys something of the excitement of her first close contact with Lloyd George:

> Now . . . he was in his heyday, revelling in the carrying out of a great scheme of reform. The atmosphere at Brynawelon glowed. In the mornings L.G. sat for his portrait to Mr Christopher Williams, a Welsh artist, in his Chancellor's robes; L.G. was always a bad sitter . . . and Megan and I would often sit and talk to him to while away the time. In the afternoons there were picnics on the banks of the Dwyfor, sheep-dog trials above Beddgelert, or drives in the wonderful surrounding country. On Sunday evenings there was the singing of glorious Welsh hymns.

At one river-side picnic:

> we all took off our shoes and stockings, the men rolling up their trousers (I noted that L.G. had a shapely calf), to cross the stream by the large stones in the river bed, careful, on L.G.'s instructions, to avoid the slippery ones – otherwise a wetting ensued. We made a fire to boil the kettle for tea. L.G. was always a good improviser and he then conceived the idea of making mushrooms on toast on a tin lid over the fire. I may add that they were uneatable, tasting of nothing but smoke. On another occasion he insisted on climbing a tree which overhung the river. He dared us to do likewise but I do not recollect that anyone accepted the challenge.[1]

After his visit to Balmoral, which was followed by short visits to Andrew Carnegie at Skibo and 'the Master' at Walkerburn, as well as a meeting with Grey at Aberdeen, Lloyd George returned – uncharacteristically – for another week at Criccieth. And when, after this, he was back again in London, he wrote to Margaret: 'I was sick to leave beautiful & friendly Wales for this dull & hostile land.'[2] It is a fair guess that he was suffering less from homesickness than from the preliminary symptoms of lovesickness, for he did not normally find Criccieth so enjoyable.

This is not the place to consider Frances Stevenson's character, or what – apart from her pretty face and youthful charm – was soon to attract Lloyd

---

1. Frances Lloyd George, *The Years that are Past*, pp. 45–6. In Lucy Masterman's version she (Lucy Masterman) not only accepted the challenge but climbed to the top of the tree alongside Lloyd George. This discrepancy shows how unreliable recollections long after the event can be. Old ladies, as well as old men, forget.
2. D.L.G. to M.L.G., 7 October 1911 (N.L.W.).

George to her so powerfully. Their love affair did not develop until the following year, and it was only by the beginning of 1913 that it was secretly formalised. But her effect upon his life was so important, for good and ill, that the moment of her first appearance in it should not go unnoticed.

Before the recess only seventeen of the Insurance Bill's eighty-seven clauses had been carried, and when Parliament reassembled on 21 October the Government's first task was to lay down a time-table for the rest of the Bill. Clearly the House of Commons was taking Lloyd George's invitation to 'fashion' it rather too seriously, and the Opposition's amending zeal could easily be mistaken for filibustering. On 25 October Asquith himself moved 'kangaroo' closure resolutions, which would have the effect of limiting to a fixed number of days discussion of each remaining compartment of the Bill. The resolutions were carried.

But Lloyd George had not waited for the reassembly of Parliament to immerse himself once again in the business of receiving deputations and tackling key people. He was hard at work in London after the first week of October, and had decided to make a fighting speech to counter Tory disparagement of his scheme. The activity of his days and the toughness of his mood are reflected in his letters to Margaret.

9 October:
Had three hours of doctors & Friendly Societies. Most useful. I am in the saddle . . . & I mean to ride hard over hurdles & ditches – & win . . . Tonight I eat a cutlet. Fire in the drawing room & on with my speech . . . Saw Redmond today. He is staunch. So is Ramsay MacDonald.

11 October:
. . . Labour Party lunched with me – their Insurance Committee. They mean to support a time limit for the Bill. That means an enormous lightening of my labours. They are thoroughly friendly. They have at last made up their minds to fight Hardie, Snowden & Lansbury. They have had an actuarial report which completely supports my scheme.

12 October:
. . . Deputationing. Lunched with Riddell & Robertson Nicoll. Breakfast Labour Party. Dinner with Grey & Haldane – a pretty full day . . .

13 October:

> . . . Fog and drizzle. Devoted day to my speech. Finished it. Lunched with Rufus. Gave him outline & passages. He thinks it best thing I have done.
>
> Off now to dictate . . .[1]

Lloyd George's way of making and preparing a speech had not essentially changed since his early days in politics. As in the past, he still delivered his speeches from memory, with handwritten notes of the main points, to be referred to only if his memory should fail. The only difference was that now, having prepared a speech, he would dictate it to a reporter beforehand so that he could be sure of a correct version in the newspapers. His old friend Herbert Lewis describes the process:

> He never sends MS to the Press beforehand, but hands it to one reporter on condition that a proof is sent. They generally put 'cheers' 'laughter' 'shame' in the wrong places. When it is necessary to prepare for a great occasion he has a 'day off', stays in bed until 10, goes out for a walk, does not think of the speech. About 2 o'clock he starts thinking out speech and makes notes. At 6 he is ready for the shorthand writer . . . if he jots down the headings at the last moment he remembers it all and has no difficulty in delivering it almost word for word as it was sent to the press.[2]

The speech referred to in the letters just quoted was delivered on 14 October at Whitefield's Tabernacle, with Silvester Horne, Congregationalist minister and Liberal M.P., in the chair. Masterman and Wedgwood Benn accompanied Lloyd George to the meeting, which went off well after a nasty incident early in the speech, when three young male suffragists had to be forcibly removed.

It began with the resounding claim that the Insurance Bill would 'do more to hinder or assuage human misery than any Bill since the abolition of the Corn Laws' – a good way to commend it to an audience of committed Liberals. Lloyd George recalled that it had been greeted at first 'by all sections of the Press and by all parties with enthusiastic acclaim'. Even now most of those who were trying to obstruct it said that they accepted it on principle, but 'whenever you accept the principle of a bill you have no right to refer to its benefits, and you must confine yourself in any

1. D.L.G. to M.L.G. (N.L.W. and partly also in *Letters*).
2. Herbert Lewis diary, undated note (N.L.W.).

allusion you make to it strictly to its shortcomings'. Since the initial goodwill had given way to 'the clamour of interests', the only course for the
reformer was 'to fight his way pertinaciously through them'.

He was ruthless in exposing the financial insecurity of the friendly
societies, and how dependent many of them were upon his scheme. But
he exulted in the proposed panel system for doctors, with only an indirect
bantering hint to show that he had adopted it as a result of irresistible
clamour by the medical interest. Under the Bill an insured person

> can have the doctor of his own choice. He is not obliged to go to Dr
> A. because there happens to be a majority of the club that prefers Dr A.
> to Dr B. He puts his confidence in B. . . . and faith is nine points of all
> healing – spiritual, mental, physical. So we say to him, 'Go to the doctor
> you believe in.' The very sight of some doctors makes you ill, and if
> you have been harried by them as much as I have been you will find
> it very difficult for any doctor to pull you through. On the other hand –
> as I find that my own doctor is in the assembly I must not say too much –
> the mere sight of some men will make you feel better the moment they
> come into the room. That is the doctor for you, and under the Insurance
> Bill you can get him.

After going into other advantages of the Bill in some detail, he discussed
the scheme's financial basis and coined a famous phrase:

> How is it all paid for? We cannot do it for nothing. From the start we
> have proposed that the scheme should be a contributory scheme, and
> that all classes should contribute to it, as all classes will benefit by it . . .
> The cost of it will be 9d. a week per insured person – that is, for men . . .
> The workman pays 4d., the employer pays 3d., the State pays 2d. . . . for
> 4d. a week the workman gets nine-pennyworth. Are you surprised that
> the Scotsmen of Kilmarnock voted enthusiastically for it? That is not
> the race to reject ninepence for fourpence.

He attacked the Opposition, ridiculing Balfour whose leadership of the
Tory Party was fast becoming untenable:

> Why do not those who are against the Bill oppose it in a straightforward
> fashion? It is because they have it in memory what they predicted about
> the old age pensions and the actual effect of them. What are they saying
> about this Bill? They are afraid of it. Mr Balfour spoke at Haddington
> the other day. He will not lift a finger to help it along, but he will not

accept the responsibility of killing it. He wants the trade unions and the friendly societies to do that. Lord Salisbury said that trade unions were cruel and tyrannical organizations. His distinguished nephew has one concern, and that is lest I should hurt those cruel organizations.

But then Balfour realised that if he said nothing his followers would say 'What is the good of keeping a dog that won't bark?' So he 'just gave a sort of yap'.

At the end of his speech Lloyd George lamented the Tories' failure to treat the Bill in a spirit of non-partisanship:

> I have endeavoured in all sincerity to make this a non-party measure. I am told that I tried to bribe the working classes. If I set out to bribe the working classes I should know how to do it. But I shall know in future that when I try to table an honest measure which calls upon the working classes for a fair share of contributions, the people who are always flaunting the honesty of their opinions are the first to join with the extremest Socialists in the land to embarrass and hinder me on the way . . . I am earnestly sorry. It would have formed such a valuable precedent. No offer of the kind has ever been made before by any Minister to the Opposition. It would have been so valuable in future for us to come together, for Bills of this kind to be framed by the best men of all parties, to see how we could save the wretched in the land.

His Liberal audience might have responded rather less warmly to this passage if they could have guessed that they were listening to a man who had tried, the year before, not simply to agree with the Tories on particular measures, but to form a grand coalition with them.

He ended on a firmly defiant note: 'The Bill is going through this year. I will fight it through or I will fall.' And he was as good as his word. Through drastic use of the closure the Bill's passage through the House of Commons was completed on 6 December. It was then swiftly passed by the House of Lords, and on 16 December received the Royal Assent. But before it eventually reached the Statute Book Lloyd George had to accept further substantial amendments, one of which was gall and wormwood to Braithwaite. This was the provision that control within an approved society would not necessarily have to be exercised by its members, but might – at the discretion of the Insurance Commission – take some other form. As a result the industrial insurance companies achieved their full aim of eligibility for approved status without any legal obligation to democratize themselves.[1] Their success was unavoidable, because they had effective blackmailing power skilfully and single-mindedly wielded.

The scheme in its final form also enabled trade unions to become approved societies, without prejudice to their collective-bargaining functions – one of a number of satisfactions that Labour obtained, though in any case most Labour M.P.s had pledged their general support for the Bill in return for the Government's action on payment for Members. Other important changes were that sickness benefit was to be paid at the full rate for twenty-six weeks, instead of at a reduced rate for the last thirteen weeks; that voluntary contributors with incomes above £160 a year were not to be accepted; that workers earning less than 2s. a day should not have to pay contributions; that the wives and children of an insured man would share his right of admission to a sanatorium; that the local insurance committees were to be somewhat differently composed, and to have rather more power; that the system of deposit insurance would end in 1915; and finally – as concessions to the Irish Party – that the Insurance Commission was to be split into four, with one for each constituent nationality of the United Kingdom, and that Irish contributors were to receive increased sickness benefit as an alternative to medical benefit.

Enactment of the measure was only the beginning of a long, complicated and at times almost desperate process of implementation, which can only be mentioned very briefly because it takes us well beyond the period covered in this volume. The business of collecting contributions had to begin in July 1912, and the payment of benefits on 15 January 1913. Both deadlines were met, though not without extreme difficulty. The first was nearly missed because of technical and administrative snags, and the second because of threatened non-cooperation by the doctors. On that occasion, however, Lloyd George judged that the B.M.A. was overplaying its hand, because he was convinced that most ordinary doctors were very keen to work the scheme. He was proved right, the revolt collapsed, and the scheme came into operation.

As chairman of the English Commission, and therefore chief executive of the health insurance system, Lloyd George appointed Sir Robert Morant. In theory, it was an inspired appointment, because Morant had made a great reputation for himself at the Education department, and was close to the Webbs, whose hostility to the scheme it would

1. Like many other changes in the Bill, this was first agreed in discussions outside Parliament before receiving legislative effect in an amendment.

be convenient to soften. Braithwaite, who had hoped for the job, was made secretary of the joint committee to coordinate the work of the four national commissions, and was then returned to the Treasury as a special Commissioner of Income Tax, in which relatively obscure capacity he languished for the rest of his career.

Lloyd George has been much criticized for not rewarding him with the post he coveted, after his loyal and dedicated labour throughout 1911. But in fairness it must be said that Lloyd George seldom allowed his personal feelings for or against a man to influence his decision how to employ him in the public service. It is beside the point, therefore, to accuse him of ingratitude in not appointing Braithwaite, and surely equally mistaken to imagine that Braithwaite would have been the right man for the job, more especially at the moment when it had to be filled. Since he was a fairly junior member of the official hierarchy, his appointment to such a responsible position would have been resented by many of his seniors and contemporaries at the Treasury, whose goodwill was needed by the Commission. His admirable qualities did not include humour, subtlety or tact. Above all, he was exhausted and on the verge of a complete break-down by the end of 1911. As it turned out, Morant was not a success in the job, but his poor showing in it was hard to predict, whereas Braithwaite's would, in the circumstances, have been predictable.

A more valid charge against Lloyd George is that he did not arrange for Braithwaite's services to be rewarded by some suitable honour. This might not have been easy at the time, for the hierarchical reason already mentioned. But it would surely have been easy enough at a later date, when Braithwaite was older and Lloyd George was controlling the honours system. In all probability he forgot about Braithwaite, who was not the sort of man to remind a Prime Minister of his existence.

Was the health insurance scheme immediately popular among those it was intended to help? In his speech at Whitefield's Tabernacle Lloyd George suggested that it was, at any rate in Scotland. But during the autumn there was clear evidence that it was doing the Government no good, electorally, in England. On 13 November, in a by-election at Oldham, a Liberal majority of about 3,500 was turned into a Unionist majority of over 1,600; and in South Somerset, on 22 November, the Unionists won a seat which had been Liberal for a quarter of a century. According to Press reports, these reverses for the Government were largely due to public disaffection with the health insurance scheme, and at the same time Unionists claimed to be receiving sackfuls of mail complaining about it.

One must remember, of course, that the franchise still excluded a large section of the working class, and that it totally excluded women. Those heroic wives of feckless working men, to whom Lloyd George had referred in his speech introducing the Bill, had no votes and were therefore unable to show their gratitude in Parliamentary elections. And the same was true of many working men who might also be grateful for the scheme, but who belonged to the 40 per cent of adult males without the qualification to vote. The franchise was heavily loaded in favour of the bourgeoisie, and of that section of the working class from which the members of friendly societies were predominantly drawn. In other words, working men with the vote tended to be working men who had already made, voluntarily, the sacrifice involved in insuring themselves against sickness, and who might not feel very enthusiastic about being obliged to contribute to a scheme from which people less virtuous and thrifty than themselves would benefit.

Moreover, it was hardly to be expected that workers who had not previously been in the habit of putting money aside would all be over-joyed at being forced to do so, even in the gratifying knowledge that employers were also having to stump up, and that the State was contribu-ting a bit as well. 'Ninepence for fourpence' would have been a very attractive proposition if it had meant that when the insured person paid his fourpence for an insurance stamp he would be handed, in exchange, ninepence to spend on whatever he liked. But of course it did not mean that. To the sort of working man who lived for the day it meant, quite simply, a deduction of fourpence a week from his wages, and the nine-pence in question was insubstantial and illusory so far as he was concerned.

But perhaps the strongest and deepest cross-current that Lloyd George had to swim against was the Victorian – and specifically Liberal – ideology of individualism, by which all classes were affected. The domestic servants' campaign, under titled leadership, against the dreadful indignity of 'licking stamps for Lloyd George', was largely a stunt stage-managed by North-cliffe; but it was also the somewhat artificial manifestation of a genuine sentiment. Human beings everywhere tend to be conservative, and the less educated, the more tenacious of traditional notions, even when it might appear to be at their own expense. Samuel Smiles's philosophy had in some degree influenced all British working men, even those who were demonstrably unequal to the task of helping themselves and looking after their dependants. Compulsory insurance was, therefore, a profound innovation, and to many unwelcome.

The Conservative Party, having lost three elections in a row, and with its pride, at least, recently damaged by the Parliament Act, was more or less bound to exploit the various sectional interests and prejudices that Lloyd George's scheme was affronting. It was on the very day of the Oldham by-election that Bonar Law succeeded Balfour as party leader, and his advent to the leadership both reflected and intensified the new spirit of militant partisanship.[1] Yet any sensible Tory knew that working-class feelings about health insurance were mixed, even at the outset, and that they would probably harden in favour of the scheme as time went on. Lloyd George was right to describe the Tories' attitude as hypocritical and ambiguous. They wanted the Bill to be halted by obstructive forces outside, but not to be lost through their own action or that of their allies in the House of Lords. Consequently Lloyd George only had to square the external pressure-groups; once he had done so, the House of Lords gave him no trouble.[2]

Whatever the immediate popular reactions to it, was the health insurance scheme as great a blessing to the British people, in the long run, as Lloyd George asserted and believed it would be? If its effect on pauperism is to be the test, it is noteworthy that the number of men and women receiving Poor Law relief, which had been rising steadily since the eighteen-eighties, began to decline after 1912. The change was not dramatic, but the reversal of such a pronounced trend cannot have been mere coincidence. In any case, one of the chief purposes of the scheme was to help those who lacked the means or the will-power to insure themselves, and who yet were too proud to turn for help to the Poor Law system. It is hard to doubt that to this very large element in the working class national health insurance was an immense boon.

One clear index of improvement is that, after the scheme came into operation, many fewer people attended hospitals as out-patients, while many more were admitted to hospital for the treatment of serious ailments.

1. But it must be emphasized that Bonar Law felt no personal animus against Lloyd George. On the contrary, he wrote on 30 November 1911 to say how glad he was that Lloyd George's health was improving and to suggest a game of golf the following weekend (Mr William Lloyd-George's collection).

2. Sir Robert Ensor writes (*England, 1870–1914*) that 'but for the change wrought by the Parliament Act' the Insurance Bill would 'certainly' have been killed by the House of Lords, 'like all the main Liberal measures preceding it since 1905'. In fact, the House of Lords was careful, after 1905, not to kill Liberal measures with an obvious appeal to the working class. Rejection of the 1909 Budget was not typical, but a gross aberration proving the rule.

This must mean that panel doctors were not only disposing of a great deal of relatively minor illness which formerly was treated, if at all, in the out-patient departments of hospitals, but also that they were diagnosing much serious illness which formerly was neglected, and allowed to become chronic or fatal, to the accompaniment of untold misery in poor families and cramped homes.

The longer expectation of life which followed national health insurance was the continuation of an existing trend, itself largely due to the control of infectious diseases by new scientific methods. But Lloyd George's scheme made an important contribution to this, through the building of sanatoria for tuberculosis patients and the provision of benefit for treatment in them. Another creature of the Act which has played a valuable and continuing role in the fight against disease was the Medical Research Committee, later incorporated as the Medical Research Council.

Bernard Shaw wrote in 1911: 'Nothing is more dangerous than a poor doctor: not even a poor employer or a poor landlord'.[1] Unquestionably the insurance scheme had a decisive effect in improving the pay and status of ordinary doctors. From the start Lloyd George offered them a large reservoir of new patients, and by hard bargaining during the gestation of the scheme they were able to escape from the system of contract practice and also to raise their basic annual rate per patient from the proposed 4s. to 9s. 6d. The change in financial conditions within the profession was soon reflected in far better prospects for young doctors and a striking increase in the value of practices, not least in working-class areas. By 1913 it was reported that doctors on completing their training, who would formerly have been glad to accept salaries of up to £300 a year, could now command nearly twice as much in panel practices, while the value of such practices had increased by about 50 per cent. 'A working-class medical practice had become at last a worthy investment for the purchase of which a young doctor could now borrow money.'[2]

One incidental benefit of the scheme was that it provided scope for the talents of a group of young civil servants, who were given the chance to prove themselves in an unprecedented field of activity. They included – as well as Braithwaite and Bradbury – John Anderson, Warren Fisher, Arthur Salter, Claud Schuster, G. M. Young and Ernest Gowers.[3] The

1. *The Doctor's Dilemma*, Preface (dated 1911).
2. Gilbert, *op. cit.*, p. 440. The figures were given in the *National Insurance Gazette*, 13 December 1913.
3. It has even been claimed that Gowers's subsequent interest in good, clear English owed something to his experience as a health insurance administrator. 'It was, I believe, the first

health insurance administration was, among other things, a nursery of future Whitehall mandarins. A more doubtful feature of the scheme, as of various other reforms put through by the Liberal Government, was that it created a number of administrative posts which could be filled, at ministerial discretion, by people who did not have to be tested or vetted by any impartial process. Bonar Law complained in 1912 that a spoils system had been brought into existence comparable with that of the United States, but he could not have foreseen the extent to which it would develop in the years ahead.

Lloyd George's prediction that his scheme would give a boost to recruitment for trade unions was amply justified, though of course it was only one of a number of forces at work. Between 1911 and 1913 membership of trade unions increased from three millions to nearly four millions. As for the friendly societies, their fortunes were temporarily revived by the scheme, but over a longer period it could not arrest their secular decline.

The system introduced in 1911 was expanded and amended until, during the Second World War, the thoughts of reformers turned to a more comprehensive system. In 1944 a critique of national health insurance appeared, in which it was said to have 'failed to be the engine for the socialization of medical progress that at one time was its expected development'.[1] The word 'socialization' can be variously interpreted, but if it is here taken to mean a larger assumption of responsibility by the State for providing and financing health services, there can be no doubt that such a development was in Lloyd George's mind as he laboured to bring his own scheme to birth. From Beachborough in March 1911 he wrote to his private secretary, Hawtrey:

> Insurance necessarily temporary expedient. At no distant date hope State will acknowledge full responsibility in the matter of making provision for sickness breakdown and unemployment. It really does so now through Poor Law, but conditions under which this system has hitherto worked have been so harsh and humiliating that working-class pride revolts against accepting so degrading and doubtful a boon.

---

time that Civil Servants had to explain novel and complex matters to the unlettered masses in plain and simple English. It is not without significance that the author of *Plain Words* began his rise to fame on the staff of the Insurance Commission.' (Sir Henry Bunbury, Introduction to Braithwaite, *op. cit.*)

1. Hermann Levy, *National Health Insurance*, p. 335.

Gradually the obligation of the State to find labour or sustenance will be realized . . . Insurance will then be unnecessary . . .[1]

Whatever may have become of State attempts to guarantee full employment, Lloyd George's comment clearly foreshadows the National Health Service.

He never pretended, to himself or anyone else, that his scheme was a definitive answer to the problem of mass poverty, of which sickness was both a cause and a consequence. He explicitly said that it was only the first step on a long road, and nobody could have been more aware of its limitations and inadequacies. Yet he achieved what was, in the circumstances, a momentous act of progress. It was also in many ways original, diverging from the German example in the method of insurance, the scale of benefits and the character of involvement by the State. It was the first scheme of State insurance in the English-speaking world, and when it was introduced only Germany, Luxembourg, Norway and Serbia had State insurance of any kind. His pioneering efforts brought relief to many suffering people, and have served as an inspiration to other social reformers, in Britain and elsewhere, who have followed in his footsteps.

1. Quoted in Braithwaite, *op. cit.*, pp. 121–2.

TWELVE
Pre-War Zenith

For David Lloyd George 1911 was an *annus mirabilis*. Despite anxiety about his health he accomplished more than in any previous year of his life, and despite the weakness of his voice he relied, as usual, mainly upon the spoken word for translating thought into action. In Parliament alone his record of work was prodigious. For the year 1911 he occupies thirty-one columns of the Hansard general index – more than Asquith and Grey put together. He steered, simultaneously, a Finance Bill and another huge piece of legislation through the House of Commons, maintaining his stamina to the very end of a gruelling autumn session. At intervals during the year he also made a number of major speeches in the country, while all the time he was exercising his incomparable persuasive arts in private, at Cabinet meetings, in conference with officials or outside bodies, receiving deputations, at working breakfasts, lunches or dinners, even when he was nominally resting or on holiday. As well as what he did within his own departmental sphere – extended far beyond its traditional limits – he stage-managed the Prince of Wales's investiture, made a most telling intervention in a European crisis, settled a crippling railway dispute and gave a lot of time to the problem of women's suffrage. As the end of the year approached, writes Elie Halévy, 'even his enemies paid tribute to his genius. Never had he appeared so great.'[1]

Contemporary evidence supports this view. Mark Sykes, for instance, a Tory M.P. returned at a by-election in July 1911, wrote soon afterwards that Lloyd George was 'the biggest man in the House by lengths'.[2]

1. *The Rule of Democracy*, p. 362.
2. Roger Adelson, *Mark Sykes: Portrait of an Amateur*, p. 143.

On his own side Winston Churchill, his acolyte and rival, described him in 1911 as 'the greatest political genius of the day' with 'more insight than any other statesman'.[1] Such tributes, coming from opposite party standpoints, show what a reputation he had at the time, and how broadly it was based. If for any reason Asquith had then been removed from the scene, it seems likely that Lloyd George would have become head of the Government in name, as many already considered him to be in fact. He would thus have had the chance, which in the event eluded him, of leading a party administration in peace-time.

His ascendancy had been quickly established. Though a lively and influential M.P. since his first election in 1890, and famous since his campaign against the Boer War, he owed his commanding position in the State to the impression that he had made during six years of high office. At the Board of Trade he had proved that he could run a department and put through legislation of value to the country. Those who had seen him only as a radical agitator and Parliamentary *frondeur* were forced to admit that he was no less effective as a conciliator and practical reformer. At the same time he never ceased to proclaim his belief in the need for a juster order of society, and it was to him, above all, that apostles of the New Liberalism looked for the realization of their dreams. Nor did they look to him in vain, for as soon as he became Chancellor of the Exchequer he set to work on an ambitious programme which, over the next three years, transformed the relationship between the British State and the British people. Tactically, he was helped by the fact that the Liberal Government needed, in the adverse trade conditions of 1908, a social radicalism of its own with which to meet the challenge from Joseph Chamberlain's radical programme. But what Lloyd George did was fully in accordance with the strategic aims that he had cherished, without formulating actual details of policy, since before his entry into Parliament.

While struggling to enact his measures he had to sustain the morale of his party through two elections, in which the open fury of his opponents was matched by the secret hostility of some of his colleagues. He could see that the future of Liberalism depended upon its appeal to the working class, much of which was still disfranchised. He was also aware that the true division between those who did and those who did not acknowledge the State's paramount responsibility for social change lay not between the two main parties, but within them. And there was another way in which his perceptions did not conform to stereotype. His genuine love of peace

1. Lord Riddell, *More Pages from My Diary, 1908–1914*, pp. 18–19.

and hatred of Imperial arrogance did not make him either a pacifist or a little Englander, as so many Liberals were. He believed in a strong British Empire (though with 'Home Rule all Round' for its subject nationalities), and he was prepared to go to war in defence of British interests. His view of both the internal and the external role of the State was, and always had been, remote from Gladstone's. Consequently, though the Liberal Party never had a more inspiring standard-bearer, there were not a few Liberals in whom he inspired mistrust as well as admiration.

Both feelings are well expressed in an essay on him by A. G. Gardiner, published in 1908. Gardiner was editor of the *Daily News,* the paper which Lloyd George had helped to secure for the anti-Boer War cause in 1901. He was not an old-fashioned Liberal, at any rate on social policy, but he was a good party man who sensed that Lloyd George's fidelity to party as such was more than doubtful. In 1915 he turned against him with a vengeance, blaming him for all the Liberals' troubles and above all for their enforced coalition with the Tories. But when he wrote his essay he was still a warm, if wary, supporter. His comments are of lasting interest, partly because some of them give us the preliminary outline of a portrait of Lloyd George which was later, through the work of other hands, to settle into a malign and accepted caricature.

The essay begins at a dinner in 10 Downing Street, with Gardiner drawing the attention of an unnamed, but 'distinguished', fellow-Liberal to the bust of Pitt the Younger and its strong resemblance to Joseph Chamberlain. 'I wonder', muses the man, 'what will happen to Chamberlain's successor.' And when Gardiner asks whom he means, he replies: 'Lloyd George, of course.'

Struck by the remark, Gardiner

> looked down the table to where Mr Lloyd George himself sat, his face lit with that smile, so quick and sunny, yet so obscure, his light voice penetrating the hum of conversation, with its note of mingled seriousness and banter, his whole air, at once so alert and self-poised, full of a baffling fascination and disquiet. Yes, here was the unknown factor of the future, here the potentiality of politics.

He evokes the 'romance' of Lloyd George's career, from 'that little village between the mountains and the sea' to his present eminence, where he is

> handling huge problems of government with easy mastery, moving great merchant princes like pawns on his chessboard, winning golden

opinions from all sides, his name always on the lips of the world, but no longer in hate – [this was 1908] – rather in a wondering admiration, mingled with doubt.

And he asks: 'What is the secret of it all?'

Answering his own question, he emphasizes Lloyd George's audacity and willingness to play for high stakes. He has 'two motives: his love of the small nationality and his instinct for the great game'. One gives him 'passion', the other 'calculation'. He has, too, 'the swiftest mind in politics', unencumbered with learning:

> He is like a runner ever stripped for the race. The pistol may go off when it likes: he is always away from the mark like an arrow. And it is not speed alone. When the hare is started he can twist and turn in full career, for the hotter the chase the cooler he becomes.

The mixed metaphors multiply:

> He is the improviser of politics. He spins his web as he goes along. He thinks best on his feet. You can see the bolts being forged in the furnace of his mind. They come hurtling out molten and aflame.

Misinterpreting a conversation with Lloyd George and Churchill, Gardiner is under the false impression that Lloyd George's speeches are not carefully prepared. The result, he says, is 'a certain thinness which contrasts with the breadth and literary form of Mr Churchill's handling of a subject, or with the massive march of Mr Asquith's utterance'.

Lloyd George 'has passion, but it is controlled. It does not burn with the deep spiritual fire of Gladstone'. His humour is coruscating, but it is 'the humour of the quick mind rather than of the rich mind':

> The soil of his mind is astonishingly fertile, but light . . . You feel that the theme is of secondary importance to the treatment. You have an uneasy fear that this wonderful fluency of execution may presently reveal another *motif*. You listen. Your quickened ear seems to catch an adumbration of change. He keeps your mind on the stretch. He fascinates you, plays with you, holds you with the mesmerism of the unsolved riddle. You would give anything to know the thought behind that debonair, gay raillery.

He is 'the least doctrinaire of men – as little doctrinaire as Mr Chamberlain':

> No anchor of theory holds him. He approaches life as if it were a new problem. It is a virgin country for him to fashion and shape. He is

unconscious of the roads and fences of his forefathers. His maxims are his own, coined out of the metal quarried from his direct contact with life. He is not modern: he is momentary. There is no past: only the living present; no teachers: only the living facts. This absolute reliance on self gives a certain sense of lack of atmosphere. There is no literature to soften the sharp lines. There are no cool grottoes of the mind, no green thought in a green shade.

After saying that, like Chamberlain, he is 'a middle-class statesman', that he is 'no Socialist', and that 'Wales looks sorrowfully on at his giddy flight', Gardiner concludes where he began:

And so I turn to the figure at the end of the table, with the smile so quick and sunny, yet so obscure. If the key to the future is anywhere it is there. If the social fabric is to be reorganized, there is the man that can do it. He stands in the furrow that Mr Chamberlain deserted. Mr Chamberlain put his hand to the plough – and turned back. He failed because he lost the vision of his youth, and treated politics as a game, and not as a gospel. Mr Lloyd George will succeed in proportion to his fidelity to the inspiration, not of Westminster with its intrigues, but of Wales with its simple faith.
I turned to my neighbour, and I said 'Yes, I wonder.'[1]

This essay, however tiresomely over-written, contains much shrewd observation and some of its judgments deserve to stand. Yet it is also an anthology of half-truths and downright fallacies about Lloyd George, which have passed into folklore and still have an undue influence even on historians. The man is presented to us as an unprincipled adventurer, with only his love of Wales and its wholesome values to redeem him from pure opportunism. His mind, though bewilderingly quick, is superficial and uncultivated; his speeches, though brilliant, lack substance. Those who listen to him are mesmerized; if he convinces, it is by magic rather than by logic. He is not a virtuous, spiritual statesman like Gladstone, but a gambler, a mountebank, a wizard. Cut off from the idealism of his Welsh Nonconformist origins, there is no telling what he may do. These opinions of Lloyd George have acquired a very wide currency, but what people have got into the habit of believing is not necessarily true.

We should take into account, for a start, two factors relating to his subsequent career which have tended to create prejudice against him. The

1. A. G. Gardiner, *Prophets, Priests and Kings*, pp. 152–60.

first is what one has to call the Asquithian mythology. The circumstances in which Lloyd George became Prime Minister in 1916, and then retained the job for nearly six years with mainly Conservative support, while the Liberal Party was irreparably damaged, have been used by many as sufficient grounds for condemning him utterly, regardless of what he did for the country. This is not the place to discuss why Asquith fell, why the Liberal Party split, or to what extent Lloyd George was responsible for either event. But since the myth dies hard that Asquith and the Liberal Party were innocent victims, while Lloyd George behaved as a combination of Judas Iscariot and Pontius Pilate, it should be said at once that no objective student would now endorse such an oversimplified and distorted view of the matter.

The other thing that has tarnished his good name is the belief that he was deeply corrupt, financially. This belief springs mainly from the Marconi affair, the sale of honours during his Premiership, and the fact that the Coalition Liberal share of the proceeds fell under his personal control, though it is also now known that he speculated irresponsibly in a Patagonian gold-mining venture even when he was a young M.P. Of course it would be absurd to suggest that he was a man of rigid scruple where money was concerned, but it is even less sensible to regard him as a man who was in politics for what he could get out of it, in the material sense. On the contrary, his interest in money consisted almost exclusively of a desire to be independent, so that he could concentrate upon politics and pursue his political aims without fear or favour. Certainly he acted improperly over Marconi shares, and then compounded his offence by prevarication. But, apart from the question of principle, the affair was trifling and there is no reason at all to suppose that it was the tip of an iceberg. Certainly he abused the honours system, but the difference between what he did and what others have done, before and since, is only one of degree. Like other Prime Ministers, he treated his honours patronage partly as a means of rewarding supporters and replenishing party funds, but he only sold baubles – never jobs – and was so unsnobbish himself that he was less hypocritical about the system than others have been. As for his control of the Coalition Liberal fund, this was largely a result of the Liberal schism and of his need to have an organization of his own. The point to be stressed is that, whatever his misdemeanours about money, they were petty and incidental compared with the dominant themes of his life. To regard him as a glorified Horatio Bottomley is to misunderstand him totally.

In 1911 there was no myth of a Great Betrayal, no talk of corruption, but already – as Gardiner's essay shows – a view in some quarters that Lloyd George was a man without principle, a man who got his way by trickery. Gardiner uses the word 'mesmerism', which suggests that he ensnared his audiences by paranormal methods. But in fact, surely, he won them over because he combined exceptional intelligence with a sense of purpose and a rare capacity to persuade people by argument, in large gatherings or small. His oratory was colourful, but seldom ranting, and there was nearly always a strong logical thread. When he spoke to people *in camera*, rather than from a public platform, he did not treat them to a monologue, but listened carefully to what they had to say and strove to enter into their thoughts and feelings. His capacity to persuade was not, therefore, an occult power, but a legitimate talent reinforced by an interest in, and curiosity about, other people, which has not always been a characteristic of great men.

After his railway settlement in 1911 Asquith's private secretary, Vaughan Nash, told Sir Almeric Fitzroy:

> The end of the Railway Strike is another triumph of Lloyd George's genius for conciliation . . . he plays upon men round a table like the chords of a musical instrument; now pleading, now persuasive, stern, playful and minatory in quick succession, he never permits one impression to tire, still less to provoke, and succeeds in carrying with him men's feelings and understandings in a way which, while keeping the common aim in high relief, makes allowance for the objects, antecedents, qualities, wishes, even prejudices of those who are working with him, until out of the clash and conflict a real harmony is struck.[1]

The truth is that he knew how to deal with human beings, and that he had a genuine desire to reconcile them. His art was not that of a magician, but that of a most highly qualified democratic statesman.

He did not, however, very much like the word 'statesman' himself, reacting against the pomposity which comes so naturally to many successful public men.[2] His light-heartedness and refusal to take himself,

1. Almeric Fitzroy, *Memoirs*, Vol. II, p. 462.
2. In 1943 Anthony Eden was having an argument with Cordell Hull, the American Secretary of State, who said at one point that he never knew Eden was such a politician, allowing it to be inferred that he, Hull, was by contrast a statesman. 'Eden asked whether the Secretary of State had not heard Lloyd George's definition of a statesman: "a politician with whom one happens to agree"? Even Hull was amused . . .' (*The Diaries of Sir Alexander Cadogan, 1938–45*, edited by David Dilks, p. 554).

or other politicians, too seriously laid him open to the charge of shallow-ness and frivolity. Gardiner dismisses his humour as that of the quick rather than of the rich mind, and feels that he is being bamboozled by his debonair manner. Perhaps Disraeli was right when he said that the British 'require grave statesmen'; certainly neither he nor Lloyd George measured up to the requirement. But in fact, both of them were fundamentally serious *about politics*, and of the two it could be said that Lloyd George was the more serious, though also, perhaps, the less profound.

Lloyd George's lack of depth should not, however, be exaggerated. He was no philosopher-king – how many great men of action have merited the description? – but he was also no smatterer. His cultural equip-ment was far from negligible, and he thought hard, as well as quickly, about problems. Gardiner's suggestion that he had no literary culture is quite incorrect. At the time he was much better read than Churchill, who probably never, even in the course of a long life, read all the English classics that Lloyd George read as a boy. It was not true that he learned nothing from the past; he was much influenced, for example, by his early reading of Burke. But it is true that he was a visual Philistine, moved only by the glories of Nature, and either impervious or hostile to the charm of old buildings. Even Nature did not reduce him to a state of aesthetic trance or daydreaming, and it is probably true that in his mind there was no 'green thought in a green shade'. But the man who wrote those beautiful words was, though later an M.P., in no way a man of action. Andrew Marvell had the temperament for green thoughts in green shades. But did Oliver Cromwell?

Though he never pretended to be an intellectual, Lloyd George made a strong appeal to academics and surrounded himself with aides and advisers of the highest intellectual quality, who served him with enthusiasm and a sense of continual excitement. He respected men of intellect, what-ever their backgrounds, and knew how to make the best use of their brains. It could never be said that he gravitated towards the second-rate, or that only the second-rate were attracted to him.

But was he no more than a brilliant careerist? Was he devoid of heart or conviction? It goes without saying that he loved 'the great game', as nearly every important politician has done. It is not unusual, or immoral, for people to enjoy doing anything that they do well, and *vice versa*. But politics to him was far more than a game. He was in it to serve causes as well as to win fame for himself. And his higher motivation was not confined to 'love of the small nationality'. His Welsh patriotism was always subordinate to his British patriotism, which was one of the supreme motives of his career. Another was his zeal for social reform. Though not exactly a man of the people, he was truly on the side of the people; though he had never experienced the worst poverty, he had the imagination to sympathise with the really poor. There was nothing bogus in his outburst to Masterman: 'All down history nine-tenths of mankind have been grinding the corn for the remaining tenth, and have been paid with the husks and bidden to thank God they had the husk.'[1] He was equally sincere when he said in Edinburgh, during the second election of 1910: 'Civilisation has no perils for property; it is not property that stands in need of defence, but poverty.' Those are not the words of a revolutionary, but they are surely the words of a genuine radical – and incidentally Sir William Anson, scholar and strong conservative, regarded the speech in which they occur as 'the finest exercise in platform oratory' of his time: evidence of Lloyd George's power to impress opponents.[2] He was, indeed, the people's champion in a Government which, without him, would never have done battle so vigorously on their behalf.

When he is accused of lack of principle, what is often meant is that he recoiled from dogma, and was flexible in his approach to an objective. In that sense there is plenty of truth in the accusation, but is it not more a matter for praise than blame? He was, as Gardiner says, 'the least doctrinaire of men', and he was *less* doctrinaire than Chamberlain, because he never developed a monomaniac fixation for any particular supposed nostrum, as Chamberlain did for Tariff Reform. He may have lacked 'simple faith', but simple faith has been responsible for many of the world's most terrible calamities and outrages.

During the period that this book has attempted to describe he achieved great results, and his splendid qualities were fully deployed. Much of his work has proved enduring and the monuments of it are visible all around us. Yet both he and the Liberal Government failed where they are generally thought to have been most successful. Having faced a showdown with the House of Lords, they then bungled the ensuing constitutional reform, so that they were doomed, after 1911, to a legislative treadmill which restricted their scope and put them at the mercy of their enemies. Though it is fair to say that Lloyd George was desperately overworked as Chancellor, he must take his share of the blame for what went wrong. It might have been impossible for him to avert, single-handed, the mistakes

1. Masterman, *op. cit.*, p. 150.
2. J. A. Spender, *Life, Journalism and Politics*, Vol. I, p. 231.

that led to the Liberals' flawed victory in January 1910, or to persuade his colleagues to tackle the Second Chamber problem as it should have been tackled. But there is no evidence that he brought to the constitutional issue the clarity of vision, allied to a sense of urgency, which mark his political performance at its best. It must also be said that he failed, despite seeing quite clearly what ought to be done, to rescue the Government from its crass mishandling of the women's suffrage issue.

The next two or three years were to be a time, largely, of political frustration for him, but at the end of 1911 he stood at the zenith of his pre-war career. Though his hair was beginning to go grey, he was still under fifty. The past was full of achievement, the future seemed full of promise.

APPENDIX

Mr LLOYD GEORGE'S MEMORANDUM ON THE FORMATION OF A COALITION, 17 AUGUST 1910.

Some of the urgent problems awaiting settlement, problems which concern intimately the happiness and the efficiency of the inhabitants of these islands, their strength and influence, can only be successfully coped with by the active co-operation of both the great Parties in the State. Parties will always disagree on certain vital issues affecting the government of this country: their respective points of view are essentially different; but at the present moment the questions which are of the most vital importance to the well-being of the great community are all questions which are not only capable of being settled by the joint action of the two great Parties without involving any sacrifice of principle on the part of either, but which can be better settled by such co-operation than by the normal working of Party machinery. This country has gained a good deal from the conflict and rivalry of Parties, and it will gain a good deal more in the future from the same cause; but I cannot help thinking that the time has arrived for a truce, for bringing the resources of the two Parties into joint stock in order to liquidate arrears which, if much longer neglected, may end in national impoverishment, if not insolvency.

What are the questions which call for immediate attention and which could properly and effectively be dealt with by some such combined effort as I indicate? There are first of all the questions which come under the category of Social Reform: they affect the health, the vitality, the efficiency, and the happiness of the individuals who constitute the races that dwell in these islands.

HOUSING

The putting an end to a system which houses millions of the people under conditions which devitalize their strength, depress their energies, and deprive them of all motive power for putting forth their best.

DRINK

The problem of excessive drinking has a most intimate relation to other questions of Social Reform. There is no doubt that a vast number of people in this country destroy their physical, mental, and moral powers owing to their addiction to alcohol. One Party has been for the moment completely captured by a rigid and sterile plan for effecting reform; the other Party's energies are concentrated upon resistance to this scheme. If both Parties put their heads together, they could discover some idea which, whilst treating vested interests fairly, and even generously, would advance the cause of national sobriety.

INSURANCE

Provision against the accidents of life which bring so much undeserved poverty to hundreds of thousands of homes, accidents which are quite inevitable, such as the death of the breadwinner or his premature breakdown in health. I have always thought that the poverty which was brought upon families owing to these causes presents a much more urgent demand upon the practical sympathy of the community than even old age pensions. With old age, the suffering is confined to the individual alone; but in these other cases it extends to the whole family of the victim of circumstances.

UNEMPLOYMENT

Unemployment might also be put in the same category. Whatever is done towards improving the trade conditions, we shall at any rate for some time to come have to face a percentage of unemployment, especially in certain precarious trades. No country has been able to avoid it, and, with fluctuations in trade, the constant improvements in machinery, the variations in public demand for commodities and many other reasons, men will be thrown out of employment temporarily, and great difficulty will be found in absorbing this surplus labour. Much misery will thereby be caused, misery often culminating in hunger and starvation. Every country ought to provide adequately against such disasters.

This question of insurance illustrates one of the difficulties that must necessarily be encountered by every Government that attempts to grapple with it without first of all securing the co-operation of its opponents. The hardest case of all is that of the man who dies in the prime of life leaving a widow and young children. She suddenly finds herself without any adequate means, very often with all her means exhausted by medical and funeral expenses, face to face with the task of having not merely to attend to her household duties and the bringing up of the children, but also with that of earning a livelihood for herself and for them. In Germany they contemplate adding provision for widows under these conditions to their ordinary invalidity insurance. It is comparatively easy to set up a system of that kind in Germany; but here one would have to encounter the bitter hostility of powerful organizations like the Prudential, the Liver, the Royal Victoria, the Pearl, and similar institutions, with an army numbering scores, if not hundreds of thousands, of agents and collectors who make a living out of collecting a few pence a week from millions of households in this country for the purpose of providing death allowances. The expenses of collection and administration come to something like 50 per cent of the total receipts, and these poor widows and children are by this extravagant system robbed of one half of the benefits which it has cost the workmen so much to provide for them. Sometimes these agents and collectors sell their books and sub-let them and make hundreds of pounds out of the transaction, all at the expense of the poorest and most helpless creatures in the land. This system ought to be terminated at the earliest possible moment. The benefits are small, costly and precarious for if a man is unable, owing to ill-health or lack of employment, to keep up his payments, his policy is forfeited. State insurance costs 10 per cent to administer, and, inasmuch as the State and the employer both contribute, either the premium is considerably less, or the benefits are substantially greater, than with the insurance companies. But, however desirable it may be to substitute State insurance, which does not involve collection and therefore is more economical, any Party that attempted it would instantly incur the relentless hostility of all these agents and collectors. They visit every house, they are indefatigable, they are often very intelligent, and a Government which attempted to take over their work without first of all securing the co-operation of the other Party would inevitably fail in its undertaking; so that, if a scheme of national insurance is taken in hand by any Party Government, it must be confined to invalidity, and the most urgent and pitiable case of all must be left out. I may add that compensation on an adequate scale is well-nigh impossible, inasmuch as it would cost something like twenty or thirty millions at the very least to buy off the interest of these collectors, and such a payment would crush the scheme and destroy its usefulness. On the other hand, the agents cannot be absorbed in the new system, there being no door-to-door collection contemplated.

This is an excellent illustration of the difficulty of dealing with some of these problems except by joint action.

THE POOR LAW

This requires overhauling and re-casting, and I can see nothing in the principles of either Party which are irreconcilable in this matter.

NATIONAL REORGANIZATION

There are several questions coming under this head which could be much better dealt with by a Coalition than by a Party administration.

There is education. Not merely could the denominational issue be thus much more satisfactorily disposed of, inasmuch as the Parties are committed to certain controversial solutions which may not be the very best, but there are questions like the raising of the age limit, which is quite essential if the youth of the country are to receive a training which will enable them to cope with the workmen of Germany and the United States of America.

The same observation applies to the development of technical instruction in this country. The raising of the age limit would excite a good deal of opposition in many quarters, and might gain for a Government great unpopularity, even amongst sections of its own supporters who benefit now largely by boy labour. The Unionist Government of 1886 discovered this, and it is only a Coalition that could, here again, have the strength to face the ignorant and selfish prejudices that will be aroused by any effort to keep the children at school instead of turning them out to make money for their parents.

NATIONAL DEFENCE

This ought to be thoroughly looked into from the point of view of both efficiency and economy.

There are undoubtedly directions in which money can be saved: there are others in which it is imperative that more money should be spent. The whole question of national defence ought to be boldly faced. I doubt whether we are getting our money's worth in any direction. I am strongly of opinion that even the question of compulsory training should not be shirked. No Party dare touch it, because of the violent prejudices which would be excited even if it were suspected that a Government contemplated the possibility of establishing anything of the kind. For that reason it has never really been looked into by statesmen in this country. The Swiss militia system might be considered and those liable to serve might be chosen by ballot. We have no such need as Continental countries labour under of organizing an Army of 3,000,000 or 4,000,000 for defence; but we might aim at raising 500,000 armed militia to supplement our Regular Army to provide against contingencies.

LOCAL GOVERNMENT

Our whole system of local government is on a very unsatisfactory basis. There are too many boards and there is no system of intelligent direction, such as is provided by the Burgomasters on the Continent. Whilst there are too many small boards and councils, there are too few large ones, and a good deal of work is cast upon the Imperial Parliament which could be much more efficiently discharged by local bodies on a large scale.

TRADE

The various problems connected with State assistance to trade and commerce could be enquired into with some approach to intelligent and judicial impartiality if Party rivalries were eliminated. We have not merely problems connected with tariffs, but we have the question of inland transport that ought to be thoroughly overhauled. In Germany, the railway is one of the most important weapons of the State for the purpose of promoting the foreign trade of that country.

THE LAND

There is no question which would gain more, by the elimination of Party strife and bitterness, than that of the land. It is admitted on all hands that the land of this country is capable of much more profitable use than is now given to it. Both Parties seem to imagine, for the moment, that the real solution lies in the direction of establishing a system of small-holdings. I think they have been rather too readily rushed by small, but well-organized, groups of their own supporters into an acceptance of this doctrine. These groups are inspired by men of no marked intelligence and with little knowledge of land cultivation. The smallholdings craze is of a very doubtful utility; and I do not think its devotees have sufficiently considered whether farming on a large scale by competent persons with adequate capital is not more likely to be profitable to the community than a system which divides the land amongst a large number of more or less incompetent smallholders. After all, farming is a business, and it requires just as much capacity to run successfully a 50-acre farm as it would to manage a 500-acre holding. There ought to be the same knowledge of the qualities of the soil, the same gift of buying and selling, the same skill in making the best of the soil in both cases. It is very rarely that men enjoy a combination of all these gifts; and it is far better that the majority of men should work under competent guidance, direction, and command than that they should undertake the responsibilities of management. Few are the men who can, if left to themselves, put their own labour to the more fruitful use. The alternatives are worthy of much more careful and thorough consideration than has hitherto been given to them. If a mistake is made, it will be irreparable for generations. Once a system of small-holdings is rooted in this country it will be almost impossible for a very long period to substitute for it a system of farming on a large scale with adequate capital, where the State might very well assist, and under intelligent management.

IMPERIAL PROBLEMS

Schemes for uniting together the Empire and utilizing and concentrating its resources for defence as for commerce might also to much better advantage be undertaken and put through by a Coalition. They are the most delicate and difficult questions that have to be settled by modern statesmanship. In many respects they are the most urgent. Now is un-doubtedly the best time to approach them. After all, there are Parties in the Colonies as well as here; there are Parties in our Colonies whose sympathies are more naturally attracted to the Liberals, and some whose views perhaps bear an affinity to the Conservatives. In one section, Conservative statesmen are viewed with some suspicion; by others, the

Liberal Party is regarded with much distrust; but a Government that represented both Parties would appeal to all sections and would carry infinitely greater weight. In this connection, the settlement of the Irish question would come up for consideration. The advantages of a non-Party treatment of this vexed problem are obvious. Parties might deal with it without being subject to the embarrassing dictation of extreme partisans, whether from Nationalists or Orangemen.

FOREIGN POLICY

Such a Government, representing as it would not a fragment but the whole nation, would undoubtedly enhance the prestige of this country abroad.

17 August 1910.

Note on Sources

The best historical sources are contemporary documents, of which the most useful, of course, are those which are naturally objective, such as Hansard or strictly factual reports in the Press. Contemporary letters are objective too, in the sense that they are themselves historical facts, however unreliable their contents. At the very least they tell us where A was at a particular moment, and what he wanted B to know or think or believe.

Contemporary diaries are equally helpful in establishing where a person was and what he was doing on which dates. But in other respects they are a trickier form of evidence, because to the extent that they provide instant history almost everything depends upon the character of the diarist. What appears to be a more or less straightforward account of the passing scene may be vitiated by faults or handicaps in the narrator, such as ignorance, stupidity, lowly or mediocre status, remoteness from major decision-making, proneness to fantasy, personal bias affecting truthfulness, or a tendency to quote gossip as fact. Any one of these defects can gravely impair the value of a diary as historical evidence, and quite often two or more of them are found in combination. All the same, even the most dubious contemporary evidence has the merit that it is not distorted by failing memory or hindsight.

This merit is absent, of course, from the recollections of politicians and others, published in later life. Such recollections may be of great value, more especially for the sense of atmosphere and personality that they can convey. But on matters of fact they are often inaccurate even when the author genuinely wishes to tell the truth and has no motive for spreading falsehood. As a general rule, any statement of fact made after a considerable lapse of time, even by an author who was in the thick of the events described, should be treated with caution unless it can be supported by good contemporary evidence. Moreover those who write memoirs, as well as being liable to forget and to be wise after the event, are also liable to suffer from the same frailties as diarists.

For Lloyd George during the period of this book Hansard is a supremely important source, because most of his achievements were legislative and he took up a very large amount of Parliamentary time. The Press is another key source, because he was always making news, though obviously allowance has to be made for editorial prejudice in newspaper commentary and gossip, as distinct from hard reporting. A close study of newspaper reports can sometimes act as a corrective to entrenched historical notions (for instance the notion, examined at the beginning of Chapter Five, that Lloyd George alone was responsible for leaking details of the Asquith Cabinet in April 1908). Another source of objective information is the Public Record Office.

The two main archives for Lloyd George students are the Lloyd George Papers, now in the House of Lords Record Office, and the collection of family letters and other documents in the National Library of Wales. The first consists of the 'Parliamentary and political' papers held by Lloyd George at the time of his death and bequeathed by him to his second wife, Frances, who later sold them to Lord Beaverbrook. While the Beaverbrook Library was in existence the Papers were housed there, but since its regrettable closure in 1975 they have found a new home in the House of Lords (where, ironically, Lloyd George's notes for the Limehouse speech have long been deposited).

For the period 1902–1911, as for the earlier period, the Lloyd George Papers are not very copious, because it was only when Frances Stevenson became his private secretary in 1912 that his records began to be systematically kept. He did, however, preserve some good things even before she took over, and the Lloyd George Papers have provided some useful material for this volume.

The Lloyd George collection at the National Library of Wales is largely composed of documents left by Dame Margaret Lloyd George to her daughter, Megan, and by her to her nephew Mr D. L. Carey Evans, from whom they were acquired by the National Library. Most of the documents are letters written by Lloyd George to Margaret, but these become much less frequent after the turn of the century, because she was then spending far more time with him in London. They also tend to be shorter and less interesting, because he was so much busier. Many of them have been published in *Lloyd George: Family Letters, 1885–1936*, edited by Kenneth O. Morgan. Since access is denied to Lloyd George's letters to his uncle and brother (see Preface), the National Library collection is the principal, if necessarily inadequate, source for private documentation of the period. In addition, it contains some non-family letters and other interesting odds and ends.

The author has been most fortunate in being allowed to draw on a smaller, but extremely valuable, collection of Lloyd George documents – public and private – inherited by the present Lord Lloyd George from his father, Richard, Lloyd George's elder son. Another small, but significant, collection which has been made available is that belonging to Mr William Lloyd-George and inherited by him from his father, Lloyd George's younger son, Gwilym (Lord Tenby).

The Herbert Lewis Papers in the National Library of Wales have been an important source for this, as for the last volume. The diary is particularly valuable, because Herbert Lewis is an excellent witness – honest, conscientious, close to Lloyd George and devoted to him, yet capable of detached observation.

The D. R. Daniel memoir, also in the National Library, throws more light upon Lloyd George's early life than upon his years of power, but it is always interesting about his character and contains, for this period, one or two notable passages. (It is written in Welsh, but was translated for the author by Dr Prys Morgan.)

A good privately owned source, hitherto unused, is the journal of Ellis W. Davies, who represented the Eifion division of Caernarvonshire from 1906 to 1918. Though never an intimate of Lloyd George, he knew him quite well and was of some consequence as a radical member of the Welsh Parliamentary group. His entries are sober but occasionally illuminating.

Among the archives of leading contemporary politicians, the Asquith Papers at the Bodleian are obviously of great importance, and the first two Companion Volumes to Volume II of the official life of Winston Churchill, covering the years 1901–1911, are the equivalent of a major archive for the period of this book. Other collections which the author has found of special value are the Haldane and Murray of Elibank Papers at the National Library of Scotland, the McKenna Papers at Churchill College, Cambridge, and the Runciman Papers at Newcastle University Library (which were, however, consulted before they were moved there).

As a background source for the early part of the story the unpublished diary of Edmund Gosse has been helpful as well as enjoyable. Gosse was appointed Librarian of the House of Lords in 1904, and the position gave him plenty of opportunity to talk to politicians from both Houses who were friends of his. Unfortunately the diary ends – apart from two later fragments – in December 1906.

For the 1902 Education controversy a good secondary source is *Nonconformity in Modern British Politics* by Stephen Koss. For general politics during Balfour's Premiership no books are more enlightening than Volumes Five and Six – by Julian Amery – of *The Life of Joseph Chamberlain*, and *Balfour's Burden: Arthur Balfour and Imperial Preference* by Alfred M. Gollin. On the 1906 election, *Liberal Landslide* by A. K. Russell is invaluable.

Lloyd George at the Board of Trade is brought to life in Lord Devonport's memoir, *The Travelled Road*, which was printed for private circulation in the 1930s. Despite the rather long interval, Devonport gives a vivid impression of the man with whom he worked closely as junior minister. Hubert Llewellyn Smith's book, *The Board of Trade*, is interesting on the organization of the department, but makes no reference to Lloyd George except in the list of Presidents in Appendix VI.

In *The Treasury: the Evolution of a British Institution*, by Henry Roseveare, Lloyd George's next department is described, and the section of Chapter 7 entitled 'The Treasury and Liberal Reforms, 1906–14' is of special relevance. On the detail of Budgets Bernard Mallet's *British Budgets, 1887 to 1912–13* is a handy source.

The two outstanding studies of the Constitutional conflict resulting from the 1909 Budget are *Mr Balfour's Poodle* by Roy Jenkins and *The Peers, the Parties and the People: The General Elections of 1910* by Neal Blewett.

The women's suffrage movement, and its impact upon the Liberal Government, are best described in *Suffragists and Liberals: the Politics of Woman Suffrage* by David Morgan. Another book on the subject is *Rise up Women! The Militant Campaign of the Women's Social and Political Union 1903–1914* by Andrew Rosen.

For Lloyd George's relations with labour, *David Lloyd George and the British Labour Movement* by Chris Wrigley is the authoritative work. Lord Askwith's *Industrial Problems and Disputes*, though important in view of Askwith's role at the time, is not wholly reliable in either memory or judgment.

Lloyd George's coalition plan in 1910 is studied in detail in Chapter VI of *The Quest for National Efficiency*, by G. R. Searle, which is anyway an important book for the whole period. Mr Searle's disapproving view of Lloyd George's methods, however, is open to challenge.

A good short study of Lloyd George's attitude towards foreign affairs before the First World War was written by M. L. Dockrill for the collection *Lloyd George: Twelve Essays,* but recently the first volume has appeared of a full-length study of *Lloyd George and Foreign Policy* by Michael G. Fry. This covers the period of the present book in some detail, and includes a chapter on the Agadir crisis.

The best books on the launching of National Health Insurance are, unquestionably, *Lloyd George's Ambulance Wagon* by W. J. Braithwaite and *The Evolution of National Insurance in Great Britain: The Origins of the Welfare State* by Bentley B. Gilbert.

In the Note on Sources to *The Young Lloyd George* the numerous general works on Lloyd George were discussed. Since then an admirable short life has appeared – *Lloyd George* by Kenneth O. Morgan – and a long single-volume biography – *Lloyd George* by Peter Rowland – which definitely supersedes the comparable works by Malcolm Thomson and Frank Owen. One of the few criticisms that can be made of Mr Rowland's book is that it gives rather less space, proportionately, to Lloyd George's ministerial career before 1914 than might have been expected from the author of two volumes on *The Last Liberal Governments* (of which the first, *The Promised Land,* covers the period to 1911). Another recent book on Lloyd George's life to 1914, is *Bounder from Wales* by Don M. Cregier. This has little to contribute in new information or interpretation.

Various other books on Lloyd George (including one or two very important ones) have appeared during the past few years, but they deal with different periods of his life and would, therefore, be out of place in this Note. Of the earlier general studies, Volumes II and III of Herbert du Parcq's life provide some useful material on the period 1902–1911, as does *Lloyd George 1863–1914* by Watkin Davies and, of course, *My Brother and I* by William George. It must, however, be said of du Parcq's work that it is of diminishing value as it approaches the time when it was written (1911–13), because its hagiographic character, of which the author was later so ashamed, becomes increasingly marked. (His shame can be presumed from the fact that he managed to suppress all mention of the book in his entries in works of reference, and even in the D.N.B.)

The later volumes of du Parcq do not, like the first, have the merit of quoting from the William George archive which was – and remains – closed to all other outsiders. But *My Brother and I* quotes a substantial number of letters from Lloyd George to his relations at Criccieth during the Edwardian period.

E. H. Spender's *The Prime Minister*, though absurdly adulatory, is not to be ignored, because the author knew Lloyd George well and was often in his company – for instance when he went to Germany in 1908.

Among published diaries, Lord Riddell's *More Pages from My Diary 1908–1914* is excellent value, though unfortunately the entries are too few and far between; Charles Hobhouse's diary, *Inside Asquith's Cabinet* (edited by Edward David), is of intermittent interest, despite the author's limitations; Beatrice Webb's *Our Partnership* (edited by Barbara Drake and Margaret Cole) provides a commentary on Lloyd George's social reforming efforts from a largely hostile viewpoint; and Almeric Fitzroy's *Memoirs* (in diary form) have quite a lot to offer. But the best diary material is in Lucy Masterman's *C. F. G. Masterman: a Biography*, which is an altogether outstanding source for the period, though it is not always clear when the author is quoting a contemporary record or narrating (less reliably) from memory.

There are many works of general political history covering the early years of the century, of which the finest is Elie Halévy's *The Rule of Democracy (1905–1914)*, translated by E. I. Watkin – the coda, as it were, to his *History of the English People in the Nineteenth Century*. Sir Robert Ensor's *England, 1870–1914* in the Oxford History of England still has many virtues, though in some respects it is a bit dated. Sir John Marriott's *Modern England, 1885–1932* has the straightforward clarity of an unpretentious historian whose understanding of politics was enhanced by being an M.P. Robert Rhodes James's *The British Revolution* (Volume I, 1880–1914) is most readable, and also the work of a scholar with first-hand knowledge of Parliamentary politics. Henry Pelling's *Modern Britain, 1885–1955* is a lucid short account.

More restricted studies worth mentioning are *The Liberals in Power, 1905–1914* by Colin Cross, and *Liberals, Radicals and Social Politics, 1892–1914* by H. V. Emy.

Of course the author has had the benefit of reading a great many other books, including biographies of Lloyd George's contemporaries. Many of these are quoted or referred to in the course of the book.

Since it was completed an important work has come out on the ideological background to Lloyd George's essentially unideological reforms – *The New Liberalism* by Michael Freeden.

Index